THE
IDEOLOGY
OF
FASCISM

THE
IDEOLOGY
OF
FASCISM

THE RATIONALE OF
TOTALITARIANISM

A. James Gregor

THE FREE PRESS, NEW YORK
COLLIER-MACMILLAN LIMITED, LONDON

Copyright © 1969 by The Free Press
A DIVISION OF THE MACMILLAN COMPANY

Printed in the United States of America

Collier-Macmillan Canada, Ltd., Toronto, Ontario

Library of Congress Catalog Card Number: 69–16920

First Printing

This book is dedicated to Gamma
and to the sacrifice of his generation

Contents

Preface

T H I S book has modest pretensions. It is intended to serve, essentially, a two-fold purpose: (1) to provide an historically accurate and objective account of the ideology of Mussolini's Fascism; and (2) to suggest a general typology of revolutionary mass movements that reflects contemporary thinking with respect to the description and analysis of totalitarian movements. If *totalitarian* identifies a recognizable political genus, with totalitarian movements representing specific types of that genus, all such movements should share phenotypic and perhaps genotypic similarities. If such similarities are to be searched out we require, as a necessary preliminary to classification, adequate description.

What results is an essay in the history of political ideas, a discursive and descriptive account of the relatively consistent and stable constellation of ideas that came to constitute the Fascism of Benito Mussolini. As such it addresses itself only peripherally to the political and institutional history of Fascist Italy. Any effort to incorporate such materials would obviously outstrip the limits of this book and would fall outside the competence of this author. There are a substantial number of English and foreign language books that provide substantive accounts of the political and institutional history of Fascist Italy. There are, on the other hand, precious few that afford a competent and objective account of the ideological vindications that animated that history and subtended those institutions.

Every political ideology has a particular history and, as a consequence, is unique in the history of ideas. But to understand the impact of a political ideology it is necessary to relate it to identifiable constants, to indicate its place in a context of forces that have a systematic relevance to other contemporary political ideas. To this end I have conceived Fascist ideology as taking on particular significance when it is seen within the context of contemporary problems which beset developing nations. Within such a context the descriptive and didactic account of Fascist ideology takes on a heuristic character that affords preliminary insights into historical and political explanation. The principal purpose of this book will be expository and descriptive; its subsidiary purpose will be heuristic. Adequate description almost invariably suggests something of heuristic purpose.

One of the principal claims made by this book will be that Fascism has been by-and-large misunderstood by Anglo-American analysts, primarily because most studies of Fascism have been conducted under the burden of preliminary assumptions which have led to the serious neglect of its explicit ideology. The first chapter attempts to indicate something of the nature and extent of the disabilities suffered as a consequence. Because the thrust of the present exposition is counter-current, all the paraphernalia of academic footnoting and extensive direct quotation have been employed. This encumbers the text and impairs legibility. It is the price paid for writing and reading a book which attempts to reorientate thinking that for some considerable time has been comfortably pursuing paths laid down over a generation ago.

Two seeming disabilities attend this effort. First and foremost, the regular recourse to a restricted collection of core conceptions by the variety of thinkers included in our account made repetition an unavoidable necessity. The same constellation of ideas appear and reappear in the works of men in both the proto-Fascist and Fascist traditions. Furthermore, Fascists in articulating their justificatory arguments, employ the same concepts in a variety of circumstances.

An analysis of each justificatory rationale necessitates a restatement of antecedent premises if the structure of argument is to be revealed without ellipses. The recurrence of these ideas is compelling testimony of the constancy of Fascist doctrine. Second, and perhaps as a consequence, the account of Fascist ideology thus produced takes on an appearance perhaps too rational and too systematic. Appearances notwithstanding, however, the account is, I believe, substantially correct. Whatever spurious neatness obtains is by and large the consequence of not having included in the exposition all expressions of dissident Fascist opinion. Mussolini's own thought, central to the exposition, is treated chronologically. References to, and quotations from his speeches and writings are provided in chronological order unless otherwise indicated by a specific reference to date. Comparisons are sometimes provided with his earlier or later doctrinal statements in the effort to evidence consistency or specific developments. A strict regard for chronology is maintained in order to establish that the development and essential consistency of Mussolini's thought is not an artifact of the exposition itself.

Given the intentions of this account, specific criticism of Fascist thought has been no more than marginal. This volume is devoted almost exclusively to exposition. To have undertaken intrinsic and extrinsic criticism would have at least doubled the size of the manuscript. In any event, substantive criticism of Fascist thought must presuppose what this volume attempts: an accurate and objective account of Fascist commitment. Most past criticism has failed to meet that first minimal requirement.

What I think clearly emerges from the evidence is that the Mussolini of Anglo-American literature is, in certain important respects, a caricature of the historic political personality. Whatever else he was, Mussolini was an interesting political thinker; as interesting (or as dull) as Lenin, with whom he shared many affinities. His thought, most frequently elliptically and stenographically expressed, did not have the breadth or depth of Lenin's. Often what is most interesting can only be revealed by disinterring suppressed premises and auxiliary assumptions. Such an enterprise is obviously hazardous. That the enterprise has not been faulted is evidenced only by reference to the literature with which we know

Mussolini to have been familiar and with which he tacitly or explicitly identified.

Certainly Mussolini was as profound (or as shallow) a thinker as Stalin or Mao Tse-tung, and there is as much profit to be obtained from reading the thirty-five volumes of his collected writings and speeches as there is in reading the collected works of either of the others.

Chapters 2 through 7 attempt a faithful reconstruction of Fascist ideology. Chapter 8 attempts to indicate the relevance of Fascist thought to contemporary political circumstances. What it suggests is that Fascism and the various variants of contemporary Marxism share substantive similarities more pervasive than any differences which obtain between them. The argument contends that Fascism represents an extreme type of revolutionary mass movement and affords a paradigm of national totalitarianism. The revolutionary mass movements of our time, it will be suggested, have taken on more and more of the species traits of paradigmatic Fascism. What the volume does not attempt, something that hopefully will be the subject of a subsequent volume, is the identification of the economic, political, and cultural circumstances that conduce to the organization and success of contemporary quasi- or proto-Fascist mass movements.

Fascism is identified as the first revolutionary mass movement regime which aspired to commit the totality of human and natural resources of an historic community to national development. Fascism's evident intention was the restoration of Italy's place in the world as a power of significance. In order to accomplish this aim, the clear purpose of the movement was productionist, developmental. It was the first mature exemplar of what, in our own time, are referred to as modernizing movements. In a calculated effort to achieve its ends it required a centralized agency of resource mobilization, allocation, and direction. The totalitarian state and the authoritarian single party made their predictable appearance. The Fascist ideology both supported and prompted change in the direction of a totalitarian state capitalism. Italy was among the first underdeveloped countries of the twentieth century to be animated by a movement of national insurgency. Its professed opponents were the favored, or "plutocratic," nations of the earth. Fascism was the first representative of those revolutions now spoken of as "revolutions of rising expectation." The Soviet Union, at almost the same time, assumed similar guise. The internationalist, libertarian, distributionist, and democratic features of classical Marxism were rapidly transformed into the nationalist, authoritarian, productionist, and elitist features of an inconsistent and incongruent fascism— what we sometimes today refer to as Stalinism. The principal victims of Stalin's purges were representatives of social democracy and bolshevism, representatives of the same political elements that were suppressed in Fascist Italy.

Fascism is here construed as a developmental dictatorship appropriate to partially developed or underdeveloped, and consequently status deprived, national communities in a period of intense international competition for place and status. In this sense the ideology of Fascism, historically and intellectually unique insofar as it was the product of a particular collection of ideas prevalent during the first decades of the twentieth century, is understood to have been operative in an environment in which general historic forces were, and in a substantial sense remain, operative. Those forces can be distinguished from the ideology which mobilized a nation to respond to the forces. Italian Fascism was historically unique but, insofar as it was a response to the general political and social problems which attend the efforts to establish a developing nation's place in the sun, it has a broader relevance than its brief political existence might suggest. Fascism was, in fact, a political phenomenon characteristic of the partially industrialized nations of Europe. It was strongest and succeeded to power in the Latin countries of Europe where the gross national product and the per capita income were lowest, and in countries marginally industrialized like Spain, Portugal, Romania, and Hungary. If this analysis is correct, one might well expect the revolutions in underdeveloped countries facing the same problems and entertaining the same aspirations toward status in international competition to take on some of the criterial attributes of, and provide essentially the same vindications as, paradigmatic Fascism. The involution of classical Marxism in the Soviet Union and the manifestly fascist features of African socialism provide presumptive evidence for such a contention. Only the appearance of National Socialism in industrialized

Germany seems to resist such an analysis. And yet the traumatic experience of Germany after World War I, its reduction to a second class power at the moment it had every promise of becoming a world power of the first rank, suggests that gross status deprivation might aid in explaining its identification with the aspiring revolutionary powers of the continent with whom it had so little in common. But it is instructive to note that National Socialism was an anomalous fascist power. Its charismatic object of loyalty (the community with which it identified) proved to be not the nation, the characteristic object of loyalty for true fascisms, but an ill-defined and ill-assessed racial confraternity. National Socialism was, in a substantial sense, more removed from Mussolini's Fascism than was the "socialism" of the Soviet Union and, as such, requires separate analysis. In a curious inversion of political intentions the Soviet Union became increasingly nationalistic while National Socialism became increasingly internationalistic. Hitler aspired to a racial internationale that would strip the world of its national boundaries. The Soviet Union on the other hand, has had to concede the historic viability and relative permanence of national communities.

Such interpretations are obviously offered as heuristic suggestions. They are intended as one possible solution to the problems suggested by this volume and by the increasing awareness that revolutionary mass-movement regimes having totalitarian aspirations share more features in common than they share with any alternate political system. Obviously the principal purpose of this book is the reconstruction of Fascist ideology. If it succeeds in providing a convincing account of that alone it will have more than fulfilled my intention.

Preparation of this manuscript has put me in debt to many more people than I could possibly publicly acknowledge. I am, however, particularly indebted to Ing. Giovanni Perona and the late Professor Corrado Gini for many insights into the content and structure of Fascist thought. To Professor Giuseppe Prezzolini I am particularly obligated. He not only read the typescript of this manuscript while it was in preparation, but provided constructive criticism which clarified a number of issues in my own mind as well. Moreover, his encouragement and kindness bolstered, on many occasions, my flagging resolve. The Institute of International Studies of the University of California, Berkeley, provided the financial support which made completion of this work possible, and my wife, Dorothy, read and reread these pages in the effort to render more comprehensible my all-too-Germanic prose. Mrs. Jean McGrath worked indefatigably in preparing this manuscript for publication. Finally, I am indebted to the many members of the Political Science Department at the University of California, Berkeley, for providing the environment and evincing the interest that made this work at all possible. Needless to say, I alone am responsible for all its shortcomings.

A. J. G.

THE
IDEOLOGY
OF
FASCISM

CHAPTER ONE

Introduction

THE TWENTIETH century is a time of troubles, a time of unsettled season in almost every range of human activity. The intensity and scope of the crisis that has beset mankind is unprecedented, but it shares with precedent crises certain species traits, the most important being an agonizing and searching reappraisal of convictions held and covenants honored. It is an age of uncertainty and misgivings. There is hardly a hallowed tradition, a cherished principle, or a hitherto established conviction that has not been subjected to destructive criticism or become the object of studied and sceptical scrutiny. Every aspect of man's social life, which in more settled times is governed by habit and effortless conformity, is open to question. This is nowhere more obvious than in the domain of political life, which, in the twentieth century, has become increasingly integrative and totalitarian, in the sense that no aspect of life is conceived to be, in principle, private and unpolitical. With the decline of religion, politics has become its secular surrogate, and where much of the world's past is the history of religious strife, the twentieth century has been, and will from all indications continue to be, the century of ideological struggle, political conflict. Mankind has divided itself along lines of ideological difference. Incalculable wealth and innumerable lives have been consumed in the attendant contest, in the catastrophic wars and sociopolitical revolutions of our time. Against the prevalent optimism of the late nineteenth and early twentieth century, our time is revealed as one of incredible turmoil.

The objective indices available indicate that the last quarter of the nineteenth century was remarkable in its orderliness, intra- and international peace, and substantial progress. Of the fifty-six quarter-centuries from 525 A.D. to 1925, only two had a slightly lower index of internal disturbance. On the other hand, during the same period only one quarter-century reveals itself more turbulent than the period from 1901 to 1925. The turn of the twentieth century brought with it a manifest increment in intra- and international disturbance. It was a period of internal revolution, highlighted by the successful Bolshevik and Fascist revolutions in Russia and Italy, and torn by World War I. Since that time the tempo has increased and, conditioned by the technological revolution in transportation and communication, revolution has become a world-wide phenomenon. Intra- and international strife is no longer geographically confined, and the crisis is no longer a crisis of the West or of Western civilization—this is a time of troubles that afflicts all mankind. The twentieth is perhaps the most tumultuous century in the history of the human race.[1]

Two world wars in the space of one generation, painfully linked by an uninterrupted series of local wars and revolutions, have been followed by peripheral wars, "police actions," and internecine strife that has dissipated all hope of eventual restoration of a world order and its binding covenants that brought peace to our progenitors during the closing years of the nineteenth century. The largely unlettered masses of five continents have been thrown into turmoil by what have been called "revolutions of rising expectations." Among these revolutions, there are those that, to one degree or another, have been animated by a secular ideology of solidarity and molded by a unitary political party to the requirements of a totalitarian or quasi-totalitarian state. Nations as unlikely as China, for so long culturally and politically anti-Western, have taken up the ideological accoutrements and the institutional accessories of a specifically European doctrine. Egypt, Syria, Senegal, Mali, and

Guinea, long outside the current of Western thought, have committed themselves to the world-view and the policies of a secular ideology. Throughout Asia and Africa, in the Western Hemisphere and beyond the Oder-Niese, secular ideologies have lit the fires of revolution. With these revolutions have come the unitary party, the planned economy, and the totalitarian or potentially totalitarian state. Gone is the ideal of the republic of free opinion and the permissive politics of conflicting ideas. Gone, too, is the aspiration toward a "pluralistic democracy," so much the hope of nineteenth- and twentieth-century liberalism. Abandoned, as well, is the market economy of free enterprise and its by-product, the state whose functions are delegated, agential, and severely circumscribed. What we have witnessed and are witnessing is a vast ideological revolution, a major dislocation in what had been the prevalent social and political world-view of the West.

A Working Definition of Ideology   In general, the term *ideology* is used to refer to a given constellation of beliefs (descriptive and normative) which, taken together, have significant implications for a wide range of conduct. An ideology implies a way of life.[2] It is a conceptual frame of reference which provides criteria for choice and decision by virtue of which the major activities of an organized community are governed. This common usage and ordinary understanding is unobjectionable and in the forthcoming discussion the term, so understood, would render passages in which it appears perfectly comprehensible. For the special purposes of exposition and analysis, however, certain stipulative distinctions are introduced. An ideology will be here understood to involve (1) an explicit value system, supported by argument, accompanied by (2) a relatively coherent system of generalizations about nature, society, and man to which a group appeals to justify the issuance of social and political directives, prescriptions and proscriptions, as well as (3) the formal and informal directives, prescriptions, and proscriptions themselves.

The first component of ideology, as it is here understood, can be identified as *social and political philosophy*, a fairly rigorous

3

and coherent body of argued judgments concerning nature, society, and man which has normative implications. This philosophical component of ideologies has a detached and intellectual quality. It is formulated in reasoned guise and attempts to meet the minimal requirements of significant discourse. Its specific distinguishing trait is its normative potential.

Speculative social and political philosophies tend to be deceptively descriptive. Argument sequences seem to be concerned with the nature and origin of the universe, society, or man. The philosopher, as a consequence, appears to be preoccupied with the issuance of descriptive utterances different from those issued by the natural scientist only in their more inclusive scope and evident lack of quantitative precision. But for the speculative social and political philosopher, such a collection of propositions is obscurely related to a set of normative judgments. The ability to negotiate the transit between descriptive and normative propositions is what distinguishes speculative social and political philosophy from political science as a science. Ideally, the natural scientist and the political scientist *qua* political scientist are concerned with description, classification, and explanation. They are concerned with descriptive or definitional propositions employed in the articulation of typologies, adequate descriptions, theory construction, and fruitful explanations. In their capacity as scientists, the natural scientist and the political scientist are *not* concerned, in principle, with what the universe, society, and man *should* be. Their preoccupation is adequate description and classification, competent explanation, and effective prediction. In contrast, the social and political philosopher or (as he is commonly referred to) the political theorist is intent upon providing standards of rectitude—serious, sober, and insistent criteria governing approbation and disapprobation, and evaluations of right and wrong. In this sense speculative social and political philosophers or political theorists are a sub-group of practicing moralists.

The second component of ideologies is *doctrine:* a relatively loose collection of assumptions, generalizations, and judgments about the general nature and the dynamics of social reality. These are conjoined with negative evaluations of the past and present which, together with some conceptions of a desired eventual state of affairs, provide a general guide to contemporary action. Doctrine differs from speculative social and political philosophy in that its value commitments are tacitly assumed rather than argued, and by the fact that the focus of its concerns are exigencies of local and contingent character. Doctrinal ideas, taken by themselves, display only rudimentary internal coherence, and are characterized by high emotional salience. Doctrinal statements are calculated to persuade rather than cognitively convince. In general, doctrine is the leading edge of a social and political philosophy that has become an ideology. Doctrine finds its way into propaganda pamphlets and undergraduate surveys. It is usually the product of a number of apprentice talents. Social and political philosophy is characteristically the product of a master hand, or of a master guild of severely restricted membership. Marxism, as a social and political philosophy, was the product of the genius of Karl Marx. Fascism, as a social and political philosophy, was essentially the product of the genius of Giovanni Gentile. Marxism and Fascism as doctrines, on the other hand, were the products of many hands. At what point doctrine becomes speculative social and political philosophy is much disputed, and the arguments need not be entered into here. Generally, the qualitative differences between social and political philosophy and social and political doctrine are so manifest that one can rest content with intuitive distinctions. That Lenin is not Marx and that Mussolini is not Gentile is evident in everything that Lenin and Mussolini wrote.

The third component of ideologies is composed of *formal and informal imperatives* issued as codified law or represented in group sentiment and supported by formal and informal sanction. This final component of ideological systems includes legislation, precepts, and social sentiments, instituted and fostered through a variety of social and political agencies. The typical response to violation of a positive standard of conduct (either a public sentiment or a codified law) is moral indignation and/or punishment. The formal and informal imperatives provide the rule context by virtue of which ascriptions of good and bad can be meaningfully made, culpability assigned, and extenuation forthcoming. The first order of justification for an act is a reference to law or common social practice. It is on this level that the average citizen functions. In a communistic

5

environment, the average citizen is a good citizen because he has adapted to a specific rule-governed context. In a fascist environment he would have been an equally good citizen. The end of World War II saw innumerable good fascists become, in a remarkably short period of time, equally good democrats or communists, depending on the doctrinal and philosophical climate which prevailed in the geographic locale in which they happened to be.

From the philosophic point of view more interesting issues are joined when the system of formal and informal rules itself is the subject of scrutiny. Laws restricting the ownership of private property in the Soviet Union, for example, are justified by appeals to doctrinal notions about the nature of capitalism and capitalist society, property ownership, and class antagonism. Implicit in this catalogue of arguments are certain attitudinal biases and certain implicit values governing the normative force of such accounts. The searching out and assessment of such an implicit constellation of values is the task of critical social and political philosophy. The analysis of justificatory argument at this level focuses upon the speculative social and political philosophy that subtends ideology.

Revolution, Totalitarianism, and Democracy

When an entire prevailing ideological system is threatened, we speak of impending *revolution*. Revolutions constitute sweeping and fundamental changes in political organization, social structure, and economic control; successful challenges to the established social and political covenants whose ultimate justification was the hitherto predominant ideology. A successful revolution, therefore, marks for our purposes a major break in the continuity of philosophical development. Of course, this does not imply that revolutions are essentially or primarily cerebral, but only that "ideas have consequences." Revolution is obviously the consequence of the intersection of a finite, if indeterminate, set of causes. Among those causes, the appeal of one rather than another ideology, its consistency and evident relevance to a given crisis situation, is no doubt of significant, if incalculable, importance. Revolution is, in general, a violent reaction to multiple dysfunctions in the prevailing social system. These dysfunctions, conjoined with the indisposition of the established elite to countenance change, create the necessary conditions for revolution.[3] A further set of local conditions, the presence of determined insurrectionary leadership and effective political organization, among others, can provide the precipitating agencies of revolution. The substitution of an alternate legitimating rationale for a new order of society is its characteristic, most manifest, outcome.

It is not our purpose to attempt to specify the necessary and sufficient conditions for revolution. In the present context all that is necessary is the indication that the mass-based radical movements of solidarity that provide the impetus for change in our time are, in a fundamental and important sense, revolutionary. They challenge the central commitments of the late nineteenth century. Against the contractualist, individualist, and permissive capitalist ideology of the last century, they oppose the tutelary, communalist, and authoritarian socialism of our time. The generic name assigned to the latter ideologies, however they identify themselves, is *totalitarianism*.

Totalitarian ideologies provide the justificatory arguments in support of a type of society minimally characterized by (1) an official and (relative to antecedent systems of political thought) highly specific official ideology based upon a radical rejection of some aspects of the past and chiliastic claims for the future, (2) a unitary mass movement of solidarity, hierarchically organized as a single party under the authoritarian leadership of a charismatic (or pseudocharismatic) leader and a directive and tutelary elite, (3) a technologically conditioned near-monopoly of the means of communication and coercion, and (4) centralized direction, under bureaucratized control, of the entire economy.[4]

One of the central theses of this book will be that paradigmatic Fascism was the first, and remains perhaps the only, fully matured ideological rationale for the totalitarian systems of the twentieth century. While Leninism could, for some considerable time, be considered an extension of liberalism and "radical democracy," Fascism from its inception was self-characterized as antiparliamentarian, antimajoritarian, and explicitly totalitarian. The early and lifelong political ideal of Marx and Engels was a "democratically constituted state," a Marxist ideal later characterized by Hans

Kelsen as a "perfected democracy" governed by the "majority principle."[5] As late as 1919, as astute a commentator as Bertrand Russell could still insist that "orthodox socialists are content with parliamentary democracy in the sphere of government. . . ."[6] The Marxists of our time never tire of characterizing their system of government and the rationale that subtends it as "truly democratic."

The fixing of an adjectival qualifier like *democratic* to a social and political philosophy is, of course, never a substitute for serious analysis, the self-characterization of Marxist political ideas as *truly* democratic is sufficient to indicate that Marxists of sundry times and places sought to distinguish their democracy from that of the prevalent "bourgeois democrats." But whatever the analysis, and whatever the extent of legitimate skepticism in the face of Marxist, particularly Leninist, protestations of democratic ideals, the fact remains that Marxism in all its variant forms has identified itself as "democratic." Lenin's anarcho-syndicalist *State and Revolution* is a sincere, if unconvincing, statement of democratic purpose. "We establish as our final aim," Lenin insisted, "the liquidation of the state, i.e., of any sort of organized and systematic constraint. . . . [We] are convinced that . . . all necessity for the coercion of men in general will disappear, all necessity for the *subordination* of one man to another, of one part of the population to another part. . . ."[7] And Alfred Meyer could recently reaffirm, "Democracy, in its most radical, anarchistic form, constitutes part of the ideal society toward which Lenin and most other Marxists were striving."[8]

Leninism as a social and political philosophy constitutes, at best, a confused and confusing rationale for the totalitarianism of Soviet and Chinese communist society. The practice of Soviet society stands in flagrant violation of the professed ideals of Leninism. Only specious and tortuous argument can give the semblance of consistency to the ideological system. The comparison of the ideals of classical Marxism and the enactments which provide form and substance to Soviet society remains a source of continuous embarrassment to contemporary Leninists. The "democratic centralism" which imparts the hierarchical organization to the minoritarian Communist Party was initially a tactic devised to meet the exigencies of an autocratic and oppressive social and political environment. That Leninism has succeeded in making a virtue of necessity and has elevated the Party to the status of the prime instrument of political domination and control remains a source of real theoretical discomfort to thinking Marxists.[9] Rosa Luxemburg, one of the foremost Marxists of the turn of the century, felt that the Leninist conception of the party constituted a betrayal of the essentials of Marxism,[10] but contemporary Leninists have been forced to make the Leninist conception central to their program for the realization of Marxism.[11]

The tensions that have accumulated within Leninism as an ideological system have become increasingly evident. Where Lenin himself could insist that "the state is a product and a manifestation of the *irreconcilability* of class antagonisms," that "the state arises where, when, and insofar as class antagonisms objectively *cannot* be reconciled," and, consequently, that "the state is an organ of class rule, an organ for the oppression of one class by another," contemporary Leninists must maintain that, "until now the state has always been an instrument of dictatorship by this or that class," but now, "for the first time in history, a state has taken shape which is not a dictatorship of any one class, but an instrument of society as a whole, of the entire people."[12] Lenin had maintained that "so long as the state exists there is no freedom. When there is freedom, there will be no state."[13] For contemporary Leninists the state is "the organ expressing the will of the whole people," and, "will remain long after the victory of the first phase of communism."[14] These evident discrepancies have not escaped the attention of contemporary revolutionary Marxists. The Chinese communists contend,

The state is a weapon of class struggle, a machine by means of which one class represses another. Every state is the dictatorship of a definite class. So long as the state exists, it cannot possibly stand above class or belong to the whole people. . . . The fact that Khrushchev has announced the abolition of the dictatorship of the proletariat in the Soviet Union and advanced the thesis of the "state of the whole people" demonstrates that he has replaced the Marxist-Leninist teachings on the state by bourgeois falsehoods.[15]

Soviet Leninism has proved manifestly incapable of producing a justificatory rationale for some of the most significant social and political developments featured in the revolutions that characterize our time. In this sense it is far less instructive than Fascism for understanding those revolutions which have been consistently *nationalistic*, or for understanding our epoch, which has become increasingly *totalitarian*. Therefore, the search for a sustained and consistent rationale for totalitarian nationalism must be sought not in the pages of Marx or Lenin, but in those of Gentile and Mussolini. Leninists are more preoccupied with explaining away than explaining, or even justifying, the totalitarian and nationalist features of the societies they govern. As the tutelary, pedagogic, enterprisory, and directive functions of the state increase and become the identifying features of the simple developmental dictatorships or totalitarianisms of our century, the Leninists insist upon the ultimate "withering away" of the state. That this "withering away" has been discretely postponed for "perhaps an entire historic epoch" documents the theoretical tension that has developed between Leninist doctrinal commitment and Leninist practice. Similarly, as the fraternity of socialist nations is increasingly riven by manifestly nationalist interests, and as nationalism reveals itself as one of the most dynamic contemporary forces, Leninists expend an increasing amount of energy certifying their theoretical commitment to internationalism and make remarkably little effort to vindicate the admonitions to "socialist patriotism" now embodied in the Decalogue of the "Builders of Communism."[16]

Fascism as an Ideology

That Fascism as an ideological system has been the object of so little serious analysis is curious. Now, more than a generation after the passing of paradigmatic Fascism, George Mosse can justifiably maintain that "Fascism has been a neglected movement," and Hugh Seton-Watson can persuasively add that "the essence of Fascism is still elusive."[17]

The prewar neglect of Fascism was in large part the result of the union of ignorance and bias—understandable under the circumstances that prevailed when Fascism was an active threat to national existence, cherished institutions, and political predilections. Immediately prior to, and during World War II, Fascism was simply equated with National Socialism and charged with every absurdity, every infamy, and every caricature that could be legitimately or illegitimately associated with the political notions of Adolf Hitler. For some time, for example, it was common for commentators to charge that the racial doctrines of Fascism were "clumsy imitations" of National Socialist racism.[18] Even as careful a postwar and contemporary scholar as Ernst Nolte could conclude that by the end of his political career Mussolini, and consequently Fascism, had adopted "*in toto* Hitler's political race doctrine."[19]

The first judgment, that the racial doctrine of Fascism was an imitation of National Socialist doctrine, although partially, and in a qualified sense, true, was made at the expense of the actual historic doctrine and it obscures the relevance of Fascist racial doctrine to more contemporary ideologies. The second proposition, that Mussolini *fully* accepted Hitler's racial doctrines, is simply false.

Only recently has the more judicious assessment of both Fascism and National Socialism led to the awareness that

because neither Fascism nor National Socialism has been thoroughly analyzed, we lack sound definitions of either and frequently confuse the two. Only the ignorant still think that Socialism and Communism, much though they have in common, are one and the same thing. But even serious scholars are liable to refer to "German Fascism," and to use Fascism and National Socialism interchangeably.[20]

Only the abatement of passion that followed the passing of Fascism as an international threat made possible the more objective and accurate study of Fascism as a political phenomenon. The last decade has produced a number of substantial works on Fascism including an objective and competent study of Gentile as a social and political philosopher. H. S. Harris' volume, *The Social Philosophy of Giovanni Gentile*, is perhaps the best exposition of Gentile's thought in any language.[21] While much remains to be said of the relationship of Gentile to both Mussolini and Fascism, and concerning Fascism itself, the basic materials for an objective and accurate appraisal are now available.

At least part of the reason for the inadequacy of treatments of Fascism to date has been the disposition, prevalent among political analysts until very recently, to give too much credence to a Marxist or quasi-Marxist interpretation of the entire political phenomenon.

The standard Marxist-Leninist interpretation of Fascism is found in works like the *Short Philosophical Dictionary* published in the Soviet Union—which defined Fascism as

the most reactionary and openly terroristic form of the dictatorship of finance capital, established by the imperialistic bourgeoisie to break the resistance of the working class and all the progressive elements of society.[22]

Similarly, for Trotsky, Fascism was "a plebeian movement in origin," but one "directed and financed by big capitalist powers."[23] Fascism was conceived to be the creature of monopoly or finance capitalism, its ideology a crude rationalization of capitalist interests. It was supposedly "directed" by "big capitalist powers." All the available documentary evidence, however, clearly indicates that Mussolini was the actual ruler of Fascist Italy.[24] Through the party apparatus he exercised ultimate control over the destiny of his country. Whatever concessions were made to capitalism or capitalists, whatever real or imagined benefits they received, were always meted out with tactical concern for the maintenance of the Regime. As became evident in the last years of the Regime, Mussolini was prepared to sacrifice capitalism, *in toto,* for the survival of Fascism. Moreover, contemporary analysts have come to recognize a "proletarian fascism" as well as a "peasant fascism" in circumstances where fascism has either been opposed by the possessing classes or where there is or was no "big capitalist" or "imperialist bourgeois" class in existence.[25] Under such circumstances the Marxist or quasi-Marxist analyst is driven into a conspiratorial interpretation of history in which he maintains that the big capitalists of Argentina were "really" directing the proletarian fascism of Peron and capitalists of Rumania "really" created the peasant fascism of Cornellu Codreanu—interpretations for which there is no supporting evidence and substantial counterevidence.

There is in fact a fascist ideology which cannot be successfully analyzed as the rationalization of the interests of any specific social class. It is a political ideology, usually articulated by declassed intellectuals, which becomes an animating force for a mass movement of solidarity of diverse population components under various historic and social circumstances. Those elements of the population which, for whatever reason, come to its support, influence its effective practice. If its most active and aggressive support originates among an aspiring or threatened bourgeoisie, fascist applications, at least temporarily, take on some quasi-conservative, anti-Marxist, even capitalist, features. If its support comes from an aggressive working class, its practice is anti-Marxist, but manifestly anti-capitalist. In this sense it would be appropriate to speak of a "fascism of the right" and a "fascism of the left." But that both would be fascist, nonetheless, indicates that there is a complex of ideas that are relatively coherent and specific and that can be identified as "fascist ideology." This volume proposes a consideration of paradigmatic Fascism, the first mature ideological statement of generic Fascism. Such an account will provide the materials for an adequate assessment of fascism and prevent the misidentification of fascism with the exacerbated conservativism of the John Birch Society or Right Wing Republicanism.

Under the crabbed influence of the Marxist or quasi-Marxist analysis of fascism—which construes fascism as an aggressive movement in the service of monopoly capital—fascist statements have never been analyzed as such. They are always "interpreted." Fascists are never to be understood to mean what they say—what they say is always understood in some Pickwickian sense. As a consequence there has been very little effort, to date, to provide a serious account of fascism as an ideology.

Fascist ideology merits attention not only in order to reconstruct an important body of modern social and political argument, but also in order more adequately to understand recent historical as well as some significant contemporary developments. Although the ideals men entertain rarely translate themselves directly into action, they do provide a frame of reference by virtue of which we can orientate ourselves in trying to understand their behavior. Most of us are prepared to grant that if an agent is introduced into a given set of political circumstances we will enjoy a certain degree of predictive advantage in anticipating his behavior if we also know that our historical protagonist is a Marxist, a Kennedy liberal, or a fascist. This increased leverage can be employed for retrodiction as well. By knowing the ideals to which knowledgeable Fascists were committed we are in a better position to reconstruct their influence in the "logic" of historical events. The implied assumption is, of course, that *some* identifiable fascist precepts and convictions exercised *some* influence over overt behavior. It is not difficult to argue in support of just such an assumption in the case of individual or collective fascist subordinates. A fascist doctrine and a fascist "style" rapidly articulated themselves and one could, with some accuracy, anticipate individual and collective fascist postures under specific historic and political circumstances. It is more difficult, on the other hand, to make a case for fascist leaders. The tendency has long been to treat fascist leaders in general, and Mussolini in particular, as unprincipled opportunists. It is a curious fact that Leninists, whose political doctrines are evidently so much at variance with their practice (advocating as they do the "withering away of the state," a perfervid internationalism, and an abiding love of peace), are rarely characterized as unprincipled opportunists. Leninist ideology is assiduously studied in order to obtain insights into Soviet or Chinese communist behavior. And yet fascists, whose ideology constitutes essentially a vindication of their manifest practice, advocating as they do an authoritarian state, a consuming nationalism, and an undeniable militarism, are regularly regarded as men with respect to whom the study of professed ideology would be unprofitable.

The fact is that the evidence available indicates that Mussolini was as principled or as unprincipled as Lenin. An adequate explanation of the behavior of either is forthcoming only if their behavior is understood as the result of an interaction of considerations of both principles and tactics. That Mussolini has, in the past, been judged simply unprincipled and opportunistic is a consequence of a number of inadequate assessments. Mussolini is understood, first of all, to have "abandoned" Marxian socialism in 1914 in order to batten on some obscure political advantage. As a matter of fact, as early as 1904, Mussolini's socialism was far from orthodox. Important elements of Fascism were already present in his *syndicalist* convictions of this early period. The evidence now available indicates that the transition to Fascism was neither as abrupt nor as dislocating as the juxtaposition of Marxist socialism and Fascism suggested in the interwar years and would suggest today. Mussolini's abandonment of socialist internationalism, on the other hand, was abrupt and dislocating, but all the evidence indicates it was the consequence of a long period of intense reflection and reassessment.[26] Nor could Mussolini gain any immediate political advantage by being expelled in 1914 from the Socialist Party in which he had achieved a position of considerable prominence. Upon his expulsion from the Party, Mussolini was all but politically isolated.

The most frequently cited instance of Fascist opportunism is, of course, the manifestation of racism after the Italian rapprochement with National Socialist Germany. That Fascist racism was, at least in part, the consequence of tactical considerations is undeniably true,[27] but this recognition should not obscure the unique character of Fascist racism in both theoretical and doctrinal distinctions which manifested themselves in application.

The Assessment of Ideologies

It must be recognized, of course, that for many Anglo-American intellectuals the study of ideologies is, at best, a fruitless preoccupation and, at worst, perverse in principle. We are counselled to be either cynical about the ideologist's motives, skeptical about his logic, or both.

There is much in the characteristic formations of ideologists that tends to support such an admonition. The normative pronouncements of ideologists tend to be couched in elaborate metaphor, effusions are deployed to conceal deficiencies in argument or fact, and there are rank appeals to emotion and recourse to elaborate ritual to augment the poverty of cognitive assessment. Such accounts constitute standard efforts at political persuasion. They are composed of tendentious metaphors and ill-concealed emotionalism. We have all been, at one time or another, exposed to such transparent persuasive strategies. In our tolerance we do not hold it wrong for a man to work in the interests of the ideology to which he is committed by personal preference, but we do hold it wrong for another man to be gulled by the performance.

Yet for all that we do not rest content with an analysis which equates statements like, "Racial discrimination is wrong," or, "Democracy is the best political system," with simple expressions of personal preference and/or emotion. Certainly any person involved in serious normative dispute does not conceive of himself as doing nothing more than defending his personal emotional preference against the simple emotional preference of his opponent. Ethical argument does not cease when contending propositions are analyzed as instances of felt preference. Disputants will insist that feelings of approbation attend their moral statements because they are right, not that their moral statements are right because attended by feelings of approbation. An ideologist will recommend his social and political conceptions by mustering *reasons* in their support. He is never content to simply iterate and reiterate no more than that he *prefers* such and such social and political conceptions. He would hardly be expected to argue in their behalf if he did not. What one expects in such cases are *reasons* in support of such conceptions, harboring as they do prescription and proscription. The distinction is understood, in fact, to mark the difference between matters of taste or preference and *bona fide* questions of legitimate commitment.

It is not necessary for the critical social and political philosopher of contemporary ideologies to resolve the meta-ethical and metanormative questions such a distinction invokes. All that is necessary to convince oneself of this is to observe the performance of contemporary ideologists and their products. What the political ideologist characteristically does, in fact, is to advance a general normative ideal, the "emancipation of man," "freedom," or, "fulfillment of the self." Agreement with such ideals is not difficult to obtain simply because agreement really constitutes nothing more, in effect, than evidence of normality or rectitude, evidence that one understands and is responsive to the language of contemporary morality. What would one oppose to such ideals? Would one advocate the enslavement of man as an emotional preference? Or the debasement of the self? Anyone who assumed such postures could hardly be conceived to be a serious disputant. He demands psychotherapy rather than persuasion. If serious moral argument is joined, our opponents do not argue for slavery or debasement—what they argue is that what we conceived to be slavery or debasement is "really" freedom and fulfillment. They characteristically tender redefinitions supported by argument. Or they might indicate the existence of equally imperative ideals that conflict with those proferred, or seek to specify what such ideals mean in terms of descriptive content, in terms of techniques for their realization, and in terms of possible cost. Once such questions are joined, however, the disputants are engaged in a cognitive exchange, involving conceptual analysis, logical rigor, factual appraisal, and predictive competence. Personal preferences, if they enter into the argument, enter as shared commitment to cognitively vague and ambiguous persuasive terms like "freedom," "fulfillment," "progress," "order," "justice," and "democracy." In effect, argument is joined when efforts are made to impart consistent content to such expressions— and such efforts are inevitably and essentially cognitive.

In other words, one need not resolve ultimate questions about the nature of normative disputes before one can undertake the critical appraisal of contemporary political ideologies. One can grant the substance of the analysis that makes normative conclusions rest ultimately upon a non-cognitive personal preference and still meaningfully consider ideologies. This is the case because ideological judgments characteristically appear as conclusions of cognitive arguments tendered to standardize the meanings of self-recommending values. The ideologist offers reasons for his stipulations and assertions. Ideologists can and do frequently contradict each other. When a political liberal insists that men can be politically free only in a situation which permits them effective choice between competing political parties and the fascist insists that such a political system is calculated to frustrate freedom, they are contradicting each other in some determinate sense. Differences may rest upon different assessments of fact or alternative definitions, but in either case they rest on intelligent and intelligible grounds. The fascist might argue (as some did) that the diversity of political parties is a ruse to thwart the will of the people, or they might argue (as some did) that the kind of freedom exemplified by periodic political competition is more appropriately identified as license or caprice, and they would support their proposed redefinition with reasons. Competing political parties in parliamentary regimes, they might argue, in order to muster the greatest number of possible votes in their support, must appeal to the basest human motives and the meanest intelligences, and must focus on the best organized particular interests. This is so because most men are base, of mediocre intelligence, and primarily concerned with their own immediate interests. But any group of men governed by their basest motives, and the meanest intelligence and driven by organized, but special, interests cannot be said to be free. To counter such arguments one would ask questions of the following kind: Do political parties in parliamentary states appeal to the basest motives and the meanest intelligences? Are most men stupid and base? Do organized, but special, interests prevail in parliamentary regimes? These again are questions of fact and definition. In other words, they are topics for intelligent disagreement. The fundamental political values which make the entire discussion normative are, in some real sense, generally shared at the outset by both parties to the dispute. Both agree, for example, that men should be free in some sense or other. Questions can be asked about the sense of "free" that is being recommended as well as the techniques suggested to effect its realization. These are cognitive matters.

Contemporary language is replete with words which have, in ordinary parlance, positive emotional force; "freedom," "justice," "happiness," and "fulfillment" are among the most prominent. They have become part of the essential vocabulary of every contemporary ideologist. Their use serves to assure unanimity of initial attitude on the part of participants involved in political dialogue. But upon this common attitudinal base each ideologue will erect a different structure composed of statemental constituents, cognitive propositions which are either factual or analytic. The non-statemental components, the "pseudopropositions," the ventings of feeling, serve only (or should serve only) to provide the original impetus to the discussion, the force necessary to negotiate the gap between factual and analytic propositions and normative conclusions. The term *freedom,* or *liberty,* has positive emotional significance. The preference for *freedom,* or *liberty,* might be construed as a simple matter of personal taste, but since no serious contemporary ideologist has ever argued for bondage or slavery *per se,* one can grant that the original commitment was simply a matter of taste without having to abandon the critical appraisal of alternative ideologies. Since all effective political ideologies commence with ideals concerning which there is no serious initial dispute—only contested definitions, factual disagreement, and a possible conflict with other equally self-recommending values—contemporary ideological arguments can be judged on the basis of their logical consistency, their relevance, and their factual truth or falsity and reasons for according more weight to one value rather than another. The statemental components are the object of cognitive scrutiny. The reasoning is open to public assessment. The emotive components are all but universally self-recommending.

The adequacy of this account can be apprised by reviewing even those ideological arguments least capable of rational analysis. Adolf Hitler's *Mein Kampf* can, in no sense, be conceived as *simply* a statement of the author's personal emotional preferences. Suggestions, admonitions, and imperatives are *argued.* The arguments may be elliptical—vital premises may be suppressed—or they may be invalid and their factual premises erroneous, but they are not simply assertions of personal preference. Hitler advocates, for example, the fulfillment of one of mankind's highest aspirations: man's continued evolutionary progress. No one seriously objects, in principle, to such an ideal. In this sense it, among others, is self-recommending. We raise objections when Hitler contends that the fulfillment of such an ideal requires the caste superordination of a specific biological race —when fulfillment of the ideal conflicts with other values. We demand evidence, for example, that would confirm that a given race is the sole repository of man's foremost creative capacities. But such objections raise questions of fact and definition and as such are subject to cognitive appraisal. No one seriously advocates thwarting man's highest aspirations or his continued evolutionary progress. Consequently, Hitler need not concern himself with advancing arguments specifically calculated to support his initial values; nor, for that matter, need any ideologist. Similarly, Marx need not support his proffered ideal of "human emancipation" with studied arguments. We are all prepared to grant the merit of such an ideal. But commitment to such an ideal no more makes one a Marxist than commitment to the fulfillment of man's highest aspirations or mankind's evolutionary progress makes one a National Socialist. Such commitments merely indicate that one understands what constitutes appropriate response to the contemporary language of approbation and disapprobation.

Should the foregoing suggestions be correct, it would be, at best, a simplism to suggest that paradigmatic Fascism "violently" rejected "humanitarian ideals, including any notion of potential human equality."[28] Certainly Fascists denied that men were equal in any descriptive sense. They recognized, as do Marxists, democrats, and Christians, that men differed in size, weight, racial traits, intellectual potential, and moral character. But neither presumptive nor procedural equality is based on any of these differences. Emphasis upon such differences does not necessarily preclude a commitment to presumptive or procedural equality. Presumptive equality requires only that men be *initially* treated as objects each having intrinsic value; that each is conceived *initially* as a repository of moral substance and has a *prima facie* claim on our consideration. Procedural equality requires only that any substantive denial of rights, the active practice of discrimination, the meting out of punishments, be justified by standard argument rather than be the product of caprice. Men are, and should be, treated as equals unless and until significant reasons are forthcoming for construing them to be, and treating them as, unequals. In practice, *equality* means little more than presumptive and procedural equality. Such an operational meaning entails no more than the requirement that the differential treatment of individuals, or groups of individuals, be vindicated by arguments calculated to win the support of any unbiased judge. It means, in essence, no more in a democratic environment than it did in Fascist Italy. Italian Fascist apologists recognized, in principle, each man as a member of the Kantian Kingdom of Ends.[29] Differential treatment was conceived to be the consequence of real and relevant differences in determinate and objective individual or group traits. Thus, Fascist treatment of the Jews was justified by arguments no different, in principle, than the justificatory arguments employed by American authorities for the wholesale removal and confinement of the Japanese-American population on the West Coast of the United States during World War II. Appeals were made to threats of collective security and survival and so forth. The real and painfully evident differences between the two circumstances resided in the fact that in the one case appeal to an unbiased agency was all but impossible to obtain. In the American situation the high emotional salience prevalent in times of national emergency can be credited with the miscarriage of justice.

In totalitarian environments appeal to unbiased agencies is effectively precluded by the institutional structure of the system itself. But this should not obscure the fact that arguments *were* forthcoming in support of differential treatments in totalitarian circumstances. And it is to the coherency, relevance, and truth of such arguments that the scrutiny of ideologies is directed.

Any classificatory schema that would distinguish between fascism, Marxism, and democracy on the basis of fascism's putative "anti-humanism" and "anti-equalitarianism" would be, in a substantial sense, mistaken. Italian Fascism was explicitly committed to a concept it called the "humanism of labor" and, as has been suggested, to the presumptive equality of all men. Real distinctions between the various political ideologies begin to manifest themselves when *humanism* and *equality* are defined and the means for the realization specified descriptively. But these are matters of fact and definition rather than irreducible and incorrigible emotional preferences. They constitute the cognitive grounds in which intelligent disagreements can be anchored.

In effect, what is being argued is that ideologies can be considered to be, in a substantial sense, rational products, and can be assessed against standards of truth, validity, and relevance. That this is a plausible posture to assume can be illustrated by one further consideration: nationalism as a sustaining political value.

The appeal to nationalism is frequently construed as an ultimate and irreducibly irrational appeal—"my country, right or wrong." But the nationalist is never content, characteristically, to rest his case on a simple pronouncement. Consider, once again, the National Socialist case. The thesis, "Germany over all," is neither morally self-recommending nor intellectually self-certifying. If it were, Hitler would not feel, as he in fact did, that it was necessary to advance arguments in its support.

He argued that the racial "core" of the German people was "Aryan" or "Nordic" (he used both formulations). He then maintained that only the Aryans were true culture creators. With their passing, culture would disintegrate and mankind lapse back into savagery. In fact, the very survival of mankind itself would be threatened.[30] Departure from the initial presumption of the equality of men implied by nationalism was thus vindicated by an appeal to an entire sequence of logically related propositions bearing on generally accepted values. One can test the logic of such an argument as well as the truth status of the constituent propositions. If the argument form fails to meet the test of validity, and the propositions the test of truth, the argument is faulted and the initial presumption in favor of procedural and presumptive human equality is restored. For this reason National Socialism defended the collection of factual assertions about racial differences with such intransigence.

If the foregoing suggestions are correct, they would imply that the critical appraisal of contemporary political ideologies can be seriously undertaken without a final resolution of the fundamental problems of meta-ethics. Ideologies are linguistic entities that can be assessed, evaluated, and approved or disapproved without lapsing into simple emotion or resolving all the problems that attend normative discussion. One's appraisal can be made substantially, if not exclusively, in the language of reasoned discourse.[31]

Description, Analysis, and Empirical Political Theory

Finally, some indication of the role played in the knowledge enterprise by descriptive studies such as that which is here forthcoming should be considered. The contemporary emphasis in political science, as well as political history, is focused on theory construction and explanation. Descriptive studies are, by and large, suspect. It must be recognized, however, that significant theory and adequate explanation require, as their necessary propaedeutic, responsible description and appropriate classification of the subject matter within the domain of discourse.

The failure to meet these minimal requirements of competent inquiry and assessment has left in a confused state the study of fascism as a political phenomenon. Most of the responsibility for the attendant confusion is attributable in large part, as has been suggested, to what has been identified as the "communist theory of Fascism,"[32] an enterprise which purports to identify the criterial attributes as well as the historic and socioeconomic functions of fascism in general and paradigmatic Fascism in particular.

The orthodox Marxist is disposed to see in generic fascism "a real working system for the maintenance of capitalism in conditions of extreme crisis and weakening," manipulated by "the business heads of finance-capital who pay the costs and pull the strings. . . ." As a consequence fascism is understood to constitute a "tactical method of finance-capital." There is therefore no specific ideology of fascism—"it represents in reality no new ideology distinct from the general ideology of capitalism."[33]

Given such an appraisal there was an almost irresistible tendency to identify all and any non-Marxist-Leninist organizations, ideologies, and individuals as "fascist." The class of "fascists" became inordinately large. Admission to class membership was forthcoming if any real or fancied posture assumed could be somehow construed as "supporting" finance-capitalism. The term was used negatively to identify all those social and political elements that were non-Marxist-Leninist. Thus the German Social Democrats were "fascists." The National Socialists were equally "fascists." Business institutes, church groups, patriotic clubs, chambers of commerce, veterans' organizations, and, on occasion, the Boy Scouts, were all catalogued under the meaningless rubric "fascist."

The net result was, of course, intellectual confusion and systematic ambiguity in the cognitive uses of the term. The term "fascist" had no intentional meaning and consequently no denotation. For lay Americans the term came to mean simply "anyone whose opinion differs materially from our own. . . ."[34] To American university students the term "fascist" came to refer, by 1940, to those who were "militaristic, nationalistic, proud, egotistical and showy."[35]

Worse still was the fact that American academicians, all too frequently influenced by Marxist-Leninist appraisals of fascism, designed scales for the measure of "fascistic" attitudes employing all the stereotypes that were its analytic artifacts. Ross Stagner, in one of the first studies of "fascist attitudes," selected items the responses to which would serve as putative indicators of the requisite attitudes. The item sample was collected from "authoritative sources," including J. P. Dutt's Marxist-Leninist "interpretation" of "fascism" as well as representative statements of German "fascists," that is to say, National Socialists. A fragmentary collection of Mussolini's speeches was also used as a resource reference but it is evident that Mussolini's statements were systematically interpreted as being "anti-radical," and as manifesting a "middle-class-consciousness, which may be defined as a superior attitude toward the working class." Because of the inclusion of National Socialist among the "fascist" items, "racial antagonism" made its appearance at a time (1936) when (as we shall see) Fascists were deploring the inhumanity of National Socialist racism. Items like "anti-radicalism, contempt for the lower classes, and opposition to labor unions" appeared and reappeared throughout the inter-war period in studies presumably designed to tap "fascist" attitudes.[36]

Whatever such items represented they did not responsibly incorporate authoritative Fascist assertions. Fascists, particularly during the decade between 1930 and 1940, never tired of affirming their radicalism, their rejection of capitalism as an economic system, and their preoccupation with the well-being and syndical organization of the working classes. Only if the scaling devices were formulated by men who ignored representative Fascist literature, or if the enterprise were governed by pervasive prejudgments, could standard Fascist assertions be "reinterpreted" to mean precisely the reverse of their literal intention. Whatever such attitude studies were studying they were clearly not studying paradigmatic Fascist attitudes.

The tacit bias governing such experiments is explicit in works like that of Dutt. He held that Fascism could not be "interpreted in its own terms . . . but only in terms of its service to finance-capital."[37] Standard university textbooks in the United States echoed this kind of appraisal and incorporated its bias without even minimal reservations. J. F. Brown's text, a contemporary work devoted to social psychology, informed students and colleagues that

liberal democracy while superficially the rule of the whole people is actually the rule of the bourgeoisie. A dictatorship in modern society can only represent the rule of a class through force alone. . . . In modern industrial society the dictator may only be the tool of the bourgeoisie, unless the underlying property relations have been destroyed through a proletarian revolution.

He went on to indicate that when "the government is taken over by the bourgeoisie and ruled in its interests," one has a "fascist dictatorship."[38] Given this assumption, "fascist movements" must needs "tend toward political conservatism." Fascism must, furthermore, be "anti-radical" and, given an indeterminate number of auxiliary assumptions that psychologically follow from this account, it must harbor contempt for the working classes.

Even after World War II the massive study of the "authoritarian personality" was conducted with the assumption that what was being assessed was "potentially fascistic" personality traits and "prefascist dispositions."[39] What was presumably discovered was that persons who were anti-Semitic tended to be generally ethnocentric, antagonistic to groups other than their own, politically and economically conservative, firm advocates of "free-enterprise," and opponents of labor unions. This constellation of dispositions seemed to hang together in empirical fact. Persons possessed of these prepotent dispositions were variously characterized as "authoritarian," "antidemocratic," and "fascistic," as though all three terms could be used interchangeably to refer to a specific class.

What seems reasonably clear is that, as Roger Brown has recently asserted, "American intellectuals generally accepted the Marxist interpretation of fascism as a movement of the extreme political right, as a conservatism driven to desperation by the economic problems of capitalism."[40] As a consequence only those "fascist" statements that could be somehow construed as politically and economically conservative entered into the item lists employed in the measurement of "fascist" attitudes. Outside of the methodological shortcomings which afflicted such work (these have been entered into systematically in a variety of places[41]) the fact remains that anti-Semitism, political and economic conservatism, and contempt for the working classes have never been necessary or sufficient conditions for admission into the class of individuals that could be historically identified as "fascists." Many prominent Fascists in Italy (Gentile among them) were never anti-Semitic, anti-radical, or anti-labor even for tactical reasons. Many movements generally identified as "fascist" were neither conservative or anti-Semitic, nor did they manifest "racial antagonism" in any meaningful sense of the term.

The fact is that we are not in any position to assign, with any conviction, a precise significance to high scores on such test vehicles as the F Scale. There is good internal evidence to indicate that convinced Fascists would not have made notably high scores. That Fascism in Italy did attract an important following among conservatives is clearly the case. But the evidence also indicates that these elements were quickly disillusioned by Fascism's radicalism. G. D. H. Cole has argued specifically against the

erroneous belief that Fascism was simply a form of Capitalism. . . . [The] great capitalists [came] to be controlled by it, and [were] compelled to subordinate their money-making impulses to the requirements of the Fascist State. . . . [Fascism was] not fundamentally a class-movement. Its claim to transcend classes is in a sense quite genuine; for it reaches back, behind the class-divisions of modern society, towards primitive conditions of tribal solidarity.[42]

Most contemporary political analysts recognize today that much of the analytic effort made to comprehend fascism as a social and political phenomenon has been simplistic. Unfortunately, those scales self-advertised as tapping "fascist attitudes" traffic on such simplisms. What is required as a preliminary to responsible empirical work and theory construction is a serious and searching redescription of historic, paradigmatic Fascism. This is the preliminary taxonomic obligation requisite to any further empirical investigation. Only out of such a reappraisal can some order be restored and significant efforts at classification, interpretation, and theory construction be forthcoming.

The forthcoming chapters attempt a restatement of the justificatory arguments of historic Fascism. They attempt to provide a summary statement of the constellation of argued beliefs Fascists were prepared to defend. Such arguments can be reasonably understood to represent the public manifestation of felt social and political attitudes.

Fascism and Its Ideologues

Fascism as an ideology was a far more complex and systematic intellectual product than many of its antagonists (and many of its protagonists as well) have been prepared to admit. At its best, in the works of Giovanni Gentile, for example, it certainly compares more than favorably with Lenin's rationale and perhaps favorably with the philosophic efforts of Marx as well. That Gentile's vindication of Fascism may well constitute an elaborate rationalization of Fascist power is a consideration which need not deter us from our account. Such a judgment could only be the consequence of a necessarily detailed comparison of Fascist practice and Fascist thought and is essentially the task of the political historian. But such an analysis requires a responsible familiarity with the historic rationale of Fascism. To this end an account of Gentile's thought is of crucial importance. Even though Gentile's efforts at pedagogical reform, for example, were faulted by the Regime, and even granted that many Fascists resisted the identification of Fascism with Gentile's philosophic system, Gentile's arguments appear and reappear in all the official Fascist attempts at rational vindications of policy. Gentile's arguments proved essential to standard Fascist apologetics. Since our principal concern is with the rational reconstruction of that apologetic, Gentile occupies a central position in the forthcoming exposition.

For all that, Gentile contributed but one, if very important, component of the mature ideology. The ideology matured only after the Fascist accession to power, and consequently succeeded in drawing into its orbit a number of competent academicians, not the least of whom were Carlo Costamagna, the jurist, Roberto Michels, the political sociologist, and Corrado Gini, the statistician, demographer, and sociologist. This is not to say that every expression of conviction issued by such men was fully compatible with the system of thought we will characterize as the ideology of Fascism— but is rather a preliminary recognition of the fact that they contributed substantial elements to the mature belief system that became the ultimate intellectual charter for the exercise of Fascist authority. Neither Roberto Michels nor Corrado Gini, for instance, were Fascist enthusiasts. Both found Fascism compatible and both contributed substantially to its ideological formulations,[43] but both entertained reservations concerning the historic Regime itself.

That the thought of such men be included in a reconstruction of Fascist ideology is required for historical accuracy. That their association to Fascism may have been an embarrassment to the Regime, or that they later renounced Fascism, is a matter of little consequence to the reformulation of the ideology as it did, in fact, develop. When Fascist Italy assumed an anti-Semitic posture, for example, there was an effort to disassociate the ideology from those men of Jewish provenience who had substantially contributed to its articulation. Roberto Michels had Jewish antecedents—as did others, like A. O. Olivetti, who were equally important.[44] As a consequence there was a tendency on the part of Fascist doctrinaires to neglect their contribution. Obviously, such a restriction will not be entertained here. Finally, the fact that many of the men who contributed to the development of the ideology were later declared "traitors" to the historic Regime is equally a consideration of little consequence for our reconstruction. Many of the original Bolsheviks, including some of the foremost theoreticians of Leninism, were later executed as "traitors" to the system to which they had contributed so much. Nonetheless, their contributions can be judged quite independently of that fact. Thus the thought of N. Bukharin and G. Zinoviev is as significant for an adequate appraisal of the historic and intellectual articulation of contemporary Leninism as that of Joseph Stalin. With the same justification, the foregoing account will incorporate arguments developed by men like Giuseppe Bottai, who, although they harbored serious reservations and were subsequently adjudged traitors to the historic Regime,[45] contributed substantially to its ideology.

Finally, because Fascism did not attain relative maturity as an ideological system until the first years of the 'thirties, and because in a real sense it continued to undergo development thereafter, any adequate account must be historical in character. There were intimations of Fascism in Mussolini's thought certainly as early as 1904 and by 1910 they had become so prominent a feature that Renzo De Felice could legitimately speak of a "Mussolinian" as distinct from a "Marxian" socialism, and Georges Roux could plausibly suggest that nascent Fascism had already begun to manifest itself under the guise of revolutionary socialism.[46] In what sense and how far such judgments are true can only be the consequence of a scrutiny of the historical development of Mussolini's thought. Similarly, the doctrinal emphasis on race theory and the radicalization of corporativism postdate the maturation of the ideology as such. Their adequate appreciation requires a historical perspective.

Each successive phase, of course, is subject to the same challenges of coherency, relevance, and truth.

Fascism loomed large in the first half of the twentieth century, the most tumultuous of centuries. Its adequate appraisal is a primary responsibility of our time, for, as this treatment will suggest, Fascism has cast its shadow across our entire historic epoch.

CHAPTER TWO

The Historic Background and Proto-Fascism

AT THE turn of the twentieth century Italy was the product of a vast and unique array of historical forces. United a scant three decades before, she found herself thrust into a European environment in which the principal nation-states had already carved out for themselves an enviable measure of security and enjoyed enormous potential for development in an industrial age. Italy was favored in neither respect. Since the time of Charles V, in the sixteenth century, the people who had given the world some of its most enduring treasures had counted no more than a cipher in world affairs. Italy was fragmented into a collection of contending states, their provincialism and insularity rising in inverse proportion to their historic viability. While Britain and France were resolving their problems of national unification, the Italian states either fell beneath the heel of foreign conquerors or became embroiled in the intrigues of endogenous secular or religious politics.

The nineteenth century catapulted Italy into the modern age. The entire peninsula was astir with demands for reform and unification. Under the leadership of a newly emergent and numerically small middle class, the *Risorgimento* effected both. By 1870 Italy joined the number of liberal and unified nation-states that made up the European continent. But Italy made its entrance into modern history beset by a deep-seated regionalism and provincialism born of centuries of division and subordination. Its unity was sustained by the efforts of but a very small fraction of its population. Moreover, Italy was incredibly poor. In 1890 per capita income in Italy was forty dollars, while the corresponding figures for Britain and France were one hundred and fifty five dollars and one hundred and thirty dollars respectively; and the prospects of amelioration were not encouraging.

Italy's very geographic configuration and location militated against her rapid industrial and commercial development. Her major cities were separated by distances that required prohibitive initial capital outlay if efficient and rapid transportation were to be achieved. Furthermore, Italy's immediate access was to the Mediterranean, which modern commerce had long since by-passed. But such disabilities could be overcome had Italy given any evidence that her soil offered any occasion for exploitation. The fact of the matter was that about one third of that soil could not be cultivated because of the mountainous Apennines. Where the soil could be cultivated it was, in large part (as in the Basilicata, Calabria and parts of Sicily), exhausted by the cultivation of centuries. Elsewhere, torrents from the mountains or desiccation precluded effective utilization. But the most significant of Italy's deficiencies was the lack of even the prerequisites for industrialization—the availability of necessary mineral resources. At the turn of the century Italy's total mineral production was one twentieth that of Germany and almost half of that total was provided by the sulphur unearthed in the mines of Sicily. In 1897 Germany produced one fifth of the world total of raw iron while Italy produced one tenth of one per cent. In 1898 Germany produced 130,928,490 tons of coal; Italy produced 341,327 tons.[1] One need but compare the rates of economic growth of Germany and Italy at the turn of the century to gauge the colossal significance of such discrepancies in available raw materials.

Conjoined with, and at least in part the consequence of, such oppressive poverty was a scandalous level of illiteracy. Even where there was compulsory elementary education there was no effective implementation, and in 1900 fully half the population of Italy could neither read nor write. In most parts of southern Italy, where the peasant population lived in conditions of the utmost destitution, illiteracy was the rule. Afflicted with gross dietary deficiency, accustomed to deprivation, and mulled by ceaseless toil, whole regions were innocent of the most elementary education and were consequently not equipped to participate in the challenges offered by the new century.

Self-government, as understood in the West, is predicated upon the supposition that effective education and a general value consensus are the necessary, if not the sufficient, conditions for the successful implementation of representative democracy. The parliamentary system instituted in a united Italy in 1870 was, however, challenged not only by the monumental problems generated by poverty, but by a potential electorate that was not only regional in its biases, but illiterate as well. In the effort to meet so ominous a challenge suffrage was initially limited by property and educational requirements to about two and a half per cent of the population. By 1882 suffrage qualifications had been relaxed so that seven per cent of the population had access to the voting booth. By 1913 suffrage had been extended to less than nine per cent of the population, of whom less than sixty per cent chose to vote. Many did not vote out of obedience to the Papal decree forbidding Catholic participation in elections, but many more failed to exercise their prerogatives because of a pervasive disillusionment with the parliamentary system itself.

It is true that during the thirty years that preceded the turn of the century Italy enjoyed an appreciable economic improvement. Italy developed a substantial textile industry, with Milan displacing Lyons as the textile center of Europe. Similarly, Genoa overtook Marseilles as the principal port of the Mediterranean. A network of rail lines connected the peninsula to the great trunk lines of the European heartland in a remarkable engineering achievement which succeeded in overcoming imposing natural barriers. Commerce, both domestic and foreign, was stimulated, and the overall wealth of the nation gradually increased. But even in 1914 the per capita income of Italy, measured in standard gold units, was only 105, while that of Britain stood at 237, and that of France at 182. The vast mass of agricultural and industrial workers lived at mere subsistence level and manpower became one of Italy's principal export items. From 1876 through 1880 yearly emigration was approximately 100,-000, from 1881–1886 approximately 150,000, from 1887–1894 approximately 250,000, and from 1895 through 1900 it attained the level of 300,000 and continued to increase until 1907, when 700,-000 Italians left their homeland to search out a more satisfactory standard of living.[2]

The steady increase in the rate of emigration is evidence of a real or fancied deterioration in the position of the Italian laboring classes. Ruled by a government effectively in the hands of a select and restricted clientele, the majority of Italians construed the state to be, at best, the executive committee of the bourgeoisie, or, at worst, a self-serving camarilla. The behavior of far too many members of the governing class did much to foster these convictions. Members of the Italian parliament frequently made government an enterprise for their own financial advantage. Corruption was prevalent and the elections of 1894 marked the nadir in political morality. The campaign was conducted on the level of personalities and it was revealed that members of the highest echelons in government service were implicated in a financial scandal involving the Banca Romana.[3]

Such shortcomings have, of course, characterized other parliamentary regimes, but under the conditions which prevailed in Italy they had portentous consequences. In a social system which provides for upward mobility, corruption and self-service in government are matters of little concern. In Italy, where the vast majority of the disenfranchised suffered real and sustained poverty, the manifest corruption in government circles constituted compelling evidence that the agencies of the state served special rather than the general interest. Consequently, the central government never succeeded in gaining the confidence of the vast majority of the Italian population. Italy seemed destined to develop into a society riven by irremediable class differences. Although Italy had only begun extensive industrialization, revolutionary socialism rapidly spread throughout the propertyless class. Alienated from the state, afflicted with urgent grievances which the middle-class government of parliamentary Italy largely ignored, the dissident elements among the working population turned to anarchism and socialism. Only years later did Italy's governing class realize that it was not the lure of doctrine or criminal disposition that made men seek membership in the "subversive" parties. By the time he wrote his memoirs, Giovanni Giolitti had come to appreciate that poverty had driven the masses into the socialist parties. For years the constitutional parties failed to offer the dissident disenfranchised the opportunity for parliamentary redress of grievances. The socialists offered them the one remaining recourse—revolution.[4]

Only in 1912 was universal manhood suffrage introduced into Italy. But by that time revolutionary sentiment had long since crystallized into reasonably well-organized political associations. Their explicit commitment to class interests was a not unexpected reaction to the evident class preoccupations of Italy's minoritarian government. Since political expression was, in effect, denied the working masses, political motives insinuated themselves into every aspect of Italy's economic life. Class antagonisms had poisoned Italian life so much that strikes were often called in situations where no conceivable economic advantage could be forthcoming. When Giolitti finally offered reformist socialists like Leonida Bissolati and Filippo Turati ministries in the government, they could not accept because acceptance would have been construed as class betrayal by the Italian laboring classes. Such belated attempts to dissipate the political frustrations which afflicted Italy had no effect and the advent of World War I found the nation cleft by chronic class strife.

Italy made its entrance into the twentieth century burdened with endemic poverty and a minoritarian parliamentary regime which exacerbated the grievances of the poor. But if its internal policies were calculated to generate structural tensions in the system, its foreign policies were hardly less disastrous. In foreign affairs Italy could hardly aspire to the role of a great power. It was an economically backward, badly organized, and ineffectively administered state. Italy came away from the 1878 Congress of Berlin, where the major powers had carved out colonial empires for themselves, with "clean" but empty hands. In 1881 the French occupied Tunis, an event which shook the Italian government. Italians had looked upon Tunisia, where the population of Italian origin far outnumbered the French, as a natural extension of the peninsula. But both Britain and Germany, seeking to divert French energies from *their* respective spheres of interest, sought to involve France elsewhere. As a consequence France, with the connivance of the other major powers, succeeded in establishing a protectorate over the disputed territory, and Italy nursed a sense of grievance and humiliation. More important, perhaps, than grievance and humiliation, the episode left Italy with a sense of isolation. Italy found herself increasingly confined in the Mediterranean. The growing pressure of Austria-Hungary in the Balkans, the expansion of France in North Africa, and finally the British move into Egypt in 1882, from which the shortsightedness and inconstancy of Italy's policy excluded her, produced a growing sense of national frustration. This was capped by the defeat of the ill-equipped Italian army at Adowa in Ethiopia in 1896, during Crispi's half-hearted essay at colonial expansion.

The best the parliamentary government of the nineteenth century could effect was a series of treaty arrangements which promised Italy some leverage in international contest. Operating from an intrinsically weak position, insecure and potentially isolated, Italy undertook policies of expediency. She signed defensive agreements with Austria-Hungary and Germany and at the turn of the century made a similar agreement with France. Whether this arrangement with the French was compatible with the commitments made in the context of the Triple Alliance remains an unresolved historical and diplomatic issue. But the major powers of Europe and the thinking population of Italy became convinced that Italy pursued a shameful Machiavellian policy, ready to sacrifice principle for any immediate advantage.

Such agreements did, of course, reflect a shrewd appraisal of Italy's international possibilities. Italy was the weakest of the major powers. Only by deploying whatever force she had on the side of the stronger, in a system of balance between rival alliances, could she hope to effect an improvement in her international position. Only where a delicate power balance obtained could Italy's negligible weight bring her positive advantage. But in the rapidly changing circumstances that characterized the turn of the century this policy required rapid and unpredictable alterations in allegiance. Italy could not entertain the role of initiator in international power politics. She could only assume the unflattering guise of a "jackal," while the major powers undertook grand initiatives. Italy became, in the eyes of the major powers and among the Italians themselves, a "nation of mandolin players," a comic opera conspirator among the greater powers. Even Italy's war with Turkey in 1911 and the consequent acquisition of Tripoli and Cyrenaica did little to enhance the Italian image, and a gnawing sense of inadequacy continued to afflict the sensitivities of Italians.

The result was increasing disenchantment with the parliamentary regime that bore the responsibility for every internal and external weakness. The mounting intensity of the internal class struggle, the appearance of insurrectionary bands in the South and organized subversion in the North, the growing sense of alienation that separated the governed from the governors, the notorious corruption and class nepotism of the ruling class, an ineffectual and sometimes humiliating foreign policy, all conspired to undermine the confidence of the Italian masses in the regime that had been established upon unification.

By the turn of the century historic circumstances had provided the social support for three potentially revolutionary forces: (1) antiparliamentarianism, (2) an intransigent revolutionary socialism and (3) an exacerbated nationalism. Each of these forces, although in some sense independent of the others, was nonetheless in a more significant sense intimately related to them. The intellectual spokesmen of one would appear as spokesmen for the others. There was a fascinating and sometimes bewildering circulation of ideas and of intellectual cadre. Originally quite distinct, the three revolutionary forces ultimately coalesced to produce the highly combustible amalgam that was historic Fascism. To reconstruct the initial doctrine of Fascism is, in large part, to recount the intellectual history of these three constituent elements.

Antiparliamentarianism and the Proto-Fascist Sociological Tradition   To have identified, however fully, the historic forces which prepared the ground for the reception of a particular constellation of ideas tells us nothing about its internal coherence or the truth of its constituent propositions. When we speak of an intellectual tradition, we imply that some systematic relationship obtains within an identifiable collection of propositions, a logic (using the word in its extended and informal sense) which relates a body of ideas in such a manner as to produce a coherent and convincing unity.

It is important to know why Italy, at the turn of the century, was so receptive to the antiparliamentarianism of Gaetano Mosca (1858–1941) and Vilfredo Pareto (1848–1923). But it is equally important to trace the implications of their ideas independent of the historic circumstances which made them so appealing.[5]

Within the complex ideas identified with the names of Mosca and Pareto there is a core of critical conceptions of which antiparliamentarianism was only one prominent expression. Subtending and logically antecedent to antiparliamentarianism were the concept of *elitism* and the concept of the historic and social function of *political myths,* both intrinsically related to lawlike generalizations concerning inter- and intragroup dynamics—generalizations which were at that time and are today identified with the concept of *ethnocentrism.*

What will become evident is that a remarkable similarity of ideas obtained among a specific group of social theorists who were to exercise enormous influence in pre-Fascist Italy. Their ideas were to appear and reappear with sometimes tedious regularity, not only among the antiparliamentarians in general, but among the revolutionary socialists and nationalists as well.

For the purposes of exposition, the ideas of Mosca can be considered first. This is not to suggest that the question of intellectual priority has been decided in Mosca's favor. Specialists have engaged in a long, tedious, and, for our purposes, fruitless debate concerning the intellectual priority of Mosca's formulations with respect to those of Pareto.[6] Mosca's ideas were mature by 1881; the text of his *Teorica dei governi e governo parlamentare* was completed by 1883 and published in 1884. By 1895 he had completed his masterwork, *Elementi di scienza politica* (translated into English as *The Ruling Class*), which appeared in print in 1896. At almost the same time Pareto published his *Corso di economia politica,* which contained clear anticipations of his subsequent ideas.[7] Many of those ideas shared a marked similarity with those of Mosca and were to influence the political thought of Benito Mussolini.

If attention is restricted to those ideas which influenced Mussolini, the question of priority becomes academic. All the ideas that significantly influenced Mussolini and Fascism are found in the books of an Austrian scholar whose work was certainly known to Mosca and in all probability to Pareto as well—Ludwig Gumplowicz (1838–1909). Intimations of those ideas, as well as some of the ideas themselves, are to be found in the writings of Henri Saint Simon, Hippolyte Taine and Karl Marx, among others. However, they are fully developed only in the work of Gumplowicz. The extent of Gumplowicz' influence on Fascist theory construction has been little appreciated. It appears almost certain that he was the initial source of almost all of Mosca's ideas and, at least indirectly, those of Pareto. And their ideas provided much of the initial intellectual substance of Fascism.

The question of priority, then, as it bears upon the relationship of Pareto's ideas to those of Mosca, need not detain us because whatever is of interest and significance for the present exposition is to be found in the antecedent work of Gumplowicz. Substantially all of the ideas traditionally credited to Mosca are to be found in Gumplowicz' *Rechtsstaat und Socialismus* and *Der Rassenkampf*, both apparently published in 1881,[8] two years before the appearance of Mosca's *Teorica* and many years before the publication of Pareto's *Corso*. Gumplowicz' *Grundriss der Sociologie*, published in 1885, together with *Rechtsstaat und Socialismus* and *Der Rassenkampf*, provides a full explication of his central theoretical concepts. When they are compared with the core concepts of Mosca's *Elementi* one cannot help but note a remarkable correspondence. Much the same can be said for some of Pareto's theoretical formulations—with the proviso that Pareto's general treatment of issues is more exhaustive and inclusive.

Gumplowicz, Mosca, and Pareto were men in the tradition of late nineteenth and early twentieth century positivism.[9] They conceived their enterprise as one calculated to yield the lawlike regularities governing societal and political phenomena.[10] Among those regularities they identified as characteristic of any organized aggregate of men was the presence in any community of a directive or strategic elite, a minority of men who arrogated to themselves the privilege of power.

Elitism   Working independently or
                                               in collaboration, as the
                                               case might be, Gumplo-
                                               wicz, Mosca, and Pareto
had come to the conclusion, immensely significant in the development of Fascist social and political thought, that

In all regularly constituted societies in which a government can be said
to exist, we find that all authority is exercised in the name of the entire
population, or of an aristocracy, or a single sovereign . . . but we also
find another circumstance without exception: the ruling class, or, rather,
those who hold and administer public power, will always be a minority,
and subordinate to them we find a multitude of individuals who never,
in any *real* sense, participate in government but merely submit to it:
these can be referred to as the ruled class.[11]

The above constituted Mosca's central thesis in the *Teorica* and
he repeated it in the *Elementi*:

Among the constant facts and tendencies that are to be found in all
political organisms, one is so obvious that it is apparent to the most casual
eye. In all societies—from societies that are very meagerly developed
and have barely attained the dawnings of civilization, down to the most
advanced and powerful societies—two classes of people appear—a class
that rules [*quella dei governanti*] and a class that is ruled [*dei governati*].
The first class, always the less numerous, performs all political functions,
monopolizes power, and enjoys the advantages that power brings;
whereas the second, the more numerous class, is directed and controlled
by the first, in a manner that is now more or less legal, now more or
less arbitrary and violent. . . .[12]

Pareto, in turn, in his *I sistemi socialisti*,[13] which became available in 1902, argued that human psychological traits were distributed in a normal Gaussian curve.[14] As early as 1897 he had
argued that it was an incontestable fact that men were not equal
physically, intellectually, or morally.[15] The distribution was that
of a normal distribution curve, with gifted individuals constituting
one end of the distribution and the vast bulk of the population
falling within the range of mediocrity and inferiority with respect
to the traits under consideration. Given this premise, conjoined with
the auxiliary assumption that the gifted have the opportunity of up-

ward social mobility, he concluded that society will always organize itself in the shape of a pyramid, with an elite or aristocracy occupying strategic positions at the apex, supported by the majority of the population at the base.[16] Society, as Pareto understood it, is composed of a ruling minority elite and a residual ruled majority.

The class of individuals who constitute a particular historical elite will, of course, be determined by the selective requirements of the prevailing social circumstances. In a primitive community where status is allocated on the basis of hunting or fighting prowess, the elite will be composed of the minority specially competent in this capacity. In a society of thieves the best thieves will constitute the elite; but in all cases the structure of the social organism remains constant. It is pyramidal in form, with the apex occupied by the select. Should this not be the case, should circumstances alter sufficiently so that the most competent did not constitute the effective elite and should the society not afford upward mobility to its most gifted members, it is threatened with multiple dysfunctions, not only insofar as it cannot meet challenges effectively but because the gifted counter-elite becomes a dissident and revolutionary minority. What results is either the extinction of the society or the erosive or explosive substitution of elites. This is one aspect of the phenomenon Pareto identified as the circulation of elites.[17] In general, such a circulation conceived a constancy of social form while constituent social elements circulate. The result was a conception of society in stable dynamic tension, forever characterized by a minority elite dominating a subordinate majority.

As we have suggested, this image of society is found in the antecedent work of Gumplowicz. As early as 1881 Gumplowicz insisted that "the state is not the mass but the ruled mass (*beherrschte Masse*)," who do not govern themselves but accord themselves to "the will of the ruling minority (*herrschenden Minoritaet*),"[18] The same thesis is argued in *Der Rassenkampf*, which appeared some time before the publication of Mosca's *Teorica*. The phenomenon of superordination and subordination (*Herrschaftsverhaeltniss, Herrschaftsorganisation*) was for Gumplowicz a constant and universal fact of history.[19] The struggle for dominance, furthermore, provided the motive force of history; it was "the pivot around which all history gravitates." By 1885, these conceptions were articulated in the conviction that

the state is a social phenomenon consisting of social elements behaving according to social laws. The first step is the subjection of one social group by another and the establishment of sovereignty; and the sovereign body is always the less numerous. But numerical inferiority [of the rulers] is supplemented by mental superiority and greater military discipline. . . . The state, therefore, is the organized control of the minority over the majority. . . . Universally there is a ruling minority and a subject majority. . . .[20]

Within the state, which is society organized, the constituent elements compete for dominance. When social and historic circumstances undermine the functional and strategic basis of existing dominance (e.g., when a society makes the transition from a military to an industrial community) a new elite is prepared to preempt positions of advantage. History reveals an endlessly long chain of just such substitutions (*einer unendlich langen Kette kuenftiger Herrschaftsumwaelzungen*).[21]

The image invoked by such conceptions is one of a social pyramid (Gumplowicz employs the same analogy Pareto utilizes in the *Corso*) composed of elements in dynamic tension (*ewige Spannung der Kraefte*).[22] The evident similarities between the theoretical conceptions of Gumplowicz and Pareto include arguments, allusions, and turns of speech. A notable instance is Gumplowicz' primary distinction between men and animals. The distinguishing characteristic of animals, he maintains, is that they have never learned to exploit members of their own species; they have never been able to organize a hierarchical society, to exercise dominance over their own kind.[23] Pareto advances literally the same distinction between man and beast.[24] Only men are capable of exercising organized tutelary and enterprisory control over society through hierarchical dominance. All human culture is predicated upon this capacity.[25] This is precisely the conclusion to which Gumplowicz' argument leads. He conceives culture and hierarchical organization to be causally related. One is inconceivable without the other.[26]

These similarities in content and form suggest that Pareto was at least familiar with Gumplowicz' antecedent work. Although Pareto nowhere cites Gumplowicz, Gumplowicz did exercise appreciable influence in Italy. Angelo Vaccaro's *Le basi del diritto e dello stato,* published in Turin in 1893, was written under Gumplowicz' influence, as was Icilio Vanni's *Saggi critici sulla teoria sociologica della populazione* (1886) and his *Prime linee di un programma di Sociologia* (1888).[27] Coupled with Mosca's work, which was admittedly influenced by Gumplowicz, these considerations suggest that if Pareto had not read Gumplowicz he was in all probability familiar with Gumplowicz' arguments through Italian sources before he wrote the *Corso* in 1895, and certainly before his *Sistemi* was published in 1902.

That Gumplowicz, Mosca, and Pareto shared some critical concepts, and that these concepts found their most explicit source in Gumplowicz is probably the case. The *prima facie* differences which suggest themselves, that Mosca was at least originally only interested in characterizing specifically political phenomena (he originally called his dominant minority a *political* class), that Pareto conceived his circulation of elites in terms of *individual* competition and selection, and that Gumplowicz was preoccupied with general *sociological* and *group* phenomena, are revealed upon more careful analysis to be without real substance.

Initially Mosca was concerned exclusively with a political class which he identified with the government[28] and, consequently, the range of application of the concept is far more circumscribed than that of Pareto, who conceived both a *governing* and a *non-governing* elite, and that of Gumplowicz, who understood aristocracy as directing *all* organized social activity. By the time the *Elementi* was written in 1895, however, it became evident that Mosca was occupied with broader sociological concepts. Mosca begins Chapter Seven of the *Elementi* with a reference to Buffon that maintains that social animals display a persistent disposition to organize themselves into self-regarding groups in constant competition. Mosca argues,

An instinct of very much the same sort seems to make its influence felt among men. Human beings have a natural inclination toward struggle but it is only sporadically that the struggle assumes an individual character, that one man is at war with another. Even when he fights, man remains preeminently a social animal. Ordinarily, therefore, we see men forming into groups, each group made up of leaders and followers.

The individuals who make up a group are conscious of a special brother-hood and oneness with each other and vent their pugnacious instincts on members of other groups.[29]

The disposition to so organize themselves characterizes not only primitive contact situations but "underlies the formation of all the divisions and subdivisions . . . that arise within a given society and occasion . . . conflicts."[30] Such intrasocietal groups constitute "social types" animated and organized by sustaining "political formulae," collections of maxims and prescriptions, as well as their vindications, that constitute reference guides for the governance of individual and collective behaviors. Mosca maintains,

Mankind is divided into social groups each of which is set apart from other groups by beliefs, sentiments, habits and interests that are peculiar to it. The individuals who belong to one such group are held together by a consciousness of common brotherhood and held apart from other groups by passions and tendencies that are more or less antagonistic and mutually repellent. As we have already indicated, the political formula must be based upon the special beliefs and the strongest sentiments of the particular portion of that group which holds political pre-eminence.[31]

These are, of course, broad sociological generalizations and Mosca identifies Gumplowicz as one of their principal sources. In fact, the theoretical account that emerges shares all the features of that given as early as 1875 in Gumplowicz' *Rasse und Staat*. Mosca's account differs only in relatively minor features and in emphasis. His interests were those of what we might call today political sociology, while Gumplowicz' were those of general or macrosociology. Nonetheless, for both the fundamental unit of analysis was the group. This is eminently clear in the work of both men (although Mosca on occasion lapses into theoretical individualism). Society was conceived as an organized collection of social aggregates that have crystallized around similarities in traits of high visibility, belief, and interest.[32] Within any particular historical society, specific needs open the path to dominance for specially endowed social elements. Thus Mosca argued that a strategic minority comes to exercise dominion over the society through the administrative and executive agency of the state. When historic circumstances alter and those qualities which once had high strategic and functional importance are no longer required, society moves into a protracted period of transition in which the old ruling class is gradually transformed by assimilating elements of the subordinate class that display the requisite talents—or there is a period of violent dislocation in which a new contending class undertakes successful revolution.[33] That such transformations involve entire classes, groups, "social types," is specifically indicated by Mosca's reference to lower class revolutions organized and directed by their own dirigent minority (*classe dirigente*).[34] Mosca had thus transformed the conception of the "ruling class." The elite which he had originally identified with the restricted intensional meaning he had assigned to "political class" finally came to mean *any* elite that organized the membership of any specific social type to some collective purpose. The range of application of Mosca's concept of a "ruling minority" is thus, in general, the same as that of Gumplowicz' dominant minority and Pareto's elite. Since the dirigent class of the contending subordinate majority does not participate in the government—which Mosca maintains is the monopoly of the dominant minority—they cannot be said to be members of what he had previously identified as the "political class." They could only be specially talented members of a contending elite in quite the Gumplowiczian and Paretan sense.

Furthermore, the social types of Mosca function in precisely the same way as the "heterogeneous social elements" of Gumplowicz. History becomes the arena of contending groups. Intersocietal conflicts are resolved by appeals to simple force. Intrasocietal competition manifests itself in political struggle, each social type attempting to arrogate for itself an increased measure of influence in the exercise of political control.

Even an elementary analysis of Pareto's *Sistemi* provides a similar theoretical account. What originally appears to be an analysis in terms of competition between individuals within the organized society is revealed as a struggle for dominance between groups.

The history of the past, and observations in the present, indicate that it has always been the case that mankind divides itself into groups, each of which procures for itself economic goods in part by producing them directly and in part by divesting other groups of them. . . .[35]

That Pareto is not referring to primitive inter- and intra-societal relations alone is indicated by his references, in the same context, to the "infinity of groups" contending for power in modern society. Each of these groups crystallizes around similarities, racial traits of high social visibility, cultural attributes, or immediate material interest. Each group contends for social power and privilege. To make successful forays into the struggle each group must be animated by an in-group solidarity; a prevailing sense of benevolence, even self-sacrifice, in the service of their "similars" (*i loro simili*);[36] as well as dispositional diffidence capable of sustaining the calculated use of force against out-groups.[37] The constellation of sentiments necessary to direct individual and group activity finds expression in a functional myth, what Pareto was later to characterize as a "derivation," speech reactions which are the variable manifestations of relatively stable prepotent dispositions or invariable "residues."[38] The vindications advanced by groups in conflict are non-logical constellations of ideas that are, in fact, "very transparent disguises of exclusively terrestrial interests."[39] Thus, Pareto speaks of the "religion" of socialism, the organizing or functional myth of the working class (what Mosca calls a "political formula"), as the form most appropriate for advancing class interests, for the protection and enhancement of group concerns. Thus the social struggle which is apparently conducted on the basis of doctrine actually exemplifies contending interests.[40]

For all three theoreticians, Gumplowicz, Mosca, and Pareto, intrasocietal group conflict comes to take on a manifestly different character than intersocietal conflict. It is this difference which is the distinguishing species trait of society. A society riven by internecine conflict between groups, social types, classes, sects, or social strata is not viable. Open and violent conflict is manifestly dysfunctional. A *modus vivendi* is established under the suzerainty of the state and the governance of law. Once mankind achieves a minimal level of civilization, contending groups no longer simply exterminate each other. One group accedes to dominance and proceeds to exploit the vanquished. The conquered are accorded a disadvantaged place in a new, larger, and more complex social configuration. The victorious group constitutes itself the sovereign power and establishes law-governed relations between the heterogeneous social elements.

These relations, established by force, define the rights and duties of the various constituent elements of society.[41] Gumplowicz maintained,

The hostile contact of different social elements of unlike strength is the first condition for the creation of rights; the conditions established by force and accepted in weakness, if peaceably continued, become rightful. . . . It is an error and a delusion to think that rights have been or can be equally distributed. They arise only in the relations which exist in the state; they express them and measure their inequality. . . . Some force is necessary to maintain the unequal condition in peace; suitable institutions must be set up and sedulously sustained.[42]

Myths and Masses

Once the relationships between the various social elements are governed by sanction-sustained rules, struggle between groups takes on a singularly "ideological" guise. Contending social elements make strategic appeal to "moral sentiments" in order to gain tactical advantage in an interminable social struggle. For the sake of exposition, any constellation of ideas to which appeal is made in the effort to standardize individual duties and obligations within a group by providing a hierarchy of effective values will be identified as a *myth*. A myth used to mobilize support behind a contending elite's challenge of the dominant elite and the rules which result as a consequence of commitment to the prevailing myth will be referred to as an *organizational* or *functional myth*. *Charter myth*, on the other hand, will refer to those political formulae used to legitimize the rules of obligation sustaining the established order. Thus, when the rising bourgeoisie contested the dominance of the established feudal nobility they appealed to "popular sovereignty" and the "rights of man." These myths served as organizing belief systems.[43] When the bourgeoisie acceded to social and political pre-eminence, the myth of popular sovereignty ceased to be revolutionary and reformist and became a charter myth, a major conservative moral force in legitimizing the newly established order. But the supersession of charter myths is merely a surface feature of the perpetual substitution of elites. That the "divine right of kings" can no longer legitimize the dominance of the feudal nobility simply means that the historic circumstances have so disadvantaged, and internal debilitation so far weakened the hitherto dominant minority that the path to succession has been opened. In the course of the contest force will be judiciously employed, but open violence threatens the entire structural fabric of society and is consequently employed only with circumspection. An astute contending elite organizes the dispossessed of a multitude of subordinate social elements behind the slogans of an organizing or functional myth. These "masses" can be mobilized in the service of the revolutionary or reformist challenge even against their own real interest, for it is in the nature of the masses to be essentially passive, non-logical, uninformed, and easily gulled by shibboleths and emotive appeals. Devoid of energy, character, and intelligence, they become the instruments of social change.[44] As instruments they *always* serve the ends of an organizing elite. Gumplowicz, Mosca, and Pareto are all equally insistent upon these points. Mosca contended,

Granting that the discontent of the masses might succeed in deposing a ruling class, inevitably . . . there would have to be another organized minority within the masses themselves to discharge the functions of a ruling class. . . . In reality the dominion of an organized minority, obeying a single impulse, over the unorganized majority is inevitable.[45]

Gumplowicz advanced the same theses.

The masses always lack unity and organization as the result partly of their great bulk, partly of indolence. Since the result of the social struggle depends on discipline, the minority has the advantage because it is small. . . .[46]

These propositions articulated in a theoretical account provide an interpretation of society, the state, and social change. Society is a system of ordered relations between heterogeneous social elements. Order is sustained by sanctions administered by the state. Each constituent element of society is maintained by a self-regarding group disposition. Under specific social and historic circumstances a particular social element accedes to dominance. In the course of its ascent it may mobilize a variety of other elements in society to its service. One of the most effective techniques employed in such mobilization is the strategic use of functional myths. Such myths channelize energies, provide precepts and maxims for the governance of conduct, specify tactical goals, and organize an aggregate into a machine for conquest. Once having acceded to dominance, the organizing minority seeks to perpetuate its power. The functional myth may become a charter myth or, depending on circumstances, a new myth may be devised for this purpose. Whatever the course, the inevitable result is the dominance of an elite, a new *de facto* aristocracy.[47] In primitive conditions where hunting and war characterize group life, a group of warriors and hunters becomes the dominant elite. Their behavior is governed by a constellation of beliefs that establishes the rules governing approbation and disapprobation. The "warrior's code" becomes a functional myth. In order to maintain the stability of the community they dominate, they foster a charter myth which traces their right of domination to the gods or to a fictive eponymic hero. The subordinate classes are traced to the inferior descendents of the hero, or are burdened with some putative hereditary sin that vindicates the superior status of the dominant minority and justifies the inferior status accorded the majority. As long as the majority of the subordinate class remains convinced of the legitimacy of established social arrangements, the continued dominance of the established minority is assured. When the proffered rationale crystallizes into a normative belief system, priests make their appearance and provide essential moral support to the regime.[48] When, under the pressure of altered social and economic conditions, circumstances change, a new element within the constituent subordinate population is prepared to contend for dominance. Settled conditions, for example, can bring an increase in the social significance of the intellectual, commercial, and enterprisory elements in an organized community, and a military class gradually gives way to an intellectual, commercial, or enterprisory elite. The sustaining charter myth which hitherto prevailed is no longer honored. Counter claims are lodged. Once the transition is effected and a new relationship between the social elements is established which better accords with the demands of a given historic situation, a new period of stabilization is initiated. A new charter myth is advanced to provide the moral ligaments binding up society. The new myth represents the interests of the new elite but must also appeal to the group-building factors, both moral and material, which constitute its sustaining force. While neither functional nor charter myths are rational in themselves, they must, first and foremost, reflect the real relations which obtain between the various elements in society. That is, they must provide rules for the allocation of rights and obligations. But they must also appeal to the persistent sentiments which characterize man as a social animal. Men must develop the minimal sense of group identity without which any group would disintegrate into contending factions. Appeals to national sentiment, tradition, historic memories, dynastic loyalties, and/or cultural affinities provide the basis for a sense of group identity which often prevails against the real and immediate material interests of the various constituent social elements which compose the larger group.[49]

By their very nature the myths which organize or legitimatize are never *simply* rational products. They must satisfy too many social requirements to be simply intellectual artifacts. Nor will there be any necessary relationship between their intrinsic rationality and their persistence. They endure, in many cases, in spite of their evident irrationality or arationality. One of their major functions is to mobilize sentiment, to initiate and govern action. Whether they are called "political formulae," "derivations," or "fictions" they constitute a necessary and inevitable factor in social stasis and evolution.

Myths, Masses, and Ethnocentrism

This entire theoretical account is predicated upon one critical concept–ethnocentrism. The term ethnocentrism is used advisedly. It is one of the most frequently employed and widely accepted concepts in contemporary sociology.[50] Generally, its modern formulation is attributed to William Graham Sumner.[51] As a matter of fact the concept occupies a central position in the work of Mosca and Pareto and is found in the antecedent work of Gumplowicz more than a generation before Sumner's *Folkways* was written. Sumner was, in fact, familiar with Gumplowicz' work and cites his publications in a number of places.[52]

Ethnocentrism refers to the disposition on the part of *any* community to conceive its shared traits and interests as the initial standard of reference in establishing a hierarchy of comparative values. The individual, through a process characterized as "socialization," identifies with his group. In its habits, customs, and usages he finds the criteria for orienting himself in the macrosocial world of individual and group contacts. Ethnocentrism is the generic term referring to the general disposition on the part of individuals to identify with a myth, the normative system of their community. Anthropologists will employ the concept as an explanatory device to explain the attitudes of primitive tribesmen, while sociologists and social psychologists more frequently extend the range of its application to *all* in-group attitudes exhibited by *any* social element, whether that element is economic, racial, political, cultural, or hereditary.

Ethnocentric dispositions have high survival value. They enhance the survival capacity of a group because they dispose the individual to accord with group strictures and to sacrifice in the service of the community that, because he identifies with its valued traits, augments his self-esteem. Any threat to the group is construed as a threat to himself.

Gumplowicz early identified these "constant psychological tendencies," characterizing them as "ethnocentrism" (*Ethnocentrismus.*)[53] In *Der Rassenkampf* he was to employ the neologism "syngenism" (*Syngenismus*) to identify the same dispositional trait-complex, and persisted in its use throughout the remainder of his productive life. Its intensional meaning remained that of ethnocentrism, for syngenism refers to the in-group sentiments of social sympathy, self-sacrifice, and devotion to the natural social community. It refers to the self-regard with which each community sustains itself. Its obverse is a diffidence toward out-groups, muted or overt hostility which at best is avoidance or simple tolerance.[54] Each self-regarding group is the product of an intersection of material and moral factors—community of interest, biological descent, and similar territorial origins, as well as manifest cultural affinities in speech, dress, practice, and belief.[55]

That men could be mobilized into self-regarding groups, whether those groups be hordes, tribes, city-states, nations, castes, classes, or political parties was, for Gumplowicz, a fact of central importance. Man was conceived to be, by nature, a social animal. The identification with group norms involves the individual intrinsically with his community. What is generally referred to in our own time as "socialization" was called "mimetism," "imitation," "suggestion," or simply "education" by Gumplowicz.[56] When the works of Scipio Sighele and Gustave Le Bon appeared during the last decade of the nineteenth century, Gumplowicz was quick to cite them as providing evidence of the group sustaining dispositional traits of man as a social animal.[57] Collective psychology provided explanatory accounts of man's behavior in the various social groups of which he was a member. Furthermore, it explained how masses could be dominated and set into motion by organized minorities.

Scipio Sighele and Gustave Le Bon provided the theoretical supplement necessary for a more comprehensive account of the processes governing the identification of the individual and his community. Le Bon's "collective hallucinations" upon which men act, the "images" which call up other "images, having no logical connection with the first," were too much the counterpart of the group sustaining myths and collective sentiments of Gumplowicz, Pareto, and Mosca to pass unnoticed. Le Bon's conception of society composed of the ruled masses, dominated by "collective hallucinations" and a dominant elite was similarly compatible with the antidemocratic conclusions which united the three. As soon as Le Bon's *Psychologie des foules* and Sighele's *Le folla delinquente* appeared (in 1895 and 1891 respectively), their results were incorporated into the theoretical structure of Gumplowiczian and Paretan thought.

To the intellectuals of Italy, disillusioned with the parliamentary system which seemed to operate in the service of minoritarian interests, cognizant of constant interclass tensions and conscious of the irrationality and suggestibility of the masses that composed both the rural and the newly urbanized populations, the set of related theoretical propositions advanced in the works of Pareto and Mosca provided an illuminating account of perceived reality. That account was provided largely by Gumplowicz and for almost the next half century his thought had more influence in Italy than anywhere else in the world. His ideas, as we shall indicate, recurred regularly in Fascist theoretical literature. His image of society was that of a complex system of elements dominated by a state apparatus that answered to the will of an organizing and dominant minority. Potential intergroup strife forever threatens the stability of society. When changed material conditions disadvantage a dominant elite, society witnesses a rotation of elites. Each such challenge is led by an organizing minority mobilizing the masses in its service. Each minority advances a sustaining myth, a myth that can act as a goad to rebellion during times of transition from the rule of an established elite to the rule of a contending elite and a legitimizing fiction once the contending elite has established its dominance. Behind the facade of representative institutions and parliamentary procedures the bourgeois government of Italy was just such an established elite.

Gumplowicz, Mosca, and Pareto felt that this account exposed democratic pretensions. All parliamentary procedures succeeded in doing was to conceal the fact of minoritarian rule. Any political movement which promised effective democracy, the "rule of the people," and any political theory which seriously conceived political and social order to be the consequence of rational and voluntary contract, traded upon illusion and sophistry. The disorganized, dispersed, and ignorant majority could no more effect its political will in contemporary society than it could have contracted away its "natural freedom" in the "state of nature" for the security of the rule of law. These are the political formulae, the moral fictions, the charter myths of bourgeois dominance.

What is curious, and also significant for our purposes, is the fact that Gumplowicz, Mosca, and Pareto were essentially conservative thinkers. Gumplowicz conceived class society, with clearly defined hierarchies of property and prestige elites, as man's natural and inevitable social environment. Pareto was a *laissez-faire* economist who saw intrasocietal relations governed by sentiments and interests rather than the normative ideals which constituted their public image. Mosca revealed himself ultimately to be a "conservative-liberal" who sought the maximum amount of individual and group freedom compatible with the laws and regularities governing man in society.[58] None could be conceived as representing lower- or working-class interests. None were Marxists or socialists. And yet, for all that, Gumplowicz, Mosca, and Pareto were to exercise enormous influence upon the intellectually aggressive and politically active socialist factions in Italy. The living embodiment of this relationship was Roberto Michels (1876–1936), a revolutionary socialist and active associate of Mussolini during the years prior to World War I. Nine years Mussolini's senior, Michels personified the relationship which obtained between the antiparliamentarianism of the conservative right and the antiparliamentarianism of the revolutionary left.

The Proto-Fascist Sociological Tradition and Marxian Socialism

In 1911, Michels published his classic *Zur Soziologie des Parteiwesens in der modernen Democratie,* which appeared in Italy in 1912 and in English translation as *Political Parties* in 1915. At the close of his study Michels indicated that the conception of the "oligarchical tendencies" in society was not original with him. The theory that a directive social group of restricted membership is absolutely essential to political and social life, he insisted, was by no means a new one.

Gaetano Mosca, the most distinguished living advocate of this sociological conception, and, with Vilfredo Pareto, its ablest and most authoritative exponent, while disputing priority with Pareto, recognized as precursors Hippolyte Taine and Ludwig Gumplowicz.[59]

Michels went on to indicate that the theory that society cannot exist without a dominant minority, that the state is the executive agency of an organizing elite which creates the moral and law-governed order that provides the structure of community life, that the masses provide the elemental energy but not the directive will of social change,

far from conflicting with or replacing the materialist conception of history, completes that conception and reinforces it. There is no essential contradiction between the doctrine that history is the record of a continued series of class struggles and the doctrine that class struggles invariably culminate in the creation of new oligarchies which undergo fusion with the old. The existence of a political class does not conflict with the essential content of Marxism, considered not as an economic dogma but as a philosophy of history. . . .[60]

Whether such a compatibility existed in fact need not detain us here. It is important that many Italian revolutionary socialists maintained that it did. Revolutionary socialists in Italy were ready to acknowledge, with Marx, the fact that history is the history of class struggles and that "all previous historical movements," as Marx maintained, "were movements of minorities, or in the interest of minorities." They were equally ready to recognize, with Marx, that "law, morality, religion, are . . . so many [class] prejudices, behind which lurk in ambush just as many [class] interests," and that "the executive of the modern state is but a committee for managing the common affairs of the whole bourgeoisie."[61] For Marx, as for Pareto and Mosca, the displacement of class and faction was the consequence of social and historic forces quite independent of the will and conscious direction of men.

Both non-Marxist and Marxist antiparliamentarians saw the entire structure of parliamentary government as an elaborate facade consciously or unconsciously designed to conceal the realities of minority dominance. It was as obvious to critics of the Left as it was to critics of the Right that the cry of "popular rule" was a snare, a piece of political fiction through which a minority sought to legitimize its rule. Critics of both the Left and the Right agreed that society had entered into a period of revolutionary transition. The analyses common to Gumplowicz, Mosca, and Pareto appeared more and more frequently in revolutionary socialist publications, and the ideas of Le Bon, conjoined with those of Michels, became common media of intellectual exchange among the most radical elements of Italian socialism. But there was one name around which all these ideas, the arguments which were to transmogrify classical Marxism, were to crystallize—Georges Sorel.

Georges Sorel

Of all the social and political thinkers of this germinal period before World War I, Georges Sorel (1847–1922), the principal theoretician of revolutionary syndicalism, was, at the same time, among the most obscure and the most stimulating. Because of his obscurity, anything said about his social thought must be qualified in a number of significant ways. First of all, Sorel was a notoriously bad writer.[62] He was, furthermore, an autodidact who pursued his ideas with an undisciplined enthusiasm that often leaves the reader completely unable to reconstruct the order of ideas and their relative importance. Much of his thinking follows psychological rather than logical sequence and, consequently, many of the essential premises of his arguments are suppressed and his discussions become perplexingly elliptical. When one surveys the complex disorder of his life's work, he becomes difficult to classify. He was at once a defender of the proletariat, an advocate of an insistent, if transmogrified, Marxism, and a protagonist of bourgeois virtues—a defender of radical libertarianism and an anti-Semite—a radical revolutionary and a traditionalist —a revolutionary socialist and a defender of monarchism. From this list of seemingly contradictory commitments it is not surprising that it has been thought possible to trace lines of influence not only to paradigmatic Fascism, but also to Leninism and, some would suggest, to National Socialism as well.[63]

Our concern here will be with the Sorel whose ideas directly influenced the political maturation of Mussolini. The discussion will be calculated to reconstruct the relationships between the two men rather than to provide an exposition of the thought of Sorel.

Sorel is generally known only as the author of the *Réflexions sur la violence,* a substantial part of which he first published in Italy between October and December, 1905, as "La lotta di classi e la violenza" and "Lo sciopero generale," and which was later issued as a pamphlet entitled *Lo sciopero generale e la violenza* with a preface by the Italian syndicalist Enrico Leone.[64] It was in this work, which exercised enormous influence on radical Italian Socialist thought prior to World War I, that Sorel developed his most characteristic Syndicalist ideas. It is a work as important for what it does not say as for what it does. The foundation of the exposition is almost entirely concealed from view. Unless the reader is aware of that foundation, however, Sorel's ideas take on a precariousness and an insubstantiality that belie his enormous impact on the development of Fascism.

The edition of the *Réflexions* which became standard made its appearance in France in 1908. The work dealt primarily with revolutionary tactics and organization. In this sense the range of

Sorel's interests was more restricted than that of Gumplowicz and Pareto, who were concerned with macrosociology, and the focus of Sorel's attention was more narrow than that of Mosca, whose interests lay in political sociology. Sorel was a revolutionary tactician who conceived himself more concerned with method than with ends.

As a tactician, Sorel had an abiding distrust of "professional intellectuals," who were apparently only concerned with an apocalyptic vision of the future society.[65] Emphasis upon this specialized preoccupation, he maintained, was calculated to afford advantage to a special class of nonproducers, the architects of utopian theories and speculative fancies. Such intellectuals advance themselves as mentors of revolutionary socialism only to become its masters.[66] The intelligentsia exploits its expertise, its ability to formulate obscure speculations on the future organization of society, in order to make itself indispensable to the proletarian revolution. Intellectuals quickly monopolize the leadership of the revolutionary movement and constitute themselves an encysted special interest. Thus a rotation of minoritarian political elites will have occurred within the organization of the proletariat.[67]

Sorel feared the dominance of the intellectuals within the revolutionary proletariat because he recognized that society, in general, is characterized by the phenomenon of minoritarian dominance. All history has been the history of the struggle for dominance on the part of minorities.[68] These minorities, whatever their origin, seek to obtain control of the state which holds an exclusive monopoly of force within the body politic. The state is the agency of effective social control and as such is the contested prize in every historic instance of social conflict,[69] for it serves those who have succeeded to social dominance by transforming the wishes of the dominant minority into law. Its explicit function is the exercise of force, and the "object of force is to impose a certain social order in which the minority governs. . . ."[70]

The image that Sorel's convictions conjure up is one in which man as a social animal is in unremitting inter- and intrasocietal conflict. Since the state has always existed and the "state has always been, in fact, the organizer of the war of conquest . . . ," society has forever been in a state of conflict, now open, now veiled.[71] The

putative "unity of society," which provides room only for intersocietal conflict concerning which the professors of jurisprudence
and the "bleating, democratic moralists" become so eloquent, is a
fiction, a political formula for inuring the inert and feckless masses
to political control.[72] Only a Europe "stupefied by humanitarianism"
could stumble into the "democratic marsh" in which such elementary
truths go unrecognized.[73] The truth is that society itself is the arena
of group competition. Each group, when it is vital, is activated by
a self-regarding ethnocentric group spirit, possessed of "that audacity of noble races, that mad, absurd, and spontaneous audacity . . .
[which shows] contempt for all security of the body, for life, for
comfort" in the struggle for dominion.[74]

This view is not incompatible with Marxism. Classical Marxism
conceived man's history as a doleful tale of unrelenting class
struggle, with elites contending for power and acceding to dominance when the array of power they could marshal overwhelmed
their opponents. Once ensconced, the will of the ascendant minority
is made into a law for all.[75]

The simple outline of such an interpretive and explanatory
account is equally compatible with the conception of society and
social dynamics common to Gumplowicz, Mosca, and Pareto. Revolutionary Syndicalists like Angelo Oliviero Olivetti could link the
names of Marx, Pareto, and Gumplowicz without provoking surprise
among the radical leftists of the Italian socialist movement.[76] All
these theoreticians were convinced that the history of society can
only be written in terms of group antagonism and that violence
provides the motive force of change. Intrasocial relations established by violence become codified in law and sustained by force.
Olivetti could argue that "violence is force seen from a particular
point of view. Repression exercised by those who dominate is
force and becomes translated into law; the resistance of those who
are dominated is called violence."[77] This is the distinction made by
Sorel as early as 1903, and it reappears in the *Réflexions*.[78] Pareto
renders a similar account in the *Sistemi* of 1902 and develops it
systematically in his later *Trattato*.[79] Similar convictions subtend
Mosca's notions of "juridical defense," an equilibrium between contending social forces that permit the widest scope for the prevalence

of law-governed relations to predominate over the interests of specific social elements. The concept implies that law is the codified expression of the will of interest groups. Sorel independently formulated a similar view in his *Introduction à l'économie moderne*.[80]

These ideas were found in the work of Gumplowicz long before the appearance of Mosca's youthful *Teorica*. Force, for Gumplowicz, is prior to, and the foundation of, law (". . . *am Anfang nicht das Recht war, sondern die Gewalt*. . . .").[81] Force is restrained only by counterforce.

Rights are a social creation, a form of communal life produced by the conflict of unlike social groups of unequal power. . . . [Each] group tends in the direction of its own interests, it tries to protect and further them, to increase its power and to acquire a corresponding influence in the state. . . . In other words each participates in sovereignty solely and exactly in proportion to its power.[82]

Gumplowicz, Mosca, Pareto, and Sorel were agreed on the rejection of the liberal, contractual, and democratic conception of the state, society, and law. In this their views were compatible with those of Marx and the compatibility explains why Italian socialists could move without theoretical embarrassment from one to the other. Just as instructive, however, are the differences between their accounts.

Classical liberalism conceived sovereignty to reside ultimately in the individual. Individuals were understood to contract with their equals, all of whom were endowed with certain natural and imprescribable rights, to generate a state ultimately responsible to the aggregate of contracting parties. The sovereignty delegated to the state was understood to be limited by the positive and natural rights possessed by the contracting individuals. Like Gumplowicz, Mosca, Pareto, and Sorel, the Marxists denied the adequacy of such an account. For them the state comes into existence when irreconcilable conflicts arise between social elements. The state arises out of conflict. It is the mechanism employed to impose the will of a dominant minority upon the defeated or powerless majority.[83] Classical Marxism, however, did not conceive this relationship as an exemplification of the primacy of force as such.[84] Such an interpretation would be simplistic.

For Marxists, the relationship between social elements was determined by prevailing economic relations which depend, in the last analysis, on the stage of development attained by the forces of production. Marxists held that political power—the rotation of elites—is dependent upon economic power, and that legal relations depend upon economic relations. The social elements put into motion during periods of social change derive their energy from changes undergone in the economic base of society. If a new contending elite appears it is evidence that productive forces have outgrown the productive relations created to satisfy the demands of an earlier mode of production. The vitality, organization, and ultimate success of this new social force is the consequence of antecedent economic development. Taken together these theses assert the primacy of economic over moral and political development.

All of the theoreticians with whom we are concerned objected to the monofactorial pretenses of classical Marxism. Gumplowicz, Mosca, Pareto, and Sorel, in almost the same language, rejected the monocausal theory of social development. They all held that the relationship between determinants of historical change was one of interdependency. Sorel conceived economic determinism, however complex its theoretical formulations, beset by difficulties. As early as 1898 he objected to the determinism that characterized the explanatory accounts of orthodox socialists.[85] He maintained that Marx himself, as well as his orthodox protagonists, employed vague and ambiguous formulations in theory construction that afflicted their arguments with equivocations. Once the equivocations were analyzed, it was obvious that empirical fact had infirmed many of their critical propositions. Pursuing arguments advanced in Benedetto Croce's *Materialismo storico ed economia marxistica*, Sorel rejected Marxist determinism.[86] By the time he wrote the *Réflexions* he could conclude,

There is no process by which the future can be predicted scientifically, nor even one which enables us to discuss whether one hypothesis about it is better than another; it has been proved by too many memorable examples that the greatest men have committed prodigious errors in thus desiring to make predictions about even the least distant future.[87]

Sorel, Anti-Intellectualism, and the **At least partly as a con-**
Concept of Political Myth **sequence of these con-**
victions, Sorelian thought
moved inexorably away
from a theory of society to a theory of motivation. The attempt to
formulate his views drove him irresistibly away from the assessment of economic factors operating in society to a consideration
of the psychological or subjective factors that govern human behavior and the moral criteria against which that behavior is to be
evaluated.[88] Sorel was, in effect, what the French call a *moraliste.*
The central preoccupation of the "apologist for violence" was the
moral life. More specifically, he was concerned to know not only
what constituted the moral life; he also wished "to determine if
there is a mechanism in existence capable of guaranteeing the
development of morality."[89] If this were known, one could more
competently assess social change.

For Sorel, morality necessarily implied autonomy. Moral approbation and disapprobation are inappropriate when applied to
actions which are not free. Where the individual does only what
he is compelled to do, moral approval or disapproval can gain no
foothold. Morality implies the possibility of human determination
of the events in the world.[90] A satisfactory theory of ethics, therefore, requires an account of human action which permits significant
choice, which admits the possibility of alternate courses of action
determined, in the last analysis, by the will of the moral agent.
Sorel believed he had at least the first formulations of such an
account. "To say that we are acting," Sorel maintained, "implies
that we are creating an imaginary world placed ahead of the present
world and composed of movements which depend entirely on us.
In this way our freedom becomes perfectly intelligible."[91]

This "imaginary world" is not a description of things, the
product of cognitive assessment, but an expression of a determination to act, a volitional affirmation[92] which results in social change.
The guide to action was provided by the vision of that "imaginary
world" which men, organized in groups, entertain as normative
ideals. This "imaginary world" to which he made recourse was
Sorel's political myth. Its descriptive content was not significant in
and of itself, but only insofar as individual and collective action

was governed by it *as if* it were an objective and accurate representation of some objective possibility. Sorel's myth functioned as an explanatory concept in his theories of motivation and collective organization.

Sorel's theories were the product of a confluence of various currents of European anti-intellectualism and antirationalism. He was markedly influenced by the thought of Henri Bergson and his conceptions ultimately took on the principal features of William James' pragmatism. Furthermore, some of Sorel's ideas bear a remarkable similarity to those of Friedrich Nietzsche.[93] All these men lived and wrote in an age buffeted by antipositivistic and anti-intellectualistic currents.

It had become increasingly evident that the study of society had in no sense attained the level of maturity of the paradigmatic natural sciences. General sociology gave precious little evidence of predictive competence and could deploy but meager explanatory force. The prevailing mood of the critics of social science was, at best, one of profound scepticism. One form of resistance to positivism in the study of society came in the form of a methodological critique which sought to dichotomize the sciences into the now familiar classifications, *Naturwissenschaften* and *Geisteswissenschaften*. Techniques appropriate to the one were deemed inappropriate for the other. The natural sciences sought out the lawlike regularities governing material and mechanistic processes; the "human sciences" were concerned with the individual and collective willed responses of "spiritual" agents.

The most radical form of antipositivism manifested itself in the anti-intellectualist movement which numbered Bergson, James, and Nietzsche among its principal adherents. The use of the designation *anti-intellectualism* has considerably obscured the nature and intention of the movement that stimulated some of the finest intellects of the turn of the century. At times, anti-intellectualism is understood to have the same meaning as *irrationalism* or *mysticism*, but the identification is transparently incorrect. All the anti-intellectuals employed reason in their analyses and expositions, and both Bergson and James emphatically denied that their views entailed any abandonment of reason as such. Rather than abandoning reason, anti-intellectualists cast it in the role of an adaptive and

creative tool; they tended to understand its products not as dis-
coveries, but as adaptive creations or contrivances. In this sense they
opposed themselves to the main current of late nineteenth century
positivism which espoused a somewhat crude reflection or rep-
resentationalist theory of cognition. For the positivist, something
was true if it "reflected" or adequately "represented" an "external
world." Anti-intellectualists, on the other hand, tended to be
pragmatic; they judged truths not as reflections or representations
of an "objective reality" but as felicitous creations, systematic
anticipations of experience that enhance and facilitate the life of the
individual and the collectivity. Anticipations which successfully
guide man through experience are true; the measure of truth is
predictive competence, confirmed by "irreducible and stubborn
facts." For the anti-intellectualists, truth could be no more than
this. Thus they employed abstract concepts and logical fictions in
the effort to anticipate consequences, but they always made regular
recourse to the concrete particulars in reference to which concepts
and fictions establish their truth and meaning. The abstractions,
universals, class names, and logical constructs thus employed were
not understood as "reflecting" reality, "representing" immutable
truth. Euclidean geometry, for example, is but one of the possible
interpretations of physical space and is itself one of an infinite
number of possible geometries. We characterize our world as
Euclidean because of the adaptive convenience afforded by the
system. Only in this sense is Euclidean geometry true. Euclidean
geometry cannot be said to be true because it more adequately
reflects or represents the world, for it cannot be meaningfully said
that the world has, in itself, a geometry to describe.[94]

Historically, intellectualists may be thought of as those thinkers
who accorded epistemological priority and ontological significance
to reason, in the sense that its products were thought to reflect a
higher and more substantial reality than that of the senses. This
position is characteristically attributed to Platonism but is equally
characteristic of positivists, who thought that true theoretical propositions shared an iconographic similarity with "objective nature."
The anti-intellectuals opposed this privative theory of reason, not
reason itself. Such theories were held to be privative because they
impoverished the fullness and meaning of experience; they either

relegated sensory experience to secondary cognitive significance or postulated an empirically inaccessible and, consequently, metaphysical reality that is external and prior to experience.

At the same time a related but not identical current, antirationalism, was influencing the development of social and political thought. As in the case of anti-intellectualism, the expression *antirationalism* is frequently employed as a term of derogation. On occasion the alternate term *irrationalist* is employed to identify those thinkers who, at the turn of the century, had begun to take cognizance of the compulsive, neurotic determinants governing individual and collective behavior. Once again the distinction must be made between the theoretical account given by psychologists and social theorists of the variables that enter into the determination of manifest behavior, and the techniques employed in searching out the variables themselves and relating them in a theoretical context. The antirationalists were, in general, men who had become convinced that "unconscious," "instinctive," or "paralogical" elements were of primary importance in determining individual and collective response to the environment. Usually Freud and Nietzsche are numbered among the most important of the theorists of antirationalism. In their case the application of the term irrational could not be conceived as descriptive of their methodological principles. Both employed rational techniques to formulate what they understood to be cognitive propositions that, taken together, constituted a theory of human motivation.

An analytic distinction should certainly be made between the anti-intellectualists and the antirationalists on the one hand and the transrationalists on the other. As the term is used here, transrationalism denotes that class of thinkers, each of whom maintains that only a source extrinsic to reason and qualitatively distinct from sense experience can provide men with "truth." These are men who tender knowledge claims whose justification rests on "faith," "intuition," "emotion," or some special "insight" which is incorrigibly correct.

With the above distinctions in mind, Bergson would qualify as an anti-intellectualist and a transrationalist, Nietzsche and James as anti-intellectualists, antirationalists, but hardly as transrationalists. Sorel, on the other hand, is difficult to classify. What is important for our purposes is the recognition that his social and political thought is largely comprehensible without recourse to special epistemological adjuncts. By 1905 Sorel claimed that a strict "science of society" was, in principle, impossible. The realities with which social theorists had to deal were so enormously complex, each social and historic event the result of so intricate an intersection of factors, that prediction was impossible. As we have seen, however, he went even further and insisted that *no* cognitive process could certify the merit of one hypothesis about the future as opposed to another. Under the influence of Croce, Sorel understood history as an art form having no scientific or specifically predictive pretensions. History is an ideal reconstruction of the past, true for those who live in a specific period insofar as it is useful in furthering their life activity.[95] History then is a collective myth. It is a projection into the past of that "imaginary world" which provides the basis for a determination to act.

History has considerable interest when it is considered as a means for coming to know the rules that given human groups probably followed in their lives; but history cannot have as its object the prediction of future facts from past facts. History is therefore, in the last analysis, a psychological summing up that permits us to reason about projected organizations, legislative reforms, and the tactics that a given class should follow to achieve a determinate end. . . .[96]

History, then, is but one form of social myth, and the purpose of myth is to provide the basis for determinate acts. The social myth is composed of a "body of images" capable of evoking "as an undivided whole the mass of sentiments which corresponds to the different manifestations of the war undertaken by Socialism against modern society."[97] The myth serves the same organizing function as military instruction. Both prepare the individual for a contest in which the actions of each are of significant (if indeterminate) consequence to all.[98] The social myth fully specifies what is expected of its protagonists.[99] It provides the basis upon which moral ascription can be made and the merit of each act adjudicated. The myth provides what Sorel calls "the ideological unity" which any revolutionary force must possess if it is to accomplish its historic task.[100] The myth, then, is essential to life activity. Only in that sense can it be spoken of as true, for it makes no descriptive knowledge claims, nor is it subject to analysis. It provides the grounds for a determination to act, a disposition to make the future that which the creative will would have it.

It is relatively clear that this treatment of history and social theory as myth is concerned with formulating an outline of a specific theory of motivation which itself makes knowledge claims. It is either true or false that men undertake collective action under the impetus of social myths. So conceived, myths—the myths of Marx's catastrophic revolution, of primitive Christianity, of the French Revolution or the Italian *Risorgimento*—are specifically historical forces. An explanatory and predictive account of historical and social events must be more adequate if it includes synthetic propositions which make references to them than if it does not. Sorel tells us that a "theory of science" which does not understand the influence of myths upon collective responses affords us only a "misleading idea of the forces which really move men."[101] This contention necessarily entails that one account of human motivation is more correct than another. It would seem, consequently, that one can distinguish more and less adequate hypotheses about the future. If either of two sets of propositions, one including and the other excluding critical and informative propositions about the function of myths in structuring behavioral responses, are equally true or equally false, such propositions would, in fact, be empirically meaningless. Sorel's contention that myths provide a more adequate account of motivation would be indefensible.

This confusion infects all of Sorel's discussion devoted to myths. On the one hand he insists that myths, to be effective, must represent "all the strongest inclinations of a people, of a party or of a class, inclinations which recur to the mind with the insistence of instincts in all the circumstances of life" through which men "reform their desires, passions, and mental activity."[102] The myth "must be made of a body of images which, by intuition alone, and before any analyses are made, is capable of evoking as an undivided whole the mass of sentiments" of a party, sect or class.[103] Now these inclinations or sentiments must be, in some sense, testable, or Sorel's contention would be empirically meaningless. The theory of social myths requires that one know, in principle, which myth would be the more effective in any given historic or social circumstance. Knowing this, however, one would be in a position to decide between alternate hypotheses about the future. Sorel cannot have it both ways. If all hypotheses about the future are equally adequate or inadequate, then his contention that effective myths invoke prevailing inclinations and sentiments is incomprehensible. In fact, one suspects that the proposition is cognitively meaningless. If Sorel claims to have correctly identified the forces that move men, then anticipations of the future which include an account of those forces must, in some sense, be truer than accounts which do not. Sorel's position would involve antirationalist theses subtended by an anti-intellectualist theory of truth, but his program would not be transrational.

This is how Pareto understood Sorel's enterprise. For Pareto, Sorel's significance lay in his *scientific* contributions. Sorel's myth was no more than a special case of what Pareto called a "derivation" in the *Trattato*. The myth was a collection of images which lent expression to the sentiments which moved men to act. It was a descriptive concept in a specific theory of motivation, the merit of which could be assessed by normal experimental techniques.[104]

Sorel denied that, in fact, reason prevails over sentiment. As a consequence, he insisted that sentiment constituted a significant historic force. This contention, as long as the nature, origin, and logic of sentiments escaped assessment, could at best make the future contingent; but it could not possibly, unless an indeterminate number of special epistemological premises are introduced, lead to the conclusion that the future is completely indeterminate.

Sorel's treatment of social myths is a special application of his general theory of motivation. The individual and the collectivity are motivated by myths, "artificial worlds," what he spoke of (in 1900) as "imagined futures."[105] These imagined futures structure the response patterns of the individual. He knows what is required of him. His life attains moral significance. In the case of individuals, such paralogical constructs are ephemeral and "generally disappear from our minds without leaving any trace in our memory; but when the masses are deeply moved it then becomes possible to trace the outlines of the kind of representation which constitutes a social myth."[106] Sorel's explicit purpose is "to find out how the feelings by

which the masses are moved form themselves into groups. . . ."[107]
But this is the process of theory construction in social science. No
transrational claims are made. The methodology employed is that
which Pareto characterized as logico-experimental.

At this level of analysis there is little to distinguish Sorel's
conception of the social myth from the "collective hallucinations"
upon which men act, developed in the work of Gustave Le Bon.
Sorel reviewed Le Bon's *Psychologie des foules* in November, 1895,
and its influence upon his thought increased in subsequent years.[108]

Le Bon spoke of "collections of images" that mobilized social
elements into activity.[109] Such a collection of images is nonlogical
in the sense that the components need share no intrinsic connection.
The function of such complex images is not cognitive; it is evocative.
The rational scrutiny of assumptions and the critical appraisal of
evidence is simply inappropriate in the attempt to understand the
motives of collective behavior.

Whatever strikes the imagination of crowds presents itself under the
shape of a startling and very clear image, freed from all accessory
explanation, or merely having as accompaniment a few marvelous or
mysterious facts; examples in point are a great victory, a great miracle,
a great crime, or a great hope. Things must be laid before the crowd
as a whole, and their genesis must never be indicated.[110]

Such images pervade the entire field of collective understanding
and tend to motivate men to act in determinate ways. Social elements are dominated by such images which are essentially impervious to reason. They possess the tyrannical and sovereign force
of being above discussion. They supply the motives of collective
action and as such constitute the "moral forces" so little understood
by social theorists who are convinced of the primary influence of
reason in man's social history. "[It] is precisely these forces that
constitute the true mainsprings of history."[111]

Le Bon's account, like that of Sorel, constitutes an effort at
theory construction. Both authors are antirationalist in the sense we
have specified above. Both sought to ground their analyses in
explanatory locutions that made myths the expression of collective
sentiment and sentiment the manifestation of a variety of group
building factors. Le Bon spoke of hereditary factors, both individual

and racial, and social and ecological factors, traditions, institutions, and education.[112] Sorel advanced a similar account and identified race, nationality, and tradition as group-building factors.[113] Le Bon made racial factors emphatic while Sorel was more circumspect in this regard. Neither conceived sentiments and the myths, formulae, or illusions which gave expression to sentiments as impervious to reductive analysis. Sentiments were the consequence of the interaction of a finite number of biological and social factors.

It is important to distinguish, in their account, between a theory about action and the descriptive account of how men, in fact, do act. In this respect neither Sorel nor Le Bon were transrationalists. They both thought they had reasoned successfully about the mainsprings of collective action.

The anomaly in Sorel's account collects around his contention that the myth delivers an insight which is, in some sense, truer than true. It is difficult to understand precisely what the "intuition of Socialism which language cannot give us with perfect clearness" might be.[114] When Sorel insists that "no effort of thought, no progress of knowledge, no rational induction will ever dispel the mystery which envelops Socialism,"[115] he need do no more than identify socialism with myth to support his proposition. It is analytically true. Myths are not rational; they are not descriptive, but evocative. They move masses to action. They specify, in a general way, what is expected of a class of men devoted to the cause of socialism. But to say that by understanding this we have attained some sort of "global knowledge" superior to any reasoned account confuses more than illuminates. When Sorel contends that the "intellectualist philosophy" cannot explain why an individual sacrifices for a cause, he is saying only that one particular explanation, based upon the model of man as a purely rational agent, is mistaken. The alternate explanation he offers, whether true or not, is perfectly comprehensible. Various determinate factors conduce men to identify with a specific community. Such a community is sustained by a belief system having all the manifest emotive traits of religion, being dogmatic, simplistic, and imperative. In its service the individual can be motivated to perform singular and compelling acts of self-sacrifice. It is a mystery why any notion of special intuitive knowledge is necessary for this account.

The fact is that Sorel's social theories are fully compatible, recognizing his special interest in revolutionary tactics, with those of Gumplowicz, Mosca, and Pareto. He was fully convinced that the history of society is the history of group conflict, that the state is the executive agency of a dominant minority. He was equally convinced that a revolutionary social element (in his case the proletariat) can accede to dominance only if organized and directed by an elite which effectively mobilizes sentiment through a compelling social myth, a paralogical derivation, or a unifying political formula which itself is not true in any cognitive sense. His entire account was cast in images appropriate to warfare. He spoke of the "rather small bodies whose members have been rigidly selected, by means of tests designed to confirm their vocation. . . ." He spoke of "elite troops . . . ," who organize and mobilize the "inert mass" to combat.[116] This elite, "less numerous and well selected, lead the class struggle; they are the ones who train proletarian thought by creating the ideological unity which the proletariat requires in order to accomplish its revolutionary work. . . ."[117] In this sense they are indistinguishable from Pareto's contending elite. Their presence is evident in the work of Gumplowicz and Mosca. Gumplowicz spoke of them as a "new minority," and Mosca referred to them as the "dominant class" of the proletariat.

Sorel envisioned society as a "multiplicity of antagonistic forces." Those forces were social elements, each animated by a self-regarding and exclusive, i.e., ethnocentric, group spirit. It was this group spirit which provided, for Sorel, the ground for moral activism. The morality of a community was the collection of precepts, maxims, prescriptions, and proscriptions implied by its sustaining belief system. That morality sustained the group in its life activity, an activity characterized by unremitting struggle against out-groups. For Sorel, "moral duty entails, in substance, hostility towards those outside one's own group, not just hidden rancor and bitterness but open aggressiveness."[118]

Sorel's myth delivers a sense of solidarity and conviction to a specific sect, nation, social stratum, or class. It endows the individual members of such groups with a sublime sense of commitment and dedication. It convinces them that they "are devoting themselves [to] a serious, formidable and sublime work; it is only on this condition that they will be able to bear the innumerable sacrifices imposed on them. . . ."[119] Such convictions make life heroic and for that reason alone can "be looked upon as having an incalculable value."[120] This explains why Sorel conceived the myth as having so profound a moral significance.[121] It creates for man the psychological state of mind which conduces toward sublimity and heroism. "Social war, by making an appeal to the honor which develops so naturally in all organized armies, can eliminate those evil feelings against which morality would remain powerless."[122] It is war and strife which create the ideal conditions for the moral life. It is the social myth which vindicates sacrifice and discipline without which man would lose all moral character, for the natural tendency of man is to degenerate.[123] It was political democracy's compulsive disposition to reduce conflict that provoked Sorel's moral disapproval. Political democracy, with its rage for unity, obscured the real lines of contest in modern society. It tended to undermine the moral fiber of all social elements and placed a premium on cunning and dissembling rather than personal heroism, forthrightness, and self-sacrifice. Democrats appeal to force or organized authority, and pretend thereby that social conflict does not exist. Sorel's contention is that organized force is simply systematic and institutionalized violence. The lines of contest are obscured, and the moral tension necessary for the ideal life is dissipated by pretending that organized force employed by the state is somehow more moral than the violence employed by a new contending social element. For Sorel,

The highest good is the heroic (i.e., aggressive) action performed with a sense of impersonal consecration to the ends of a restricted, delimited group bound together in fervent solidarity and impelled by a passionate confidence in its ultimate triumph in some cataclysmic encounter.[124]

It is evident that, for Sorel, the perfect moral life is the life lived in the *ethnocentric* community. Sorel's model of man displays all the species characteristics of Gumplowicz' syngenetic group animal, animated by in-group amity and out-group enmity. Organized around a functional myth, man's life is passed in a state of high moral tension, in an affect situation of high salience. That such myths can activate tribes, castes, social strata, sects, parties, and classes is evident in everything Sorel says. Consequently, the association of social myths with the proletariat is a contingent relation. *All* collective activity requires an organizing or functional myth. Sorel applied his analysis to the organization of the proletariat because he conceived the proletariat as possessed of elemental energy. But, by 1910, his disillusionment with Syndicalism led him to associate himself with the nationalists of the *Action Francaise*. It was possible for other social elements to evolve appropriate myths. What Sorel sought was an agency for moral regeneration. That agency need not be the proletariat. It could be any organized group of consecrated warriors bound together in exclusive solidarity. They would constitute the Homeric heroes of our decadent age; they would see life as a struggle and not as a pleasure nor a seeking after pleasure.

Morality is not doomed to perish because the motive forces behind it will change; it is not destined to become a mere collection of precepts as long as it can still vivify itself by an alliance with an enthusiasm capable of conquering all the obstacles, prejudices, and the need of immediate enjoyment, which oppose its progress.[125]

Sorel's tactical concerns and his preoccupation with moral regeneration should not obscure the fact that the model of man and society he entertained was fully compatible with the central theoretical conceptions advanced by Gumplowicz, Mosca, and Pareto. Through Sorel, their ideas became vital constituents of radical socialist thought in Italy. As a consequence, the radical socialists of Italy manifested a unique temper and their thought evinced a unique content. Under such influence Marxism was transmogrified, but Sorel's thought could equally well animate non-Marxist revolutionaries. His social theories could equally well provide the rationale for any contending social element which advanced an alternate vision of the future. One such revolutionary element formed under the leadership of Enrico Corradini. It was Italian nationalism.

The Proto-Fascist Sociological Tradition and Nationalism

The intellectual voice of nationalist sentiment in Italy prior to World War I was Enrico Corradini (1867–1931). In 1909, Sorel characterized him as "remarkably intelligent," a man who "realizes very well the value of my ideas."[126] Corradini, already an adult, had suffered grievously at the news of Italy's humiliating defeat at Adowa at the hands of the Ethiopians (1896). His personal experiences among Italian immigrants in South America had further chaffed his wounds. He found Italians serving everywhere as hewers of wood and drawers of water in the interests of alien peoples. Hundreds of thousands of Italians were being driven from their native land under the goad of poverty. Once outside the confines of their native land, a weak and ineffectual government offered them no protection against the discrimination of the people they served.

Corradini interpreted Italy's distress almost exclusively in political terms. National poverty was primarily the consequence of an ineffectual government, a government animated by a political philosophy which conceived the state as an agent of purely individual or special interest concerns. It was understood to have neither interests nor functions which were primarily *national*. It reflected only the immediate class, sectional, category, or individual interests that had insinuated themselves into power at any particular time. Its policies and efforts were, therefore, inconsistent and discontinuous. Policy ineptitude had permitted Britain to control Egypt while Austria and France extended their sphere of influence into the Balkans and North Africa, respectively. While the aggressive nations to the North were carving colonies out of the underdeveloped world, Italy was impoverishing herself still further by forcing massive emigration of labor.

An aggressive foreign policy would have won for Italy the raw materials supplement required to permit the nation to compete effectively with the advanced industrial powers. The availability of necessary raw materials would promote the massive industrial development of the peninsula and the labor power of Italians would be turned to their own material advantage and the glory of the fatherland. Only within such a context could Italy's urgent internal problems be solved and her status as a great power assured.[127]

More significant for our interests is Corradini's conception of the nation and the state, and the social and historic forces which produce change, for his account synthesized intellectual elements taken directly from the work of Pareto, Mosca, Sorel,[128] and, in the final analysis, Gumplowicz as well. Corradini, commencing his serious political efforts with the founding of *Il Regno* in 1903, had access to the mature thought of all these men and his conclusions follow arguments which include premises culled from their works.

Corradini conceived man an essentially social animal, a denizen of organized aggregates of similars (*i nostri simili*). Similarity can be the consequence of shared racial or ethnic provenience, geographic origins, cultural similarities, or economic interests.[129] The disposition so to associate is spoken of as an "instinct of association," which manifests itself as intracommunity amity and extracommunity enmity.[130] In complex communities, composed of diverse social elements, groups can coalesce around shared cultural traits, economic interests, or ethnic characteristics, and society appears as an aggregate of groups rather than an organic unity. This occurs when cohesion is not disciplined by external pressure. Corradini insisted that the development of organic and integral national communities was as much the result of external pressures as the disposition of individuals to identify with a community of restricted membership.[131]

The disposition to identify with a community of select members is the consequence of man's life circumstances. The limited availability of the means of subsistence and the satisfaction of wants coupled with the potentially unlimited desires of men created, through evolutionary time, a situation in which group conflict was an inevitable result. When men lived a marginal existence the struggle for life was open and unremitting. In-group cohesion had an immediate survival value in the struggle for existence. Out of sheer necessity mankind became a race of warriors.[132] Only those creatures capable of identifying themselves with a compact and self-regarding community could survive under such arduous natural selection. In the subsequent competition for space and sustenance there was an evolutionary substitution of local types which favored those more disposed to integrate themselves in communities of disciplined and hardy warriors. Men became characterized not only by "instincts" of ethnocentric association, but by a disposition to struggle and conquest as well.[133] As active social agents, men developed specific dispositions of intragroup amity and extragroup hostility. Such circumstances conduce to the self-regarding social organization required by a life of unremitting and merciless challenge.

From a central point of diffusion each such group radiates outward. Only those who evince superiority in some sense survive and succeed to dominion. The defeated are assimilated and come to share, in some measure or another, the gifts of the conqueror. In this manner mankind attains to the higher levels of civilization.[134] The constant challenge of external pressure, the devotion to the community with which a man identifies himself, act as goads to the accomplishments which will ensure group survival. Expansion diffuses these accomplishments beyond the confines of their original source. This diffusion constitutes what Corradini calls the "sacred function" of imperialism.[135]

Corradini insisted that life circumstances defined the nature, extent, and intensity of group struggle. Immediate circumstances might, however, obscure the clear lines of contest. The essentially ethnocentric struggle is perpetual, but its forms are varied. Groups that have attained dominance through violence will, once ensconced, become purveyors of doctrines of universal harmony and enlightenment in the effort to insulate their control from challenge. The immediate illustration Corradini employed was one drawn from the European history of his time. Those nations which had seized colonies throughout the world strenuously opposed any further forceful seizure of territory. They became the advocates of negotiation.[136] Conversely, a weak and defeated people, reduced to impotence, will preach, as the ancient Israelites preached, a doctrine of resignation in the effort to afflict its conquerors with all the inhibitions which attend bad conscience. A botched and ineffectual community of men, shorn of the vitality which life demands, seeks to insure its survival at the cost of the sacrifice of manhood. Such strategies mask the will to dominance by effusions of piety.[137]

Nothing in this account is original. All its propositions were commonplaces among the "social Darwinists" of the turn of the century, and Corradini could have culled them from the available works of Pareto. But the entire constellation is notably Gumplowicz-ian, and there is some internal evidence that Corradini was cognizant of Gumplowicz' thought either in the original or through one of his Italian exponents. In *Il volere d'Italia* there is a passage clearly reminiscent of Gumplowicz. Corradini contends,

Throughout history the state has been a dominion of class. The dominant class of a nation derives originally from an alien and conquering people which imposes itself upon an invaded and conquered people and with whom the conquerors finally intermingle to constitute a nation. . . .[138]

This is clearly and specifically a Gumplowiczian thesis. Not only are Corradini's ideas in this tradition, but they defend specifically Gumplowiczian contentions. The remainder of his account is compatible with that of Pareto and Mosca and we know, from direct testimony, that it was thence derived. The priority of sentiments, Pareto's dispositional constants, intra- and extrasocietal conflict, the function of organizing and charter myths, and the rule of minorities are all ideas which Corradini shared with those men.

Corradini's account emphasizes the necessity of organization for social struggle. Successful struggle necessarily entails organization —and organization requires discipline and hierarchical social arrangements. A community so organized is preeminently viable, for compact solidarity is a prerequisite to struggle and to dominance. The community so organized, whether a class, sect, party, or nation, becomes the agency of historical evolution. The struggle for upward class mobility takes on the form of revolutionary socialism, or, in its more radical expression, revolutionary syndicalism, which is the theoretical rationale for class warfare. It provides the functional myth of working class organizations of assault. The myth provides the principles upon which association is based and it affords the stimulus to the maintenance of high moral tension.

The syndicalists conceive the myth of the general strike in grandiose and religious terms affording the principles of a proletarian morality that would render workers disciplined, patient, self-sacrificing, and disposed to group solidarity. . . . what Sorel calls a sublime or heroic morality. . . .[139]

75

The syndicalist myth became paradigmatic for Corradini. It constituted a belief-system of solidarity.[140] It exemplified the fullness of political and social realism. It was opposed to bourgeois liberalism that, at best, constituted a charter myth behind which minoritarian rule concealed itself and that in its decadent form sought to disarm the new contending elite. Furthermore, liberalism was characteristically unrealistic and unconvincing. Its rationale was predicated on a false conception of man, a conception that construed man to be uniquely individual and society to be an aggregate of contracting individuals. In its conflict with the vested nobility of pre-revolutionary Europe, such a view of man served to activate the masses in the service of the bourgeoisie. It mobilized the "producers" against the "non-producers," the "disinherited" against their class oppressors. For a time it constituted a rationale for a new solidarity among the contending social elements that the changed conditions of society had generated. Once ensconced, it became the justification for the meanest egoism, an egoism that threatened the viability of the greater social complex that was the nation-state.[141] In its decadent contemporary form it makes personal advantage the sole measure of moral ascription—that which enhances the individual's personal well-being is accorded approbation, that which demands personal sacrifice and discipline his disapprobation. Liberalism thus threatens the very existence of the collectivity. More engaging myths promote the articulation of competing social elements within the body politic and the social fabric is rent by contending groups. The subsequent disaggregation of the nation-state weakens it before external force, and the consequent decline in national fortunes exacerbates the competition for available goods. The conclusion can only be, at best, collective destitution; at worst, national extinction. Before the process can proceed to this point a new elite mobilizes the available social forces behind a new myth and society is precipitated into revolution. A consistent liberalism thus ultimately results in international defeat or intranational revolution.[142]

Corradini's appraisal of liberalism was amplified in the work of Scipio Sighele (1868–1914), one of the founders of collective psychology as a discipline and nationalism as a political ideology. Based on his researches, published in 1891 as *La folla delinquente*, Sighele set forth a critique of parliamentarianism as early as 1895.[143] He thus anticipated the analysis of Le Bon by several years.[144] Both men developed anticipations found in the work of Gabriel Tarde, particularly his *Le Lois de l'imitation,* published in 1890.

Sighele's principal contention was that an adequate explanation of group responses could not be based on an analysis which made individuals its referents. The laws of group phenomena are irreducible and are amenable only to group analysis. He specifically objected to Herbert Spencer's insistence that the character of any aggregate of men is explicable in terms of the characters of its constituent components.[145] Sighele denied that an adequate analysis could be forthcoming out of such an individualistic bias.[146] In raising this methodological objection he selected the precise passage to which Gumplowicz was objecting at almost the same time. Gumplowicz argued,

Herbert Spencer errs when he maintains that with respect to "human society" the characteristics of the units (understood as individuals) determine the characteristics of the aggregate that they constitute. The relationship is precisely the opposite. The characteristics of the group, its strivings and its perspectives, determine the characteristics of the individual. . . . Aristotle more correctly conceived the relationship when he maintained: "the whole is necessarily prior to its parts."[147]

The interaction of men in association did not produce a *sum* of influences. On the contrary, what resulted was a *product,* something quite unique. Mimetism, suggestion, and contagion were influences which made the mental products of the group distinct from the responses of the constituent individuals taken singly. A crowd undertakes acts that the individuals of which it is composed would never countenance when acting individually. The anonymity of the crowd, shared responsibility, are factors acting to significantly modify collective response. Furthermore, sentiments graphically and forcefully expressed conduce, through suggestion, to moral contagion. The disposition of the individual to identify with a collectivity in which he finds security and ego strength further promotes imitation. As group members express supporting sentiments, the force of suggestion generates an influence against which the solitary individual is all but helpless. What can result is a unanimity of conviction of epidemic proportions. Individuals in a group are thus more readily subject to affective stimuli than intellectual appeal. All these interactive influences reveal the critical role of emotive factors in group behavior.

What is true for heterogeneous crowds is equally true for structured groups, for assemblies, parliaments, and committees. The larger the group the more effective is its influence on its constituent individuals. From this vantage point Sighele raised objections to parliamentarianism in principle. His objections were not directed against the specific defects of the system, but against the system itself.[148] Parliaments were, in essence, collectivities, and as a consequence subject to the laws of collective psychology. Even if only the most intelligent and moral men entered parliament, the results of their deliberations would not reflect the sum total of their intelligence and moral rectitude. What would result would be a collective product, the result of the potent influences of mimetism and moral contagion. But the fact is that the men chosen as popular representatives are selected, in large part, as a consequence of public opinion formed by the information media that by their very nature, appeal to the lowest intellectual denominator among their potential readership, or through the influence of oratory that is calculated to appeal to that pliant collective sentiment so subject to its influence.[149] The prevalence of lawyers in the legislatures of all the parliamentary states is ample evidence of the decisive influence of oratory and histrionics in the election process.

Thus, a representative legislature is not only open to all the group influences so prejudicial to the exercise of dispassioned intelligence but it is composed of mediocre men as well. The normal distribution of talent suggests that such a body would be composed, by and large, of men of mediocre abilities. Their system of selection all but insures such an eventuality. Their mutual influence on each other can only produce results which are at best representative of the talents of the meanest member of the legislative body; at its worst the product is inferior to that which could legitimately be expected of any individual member.

The operation of a large group permits a degree of anonymity that allows the individual to surrender to the extraneous influence of material and personal interest. The emotional atmosphere of public oratory and the constant threat of group suggestion and sentimental contagion all preclude the effective employment of intelligence. The possibility that a piece of legislation results which is the consequence of a dispassionate assessment of fact is very low. "The [parliamentary] system," Le Bon argued in terms almost identical with those of Sighele, "is the expression of the idea, psychologically erroneous, but generally admitted, that a large gathering of men is much more capable than a small number of coming to a wise and independent decision on a given subject."[150]

Parliamentary assemblies are characterized by intellectual simplicity, suggestibility, and the exaggeration of non-cognitive contagion. That parliamentary oratory will reach the collective readership of the parliamentarian's constituency leads him to further reduce the intellectual level of his performance in the effort to more effectively influence the largest number of voters. Since his constituency is composed of those more influenced by sentiment than reason, his appeals will be emotive, more calculated to generate enthusiasm than cast light upon complex social and political issues. In the resulting rhetoric the only fixed points are the explicit material interests of the respective parliamentarians. Principles will be surrendered, precepts abandoned, maxims modified under the influence of the conceptual vagueness in which business must be conducted. But material interests abide and the entire enterprise becomes essentially a systematic pursuit of local and specific material interest.[151] Since each parliamentarian pursues his own interests, since they constitute the one element in which he maintains abiding faith, there will be a mass of conflicting demands made upon the collective body. Since the majority does not share the special interest to which each individual is committed, he undertakes to persuade his colleagues by evoking in them sentimental, but conceptually empty, images, typically employing gross exaggerations, moral pronouncements, and radical simplifications. Such eloquence has sovereign effect in assemblies so constituted.

What results is "personal immorality—the immorality of political parties—and immorality of the government itself—all as the necessary and fatal consequence of a system that seems to have been so contrived that it corrupts rather than edifies."[152] The only conceivable mitigation results when such an assembly is animated by the fire of a man of genius. Possessed of political acumen, inflexible will, and indomitable courage, he can come to dominate. Should such a man advance a program of national regeneration and, by virtue of the awe in which he is held, mobilize the heterogeneous collection of parliamentarians with whom he must deal behind his program, the fatherland has taken the road to greatness. "Happy are the times and peoples," Sighele concluded, "that possess a genius capable of polarizing all their desires, all their sentiments, and succeeds in leading masses that blindly follow."[153] Man, for Sighele, is a group animal, sensitive to group influence and disposed to be led. His studies in collective psychology explicated the meaning of many of the propositions employed in the explanatory accounts advanced by the social theorists of the period.

A variety of factors conduce to stable group formation. Sighele concerned himself with the psychological factors which stabilized groups. The principal group sustaining influence is evinced in group sympathy or collective suggestion. Individuals attempt to identify with the collectivity. For two generations after Le Bon and Sighele, social psychologists were to speak of "social facilitation," "rapport," and "identification" to characterize the behavioral trait complex to which Sighele referred. But collective responses are made to perceptual cues and suggestions which have their source in some agent or agents. Sighele spoke of the *meneurs* and the *menes,* those who initiate and those who respond to suggestion. By its very nature the collectivity can have but few leaders as an effective elite. A multiplicity of leaders would generate conflicting patterns of suggestion and the unity of the collectivity would be forfeit. As a consequence, minorities come to dominate collectivities, whether those collectivities are transient, heterogeneous crowds or stable, homogeneous, structured aggregates. These minorities can change the inert masses with sublime and heroic ideals and lead the collectivity to display traits that could not be predicted from an inspection of its individual members.

This entire system of ideas was not only compatible with, but also supplemented, that found in Pareto's *Sistemi* of 1902. Pareto cites Sighele's work and the subsequent work of Le Bon.[154] Gumplowicz devoted almost an entire chapter to the exposition of Sighele's ideas in the second edition of *Die sociologische Staatsidee* published in 1902, and Sorel's conception of the social myth and the organization of collectivities, formulated as early as 1903, rests on the account afforded by Le Bon.[155] When Sighele joined forces with Corradini to found the National Association, he brought this constellation of ideas with him and by the time of the First Congress of the Nationalist Association in 1910, these ideas had crystallized into doctrine.

It was not difficult for Corradini to identify the kinship shared by revolutionary syndicalism and nationalism. Sorel's conceptions limned a world in which groups contended for dominance. Each group was led by an active minority that mobilized inert masses in its service. Sorel identified the new contending elite with an aristocracy of the proletariat, and the upwardly mobile collectivity was the working class. Revolutionary syndicalism was the doctrine of an aspiring solidarity defined in terms of class. Corradini accepted the Sorelian account but identified his historical collectivity with the *nation* rather than with a *class*. He insisted that all the available historical evidence indicated that contending nations would constitute the principal ethnocentric antagonists of the twentieth century. Rather than a conflict between proletarian and capitalist classes, the future was to see a contest between proletarian and plutocratic *nations*.

As early as 1897, in the second volume of the *Corso,* Pareto had maintained that the problems of the lower classes involved questions of increased national production rather than distribution. In effect, what he suggested was that an increase in the gross national product, rather than any socialist program of redistribution, would ameliorate the conditions of the working classes.[156] Corradini regularly invoked this theme. Socialism was a program adapted to the conditions of advanced capitalist countries where maldistribution may constitute a real issue. For underdeveloped countries like Italy, socialism was maladapted. Italy did not require internal class warfare which could only undermine her international position still further and impair her productive potential. What was required was national solidarity and a program for massive social and economic uplift. Corradini's preoccupations were productionist rather than distributionist.[157]

Corradini maintained that the group-building factors, ethnic identity, geographic attachments, cultural similarities, provided national rather than class solidarity. The nation was the most effective viable union of similars (*la nazione* [*è*] . . . *massima unità del massimo numero di nostri simili* . . .).[158] The solidarist and moral aspirations of Sorelian syndicalism, to be effectively applied in the context of the twentieth century, must have national units as their subjects. Nationalism, like syndicalism, was antidemocratic and antiparliamentarian and its organizational and tactical principles accorded well with what was known of man's collective life. Sorel fully understood the critical organizational and moral responsibilities of strategic elites and the myth of the general strike provided the moral frame of reference conducive to the sublime and heroic ethic to which nationalists aspired.[159]

But an extension of the analysis was necessary. Sorel had originally conceived the agency of moral regeneration to be the proletariat, when it was really the nation. Nationalism required only that the focus of analysis be turned to the nation rather than a specific component class. Rather than international class solidarity, the contemporary imperative was national solidarity. The internal unity which revolutionary syndicalism advocated for effective conduct of the class war was to be applied to the nation. The internal unity of the nation was to be fostered and sustained in order to effectively prepare for and conduct international war. The nationalist conceived the lines of contest in terms of proletarian nations versus capitalist nations. This transmutation of *class* syndicalism into *national* syndicalism was already clearly developed in 1909.[160] Corradini suggested,

One is asked to imagine a syndicalism that confines itself to the limits of the nation and does not extend beyond; which ceases, that is to say, to operate internationally and operates nationally. The workers unite, but no longer internationally, but only within the confines of the nation; they unite to aspire toward dominion, but not dominion of the entire globe, but rather of the nation. A syndicalism so understood suppresses the opposition between [revolutionary and national syndicalism].[161]

For the myth of the proletarian general strike one substitutes the myth of the victorious international conflict.[162] Such a myth establishes the grounds of obligation; each citizen understands, almost intuitively, what is required of him. The nation becomes an ethno-centric association infused with high moral tension. From a norm-less aggregate of men, the inert and flaccid masses are welded into an integrated and compact organism. Each individual assumes an obligation in the defense and enhancement of collective life. "Na-tionalism is, in essence, a school of moral values. . . ."[163] Like revo-lutionary syndicalism it would see men dedicated and disciplined, committed to interests other than their own immediate well-being; it was conceived as radically antibourgeois, and thus anti-liberal and antidemocratic. It was an aristocratic conception which saw a minority of dedicated men establish themselves as models for a shapeless aggregate of individuals.

The basic denominator of solidarity is the belief system which establishes the unity of all and the leadership of some. Liberalism had reduced the nation to a collection of individual consumers con-cerned only with obtaining increased access to available economic goods. The nation was no longer a community but a congeries of competing and mutually antagonistic elements. The state was re-duced to serving the selfish interests of individuals and groups. The result of the introduction of this system in Italy was the shameful immorality of representative bodies, the humiliating debility of the nation before the international community, and increasing poverty. A corrupt parliament, the doleful emigration of Italian labor, the diminution of Italy's influence in the Mediterranean were construed as effects of liberal policies. Italy was a community in disintegration with no common values which could effectively govern conduct.

During the first decade and the first half of the second decade of the twentieth century Corradini had synthesized the elements which we have discussed into a set of related propositions that provided the doctrinal basis of a mass movement of solidarity. He expressed ideas that were current in the intellectual community. As these ideas radiated outward and came to influence peripheral groups they became increasingly simplified and increasingly charged with emotion.

The most representative instance of this development mani-fested itself in the literature and activities of the Italian Futurists under the leadership of F. T. Marinetti (1876–1944). The *Futurist Manifesto* of 1909 was little more than an exacerbated expression of the Italian nationalism of Corradini. "We want to sing the love of danger, the habit of energy and rashness," the *Manifesto* proclaimed.

The essential elements of our poetry will be courage, audacity and revolt. Literature has up to now magnified pensive immobility, ecstasy and slumber. We want to exalt movements of aggression, feverish sleeplessness, the quick step, the perilous leap, the slap and the blow with the fist. . . . Beauty exists only in struggle. There is no masterpiece that has not an aggressive character. Poetry must be violent assault on the forces of the unknown, to force them to bow before man. . . . We want to glorify war—the only cure for the world—militarism, patriotism. . . . We will sing of great crowds agitated by work, pleasure and revolt. . . .[164]

Futurism was the hyperbolic literary expression of nationalism. Its "sole political program was national pride, energy and expansion," reiterating Corradini's "the [nationalist] program involves but one plank: the grandeur of the fatherland."[165] War was conceived as the grand challenge that constituted a "moral hygiene" that restored the heroic posture to men that had become enfeebled by liberalism and democracy and that had permitted their manhood to be bartered away through parliamentary subterfuge.[166] The only historic value parliamentarianism has had has been negative; it has made evident the fiction that the masses can rule themselves. Parliament is the tool of the basest class interests—interests which conceal themselves behind the facade of popular government.[167] Only the "intoxicating intuition" of revolution and war can restore the real vision of life as a constant struggle. It alone can reinvigorate men. Violence, then, becomes a moral necessity. It tears away the veil of illusion that conceals the truly vital forces that have made life the progressive and evolving reality it is.[168] Against the normlessness of bourgeois society, the Futurists offered violence as a corrective. Against the torpor and somnolence of Italian life, the Futurists offered strife, war, the "formidible symphony of shrapnel."

All these effusions were the protests of men suffering from gross inferiority feelings, but they were also transliterations of Corradinian themes. They were Wagnerian appeals to a Sorelian myth of heroism and virility. It was an invocation for a new aristocracy, an aristocracy of merit compatible with the demands of a technical age, a national aristocracy drawn from every stratum of

Italian life, an aristocracy animated by a myth of Italian grandeur.[169]
Futurism provided bizarre orchestration for themes that had
been current in Italian intellectual life for over a decade. Its
grotesqueries did not obscure that fact and, as a consequence,
Futurism attracted at least the temporary support of men like
Giuseppe Prezzolini and Giovanni Papini, men who were significantly to influence Italian life and letters through journals like
Leonardo, La Voce and *Lacerba*. They were men who had collaborated with Corradini in the publication of *Regno*. They were
nationalists who had called Italy's attention to the importance of
the works of Gaetano Mosca and Vilfredo Pareto. They were the
men who were to popularize the syndicalist ideas of Georges Sorel.
And they were the men who would publish in the pages of their
journals the work of a then little known revolutionary socialist—
Benito Mussolini.

The Proto-Fascist Synthesis

The ideas current in Italy
immediately prior to the
advent of World War I
were synthesized in the
political sociology of Roberto Michels. His *Zur Soziologie des
Parteiwesens* appeared in 1911 and the Italian edition, *Sociologia
del partito politico nella democrazia moderna,* in 1912. In the years
prior to the publication of the work now considered Michel's foremost contribution to political analysis, he contributed anticipatory
partial accounts to professional and socialist journals in Germany
and Italy, accounts based substantially on the work of Gumplowicz,
Pareto, Mosca, Sorel, Sighele, and Le Bon. His specific application
was to the nature of political parties, but his interpretation rests
upon a view of man and society shared by those men whose views
we have briefly considered.

Michels' central thesis was that our age, an age of mass-based
political parties, is one in which the oligarchical tendencies of
human organization become most manifest. "Democracy," he insisted, "leads to oligarchy, and necessarily contains an oligarchical
nucleus."[170] This is because society is an arena of group competition,
a perpetual struggle for group advantage. In such a context, organization becomes a primary strategic and tactical necessity. But

organization necessarily requires a relatively stable hierarchical order in the form of governance by a dominant minority. The measure of success in any protracted conflict will necessarily depend upon the degree to which the struggle is conducted on the basis of group solidarity, disciplined obedience, and consistent and decisive leadership. Solidarity is the by-product of empathy, mimetism, or suggestion, a conclusion "luminously discussed," Michels indicated, in Sighele's *Contro il parlamentarismo* and Gumplowicz' *Sozialphilosophie im Umriss*.[171] Such a contention illustrates Pareto's general thesis that men in association cannot function without a dominant and directing elite.[172]

Democratic theory, according to Michels' analysis, provides the charter myth of minoritarian rule. By disseminating the fiction that sovereignty resides in the electorate, the dominant minority, while effectively affording the masses the dubious privilege of periodically choosing for themselves a new set of masters, persists in its position of dominance by incorporating the elected representatives into the ensconced minority. At best, in times of crisis, a revolution can transform class, category, and strata relationships to the extent that a new directive minority accedes to dominance. But society is no more "democratically" constituted than it was before. A new minority, untrammelled by association with the hitherto established dominant minority, has succeeded to suzerainty. The factors that conduce to this circumstance are varied. First of all, the number of those among the enfranchised who take an interest in political affairs is always insignificant. Most people are either too stupid or indisposed to occupy themselves with political concerns. Consequently, it is only a minority that participates directly in the organizational and administrative work of political parties. In those parties a minority participates in the decision-making process. In general such decisions require an active interest and a measure of expertise that systematically excludes the vast majority of men. Furthermore, collectivities regularly seek out leaders who will relieve them of the responsibilities of choice. This is particularly true in crisis situations which are affect situations of high salience. The leader becomes the repository of religious fervor and he is exalted as the embodiment of collective ideals. Since the mass-based party influences public opinion through the written and spoken word, ideally the leader will be proficient in both capacities. It suffices to mention Gambetta and Clemenceau in France, Gladstone and Lloyd George in England, and Crispi and Luzzatti in Italy. Except for the fact that it would be anachronistic (since Michels did not have our contemporary examples), a number of more compelling instances could be adduced.

The sentiments of collectivities are influenced by emotive suasion. As a consequence, an organizing or functional myth is generated which captures the collective imagination. Such a myth is a collection of propositions, neither necessarily consistent nor true, that effectively mobilize sentiment. They need only be sufficiently consistent to provide the basis for general principles of political conduct. Their chief function is to reduce the collective will to obedience. The incompetence of an unstructured mass to order its political behavior in an effective manner constitutes the natural foundation for the role of leaders and the necessity for an organizational myth.[173] A mass-based party thus undergoes transformation into a hierarchically structured oligarchy. Democracy tends to produce, particularly under crisis conditions, a plebiscitary Bonapartism.

Michels employed revolutionary syndicalism as a signal instance of this process. Sorel had revealed the endemic oligarchic tendencies in democracy and had maintained that bourgeois parliamentarianism constituted the hegemony of a minority ultimately wedded to specific class interests. As a consequence, syndicalism was explicitly anti-democratic and anti-liberal.[174] It sought to circumvent minoritarian control by displacing the axis of working-class policy from political to economic struggle. But by absenting themselves from the political struggle, the syndicalists found themselves deeply committed to economic struggle. Such an arduous struggle necessitated an almost military organization. The economic strike tends to facilitate the formation of an organizational cadre, a directive elite. Originally based upon the desirability of freedom from extraneous and hierarchical control, syndicalist organizations rapidly transformed themselves into disciplined battalions under the all but absolute leadership of a dominant minority. The characteristic passivity of the mass of workers led to an effective minoritarian organization of syndicalist cells. The syndicalists proceeded to make a virtue of necessity with the realization that the masses are too vast in number and politically and intellectually too immature to comprehend the nature and significance of the ensuing struggle. The defeat of the dominant minority was to be the work of an alert, enterprising, and bellicose contending minority. By 1909, A. O. Olivetti and the Italian revolutionary syndicalists spoke unreservedly of the advent of socialism as the result of the action of working-class elites.[175]

Events only served to confirm Pareto's conviction that associations, by their very nature, must evince hierarchical structure and oligarchical features. This is nowhere more apparent than in mass-based political parties.

These phenomena would seem to prove beyond dispute that society cannot exist without a "dominant" or "political" class, and that the ruling class, whilst its elements are subject to a frequent partial renewal, nevertheless constitutes the only factor of sufficiently durable efficacy in the history of human development. According to this view, the government, or, if the phrase be preferred, the state, cannot be anything other than the organization of a minority. It is the aim of this minority to impose upon the rest of society a "legal order," which is the outcome of the exigencies of dominion and of the exploitation of the mass of helots effected by the ruling minority, and can never be truly representative of the majority. The majority is thus permanently incapable of self-government. Even when the discontent of the masses culminates in a successful attempt to deprive the bourgeoisie of power, this is after all, so Mosca contends, effected only in appearance; always and necessarily there springs from the masses a new organized minority which raises itself to the rank of a governing class. Thus the majority of human beings, in a condition of eternal tutelage, are predestined by tragic necessity to submit to the dominion of a small minority, and must be content to constitute the pedestal of an oligarchy.[176]

Michels' analysis was amplified in 1915 by an assessment of the impact of the world conflict on the articulation of organizational myths. Such myths, while not necessarily true in the sense of truth normally accorded a scientific theory, must, in some sense, correspond to some evident and urgent reality in the life circumstances of a community. Socialist parties had organized themselves around the concept of *class*, ascribing it a predominance over other candidates. In circumstances of latent or overt class struggle such a concept did exercise effective influence over the imagination of the masses. But with the coming of the catastrophe of 1914, the effectiveness of *class* as a reference point for political organization and political contest was definitively dissipated.[177] The socialist parties of the various belligerent nations opted to identify with their respective nations rather than with the international working class. Historic circumstances conspired to divest the myth of the class war of its functional and organizational capacity. The allegiances of the masses could be mobilized only in the name of a more urgent and compelling reality—the nation. The concept *nation* would constitute the core concept of political organization in the twentieth century. Michels thus moved from the ranks of Italian socialism into the ranks of Italian nationalism. Years later, as one of the foremost political sociologists of Fascist Italy, he was to characterize the nation as a "community of will, the will to the Fatherland. This community, subject to the laws of mass suggestion and consequently of variable emotional manifestation, is the decisive one."[178] A peculiar intersection of theory and historical circumstance provided a minoritarian political party with its functional myth. That same myth was employed, upon accession to power, to legitimize dominion. The functional myth became a charter myth.

Proto-Fascist Thought and Fascist Doctrine

Recently, René Albrecht-Carrié maintained that, given the circumstances prevailing in the first two decades of the present century, the advent of Fascism was the "perfectly logical consequence" of the conduct of Italian political life.[179] Our contention here is that it was more than the perfectly logical consequence of the circumstances surrounding political conduct; it was the perfectly logical consequence of the interaction of intellectual, social, and political currents. For a variety of reasons, contemporary commentators have neglected the influence of political ideas on the development of Fascism as an ideology. The Marxists insist on a circumscribed class analysis and consequently focus attention primarily upon the nationalistic components of Fascist ideology, since nationalism had evident origins among the disaffected Italian bourgeoisie.[180] Scant attention is paid to the currents of proletarian syndicalist and socialist thought in the articulation of Fascist doctrine and proletarian participation in the Fascist ranks and in the Fascist cadre. To trace Fascist doctrine exclusively to nationalist origins is to do considerable violence to the facts and gives the mistaken impression of gross discontinuity in the evolution of Mussolini's thought.

Non-Marxist commentators sometimes pursue a similar analysis. In order to level an unqualified moral indictment, the doctrine of Fascism is traced exclusively, for example, to that source best calculated to outrage public decency—Marinetti's Futurism.[181] The attempt to reduce Fascist doctrine, even in its most primitive expressions, to nothing more than a variant of Futurism is grossly misleading.

More characteristically, however, non-Marxist commentators simply dismiss the possibility that *any* social or political conceptions influenced Mussolini or Fascism. Characteristic are judgments like those of Roy MacGregor-Hastie. He insists,

Mussolini fluttered from philosopher to philosopher, as he did from woman to woman, deriving nothing but momentary gratification from them. . . . Mussolini had neither philosophy, policy nor programme; he was *ad hoc* in these human disciplines as he was in any other. His superb *ad hoc*-ness eventually enabled him to create a party machine, and his intuitive understanding of the semi-literate masses enabled him to devise the trimmings, the shiny boots, the slogans and the noise.[182]

They repeat in 1963 judgments made a quarter of a century ago by Gaudens Megaro:

All Mussolini's doctrinal and moral somersaults and divagations, all his outward allegiance to varied and contradictory political theories become intelligible only if it is borne in mind that he cannot pay even lip-service to ideas unless he can utilize them as instruments of his ambition to power, unless he can convince himself of the identity between an idea and his will for power.[183]

Similar judgments could be collected from a dozen authors. One is impressed by the confidence with which such judgments are tendered, for unrestricted generalizations are always hazardous. One counterinstance defeats them. Was there perhaps *one* philosopher from whom Mussolini derived something more than momentary gratification? Did he never have a conceptual understanding of collective psychology? Were his understandings of crowd phenomena *all* intuitive? Was Mussolini's concern with theory *exclusively* cynical and self-serving?[184]

The fact is that Mussolini's thought underwent development. Any random selection of his formulations dating from different periods of that development can deliver the impression of contradiction. Anyone familiar with the writings of any thinker is aware that this sort of "contradiction" is easily documented and just as easily exposed for what it is. What one finds more characteristically in Mussolini's thought is confusion. He was not a systematic thinker. He was primarily a journalist. The vast bulk of his output is in the form of brief pieces for daily or weekly papers. Rarely did he venture on a more extended exposition of his ideas. As a consequence, one has only an outline, the sketch of a world-view. When an attempt is made to develop his ideas in any detail, one finds oneself dealing with an enormous collection of fragmentary and fugitive impressions. The course of reconstruction is tedious and the results are not completely satisfying.

Mussolini liked to fancy himself a political realist, a Machiavellian, what the Italians call a *tempista:* a man with his fingers on the pulse of an epoch. In a certain sense this was true. He was extremely sensitive to his political and theoretical environment. He reflected moods and ideas and frequently gave men the impression that he was leading them where they had intended to go in any event, and this frequently generated confusion. Men left Mussolini with the impression that his position was theirs while in fact what had happened was that Mussolini had simply not chosen to enter into dispute about matters of principle or theory, concerns which were relatively far removed from the immediate matters at hand. This was the "anti-dogmatism" that was so attractive to George Bernard Shaw. It was the feature of Fascism that appealed to Fascist sympathizers in Britain and America. One can applaud or deplore it as one fancies. It can either be deprecated as "unprincipled" or extolled as the prevalence of "pragmatism" over "dogma."

In fact, however, Mussolini's ideas can be most effectively analyzed as a relatively consistent synthesis of core conceptions central to the sociological, revolutionary syndicalist, and ultimately nationalist traditions of his time. In him the ideas of Pareto, Mosca, Sorel, Michels, Le Bon, and Corradini were to find expression. These were the ideas critical to his youthful social and political thought. They were the ideas that were to constitute the first doctrinal statements of Fascism and were to ultimately provide the doctrinal rationale for the first frank totalitarian nationalism of our time.

CHAPTER THREE

The Social and Political Thought of the Young Mussolini

BENITO Amilcare Andrea Mussolini was the first born child of Alessandro and Rosa Maltoni Mussolini. He was born in Dovia in the Italian Romagna on July 29, 1883. In March of that year Karl Marx had died in London. Vladimir Ilyich Ulyanov, known to history as Lenin, was an adolescent. Adolf Hitler would not be born for six years. Gaetano Mosca had just completed the *Teorica*, Ludwig Gumplowicz had already published his classic *Der Rassenkampf*, and Vilfredo Pareto was preparing his *Corso* for the press. Revolutionary socialism had begun to infuse the Italian working classes with the sentiments of class warfare. The working class movement, more enthusiastic than enlightened, linked the names of Mazzini and Garibaldi with that of Marx.

Alessandro Mussolini was a revolutionary much like those common in the Romagna during the turbulent years that marked the close of the nineteenth century.[1] At that time, under the inspiration of Bakunin, the revolutionary socialism that developed was more anarchistic than Marxist, more a felt ideal than a specific theory, more a way of life than an economic analysis. Such was the socialism of Alessandro Mussolini.

Largely self-educated, Alessandro exercised considerable influence in local socialist circles. In May of 1889 he began to contribute articles to the socialist weekly, *Rivendicazione*. In February of 1891, he offered the following definition of socialism:

Socialism . . . is the open, violent, and moral rebellion against the existing inhuman order of things. It is the science and the excelsior that illumines the world. It is reason that imposes itself upon faith. It is free thought that rebels against prejudice. . . . It is the voluntary contract between all men to live a truly civil life. It is true justice become sovereign over the earth. According to us, socialism is the sublime harmony of concepts, of thought and action, that precedes the great vehicle of human progress in its triumphal journey toward the great ideal of beauty, justice, and truth.[2]

Socialism was an ideal, a protest, and a norm of life that could be realized only through open and violent revolution on the part of the oppressed. It was anarchistic in orientation and violent in intention. It was antireligious, anticlerical and antibourgeois. It was populist and charged with moral sentiment.

In this environment the child, Benito, spent his formative years. As he indicated years later, on the occasion of his father's death, ideas were the only patrimony his father left him.[3] At times the Mussolini household was desperately poor, and it never enjoyed more than adequacy. The very atmosphere bred the attitudes necessary to rebellion—and rebelliousness was fostered by an intellectual fare of revolutionary literature. While still a child, Benito Mussolini was exposed to the writings of Marx. The first volume of *Capital* had become available in a compendium prepared by the anarchist Carlo Cafiero, and Alessandro Mussolini read passages aloud to his son. Under such influences, particularly those of his father, Benito Mussolini became, inevitably, a revolutionary. Like the Romagnoli, he was violent, irredeemably political, obsessively single-minded and domineering. Even the gentleness of his mother, a patient, if inflexible, school-mistress, could hardly prevail against dispositions reinforced by every influence in his environment.

By the time Mussolini was seventeen he had, apparently, officially enrolled in the Socialist Party. At eighteen he had graduated with honors from the technical school at Forlimpopoli. He was a rebellious, but more than competent, student and displayed special ability in history, geography, literature, and moral philosophy.[4] He read widely and apparently well. He is known to have read with care Roberto Ardigò's *Morale dei positivisti* and a history of philosophy by Francesco Fiorentino. Students who knew him at this time recall periods when he would seclude himself with his books. In class when he found a subject disinteresting he would read one or another of the pamphlets or books with which his desk was forever crammed. In December, 1901, when he was eighteen, a teachers' professional journal, *I Diritti della Scuola*, published his first brief article.[5]

After his graduation from the Royal Normal School at Forlimpopoli he pursued a program of self-education. Except for periods when he was undergoing special instruction in language (French, German, and Latin), and a brief period of attendance at the University of Lausanne, Mussolini received no further formal instruction. His reading was governed by his political interests. His published writings during the period between 1902 and 1914 indicate that he devoted his attention to the socialist literature published in Italian, French, and German. A substantial portion of that literature was reviewed by him for various Italian socialist journals and the reviews themselves give clear evidence of his adequate grasp of content and of the essentials of argument. Even Megaro, a severe critic, speaks of Mussolini during this period as a "young man of uncommon intelligence and discernment. . . ."[6]

The period between 1902 and 1914 was a period of impressive intellectual activity. During that time Mussolini wrote the articles devoted to socialist theory, contemporary politics, reviews, and expositions that now fill seven volumes of his collected works. He wrote three long monographs, *L'uomo e la divinità* (1904), *Il Trentino veduto da un socialista* (1911) and *Giovanni Huss il veridico* (1913), and a novel, *Claudia Particella, l'amante del Cardinale* (1910).[7] He translated at least eighteen pieces from French and German, including Petr Kropotkin's *Paroles d'un révolté* (1904), Karl Kautsky's *Am Tage nach der sozialen Revolution* (1905), and Wilhelm Liebknecht's *Karl Marx und der historische Materialismus* (1908), as well as large selections of the poetry of Friedrich Gottlieb Klopstock. He also began an ambitious "History of Philosophy" which has not survived. In his private correspondence there are allusions to the works of a host of Italian authors, and he speaks of translating selections (which have not survived) from Arthur Schopenhauer's criticisms of Kantian and Fichtean ethics.[8]

This mass of material has been given little serious attention for a variety of reasons. First and foremost, until very recently it has been very difficult to obtain. The collection of Mussolini's works published prior to World War II, and characterized as "definitive" at that time, does not, in fact, include any of his publications prior to the fifteenth of November, 1914.[9] The collection was not, therefore, in any sense, definitive.[10] Whatever material from this early period has been available has been exploited in curious ways. Yvon De Begnac's *Vita di Benito Mussolini* refers to this early period and quotes excerpts of Mussolini's pre-Fascist writings, as does Gaudens Megaro in his *Mussolini in the Making*. De Begnac employs select material from this period in an attempt to establish that Mussolini was always a Fascist, while Megaro employs an alternate selection to indicate that Mussolini betrayed his early convictions. Fascist biographers seriously distort Mussolini's thought to establish consistency; Megaro provides counterinstances to argue Mussolini's fecklessness. Neither tactic provides an adequate treatment of the thought of the young Mussolini. Apologists see only the Fascist and detractors see only a tissue of contradictions. The truth lies, as is frequently the case, somewhere in between. The young Mussolini, as will become evident, was far from a Fascist before 1914. Even after that date there was considerable development. It would be difficult, in fact, to establish the hard lines of Fascist doctrine before 1921. On the other hand, as early as 1902 Mussolini entertained doctrinal elements which would render it difficult to equate his socialism with the orthodox socialism with which we have become familiar. Throughout this period there was regular and fairly consistent development. By 1914 Mussolini's political convictions were quite unique, but not personal. There was an entire faction among Italian revolutionary socialists that traversed the same development. Mussolini was one among a considerable group of socialist intellectuals who had followed the trajectory that was to lead to Fascism. The most important of this group of revolutionary socialists were to follow him into Fascism. Lenin, rejecting orthodox democratic socialism, was to lead a similar faction of the international socialist movement into Bolshevism. Only in 1924, after Lenin's death, did Leninism become the system of thought we identify with it today.

It is essential to recall that Mussolini was only thirty at the beginning of 1914, approximately the same age as Marx when he wrote the *Communist Manifesto*. When one compares the collection of ideas identified with the young Marx with those of the mature Marx, one appreciates the extent of significant change in perspective that can be documented. Mussolini's thought evidences a similar, if more significant and spectacular, development. A similar case can be made for the development of Lenin's thought. Certainly Lenin's assessments of the implications of Marxism underwent significant modification even after the writing of *The State and Revolution*, in 1917, when he was forty-seven.[11] Alfred Meyer is only one of the commentators who indicates the full measure of the "acute discomfort" that *The State and Revolution* still occasions among Leninist ideologists.[12]

For more than a decade, between 1902 and 1914, Mussolini conducted his education in public. Between the ages of nineteen and thirty-one the anarcho-populist ideas he had inherited from his father underwent the development that was to manifest itself as Fascism. Today, that development can be traced with considerable specificity. The period begins with a conception of socialism much like that of Alessandro Mussolini, a conception modified by the revolutionary syndicalism of men like Arturo Labriola to ultimately become the national syndicalism of the revolutionary wing of Italian socialism. It will be the purpose of this chapter to indicate the initial stages of that development from anarcho-socialism to Fascism, and to provide an account of the social and political thought of the young Mussolini. In the course of this exposition it will become obvious that much of the literature devoted to the thought of Mussolini involves a number of critical errors and misjudgments. Truth, generally, lies between the rival claims of Fascist apologists and orthodox Marxist detractors. For example, in 1939 Rino Alessi insisted that "Mussolini, in fact, never was a Marxist," and Margherita Sarfatti, his first "official" biographer maintained that the young Mussolini was more interested in Babeuf and

Proudhon than Marx. Paolo Alatri, on the other hand, a doctrinaire Marxist, insists that "the socialism of Mussolini never had a truly Marxist character (since he had not read anything other than the *Communist Manifesto* of Marx)."[13]

The fact is that as a young man Mussolini accepted all the essential theoretical and interpretive propositions of Marx. His published writings between 1902 and 1914 contain innumerable references to Marx and only seven allusions to Babeuf and eight to Proudhon. Both his published writings and what we can reconstruct of his reading during this period indicates a preoccupation with the ideas of Marx that far exceeds any concern he had for other thinkers. Mussolini's point of departure was unquestionably Marx. No adequate reconstruction of his thought is possible if that fixed point is neglected. Not only was he a convinced Marxist, he was a knowledgeable one as well. His published writings contain regular references to the works of Marx and Engels. He specifically refers to every major piece of Marx's published writings available at that time. He alludes to Marx's writings in the *Neue Rhenische Zeitung*, the "Theses on Feuerbach," "Contribution to the Critique of Hegel's Philosophy of Right," *A Contribution to the Critique of Political Economy, The Class Struggles in France*, as well as *Capital* and the *Communist Manifesto*.[14] In a number of places he not only alludes to *The Poverty of Philosophy*,[15] but provides extensive quotations as well.[16] He also provides quotations from the *Contribution to the Critique of Political Economy*, the Marx-Engels correspondence, Marx's articles in the *New York Tribune*, and the *Communist Manifesto*.[17] There are references to Engels' *The Conditions of the Working Class in England in 1845*, quotations from the *Anti-Duehring* and Engels' famous introduction to Marx's *Class Struggles in France*.[18] He was not only familiar with the most important Marxist authors of the period, including Karl Kautsky and Wilhelm Liebknecht, some of whose work he translated, but he had read the works of theoreticians such as G. Plekhanov and Rosa Luxemburg, and Marx critics such as Werner Sombart.

That Mussolini's socialism never had a truly Marxist character could only be maintained once a definition of "truly Marxist character" was formulated. The formulation of such a definition is a thankless undertaking and could only be accomplished from a doctrinaire point of view. To say that Mussolini had never read anything other than the *Communist Manifesto* is simply untrue. Whatever one thinks of his Marxism today, Mussolini was accepted by his socialist peers as a Marxist theoretician. He rose to leadership in the Italian Socialist Party at least in part on the basis of his recognized capacity as a *socialist* intellectual.

In the expert judgment of Roberto Michels, the Italian literature devoted to Marxism written during this period compared favorably in quantity and quality with that produced in Germany, so that criteria for the measure of theoretical competence were available to the members of the Italian Socialist Party.[19] Italian scholars, in fact, produced literature that achieved international reputation. Antonio Labriola published his *Essays on the Materialist Conception of History* in 1896, quickly followed by his *Socialism and Philosophy*.[20] In 1896 Benedetto Croce published his critical essays on Marx that were later collected in the volume *Historical Materialism and Marxist Economics*. A spate of similar expository and critical writings were available throughout this period, yet Mussolini's socialism was accepted as radical, but nonetheless Marxist. The elements we discover in retrospect as harboring the germs of Fascism were not recognized as any more heterodox than the views of many syndicalists all similarly regarded as Marxist. Mussolini can be characterized, during this period, as a radical Marxian socialist, an exponent of then contemporary Marxist opinions shared by a significant number of compatriots all of whom were considered, and considered themselves, Marxists. In this sense, Mussolini *was* a Marxist. And yet there are elements of his thought that were to generate increasing theoretical and doctrinal tensions as long as they were confined within Marxism, however understood. By the time his definitive break with organized socialism came (with the advent of World War I) he had already synthesized the elements which were to constitute the core conceptions of Fascist doctrine.

Edoardo Susmel is probably correct in making 1914 the critical point in Mussolini's development. Prior to that date Mussolini was, with considerable qualification, a Marxian socialist,[21] but his reorientation had been gradually maturing for a decade before the decisive realignment. The break with socialism came with Mussolini's explicit recognition of the influence of national sentiment in the political and social evolution of man. Socialism could no longer afford a satisfactory vehicle for Mussolini's conceptions. His socialism had undergone a qualitative change, the consequence of an accretion of theoretical modifications that had accumulated since 1902.

The Young Mussolini and Classical Marxism

Immediately following his graduation from the Royal Normal School at Forlimpopoli Mussolini obtained employment as an elementary school teacher in Gualtieri, where he remained from February until June, 1902. From July, 1902, until November, 1904, he remained in Switzerland as an emigrant laborer and a socialist organizer. It was in Switzerland that he published his first socialist article, and it was there that he immersed himself in the currents of thought that were to have decisive influence upon his subsequent development. Both Megaro and De Felice argue for the decisive influence of revolutionary syndicalism on Mussolini during these years when he was between nineteen and twenty-one years of age.[22]

Mussolini returned to Italy at the end of 1904 and began compulsory military service in the Italian army. In 1906 he returned to school teaching at the elementary and high school levels. During 1909, for a period of approximately nine months, he remained in the Trentino where he occupied himself as a socialist journalist and labor organizer. He returned to his native province of Romagna in 1910 to become editor of a socialist weekly. He attained national recognition at the Socialist Congress at Reggio Emilia in 1912 as the leader of the revolutionary socialist faction and became a member of the Executive Committee of the Socialist Party. That same year, at the age of twenty-nine, he became Editor of *Avanti!*, the official organ of the Socialist Party.

Mussolini's rise from the ranks, from Party member to Party leader, was a consequence of the varied talents he displayed. He was a gifted orator and a competent journalist and he had the ability to inspire confidence. He was knowledgeable and well read and had the faculty, which he shared with Lenin, of reducing complex issues to their simplest formulations. A restless and intolerant personality, he had the disposition and the ability that permitted him to dominate rather than be dominated.

Mussolini read widely and wrote prodigiously. His first publication, as we have seen, appeared when he was but eighteen. When he was twenty-one he published his first long essay, entitled *L'uomo e la divinità*, containing his arguments against religion advanced in his debate with Alfredo Tagliatela, a Christian Socialist who had undertaken evangelical activities among Italian emigrant workers in Switzerland. Mussolini's explicit intention in this youthful essay was to "oppose the forces of darkness with the forces of light; to oppose the absolute with free thought; and to oppose dogma with reason"—an intention that echoed the sentiments of Alessandro Mussolini, his father.

Under the influence of the revolutionary syndicalists with whom he early associated himself, Mussolini's Marxism did not remain at the unsophisticated level at which his father had left it. His early writings do more than provide evidence for the influence of his father and syndicalism: they also help to establish the theoretical Marxist orthodoxy of the young agitator. Coupled with the theoretical formulations scattered through the writings of the period from 1902 through 1908, the theses advanced in *L'uomo e la divinità* exemplify classical Marxism as it was generally understood at the turn of the century.

During this early period Mussolini adopted a form of positivism that was common among free-thinkers and Marxists. He expressly committed himself to positive science and opposed metaphysical speculation and fictive presupposition. Science, he argued, provided compelling evidence that the universe, instead of being the creation of a transcendental deity, was

nothing more than the manifestation of matter, eternal and indestructible, that never had a beginning and that will have no end. Matter has its "modes" . . . that transform themselves, evolving from form to more complex form. In this immense and continuous process of dissolution and reintegration, nothing is created nor destroyed. Life, therefore, in its universal significance is nothing more than the perpetual combustion of energy. . . . The universe is to be explained by such forces. All the phenomena studied by physics (heat, light, sound, electricity) are reducible to vibrations of variable intensity . . . dominated by eternal and immutable laws that recognize neither morals nor benevolence. . . . These laws govern universally: from the smallest to the most complex phenomena. . . . Against them man can accomplish nothing. He can come to understand them and put them to his service, but he cannot alter their beneficent or malevolent actions. . . . Evolution dominates the "modes" of matter. Through evolution the first primordial cell representing the first moment of animal life attains, through successive transformation, its highest expression: man.[23]

These propositions are, of course, common to a considerable number of authors writing around the turn of the century. They are also the cosmological theses advanced by "dialectical materialism," and are found, formulated in essentially the same language, in Engel's *Anti-Duehring*.[24]

Within this context Mussolini developed his conception of man and society. Man, the young Mussolini maintained, is the by-product of an organic process. His distinguishing species trait is his reasoning capacity, which is contingent upon his brain weight and cerebral architecture, the product of a long evolutionary development. A thinking animal, man is a social animal as well. He is, by nature, a member of a community.[25] Mussolini maintained

The individual can never be "unique" ["*unico*"] in the Stirnerian sense of the word, for he is bowed and subordinated by the fatal laws of solidarity. According to Darwin, the social instinct is inherent in the very nature of man.[26]

This fact is evident in the vagueness that afflicts the terms *individual* and *society*, and the adjectival qualifiers *individual* and *social*. The individual is inextricably involved in his community and all attempts to separate the individual from his social context—as was attempted, for example, by the theorists of the social contract—have failed.[27]

The characterization of man as a social animal is, of course, common to a number of philosophers. It is also a Marxist tenet. Marx contended, in writings with which Mussolini was probably familiar, that "Man is the human world, the state, society" and that the human essence was "the *ensemble* of social relations."[28] We are now in a better position than Mussolini was to recognize how seriously Marx took this conviction. In the *Economic and Philo-*

sophic Manuscripts (which were published in their entirety only in the nineteen thirties), Marx maintained that "the individual is the social being. His life . . . is . . . an expression and confirmation of social life."[29] In the notes written for his *Contribution to the Critique of Political Economy* he reiterated, "Man is in the most literal sense a *zoon politikon,* not merely a social animal, but an animal which can develop into an individual only in society."[30]

For Mussolini, individuals organize themselves into groups sharing similar characteristics, interests, and needs. A perpetual struggle for existence activates these social elements and renders the "world a vast battleground" of contending groups. When society has attained a particular level of economic development, the antagonistic interests of disparate groups generate intrasocial competition which takes on a multiplicity of forms.[31]

All men who have an identity of interest tend to defend themselves collectively to afford a greater guarantee of success. This principle demolishes that individualism which has reduced itself to a theory entertained only by literati. . . . "Cooperation" reveals contradictory elements: one positive and the other negative. The first manifests itself in the practical solidarity between members of the group, the second in struggle against antagonistic out-groups.[32]

With the maturation of capitalism the disparity of interests that separate the proletariat from the bourgeoisie has become increasingly evident. The fact is that "more or less profound differences obtain between the various parts of the social aggregate . . ." that generate the class struggle.[33]

Class differences produce class interests, interests produce contrasts, and antothetical contrasts produce the class struggle. . . . The proletariat, or the new class . . . is produced by capitalist production [itself]. . . . Socialism is the inevitable consequence of the new economic relations. . . .[34]

Socialism is true because it reflects the new productive conditions inherent in industrial development itself.[35] The thesis that Mussolini is defending is a central conviction of classical Marxism. ". . . Material interest," Mussolini maintained, "[is] the prime mover of human actions and . . . all the ideological superstructure of society (art, religion, morals) is a reflex and the consequence of economic conditions, more precisely, of the mode of material production."[36]

These are specifically Marxist theses and, conjoined with the antecedent cosmological conceptions, deliver an outline of dialectical and historical materialism that would be considered faithful to Marxism by socialist theoreticians. Mussolini's specific applications of these theoretical convictions also tended to be consistently Marxist. Mussolini construed morality, for example, as a superstructural element explicable on the basis of prevailing ecological and economic conditions.

A morality that arises out of such conditions can live and exercise dominion as long as the conditions persist that determined it; but with the disappearance of those conditions it becomes an anachronism. . . . Every epoch has had its own "morality". . . .[37]

When society enters a new epoch the old morality can be employed only as a formula for containing the revolutionary fury of the aspirant class. In this sense orthodox morality can be not only reactionary, but profoundly immoral as well. By way of illustration, in periods of restricted productivity the religious admonitions which advocated abnegation and docility in the face of privation had some warrant. With the advent of new productive forces, such a code serves only to enhance the survival capacity of antiquated discriminatory class relationships and the unnecessary oppression of man by man. In opposition to such a code a new morality arises, based upon and adapted to the needs which altered material circumstances have occasioned in the human community. This is the "human morality" to which Mussolini referred, and his entire treatment of the issue constituted a paraphrase of Engels' account in the Anti-Duehring.[38]

The rising proletariat, animated by the new precepts, organizes for a social revolution more general, more inclusive, than any antecedent uprising; a revolution that will expropriate the bourgeoisie and abolish the state, which today functions "as the committee of defense for the possessing classes. . . ."[39] These theoretical convictions, allied to specific tactical postures, and infused with socialist values, constituted a relatively coherent and relatively orthodox Marxism. Mussolini insisted upon the irreconcilability of class differences and the inevitability of class struggle. He was an internationalist in sentiment, rabidly antireligious, specifically anti-Christian, and frankly collectivist.[40]

All of these elements, culled from the articles Mussolini published before he was twenty-six, support the contention that he was both knowledgeable and a convinced Marxist. For their own reasons, both apologists and detractors have sought to obscure this fact. But it must also be added that Mussolini was a Marxist with a difference. In his very first articles there are elements which ill suit orthodox classical Marxism. In retrospect they take on a singular importance, for they constitute loci of tension that ultimately transformed the entire theoretical system.

The Young Mussolini and the Proto-Fascist Sociological Tradition

As early as 1903 and 1904, when he was approximately twenty-one, Mussolini advanced two conceptions which, with hindsight, seem to constitute a point of departure for his more mature social and political convictions.

In an essay written in 1903, he stated, "Psychology has demonstrated that the sentiments constitute the dynamic motives of human action."[41] Without attempting to extract too much from the statement, it does seem to constitute an initial move toward an antirational theory of human motivation, which would ill accord itself with classical Marxism. Whatever else it harbored, Marxism entertained an essentially rationalist view of motivation. On various occasions both Marx and Engels argued that the ultimate triumph of socialism was predicated on "the intellectual development of the working class. . . ."[42] In a variety of critical instances they both maintained that the proletariat would be driven to revolution by the clear comprehension of issues.[43]

The contention that the prime motives governing conduct are sentiments was, of course, advanced by Pareto in his *Sistemi socialisti* (published in 1902). That Mussolini read the *Sistemi* is suggested by the appearance in his articles of the term *elite*, employed in a specifically Paretan context. This conception of the elite is the second of the conceptions alluded to above. In April, 1904, Mussolini maintained that the "socialist revolution" is to be "initiated by a minority."[44] In July of that same year he specifically identified that minority as the "proletarian elite."[45] In October he specifically referred to Pareto's volume by name,[46] and it was during this time that Mussolini attended two courses conducted by Pareto at the University of Lausanne. Both Gaudens Megaro and H. Stuart Hughes are wrong when they suggest that Mussolini may not actually have attended those lectures.[47] In a letter to a friend, written on the fifth of January, 1923, Pareto reported that "Mussolini remained for some time at Lausanne and attended my courses, but I didn't know him personally,"[48]

It is almost certain that Mussolini read Pareto's *Sistemi* at this time. It is certain that he was exposed to Pareto's influence. During his sojourn in Switzerland Mussolini was occupied with the study of social science. We not only have his testimony to that effect, but also the testimony of those who knew him at the time.[49]

In 1908 Mussolini referred to "Vilfredo Pareto's theory of elites" as the "most ingenious sociological conception of modern times. History," Mussolini maintained, "is nothing more than a succession of dominant elites"; he went on to add, "progress has been possible only because the vanguard of the human species has not remained to sleep a lethargic dream at the level of civilization arduously achieved."[50]

Pareto had advanced a vision of the world as a constant competition between social elements in the struggle for dominance. He went on to add that the twentieth century was witnessing the advent of a new contending class led by an elite which challenged the minoritarian rule of the bourgeoisie. He conceived the ensuing struggle as a contest of force in which the weaker must succumb, a notion fully compatible with Mussolini's assessment of the class struggle. Mussolini argued,

. . . The socialist revolution was a pure and simple question of "force."
. . . Between the [bourgeoisie and the proletariat] no accord is possible. One must disappear. The weaker will be "eliminated." The class struggle is therefore a question of "force."[51]

Mussolini did not hesitate to call his conception "a new socialist conception, one profoundly 'aristocratic'."[52] Pareto had, of course, used the terms *elite* and *aristocracy* interchangeably. Having accepted at least some of the essentials of Pareto's position, it was not difficult for Mussolini to find the volume of Alfredo Oriani, *La rivolta ideale*, "magnificent."[53] Oriani's conceptions were characteristically elitist.

Through all history and in every human group, the special gifts of select individuals have rendered them masters over the others, who instinctively obey, bartering away liberty for security. . . . Human instincts and the necessities of history thus create an aristocracy responsible for the life of all . . . an aristocracy that must think and will for the others. . . .

Only by virtue of such an elite can the mass of men be lifted to the more sublime responsibilities of the spirit.

The function of the aristocracy is therefore dual—to develop the idea that forms the essence of a people and to lead it to express its essential character in that idea. Often there is a tension between political and moral virtue. At given moments the heroism of the species and the nation must be turned, without pity, against those destined to succumb. . . . Whatever the form of government an aristocracy forever formulates its laws. . . .[54]

Mussolini's association with these ideas is significant only in retrospect. At the time they were not considered unusual ideas for a socialist to entertain. First of all, there was alive in the Marxist tradition a Blanquist current (which reappeared in the formulations of Lenin). In Marx's essay of 1844, devoted to Hegel's philosophy of right, there are clear intimations of an imminent proletarian revolution in the backward Germany of the period. Germany was an industrially backward nation, and yet Marx spoke of a proletarian revolution. Clearly the revolution must be minoritarian. The German working class at that time was still in its infancy; it constituted only a minority faction in the total population. Yet Marx proposed an alliance of philosophers and proletarians to bring down the established social order and lift mankind to the stature of true manhood in "universal emancipation." "Philosophy," Marx maintained, "is the head of this emancipation: its heart is the proletariat."[55]

Prior to the Revolution of 1848, an entire generation of revolutionary Frenchmen had been nurtured on the radicalism of Babeuf and Buonarroti. Among them was August Blanqui. Blanqui's conception of revolution, of revolutionary tactics and organization, was elitist. He conceived revolution to be the consequence of the effective organization of the most radical members of the proletariat under the guidance of declassed bourgeois intellectuals. This union of head and heart would carry everything before it and establish a minoritarian dictatorship that would uplift the passive and inert masses.

Between 1844 and 1850, Marx and Engels were clearly under the influence of this tradition.[56] Many of their pronouncements concerning revolution in largely agrarian countries are comprehensible only if a form of minoritarian dictatorship were envisioned. Majoritarian revolution could be appropriate only for countries in which industry had reduced the majority of the population to proletarian status. In largely agrarian countries the peasant masses would have to be led by a minority of proletarians because the peasants were conceived to be intrinsically reactionary when left to their own devices. Thus, while it would not constitute an exhaustive or exclusive interpretation, a case could be made for a Blanquist or elitist tradition in classical Marxism.

Whatever the case, Mussolini's espousal of the specific Paretan theses with which we are concerned was neither unusual, nor would it have been considered heterodox. During his sojourn in Switzerland Mussolini had established a working contact with the revolutionary syndicalists under the leadership of Arturo Labriola. At this same time Sergio Panunzio (1886–1944), Mussolini's junior by three years and still a student, associated himself with Labriola's *Avanguardia Socialista*, to which Mussolini made regular contributions. At the Socialist Congress at Zurich in March, 1903, Mussolini met Angiolo Oliviero Olivetti (1874–1931), who was soon actively associated with the syndicalists. All three men, Labriola, Panunzio, and Olivetti, exercised significant influence on Mussolini, and Panunzio and Olivetti were to be numbered among the principal doctrinaires of Fascism.

The revolutionary syndicalism these men represented was a radical wing of Italian socialism. It was composed of antidemocratic, antiparliamentarian, activist, and ultimately elitist currents in which Mussolini found himself eminently at home. The antidemocratic and anti-parliamentarian theses of revolutionary syndicalism had their origins in orthodox Marxist theory and the peculiar historical and political circumstances that characterized Italy at the turn of the century. The founders of classical Marxism had made clear, even in their most mature writings, that a democratic republic was the most sophisticated and pernicious form of bourgeois domination. Behind the facade of democratic institutions the bourgeoisie exercised domination by corrupting public officials, by allying government and finance, and by inextricably entangling the state in the affairs of domestic and international capitalist enterprise. In effect, Engels insisted, "the possessing class rules directly through the medium of universal suffrage."[57] To disguise its dominance, the bourgeoisie fabricates political fictions to convince the exploited class that any rebelliousness would be "the basest ingratitude to its benefactors, the exploiters."[58]

At best the entire machinery of public elections could only serve as an index of the maturity of the working class. When it becomes evident that the class consciousness of the proletariat has attained that appreciation of its interests which makes it a threat to the essential interests of the possessing classes, the possessing classes resist and only violent revolution can resolve the issue. Elections, parliaments, the entire fabric of bourgeois democratic institutions are employed, by a class no longer possessed of the vitality to rule without them, to obscure the dominance of the minority over the producing majority.

The historical and political circumstances in Italy seemed to bear out such an analysis. Gaetano Mosca had revealed that the "democratic theory" was a ploy to obscure the fact of minority dominance, and his work is referred to time and again in the syndicalist literature of the period. The conduct of representatives in the Italian parliament corroborated his judgment. Parliament was afflicted with corruption and its members were frequently, if not regularly, self-serving. The industrial and commercial advances Italy made during the last two decades of the nineteenth century brought little succour to the working classes; finally, the restrictions on the suffrage made it mathematically impossible for the working class to effect substantial changes in the government or in the prevailing productive relations that governed the distribution of Italy's economic wealth.[59]

The syndicalists were therefore unalterably opposed to involvement in parliamentary maneuvers. The reformist socialists who opted to navigate ameliorative legislation through parliament were looked upon as traitors to the class interests of the proletariat. Involvement in the machinery of parliamentary government was construed by syndicalists as providing the semblance of legality for the machinery of class exploitation. They demanded a direct assault upon the agencies of the bourgeois state through autonomous workers' organizations. The principal weapon would be direct action—the strike and, in the final analysis, the general strike—which would render the entire capitalist enterprise inoperative.[60] This constituted the tactical and theoretical base of syndicalist activism.

The decision to employ the strike as the primary revolutionary weapon of the proletariat entailed a number of considerations. First and foremost, effective mobilization of the working class required organization. The syndicalists remembered Engels' admonition, ". . . Whoever mentions combined action speaks of organization; now, is it possible to have organization without authority?"[61] The answer was obvious. Effective organization required authority, and that authority, the authority of a field command in the social war, was to be arrogated to a minority of class conscious leaders—what Panunzio called a "new social aristocracy." In July, 1909, in the pages of *Pagine Libere* (a publication to which Mussolini contributed), Olivetti argued:

We do not intend to advance a program but only to affirm a fact, a fact which cannot be otherwise because syndicalist mentality cannot mature anywhere else than in the factory and in industrialized agricultural enterprise: large scale industry . . . will leave behind it a grey zone of minor industries and agriculture, artisans and petty bureaucracy, salaried domestics, and so forth, that is to say, a proletarian mass incapable, by virtue of its structure and economic position, to feel the pulse of that special revolutionary call that is syndicalism. Syndicalism is more a state of mind [*stato d'animo*] than a doctrine, a manner of social sensitivity that tends to translate itself into an operative will. Therefore it arises out of a sensitivity that not all can share, a concentration of energy that the very historic and physiological conditions of the working class impedes from becoming common, still less universal. It would be excellent if all workers were conscious of their condition and wished to change it. But who does not recognize that this is an unattainable dream? Of the thousand men who compose a collectivity, nine hundred will adapt themselves to any misery and remain content to be slaves, servants, proletarians. Of the remainder, the majority seek individual salvation and seek upward mobility without concerning themselves with the others or with any ideal aspirations. There remains only a small minority that transmits from epoch to epoch and generation to generation the torch of an ideal of perfection, of integral humanity. . . . An aristocracy? And why not? An aristocracy not proclaimed by law or possessors of material wealth; but a true aristocracy of blood and nerve open to all the strong. . . . A supremely human elite, composed of those possessed, in heart and mind, of greater humanity. . . .

Every social battle is a struggle of two minorities over the inert body of the great anonymous mass. . . . When we observe instances of admirable audacity that appear miraculous, catastrophes that appear unanticipated, it only means that the great beast has taken up a triumphant and vibrant idea. Men of historical stature are those who possess the solemn and mysterious fascination that arouses, spurs, and elevates the dormant. . . . From this vanguard cadre [*manipolo di avanguardia*] an idea and action must emanate. . . .[62]

In the context of his time Mussolini's elitism was not unusual, nor was his recourse to Pareto. The complex of ideas entertained by the revolutionary intransigents of the Socialist Party shared critical elements with the views of Pareto and Mosca as well. The presence of Roberto Michels among the revolutionary syndicalists certifies to that fact. During this period, Michels was recognized as a revolutionary "comrade" by the syndicalists,[63] and it was in this capacity that Mussolini knew him. H. Stuart Hughes errs when he suggests that Mussolini "may simply not have heard of [Michels]."[64] Mussolini was not only familiar with Michels' works of the period, but reviewed his *L'uomo economico e la cooperazione* for the socialist publication *Il Popolo*.[65] It was this work, written in 1909, which provided the basis for Michel's classic study of the oligarchical tendencies of modern political organization. The central theses of Michels' *L'uomo economico* were taken from Gumplowicz: (1) the abstract individual of the contract theorists is a fiction; (2) man is quintessentially a group animal; (3) as a member of an organized group man possesses group sustaining dispositions which manifest themselves as in-group amity and out-group enmity.

We have no direct evidence that Mussolini ever read Gumplowicz, but it has already been suggested that the ideas of Pareto, Mosca, and Michels shared common Gumplowiczian elements. Mussolini's commitment to Michels' ideas establishes at least a secondary acquaintance with those of Gumplowicz. It was indicated earlier that syndicalists like Olivetti did not hesitate to link the names of Gumplowicz, Pareto, and Marx. This is true of Panunzio as well. Panunzio, who collaborated with Labriola on his journal during the period of Mussolini's most active participation, specifically cites Gumplowicz' *Grundriss der Sociologie* and the *Sociologische Staatsidee* in their French and Italian editions to support his social and political contentions.[66] He also cites the works of Icilio Vanni. Vanni, as has been indicated, was a student of Gumplowicz and introduced his ideas into Italy during the last quarter of the nineteenth century. Since Panunzio, as will be indicated, went on to become one of the principal ideologues of Fascism, this direct contact with Gumplowiczian concepts is of critical importance in reconstructing the genesis of Fascist doctrine.

Olivetti and Panunzio were among the foremost theoreticians of syndicalism and the conceptions they articulated contained elements which originated in the work of Mosca, Pareto, Michels, and Gumplowicz. Of special interest at this point is the possible influence of the collective psychologists like Le Bon and Sighele on the young Mussolini. Since the syndicalists were favorably disposed toward Gumplowicz and Pareto, and included in their number men like Michels, the theoretical formulations of Le Bon and Sighele could be expected to exercise some influence.

In the case of Panunzio we have direct internal evidence that this was the case. In the same passage in which he makes explicit reference to Gumplowicz, he cites the "psychological laws" illustrated in the works of Tarde, Le Bon, and Sighele. Any theoretician who read Gumplowicz' *Sociologische Staatsidee* could hardly avoid taking up the ideas of Le Bon and Sighele. Years later Mussolini indicated that as early as his student years at the Royal Normal School at Forlimpopoli he had an "intense interest in the psychology of human masses—the crowd," and then went on to indicate that "one of the books that interested me most was *The Psychology of the Crowd* by Gustave Le Bon."[67] Unfortunately, the early publication of the volume precluded the possibility that Mussolini would review it for any of the journals and newspapers to which he contributed between 1902 and 1914, but it seems evident that he had read the book some time during or immediately prior to this period. There is no direct evidence that he had read Sighele, but so many of Sighele's ideas were contained in Le Bon's work that Sighele charged Le Bon with plagiarism. Mussolini's recognition of the merit of Le Bon's study entailed a similar recognition of Sighele, a consideration that is important in explaining the maturation of Mussolini's transition to Fascism. Le Bon, like Sighele, was antiparliamentarian, antidemocratic and antirationalist. He was also, as was Sighele, elitist. The syndicalist atmosphere was charged with these ideas. If they had not been transmitted through the work of Gumplowicz, they would have entered through Pareto's *Sistemi,* which made regular reference to Le Bon. Had they not been introduced by either of these secondary sources, they would have become elements of syndicalist doctrine through the work of Sorel.

The Young Mussolini and Georges Sorel

Sorel, of course, was the acknowledged master of revolutionary syndicalism. His ideas probably had more influence in Italy than they did in his native France. Mussolini was familiar with Sorel as early as 1904, at which time he ranked him alongside Marx, Engels, Labriola, and Kautsky.[68] Pini, Susmel, and De Felice suggest that Mussolini read Sorel's *Réflexions* in Switzerland, some time between 1902 and 1904, but the suggestion seems mistaken.[69] Whatever Mussolini read of Sorel's that year, it could not have been the *Réflexions,* which was first published in Italian in *Divenire Sociale* in 1905—*after* Mussolini had left Switzerland. In 1906 it was published in French in the *Mouvement Socialiste* and again in pamphlet form in Italian, with a preface by Enrico Leone, under the title, *Lo sciopero generale e la violenza.* In 1908 the French edition, entitled *Réflexions sur la violence,* appeared, and in 1909 another Italian edition, with a preface by Benedetto Croce, was published, entitled *Considerazioni sulla violenza*. It was this last edition that Mussolini reviewed for *Il Popolo* in that same year.[70]

Mussolini's review, which bore the title, "Lo sciopero generale e la violenza," harks back to the 1906 edition and suggests he had already read Sorel's *Réflexions* in the earlier edition. As a syndicalist he could hardly have avoided this earlier rendering which was so much the topic of syndicalist discussion. His review in *Il Popolo* indicates Mussolini's confident familiarity with Sorel's ideas. He not only refers to Sorel's previous works, including the *Ruine de monde antique* and the *L'introduction à l'économie moderne*, but, as Megaro indicates, his grasp of the central ideas advanced by Sorel is sure and his treatment insightful.[71]

Mussolini discussed those elements of Sorel's work that were to remain central to his own mature social and political views. In the very first paragraph he indicated that Sorel did not offer a doctrinal "system," but instead concerned himself with problems which compel one to abandon the role of spectator and commit oneself to action. This "pragmatic" disposition remained central to Mussolini's political activities, and it was the same pragmatism that characterized the thought of the major exponents of syndicalism. As early as 1902, Mussolini, already under the influence of Labriola, had maintained that syndicalism eschewed "formulae," and sought only the solution of problems.[72] This was a posture assumed by all the major exponents of syndicalism.

Mussolini then outlined the conception of the Sorelian myth. A myth is an "idea" capable of activating the masses. It affords the masses with a guide to action for the realization of specific collective programs. Thus the Christian myth inures Christians to obedience and instructs them in the performance of duties in anticipation of the apocalypse. Similarly, the French Revolution and the Italian Risorgimento were activated by political myths. All of them elevate the masses to a conception of life as a struggle, a sacrifice, a conquest, a self-transcendence. Sorel's myth of the general strike, which prepares the masses for the suppression of the state and private property, is a paradigmatic social and political myth.

The Sorelian myth sought to create a compact revolutionary movement which was at once antidemocratic, antiparliamentary and antihumanitarian in the sense that it opposed the conventional hypocrisies of the bourgeoisie. The institutional paraphernalia of the parliamentary and democratic state, with its periodic electoral subterfuges, was conceived as a mask for class oppression; its humanitarianism and pacificism was considered a device for pacifying the restive and exploited masses. If socialism were to survive as an ideal, and if its organizations were to be successful in the social struggle, it "must have the courage to be barbaric." It must have the strength of its convictions and defend them with violence against the debilitating impostures of the dominant class which controlled every major agency of public communication and held a monopoly of institutionalized force. The violence of the contending proletariat was to take on the character of the violence which attends a just war. It was necessary; surgical. Its function was to excise the evils which afflicted the social order as it was then constituted.

The state was organized force, which imposed on the social order the will of the bourgeois minority. Once vested, that force had become self-perpetuating. Its influence was all-pervasive and corrupting.[73] "Democracy" had become the charter myth of the system. The leaders of the new contending classes were drawn into the parliamentary arena and their activities confined by the "rule of law," a law which codified the property relations of capitalism itself. What resulted was a fugitive and dilute reformism which sought to ameliorate rather than abolish the system.

The myth was the organizing formula of the aspirant class. "Socialism is no longer a system located in some more or less distant future, but revolutionary orders of the day [*un tirocinio di preparazione rivoluzionaria*] in the continuous and violent class struggle."

This conception of revolution would, of necessity, alienate the sentimentalists so much addicted to reasonableness, the reformists so prone to compromise, and the intellectualists so convinced of the efficacy of reason. The prospect of such struggle was calculated to attract only men of energy who were prepared to enscribe new tables of values; *New Men* who, like the heroes of antiquity, were prepared to conceive their labors as something grave, terrible, and sublime.

115

Fifteen years after Mussolini wrote his review of Sorel's *Réflexions,* he said,

That which I am . . . I owe to Sorel. . . . He is an accomplished Master who, with his sharp theories on revolutionary formations, contributed to the molding of the discipline, the collective energy, the power of the masses, of the Fascist cohorts.[74]

In fact, Mussolini's mature concept of the mass-based movement of solidarity exemplified a special application of Sorel's functional myth.

In early 1914, in the months before his break with the Socialist Party, Mussolini gave mature expression to his views on the nature of revolution and the organization for social struggle.

There are those who would wait until they had the support of the absolute majority before undertaking revolution. That is absurd. First of all, the mass is simple quantity; it is inert. The mass is static; only minorities are dynamic. Furthermore, economic organization can hardly pretend to collect all potential members into labor organizations. . . . The problem takes on the following character: it is necessary to oppose a bourgeois minority with a revolutionary and socialist minority; those who occupy themselves with politics in Italy and those who govern in all the civilized nations are a minority as opposed to an enormous mass that submits. Since this apathetic and indifferent mass accepts and submits to a regime of inequity and injustice, why would it not submit to better rule?

We must create a proletarian minority sufficiently numerous, sufficiently knowledgeable, sufficiently audacious to substitute itself, at the opportune moment, for the bourgeois minority. The mass will simply follow and submit.[75]

Such an account could have been culled from the works of Gumplowicz, Pareto, Mosca, Michels, *or* Sorel. Gumplowicz said essentially the same thing in essentially the same words in his *Rechstaat und Sozialismus.* What distinguishes Mussolini's social and political conceptions from those of Gumplowicz and Mosca, for example, is his preoccupation with motivation. In this regard his more intimate knowledge of the work of Pareto, Michels, and Sorel is reflected in the following account written in early 1914.

. . . "Theoretic consciousness" can only be the privilege of an exiguous minority, a luxury of thinkers who are, in a certain sense, detached from reality; but the vast masses called upon to establish a new order require not so much to "know" as to "believe." In the mind of the proletariat the "theoretical consciousness" of socialism will be forever amorphous, rudimental, dull. Just as it is not necessary to have read and understood all of theology to be a good Christian, one can be an excellent socialist even ignoring the works and master works of socialist literature. . . . The *sans-culottes* who assaulted the Bastille probably possessed no "theoretical consciousness." The social revolution is not a mental schema or a calculation but, more than anything else, an act of faith.[76]

From 1902, when the first intimations of Mussolini's conception of socialism were expressed, until 1914, two themes became increasingly important: (1) the nature of human motivation and the psychology of revolution, and (2) the nature of the revolutionary struggle, that is to say the relationship between the leaders and the led. Under the direct influence of Pareto, Michels, and finally Sorel, Mussolini's conceptions matured until, in 1914, they provided the guide for the organization of a mass-based revolutionary movement. In the maturation of his ideas the influence of Labriola, Panunzio, and Olivetti were particularly significant. Their influence persisted even after Mussolini broke with the syndicalist wing of the revolutionary movement because of their refusal to participate in anything other than specifically economic forays against the bourgeoisie. Mussolini rejected the syndicalist insistence upon the exclusive use of the strike as a revolutionary weapon. It was evident, however, that he did not reject syndicalist conceptions on minoritarian leadership and the organizational function of political and social myths.[77] This was clear in 1912 after Mussolini opposed both Sorel's rapprochement with the nationalists of France and the specific tactics of Italian syndicalists. At that time he maintained that "we recognize the task and we appreciate the importance of audacious minorities and vanguard elites [*elites precorritrici*] in history," and ". . . humanity has need of a faith. It is faith that moves mountains because it induces the illusion that the mountains move."[78]

Between 1902 and 1914 Mussolini's ideas crystallized around core concepts now identified with Sorel: the view of life as a constant and arduous struggle against an indifferent external environment as well as antagonistic outgroups, with the contest between groups directed by elites capable of inspiring the inert masses with a vision of the future and possessing the will capable of disciplining those masses to the efforts necessary for the fulfillment of that vision. Yet the Mussolinian conception of the myth was different in at least one important respect. He understood the functional myth to be a necessary tactical adjunct in the organizational program of the revolution. The myth answered the requirements of mass motivation, but the myth could not provide the strategic program of the party leadership. The leadership "requires a specific knowledge that governs and is adequate for action. For those who conceive socialism in terms of Sorel's myth nothing obtains other than an act of faith. . . ." What is required is a "pragmatic realism."[79] Mussolini thus opposed the "realistic" Guicciardini to the "visionary" Sorel.

Sorel's myth satisfies the requirement obvious to those who accept a nonrationalist theory of collective motivation. But the myth is neither true nor false; questions about its truth or falsity are simply inappropriate. The activities of the organizational elite cannot be governed by such myths. The vanguard of the revolutionary movement, if it is to provide effective leadership, must have adequate techniques for the determination of truth values. Any action which results from a simple commitment to myth is hazardous. Revolutionary action must be based on an accurate assessment of the social forces in act at any given time.[80] It is necessary to possess that "theoretical consciousness" adequate to the direction of practical affairs.[81] In order to attain an adequate appraisal of circumstances it is necessary to "suppress sentiment [*far tacere il sentimento*], because only reason inquires, discovers, confronts."[82] The fact is that "Georges Sorel has not delivered a system from which one could draw tactical norms."[83] Sorelianism provides a theory of mass organization and motivation, not strategic and tactical norms for revolutionary leadership.

Mussolini indicated that his adherence to syndicalist ideas dated from his association with Labriola and Panunzio in 1904.[84] Yet in 1908 he rendered the following account:

. . . to love an idea it is necessary to understand it. To love socialism it is not enough to issue a superficial profession of faith. . . . To love socialism it is necessary to understand it, study it, pursue its practical manifestations and its doctrinal commitments. To love socialism it is necessary to live its life.

To believe out of sentiment means to have religious faith. To believe as a consequence of a determination of will and reason is to have the faith of free spirits, the conscious faith that does not delude itself. . . . It is necessary to make socialism a reasoned faith. . . . To believe is not enough; it is necessary to reason. To those who cry: "Believe!" we reply, "Demonstrate!"[85]

Mussolini, like Sorel and Pareto, was an antirationalist. Men, particularly in the mass, were motivated primarily by sentiment rather than reason. But a movement directed solely by sentiment courts disaster. With such a conviction in mind, Mussolini was sufficiently concerned with theoretical matters to found, in 1914, the journal *Utopia* in order to formulate his own doctrinal views.[86] He recognized that since 1912 he had held a theoretical position which he claimed was dictated not by sentiment but by doctrinal and philosophical reasons.[87] He held that while the party must be capable of "surrounding the revolutionary proletarian movement with an heroic, religious atmosphere," the party leadership must constitute itself "an aristocracy of intelligence and will. . . ."[88] While effective organization of the masses can only be accomplished via myths, their leaders must employ every rational tool in the formulation of policy.

Mussolini's mature conception of a political movement as a disciplined, hierarchically organized force rested upon the theoretical convictions which matured in the decade before World War I. In 1932, in his conversations with Emil Ludwig, Mussolini maintained,

The mass, for me, is nothing more than sheep as long as it remains disorganized. I am not against it. I only deny that it can govern itself. But if one is to lead it, two reins are necessary: enthusiasm and interest. Whoever contents himself with one runs a risk. Mystical and political aspects condition each other. One without the other is arid, the former without the latter loses itself in the fluttering of flags.[89]

This is a reformulation of concepts he entertained as early as 1902. Sentiment and interest provide the motive force for collective action. If a movement is to be disciplined, it requires a

certain irreducible unanimity provided by enthusiasm or sentiment. Mussolini maintained, in 1934,

It was I who gave the order that it be said that I never made mistakes.
My subordinates gave expression to this through another: "The Duce is
always right." Dictatorial regimes, more than an army of pretorians, require an aliquot of faithful fanatics. Criticism is left to those capable, and
possessed of the courage, of undertaking it. But the mass must obey: it
cannot be conceded the luxury of losing time in the search for truth.[90]

The distinction was clear. The mass responded solely to sentiment and an appeal to interest. A minority, on the other hand,
was charged with the responsibility of the search for truth. In that
same year (1934), Mussolini indicated that a distinction must be
made between the certain conviction, born of sentiment, that
animates the mass, and the reasoned conviction of the political
elite. "If by mysticism," he contended, "one means the ability to
recognize the truth without the aid of reason, I would be the first
to declare myself opposed to every mysticism."[91] Mussolini thus
entertained a theory of motivation *and* a theory of truth. One could
not be conflated with the other. There are points of contact that
are critical, but the distinction was relatively precise.

The Young Mussolini, Anti-Intel-lectualism, and Antirationalism

Coupled with Mussolini's
antirationalist theory of
motivation was an anti-
intellectualist theory of
truth. Intimations of this latter conception are to be found among
his earliest published writings.[92] His early association with the
revolutionary syndicalists reinforced a disposition to look upon
intellectualistic formulations with considerable reservation. The
movement from a form of strict positivism, as exemplified in the
conceptions of Ardigò, to pragmatism is evident in his writings
published between 1902 and 1909. In 1903, Mussolini still spoke
of the "inevitable" ascent of socialism as a consequence of the
capitalist productive process itself.[93] In 1904 he could still applaud
the "sound positivism" of Pareto.[94] As late as 1908 he could still
appeal to Marx's "economic determinism" for an adequate explanatory account of all collective human actions. "Examine all the

thoughts and movements of human thought and you will find that they were 'determined' by economic and profane motives."[95]

One could, in principle, predict the course of events by selecting a finite class of variables in the form of economic interests and, by systematically relating them, generate predictive propositions of a relatively high order. Knowing something of the degree of maturation in the productive process one could predict something of the degree of maturation concerning social theories and collective behavior.[96] The privileged variables were construed, in some sense, sufficient to produce specific effects. The relationship of economic variables to motives as immediate determinants of conduct was conceived initially as sequential, necessary, and irreversible.

That Mussolini held some version of this position between 1902 and 1908 is evident from an inspection of his published writings. Under the influence of the revolutionary syndicalists, particularly Sorel, and the antirationalists, particularly Pareto, his convictions underwent substantive alteration. In 1908 Mussolini was prepared to grant that "some of [Marx's] economic notions were incorrect."[97] In 1909 he admitted that "We do not exclude that some parts—secondary elements—of the Marxist economic doctrine are faulty. . . ."[98] Given, however, a consistent economic determinism, errors in the economic theory, however minor, entail alterations in the general conclusions. When this awareness, however vague, is conjoined with a conviction that *sentiments* constitute the dynamic motives of behavior, the original theory begins to take on an entirely different complexion. At some imprecise point during this period, according to his own testimony, Mussolini gradually abandoned positivism.[99] With this abandonment, the economic determinism of classical Marxism was sufficiently loosened to permit the insinuation of extraneous variables—in this case moral sentiment, the consequence of willed conviction. In April, 1909, Mussolini voiced his reservations with respect to Comtean positivism and Spencerian social evolution and the "verbal constructions" of sterile and solitary intellectuals. He opted for "a philosophy of action, a pragmatic philosophy."[100] In May of the same year the implications of this conversion were evident.

Socialism, out of an addiction to economic determinism, subordinated men to inscrutable laws which were cognitively obscure but to which they had to submit. Syndicalism restored to history the willed activity of man, determined and determining in turn; of man who can leave the imprint of his modifying power on things and institutions that surround him; of man who can will in a given direction. Syndicalism did not reject "economic necessity," but added "ethical consciousness."[101]

From 1909, Mussolini's conception of social and historical dynamics was framed in terms of an interdependency of variables. In 1913, he contended,

Historical materialism does not intend to establish between economic phenomena and all others a connection of causal necessity, that is to say, logical and sequential, but rather a specification of relative importance. In other words the economic factor is the most important, but it does not determine, of itself, the other social factors.[102]

Marx, Mussolini continued, had erred in "attributing a hyperbolic importance to *Homo oeconomicus*. . . ."[103] Men, in substantial if indeterminate measure, are moved to action by moral considerations, by willed convictions. Such acts, individual and collective, function as independent determinants in any historical and social situation. Political action requires such individual and collective acts, acts which cannot be plausibly construed either as the inevitable consequence of the economic process itself or of reason alone.

Mussolini identified this interpretation of Marxism with the one entertained by revolutionary socialism. In 1906, Enrico Leone had argued that ". . . socialism excludes—as Sorel has demonstrated—neither the human will nor the intersection of extrinsic variables [*cause occasionali*] in the determination of social facts."[104]

Marxism, for Mussolini, did not "conduce to a species of fatalism. Marxism is rather a doctrine of will and of conquest. . . ."[105] Marx was a "voluntarist," a revolutionary who could hardly content himself with the positivistic formulations of his epigenes.[106] The intrinsic analysis Mussolini offers which supports this interpretation is interesting. He refers to the passage, in the *Poverty of Philosophy*, in which Marx maintains, "Of all the instruments of production, the greatest productive power is the revolutionary class itself."[107] If the economic base of society, that set of ultimate determinants of man's entire history, includes the activity of the revolutionary class itself as a prime constituent, the materialist interpretation of history can be construed as essentially voluntaristic. Certainly the cited passage complicates any simple interpretation of the relationship between economic and collective response variables. Any construction which conceived collective response to be the simple consequence of the influence of productive forces (even conjoined with productive relations) on group dispositions would be in error, since the revolutionary class, itself, is the greatest productive force.

By 1914 Mussolini recognized that his voluntaristic interpretation of Marxism was one interpretation among several. Referring to his opponents, he insisted,

You conceive Marxism in accordance with an evolutionistic and positivistic interpretation of history, while we conceive it . . . in accordance with a more modern idealistic interpretation. . . . Even in Marxism there is the letter and the spirit. . . . [It] is the spirit of Marxism, and not so much Marxist doctrine in its formal and transient expression, that structures our *Weltanschauung*.[108]

This theoretical reinterpretation of Marxism was not only an abandonment of positivism, it was also an espousal of pragmatism. The reassessment of the function of willed conviction in the context of political activity suggested a reinterpretation of the entire cognitive process. Certainly Mussolini's accession to an antirationalist political activism was coeval with his adoption of an anti-intellectualist epistemology. Reason without the will not only conduced to political quietism,[109] but also proved incapable of an adequate appraisal of reality. This proposition is more far-reaching in its implications than any antirationalist commitment in interpretation of the motives of collective behavior. One can, like Pareto, entertain an antirationalist appraisal of collective conduct without entertaining anti-intellectualism. Mussolini, on the other hand, was an anti-intellectualist. He came to conceive reason as adaptive and instrumental, as neither exclusively nor primarily concerned with the delivery of final, exhaustive and infrangible truths. Reason is an instrument for changing the world and, by changing it, understanding it. The fabrication of arcane, abstruse, and abstract systems is the preoccupation of intellectuals, men untrue to the world, more concerned with formulating metaphysical theories than with confronting the immediate problems which beset humanity.[110]

Mussolini advocated a "philosophy of action, a pragmatic philosophy."[111] We know that he was familiar with the journal *Leonardo*, published by Papini and Prezzolini, an Italian journal which actively propagated pragmatism during the first decade of our century.[112] Under its impetus, pragmatism became a popular philosophical posture. Mussolini probably read Papini's "Crepuscolo dei filosofi," in *Leonardo*, and we do know that he read Papini's *L'uomo finito* which he considered "extraordinary and admirable."[113] William James, the founder of pragmatism, found Papini's representations accurate enough to cite them in his *Pragmatism*.[114] Moreover, by 1909, even before Sorel himself had indicated his specific debt to pragmatism, pragmatism had passed into the formulations of Italian syndicalism. Panunzio characterized syndicalism as "above all pragmatic," and Prezzolini, in the volume Mussolini reviewed for *Il Popolo*, interpreted Sorel in an unequivocally pragmatic fashion.[115]

In all probability Mussolini's familiarity with pragmatism was of a secondary or derivative sort. There is no evidence that he had read any of James' works himself, although James' works became increasingly available in French and Italian translations. In 1924, when he was questioned about the influence of pragmatism on the development of his thought, Mussolini indicated that it had been important insofar as it taught him "to judge actions rather from their results than any doctrinal basis."[116] Mussolini identified pragmatism more with a method, with an attitude, rather than with any specific results. In this, of course, he was faithful to at least a substantial part of what James himself maintained. James held that

[Pragmatism] has no dogmas, and no doctrines save its method. . . . No particular results then, so far, but only an attitude of orientation, is what the pragmatic method means. The attitude of looking away from first things, principles, "categories," supposed necessities; and of looking towards last things, fruits, consequences, facts.[117]

A similar emphasis is to be found in Papini's essay of 1906.

[Pragmatism] is very much occupied with methods, with cognitive and practical instruments, because it is convinced that it is far more important to perfect or create methods having high predictive competence or for changing ourselves and others than to play with empty words about incomprehensible problems. . . . [Pragmatism] excites men to act rather than talk, to transform rather than contemplate. . . . [118]

This was essentially the manner in which Mussolini interpreted the pragmatism of syndicalism. ". . . [It] is a method and not a doctrine, a program and not a dogma, action and not a formula."[119] Thus "our intelligence is not provided finished doctrinal 'systems' but excited by 'problems' that compel us to think and transform us from 'spectators' into 'actors.' "[120]

Pragmatism, particularly as it was understood by Papini, and as it came to be understood by Mussolini, was eminently suited to political voluntarism. Papini's essay of 1906, devoted to James' *Will to Believe,* emphasized the fact that there are human situations in which "a fact cannot come at all unless a preliminary faith exists in its coming," in which "the faith in a fact can help create the fact."[121] In a political context such a conception satisfies the requirement of Mussolini's interpretation of historical materialism as willed conviction on the part of the revolutionary minority and faith on the part of the masses.

As has already been indicated, Mussolini made a distinction between the willed conviction of the revolutionary elite and the faith of the organized masses. In making this distinction, Mussolini was reflecting the influence of Papini's interpretation of pragmatism. In an essay published in *Leonardo* in 1905, Papini had indicated that pragmatism was essentially a concern with "augmenting our power to modify things," but he also went on to indicate that in order to act effectively it was necessary to have a competent grasp of facts. A competent grasp of facts provides adequate leadings (anticipations), and affords greater predictive confidence.[122] Mussolini relegated this concern to a revolutionary aristocracy. So equipped, the elite can activate the masses to its determinate purposes by employing functional myths.

By 1914 Mussolini had developed a particular constellation of social and political conceptions that, in a qualified sense, could be considered his own. None of the elements was original, any more than any one in the peculiar collection of ideas contained in the

Communist Manifesto could be considered original—but in the form in which they were articulated, and in the respective emphasis given to each, Mussolini's social and political thought was peculiarly his own. His was a view of society conceived in terms of continual and implacable conflict between heterogeneous social elements. These diverse elements crystallized around specific needs and interests and, stabilized by sentiments of identity fostered by functional or organizing myths, each manifested persistent in-group amity and out-group hostility. In each of these hostile elements leadership was the privilege of a strategic political and intellectual elite. A social element steeled in conflict, animated by a myth which fostered discipline and sacrifice and staffed by a gifted cadre was destined to accede to dominance in the perpetual rotation of elites that characterized the whole of history.

A society is composed of these heterogeneous elements. Its limits are determined by more inclusive sustaining needs and interests, exemplified in common geographic origin, community of blood, language, and culture.[123] Society's first requirement is economic viability. All its subsequent activity is predicated upon its capacity to insure at least minimum subsistence to its members. As the economic base of society matures with the development of its material productive forces, the pre-established social relations, characterized by the dominance of a select minority, are destabilized and the road to succession is open. A vested elite, competent within the context of the hitherto existing social order, may not prove adequate to the new. Society may enter a period of transition during which a new society literally grows up within the confines of the old.[124] Under the governance of a contending elite, new institutions, appropriate to new conditions, make their appearance. Their appearance invokes a period of more or less protracted violence because the vested elite does not voluntarily surrender its privileges.[125] The contending elite mobilizes the elemental human energies embodied in the new social forces and opposes institutionalized force with revolutionary violence. The exercise of violence not only throws into sharp relief the real interests of the ensconced minority; it generates increased in-group sentiment in both factions, thereby defining, with utmost clarity, the responsibilities of their respective members. It conduces to the "creation of new characters, to new values, to *homines novi*."[126] The contending class opposes new values and new men to the values and the men of the moribund order. Within that ascendant class an "idealistically privileged" minority exercises revolutionary initiative.[127] A "small resolute nucleus, both audacious and possessed of reasoned faith," assumes hierarchical control over the revolutionary masses.

Because of its restricted social base, the vested elite seeks to undermine the united action and dilute the strength of conviction of the challenging revolutionary elements by employing systematic corruption and making regular appeal to conventional hypocrisies. In the twentieth century, the parliamentary system corrupts and democratic and humanitarian humbug deludes. Only violence and the threat of violence can serve the revolutionary elements as an adequate prophylactic against such tactics. The responsible use of violence, and the real threat of its use, become a moral obligation.

At each critical juncture in the development of society and the circulation of elites that attends its successive stages, human will and creative capacity exercise significant, if indeterminate, influence.

Mussolini's social and political conceptions shared essential common elements with the revolutionary syndicalism with which he identified between 1904 and 1910. The ultimate source of those conceptions can be traced to Pareto and Mosca, and ultimately to Gumplowicz. Combined with elements of pragmatism, the collection of descriptive propositions, definitions, and normative injunctions with which Mussolini identified present a fairly coherent political *Weltanschauung*. Nietzsche provided, by and large, no more than the emotive overtones for a world-view that was fundamentally anti-individualistic.[128] Nietzsche was conceived the herald of a new *pragmatic* transvaluation of values.[129] His was the voice of rebellion and uncompromising dissent.[130] He made, however, no substantive contribution to Mussolini's social or political views. Nietzsche gave expression to a mood; he exemplified an attitude. He was the poet laureate of revolutionaries of all sorts.

To what extent the young Mussolini was influenced by Henri Bergson is difficult to say with any confidence. The few times he refers directly to Bergson it is only to say that he *was* influenced.[131] Nowhere is there any indication of what effect that influence might have had on his thought.

The Young Mussolini and the Class Concept

The entire complex of ideas with which Mussolini identified qualified as Marxist largely because the central theoretical and analytic conception around which the account turned was "class." The heterogeneous social elements which provided the dynamic force of social change were classes. The struggle in which they were joined was the class struggle. The imminent victory was the victory of the proletarian class. The class fated to succumb was the bourgeoisie.

In 1910, when Mussolini assumed editorial responsibility for the organ of the regional socialist federation of Forli, he entitled his paper *La Lotta di Classe* (the *Class Struggle*). It was the class struggle which constituted the essence of Marxism for Mussolini.[132] In 1911, when he specified those elements of Marxism which he considered still viable, he identified them as (1) the doctrine of economic determinism (2) the class struggle, and (3) the concept of catastrophic social change.[133] By that time, however, the determinate influence of human will and intelligence were included among the variables that together constituted "causes" in the schema of Mussolini's "economic determinism." In effect, Mussolini tendered a "more modern, more idealistic" interpretation of determinism that was not a determinism in any significant sense—unless determinism is construed as admitting as causes the reasons, both conscious and unconscious, rational and irrational, which motivate individuals and collectivities to action. His interpretation was essentially Sorelian, with emphatic pragmatic overtones and distinctions. What remained was the concept of the class struggle and catastrophic or revolutionary change, but revolutionary change is, itself, contingent upon class struggle.[134] The class struggle, in other words, was the single surviving constituent of classical Marxism. This is evident in everything Mussolini wrote in the years between 1910 and 1914. It was his commitment to this concept which characterized his social and political thought as Marxist. Class was the core conception of his world view. It is "class," Mussolini maintained, "which is the instrument of human regeneration."[135]

By 1911, Mussolini rejected "Marxist theology." He insisted that "Karl Marx is not necessary for socialism."[136] It was necessary to "interpret Marx," and it was "not necessary to interpret Marxist theories to the letter."[137] Socialism remained socialist as long as class remained the central theoretic and analytic concept of one's social and political thought. As long as this remains the case, socialist goals and socialist values remain intact. Class association becomes a privileged association in the sense that all other associations have only derivative or instrumental normative importance. The responsibilities which define the specific content of man's moral universe are established by his class obligations. Since it is the class struggle which structures his moral universe, all other associations enjoin only secondary obligations. Thus obligations to family, religion, and nation are binding only when they do not conflict with class obligations.

Under these conditions, Mussolini could only be unalterably opposed to any claims made on the individual not enjoined by class membership. Nationalism made the association in the nation primary and made class association contingent. Nationalism required that class identification be sacrificed for the individual's identification with his "people." When "class" dilates into "people," the nation becomes man's morally privileged association.[138] The nation becomes the unit for moral regeneration and the integrating myth becomes one which appeals to the historic, traditional, and political continuity of the nation. Should the nation accede to this morally privileged status, the individual would be committed to its defense. Its defense would require effective unitary organization that, in turn, would require a value consensus, a disposition to put the interests of the nation before the interests of class and category. Should such a necessity obtain, continuing the class struggle would constitute a contingent rather than a primary obligation. The class struggle would be defaulted and socialist values would have to be surrendered. Mussolini's initial opposition to Italy's involvement in World War I was predicated expressly upon this recognition. ". . . War," he insisted, "requires the most insistent class collaboration. . . ."[139] "War between nations," he went on, "necessitates the collaboration of classes in its most acute, grandiose and sanguine form. . . . This is the profound reason why we detest the war. We are far removed from the vagaries of professional pacificists."[140]

International war divests the proletariat of its autonomy. The proletariat becomes a unit in the disciplined ranks of the nation. It must abandon its special interests. The war in which it is involved is no longer *its* war, no longer a *class* war. International war would thus displace the locus of loyalty. Class loyalty and solidarity would no longer satisfy the group sentiment of individuals. The nation would require the dissipation of intrasocietal group exclusiveness in the service of intersocietal conflict. The nation would become the charismatic object and national, rather than class, victory the goal. For socialists of all European countries such an eventuality was conceived impossible. The international class consciousness of the proletarian class precluded such an eventuality. The unity of interest that provided the real basis of collective identity was class interest, the material interests of the exploited and dispossessed of all nations.[141] Mussolini's contention during this period was that "There are but two nations in the world: that of the exploited and that of the exploiters."[142] Such a contention was thought to follow from the reality of the interests which united the proletariat. The reality of interests manifested itself in the moral sentiments that moved men to action and the political formulae in which those sentiments found expression must reflect them. "It is not formulae which create a state of mind, but a state of mind that creates formulae. . . ."[143] "Formulae," Mussolini insisted, "must adapt themselves to realities. To pretend to fit realities to formulae is sterile . . . , vain, folly, a ridiculous enterprise."[144]

If the theoretical formulations of international socialism were correct, their test would be the response of the respective national proletarian classes to international war. It was with this conviction that Mussolini, as a youthful pragmatist, faced the impending threat of World War I. For orthodox socialism the issue was clear. There could be no war. Years before Napoleone Colajanni had contended that international struggles, with the inevitability of natural law, would diminish in frequency and destructiveness until they ceased entirely.[145]

The position of the Second International was unequivocal. For the last two decades of the nineteenth century there had been a notable increment of internationalist sentiment. The founding of the Second International was heralded as the initial move in the direction of an operative proletarian internationalism. Representatives of the various national socialist parties strove to integrate into a unit of class solidarity that transcended political and cultural boundaries. The International lived over forty years, during which there was relative peace among European nations. Every international socialist congress heard, in steadily increasing profusion, protestations of international peace and solidarity. The Stuttgart Congress of 1907 had voted to oppose "in a revolutionary spirit" any imperialist ventures on the part of the capitalist class. In 1912, the socialist opposition to international war was reiterated in a special meeting called to face the growing threat of armed conflict precipitated by the vertigenous arms race and the interlocking military treaty agreements among the great powers.

But when the war descended upon the continent, these sentiments went into immediate eclipse. At the Stuttgart Congress Gustave Hervé, the French radical socialist, had proposed the insurrectionary general strike in the event of a declaration of war. In 1910 he declared that the "national flag of France is a rag to be planted on a dunghill." But with the advent of war in 1914, Hervé immediately changed the name of his paper from *La Guerre Sociale* to *La Victoire*—national victory. Hervé requested the opportunity of being among the first volunteers to reach the battle front. In Germany the socialist delegates in parliament voted (just one vote short of unanimity) war credits to the Imperial Government, and the Socialists Paul Lensch and Alexander Parvus-Helfand became ardent war propagandists. At the same time Vladimir Burtsev, the Russian Social Democrat, returned to Russia with the proclamation that all workers should support the war effort of the nation in arms. Kropotkin, Plekhanov, and Kautsky aligned themselves with their respective countries in the tragic conflict that set Europe aflame. The entire structure of international working-class solidarity collapsed. The streets of Vienna, Berlin, and Paris were filled with milling throngs of workers rejoicing at the prospect of international carnage. International working-class sentiment dissipated with the first flash of gun-powder. International socialism went into a crisis from which it never emerged.

The Young Mussolini and Nationalism

Mussolini's first, and immediate, response, as a leader of Italian socialism and editor of its principal publication, was a call for "absolute neutrality." His posture was that of the responsible party functionary. By the beginning of 1914, he had become increasingly conscious of the distinction between his roles as a party spokesman and as an independent socialist theoretician. In founding his journal, *Utopia,* he indicated that "here I can speak in the first person. Elsewhere I represent the collective opinion of the party. . . ." In *Utopia* he could

represent my own opinion, my own *Weltanschauung,* and whether or not it accords itself with the standard opinion of the party is of no consequence. Elsewhere I am a soldier who "obeys" . . . here, however, I am a soldier who can also "discuss"; but then I am not a soldier and I am not occupied with orders in the proper sense. There are certain orders one does not discuss in the presence of the army, just as one does not argue about certain truths or heresies in church.[146]

There is considerable evidence to indicate that Mussolini's intransigence in the face of Italy's possible involvement in the war was more apparent than real, but he could not discuss the issue in the presence of the "troops." During the first days of crisis in July, he moved to have the leadership of the party convene and take a decisive stand. There was considerable delay and much vacillation. Mussolini proposed that in the eventuality of Italian involvement a general strike be called (in an echo of Hervé's anti-war proposals at the Stuttgart Congress in 1907). The party directorate hesitated and the official order of the day did not include Mussolini's proposal. By August, the war had extended to Germany, France, and Russia, and England's entry was imminent. In Brussels, where the International convened, an emergency session was called. Angelica Balabanoff (who had worked with Mussolini in editing *Avanti!*) raised the issue of the general strike. Her proposal was rejected by the representatives of the working class (with the exception of the English delegates). The working class was preparing to support the "bourgeois" governments of their respective fatherlands. The international working class movement was either impotent to influence the course of events or had opted to precipitate them. In substantial part the working-class movement had espoused the thesis of national defense and assumed a "patriotic" posture. The international features of the proletarian movement became increasingly obscured and the traditional national profiles reappeared. In Italy, the members of the working class began to talk in terms of collective responsibilities. They spoke of the German military machine, of German oppression, of German autocracy. All became the subjects of disapprobation. There was little talk of the international capitalist class as the responsible moral agent. Culpability was assigned to *nations*, not to *classes*. The language they had spoken only a few months previously had become inappropriate, almost incomprehensible. Papini and Prezzolini, at one time nationalists, syndicalists, futurists, and pragmatists, the men who had called Italian attention to the significance of the work of Mosca, Pareto, and Sorel, quickly passed into the ranks of the interventionists. Defections began in the very ranks of orthodox socialism, and Massimo Rocca, a collaborator with Mussolini's *Avanti!*, passed over to the interventionists. Olivetti quickly followed, and soon the entire Left Wing of the syndicalist movement actively supported Italy's entry into the conflict. Even Filippo Corridoni, the young leader of the revolutionary syndicalists, joined the interventionist clamor. It was the same Corridoni who in 1911 had called upon the proletariat "to raise the red flag, symbol of all the blood spilled and that will be spilled in the social struggle, shouting a cry of rebellion: the tricolor to the dungheap."[147]

Cesare Battisti, the socialist with whom Mussolini had collaborated in the Trentino, made his headquarters in Milan and actively stoked irridentist fires among the socialists there. The entire socialist movement in Italy began to disintegrate under the impact of events that had overtaken it. The position of the officials of the party, nevertheless, remained unchanged. Throughout August, Mussolini obediently continued to call for absolute neutrality.

Nonetheless, Mussolini's personal judgments were profoundly troubled. In view of the circumstances he reconsidered the alternatives left to socialists. Socialists might call for a revolutionary general strike upon the declaration of war. The forces mobilized by the government for war would drown the revolutionary uprising in blood—or the uprising might be successful and the socialists accede to power. They would then face the problem of a possible enemy invasion. The socialists might "martyr" the nation, open the way for the enemy, and attempt, by moral suasion, to attain an honorable peace (a tactic later employed by Lenin). Such an alternative was extremely hazardous. The victorious invaders might simply restore a reactionary regime and the working class, after the protracted bloodletting of revolution, would find itself, at best, no better circumstanced than it was before revolution. To Mussolini, the revolutionary general strike did not appear to be an auspicious alternative.[148] Finally, on September ninth, some of these misgivings appeared in the official organ of the party, *Avanti!*. Socialists could not seriously entertain the prospect of the revolutionary general strike in the event of a declaration of war. That seemed to leave but one alternative. Mussolini conjectured,

We might accept war, but to accept it would mean crossing over the barricade and would confound us with those who conceive the war . . . as the only cure for the world [*igiene del mondo*]! We remain on the right course, a socialist course. That is not to say that our ideas cannot alter. Only the lunatic and the dead never change.[149]

If socialists accepted war it would mean they would make common cause with nationalists and Futurists. His allusion to the Futurist slogan, *"la guerra è la sola igiene del mondo,"* indicated that he was fully aware of the implications of such an alternative. Syndicalists like Olivetti had already faced such an alternative during the war in Tripoli in 1911. At that time, Olivetti conceived the war as the occasion of mobilizing disciplined force in the service of expanding life and vitality. The moral regeneration that Sorel had conceived to be the result of organized group violence could be the consequence of a war between states as well as in a war between classes.

Both imply force, an impulse to dominate, a will to power that abhors the pallid conventional equality that is the sterile dream of collectivism. . . . [Such a struggle would constitute] the prelude to the formation of aggressive and conquering elites, driven to conquest by expansiveness and vitality. There is something of this in the program of the so-called Futurists, but they are limited to an esthetic and literary conception of life; syndicalism conceives the warrior hosts as originating in the aristocracy of the working classes, possessed of the superior technical skills destined to dominate and control contemporary life. In this regard, and in order to be truthful, one must concede that there are two currents in syndicalism: one is but a form of revolutionary democracy, and the other of revolutionary aristocracy. The latter is the authentic and original syndicalism that is spokesman of the most audacious philosophy of will and action, that rejects democracy, . . . that makes recourse to Nietzsche, Marx, and, in part, to Schopenhauer, that places itself beyond good and evil, that begins once more to undertake an audacious rebirth. . . . [150]

In the face of the infinitely more challenging events of 1914, the radicals of socialism, the revolutionary syndicalists, had refused to remain spectators of events of such historic magnitude. Not only had the theoreticians of socialism failed to take cognizance of the historic realities so manifest in the war that had been sanctioned by every socialist party in Europe, but the position of the Socialist Party had condemned socialism in Italy to abject inactivity. The socialists were not to make history, they were to submit to it. The radicals demanded decisiveness. If the socialists were to stand fast on absolute neutrality, they must announce their intention to see to it that a declaration of war would be the signal for popular insurrection. This the Party flatly refused to countenance. Socialist internationalism had been predicated upon the putative identity of interests of the international working class. That identity had proved a fiction. In September, Mussolini had been forced to admit that "the socialist International is dead . . . ," and proceeded to query, "But was it ever really alive?"[151] Theory found itself opposed to fact. A theory that is true, that provides a felicitous anticipation of events, cannot find itself in flagrant contradiction with the facts.

By the middle of October Mussolini insisted that the concept of absolute neutrality could no longer be defended. Socialists could not assume a posture of complete and cynical indifference in the face of the catastrophe that contained such forbidding portent. The war had not only challenged socialist theories, it had also invoked forces the effects of which could hardly be foreseen. To passively permit these forces to operate without the willed intervention of socialists was irresponsible. Not to act was also a choice. Socialism was compelled by a momentous, forced, and living option. Continued inaction would aid and abet the Central Powers and socialism would be morally responsible, at least in part, for the victory of reaction in Europe.

But the most fundamental theoretical and moral issue with which Mussolini grappled during this period was the question of nationality. As long as class constituted the primary unit of collective identity, the nation could hardly be considered a serious candidate for the individual's loyalty. Class obligation defined the range of the individual's responsibilities. The logic of obligation, while it might appear "heretical, paradoxical, sacrilegious" requires that one "reject the Fatherland."[152] "The proletariat must never again spill his precious blood for the Moloch of patriotism," Mussolini maintained. "The national flag is for us a rag to be planted on the dunghill. There are only two nations in the world: that of the exploited and the other of the exploiters."[153] Nationalism could only be conceived as a political fiction motivated by the conscious or unconscious desire to retard the inevitable federation of nations toward which the working class aspired.[154]

As long as class constituted the unit of loyalty the logic of obligations was clear. Yet the advent of the first major intra-European war in almost half a century had revealed that the proletariat did in fact identify itself with the nation. As a pragmatist, Mussolini could not dismiss this evident, if painful, reality. He had frequently insisted that facts, not dogma, confirm or infirm the theoretical propositions advanced by responsible political leadership—only "facts can confirm Marxist theories."[155] It had become obvious, Mussolini insisted, to those who were neither "blind nor dogmatic," that "national problems" existed even for socialism. The theoretical conviction that the concept "nation" was "transcended [superato]" was a fiction that compelled its adherents to the utterance of absurdities in the face of reality.[156]

Mussolini realized that socialism had been overtaken by "a new reality" that threatened all its convictions.[157] The obvious consequence was a recognition that he could no longer speak as a party functionary. The day following the publication of his article calling for an abandonment of the formula "absolute neutrality," Mussolini resigned as editor of Avanti! even though the Party had offered him the prospect of reconciliation.[158]

On October twenty-fifth he contended that events must be considered from a *national* point of view. On the evening of November tenth he addressed an assembly of the Milanese section of the Socialist Party, where he attempted to offer an account of socialism's dilemma. "The source of our psychological ambivalence is this," Mussolini maintained, "we socialists have never examined the problem of nations. The International never concerned itself with them. The International is dead, overcome by events. . . . It is evident that the nation represents a stage in human progress that has not yet been transcended. . . . The sentiment of nationality exists; it cannot be denied! Anti-patriotism of the old sort has been eclipsed. . . ."[159]

On November eleventh he admitted, "I ask myself if internationalism is an element absolutely necessary to socialism. The future socialist theoretician might very well concern himself with finding an equilibrium between nation and class."[160] Mussolini had finally discovered the most portentous reality of the twentieth century—the nation.

The Transition to Fascism

It is obvious that World War I generated critical theoretical tensions for orthodox socialism. Out of that tension both Bolshevism and Fascism were born. One of the essentials of historical materialism was the contention that class constituted the principal theoretical and analytic tool in the assessment of world history. Such a conviction provided the grounds for the tactical orientation of the various socialist movements, defined the values and provided the basis for moral obligation. Class analysis afforded the guide for tactical and strategic orientation of the revolutionary movements of the first decade of the twentieth century. That orientation was predicated upon the community of socioeconomic interests possessed by the working class as opposed to the international bourgeoisie. Historical and social reality was horizontally stratified, with classes cutting across the vertical separation of nations and peoples. The principal distinction between the adherents of the various forms of contemporary nationalism and those of orthodox socialism originated in the fact that the former accorded moral and theoretical priority to the concept *nation* as opposed to the concept *class*, while the latter subordinated the concept and the reality *nation* to the more urgent historicity and theoretical fruit-fulness of *class*. Orthodox socialists argued as though the class consciousness of the working class was the foremost reality of our time. It was the reality of World War I which shattered that belief with one terrible blow.[161]

The war revealed the many intimate ties which bound the working class to their national bourgeoisie. The defeat of the national bourgeoisie, under the historic conditions which obtained, would be a working class calamity. The divestment of colonies, the amputation of whole provinces, the incursion of reparations obligations—all would fall heavily on the working classes. The immediate and evident interests of the working classes made them nationalistic. But more than that, the sentiment of nationality prevailed even where no conceivable material interest was involved. The fierce nationalisms of the Slavic peoples with which Mussolini had become familiar, the clamorous and irrepressible demand for national autonomy and for the restoration of irrident provinces, all suggested that nationalism was not first and foremost an economic phenomenon. Certainly, any nationalism that is to survive must have a viable economic base and, consequently, it can be said that nationalism is, in that sense, conditioned by economic considerations. But any adequate appraisal of nationalism would require a far more substantial analysis of its determinants. The reductionist attempt to construe nationalism as a superstructural product of the economic base is defeated by instances of paradigmatic nationalism that are not amenable to such analysis. The history of the Jews is the classic case in point. All Marxist theoreticians, from Marx to Stalin, have denied that the Jews could constitute a nationality. They possessed neither a common territory, a common economy, a common culture, nor even a common language. And yet the Jews exemplify a paradigmatic nationalism.

The fact is that in 1914 the historic reality of national sentiment forced Mussolini to abandon the concept of class as the primary unit of analysis. He conceived man a social animal, disposed by nature and circumstance to associate in a community of select membership sustained by a pervasive sense of common destiny. To share common glories in the past, evident affinities and a common purpose in the present, to have done notable things in communion and to project common plans into the future—all these provide the grounds for achieving the fullness of life. Until the crisis of World War I that unit of primary loyalty was, for Mussolini, an international class. In the crisis of 1914 it became evident to him, as he stated years later, that "the unit of loyalty was too large."[162] The international working class did not share the requisite affinities, the common traditions and aspirations which sustain the moral community. It is the moral community that constitutes the Sorelian vehicle of regeneration, that charismatic object that defines the range and character of obligation, that disciplines men to purposes beyond themselves, that gives meaning to life. The reality that had overtaken orthodox socialism was the reality of national consciousness, the reality of national sentiment. It was a sentiment infinitely more powerful and demanding than the sentiment, revealed in the crisis to have been artificial, of international working class unity. The heterogeneous social units which struggled for dominion, in a world in which struggle was an irrepressible reality, were revealed as nations and not classes. Those units marshalled behind warrior elites, disciplined by functional myths, or given certificates of rectitude by charter myths are nations and not classes.

In 1910, when Mussolini had to choose a name for the paper he edited, he chose *La Lotta di Classe*, the *Class Struggle*. In 1914, after having been divested of his post with *Avanti!*, he chose as the title of his new daily, *Il Popolo d'Italia*, the *People of Italy*. *Class* had dilated to *People*. As he himself had indicated years before, he who says *people* has the nation as his reference. Mussolini was no longer only a proletarian; he was also an Italian.

CHAPTER FOUR

The Development of Fascist Doctrine

DURING the years between Italy's entry into World War I in 1915 and the March on Rome in 1922, Mussolini's social and political thought took on the specific doctrinal features that were to characterize Fascism. From 1915 until the founding of the *Fasci di combattimento*, on March 23, 1919, Mussolini traced the first outlines of Fascist doctrine. The subsequent period, during which the movement was transformed into the *Partito Nazionale Fascista*, saw the articulation of the specific fundamentals of Fascism. The development during this period was continuous and pursued a fairly consistent logic. It was an evolution which did not cease with the accession to power. Nonetheless, it is instructive to focus attention on this initial period of doctrinal development because it enables a more precise and competent assessment of the judgment, frequently tendered in the literature, that Mussolini lacked *any* clear positive social and political doctrine behind the organization of the Fascist cohorts.[1]

Until 1914, Mussolini had had experience with but one complex social and political doctrine, that of Marxism as it was then understood. As he himself indicated, no *one* interpretation of that doctrine had been, at least since the death of Engels, generally accepted by thinking socialists.[2] A variety of contending schools, influenced by a variety of intellectual currents, had grown up within the socialist movement itself. Mussolini's interpretation of Marxist thought, as unique as it came to be, represented the thinking of a significant number of revolutionary socialists of prewar Italy. Mussolini's socialism, however, remained socialism only as long as class membership was understood to constitute the fundamental social and historical relationship into which individual men could enter. The entire fabric of his socialism hung upon this critical conception. As long as class was the unit of loyalty, as long as class was construed as the vehicle of moral and social regeneration, Mussolini could remain a socialist, however novel his interpretations and however extensive his revisions. Once his conviction in the primacy of class relations was weakened by the traumatic events attending the outbreak of the European conflict in 1914, his socialism was fatally compromised. As the nation loomed larger and larger in his thinking, his socialism underwent corresponding disintegration. In 1914 this process was by no means obvious to Mussolini himself. In retrospect, however, it seems quite inexorable.

On November 24, 1914, when he was expelled from the Socialist Party, Mussolini insisted that his expulsion could not divest him of his "socialist faith."[3] He made the subtitle of his new paper, *Il Popolo d'Italia,* "A Socialist Daily." National intervention in the European conflagration was an immediate issue and as a problem it divided socialists, but since most continental socialist parties had opted for war, Mussolini conceived at that time that interventionism was not a commitment sufficient to require the abandonment of socialism. He maintained that after the conflict then raging in Europe, the interventionist socialists would reorganize and formulate a program which would include one certain plank: "to prepare and arm the proletariat for the social revolution."[4] As late as December, 1914, he suggested that the class struggle would be resumed after the war.[5] Through January, 1915, he continued to speak of the socialist international as the "ineluctible reality of tomorrow."[6] He felt justified, therefore, to continue to refer to himself, throughout the period immediately following his expulsion from the Socialist Party, as a socialist.[7]

But the theoretical tensions engendered by the commitment to

Italian intervention in the War exercised their inescapable influence, and his thought underwent that final, but critical, transformation that made of his socialism, Fascism.

The First Fascism

Before the advent of World War I Mussolini had already formulated a body of social and political convictions that persisted with remarkable stability throughout his political life. It was a socialism informed of, and transformed by, elements found in the thought of Pareto, Sorel, and Michels and represented in the writings of a number of revolutionary syndicalists, among whom A. O. Olivetti and Sergio Panunzio were the most important. It was a socialism more pragmatist than rationalist, more concerned with moral regeneration than with the equitable distribution of economic goods; a socialism convinced that historic change is more the consequence of willed commitment on the part of a strategic elite than of maturation in the economic base of society. It was socialist insofar as the vehicle of moral regeneration was the class with which the individual identified, and insofar as the dynamic strategic elite was the vanguard of the proletariat.

This revised socialism remained compatible with socialism as it was then conceived only as long as class was understood to constitute the principal vehicle of historic change. That class functioned in this critical capacity seemed borne out by the protracted class violence that afflicted Italy during the last decade of the nineteenth and the first decade of the twentieth century. International class solidarity had been used to substantiate the dynamic and decisive role of class membership in the historic development of Europe in its entirety. It was only with the coming of World War I that compelling disconfirming evidence of these theses was forthcoming. The events that followed fast on the outbreak of hostilities cast serious doubts on the fruitfulness of class as a fundamental unit of analysis for theoretical or practical purposes.

Almost immediately after his expulsion from the Socialist Party, Mussolini noted that the war had crystallized whole populations into national units in which intragroup class distinctions had been by-and-large obliterated.[8] In effect, Mussolini began to argue that national rather than class units constituted more adequate subjects of analysis. Men, Mussolini argued, are mobilized to action not only by their immediate material, i.e., their class interests, but by psychological and moral considerations that transcend them. He recognized a relatively stable complex of motivating psychological and moral sentiments as historic and national products that provide for the temporal and spiritual continuity of peoples. Each historic people, Mussolini contended, is the product of a unique constellation of material and spiritual elements and shapes its own bourgeoisie and its own proletariat.[9] Class interests are conditioned by and in some significant sense subordinate to national interests. "Class," Mussolini maintained, "is based on the community of interests, but the nation is a history of sentiments, of traditions, of language, of culture or race."[10] One could not plausibly argue for the priority of class interests as opposed to national interests. Every event in the recent history of Europe infirmed such a claim. Only a dogmatist, he contended, could deny the evident reality of the sentiment of nationality so eloquently confirmed by the disposition of Europe's proletariat to sacrifice in its service. He spoke of a reassessment of the European situation from a national as well as a socialist point of view— and gave the first intimations of the possibility of a "national socialism" that would better accord with the evident realities with which socialist theoreticians were compelled to contend.

Furthermore, the significance which the concepts *nation* and *people* assumed in Mussolini's thinking forced him to re-evaluate the reality of international working class solidarity upon which much of his prewar thinking had been based. As early as December, 1914, he admitted that there had been, in fact, little substance to such internationalism. By January, 1915, he could maintain, "The Working Class International . . . has not only demonstrated its impotence in the face of events and its inability to prevent the war, but its literal nonexistence as well."[11] The reality of the then current conflict made it obvious that the peoples of Europe were striving to fulfill their national and not their class aspiration. In view of such a realization, the advocacy of class war was a vain prescription. What the circumstances demanded was national unity.[12] The consequences of this re-orientation were obvious. Mussolini advocated a return to the nationalism of Mazzini and a rejection of Marx if the reality, complexity, and urgency of contemporary events required it.[13]

By May, 1915, these convictions were firmly established. Only those men disposed to lie to themselves and delude others could fail to recognize that internationalism as a real political alternative was defunct. On the day of Italy's entry into World War I Mussolini wrote,

Never before as in this moment have we felt that the fatherland existed, that it is an irrepressible and insurmountable [datum]; never before as in this moment of conflict have we felt Italy to be an historic personality, living, corporeal, immortal.[14]

A month later he wrote,

The fatherland is the hard and solid ground, the millenarian product of the race; internationalism was a fragile ideology that did not survive the tempest. The blood that vivifies the fatherland has destroyed the International.[15]

The nation was real in a sense that the International could never be. The nation was an enduring historic, physical, and moral reality. United in culture and tradition, based upon the complex and systematic interactive patterns fostered by contemporary economic development, the nation enjoyed the prerequisites of long-term viability—and war had revealed it to be a primary object of loyalty for the vast majority of the national proletariat.[16] The nation, Mussolini argued, was the "great product of history," the value of which, though long "unrecognized and despised," was revealed on the occasion of the ultimate challenge afforded by World War I.[17]

Opposed to this monumental reality was the International, an organization that existed only on paper, responsible for little more than the sometimes issuance of a theoretical treatise in one of its "official" languages (which did not include Italian). But the International was unreal in a more significant sense. It was predicated on the putative existence of a specific real entity: class. As a matter of evident fact, Mussolini maintained, specific classes, as such, did not exist. What existed were groups and subgroups, mutually distinguishable on the basis of interests and mentality, related to each other in obscure and complex relationships. The concept *proletariat* represents an abstract ideal type, an abstraction that perhaps serves mnemonic or heuristic purposes, but corresponds to nothing in reality. If such is the case, any talk of *the* class struggle is unintelligible.

If classes do not exist, the class struggle does not exist. There is a struggle that is not a class, but a human struggle. Each individual or group attempts to maximize for itself the acquisition of goods. . . . To obtain this maximum it frequently happens—as has happened in the past—that men, so-called bourgeois, struggle against other men equally bourgeois, and men characterized as proletarian find themselves in conflict with others equally characterized as proletarian.[18]

Mussolini had come to recognize the nation as a particular kind of social system; one rooted in tradition and sentiment, which is comprehensive and differentiated enough to be self-sufficient with respect to the functional needs of its members. The nation satisfied material, psychological, and moral imperatives. Less than a month after his expulsion from the Socialist Party, Mussolini wrote that the War had revealed the "germ of new unanticipated political constructions" based upon the objective fact "that 'peoples and states' had everywhere achieved their fusion in a block of 'national unanimity.'"[19] Germany, Belgium, France, England, Switzerland, and Russia manifested the same fusion of people, state, and nation. War had revealed the infrangible material, psychological, and moral community of interests that sustained national unity.[20] This community of material and spiritual interests arched over class, category, and regional interests.

During the initial period of the development of Fascist doctrine, these ideas, which subsequently became increasingly precise, were applied to the nation at war. The nation is not, Mussolini insisted, quoting Jean Jaurès, exclusively the product of economic variables. It has an essentially moral substance.[21] Like our parents, the nation provides us not only with our sustenance but with the foundations of our moral personality. We can, he maintained, no more renounce it than we can renounce them.[22] The nation, rather than class or category, is the morally privileged object of loyalty. In its service all forces are to be marshalled. In its service all local and special interests are to be subordinated. Thus by July, 1915, Mussolini, so long an ardent advocate of the strike as a weapon in the class struggle, inveighed against work stoppage that might jeopardize the nation which, he admitted, he himself had long defamed.[23] What the nation demanded was dedication to its service not only on the part of the workers but on the part of parliamentarians as well. If the nation's laboring masses were to dedicate themselves to the collective interests, no less could be required of the political class. The minoritarian governing class of the nation must govern. It must mobilize the efforts of the nation in the service of victory. It was in this capacity that the governing class had proved itself, in Mussolini's judgment, incompetent.[24] He declared himself anti-parliamentarian because parliament had failed the nation.[25] Parliament in Italy had become "a plague that poisoned the blood of the nation." It was necessary to extirpate it.[26] His objection to parliament was no longer based upon a conception which construed it as representing special class interests; it turned on the judgment that parliament was incapable of representing and defending the vital interests of the nation.

Mussolini had always opposed parliamentarianism. His conception of social change, political organization, and rulership was consistently elitist, and he remained consistently elitist in his analysis of Italy's situation during the crisis of the war. As early as January, 1915, with the organization of the interventionist *Fasci d'Azione Rivoluzionaria,* Mussolini spoke of a resolute minority of men, animated by a sure consciousness of the national interest, invoking in the masses a state of being that would conduce to the fulfillment of collective purpose.[27] For the first time in history, Mussolini argued, the "anonymous masses" had made their appearance as the instruments of history.[28] Their leaders could only be apostles or soldiers.[29] Everything he had learned from Pareto, Sorel, and Michels compelled him to such an opinion. By December, 1917, his conviction had matured to the insight that the nation's future would be determined by a new aristocracy, the "aristocracy of the trenches," an elite composed of men in whom the reality of the nation had become a living and momentous conviction. Only the short-sighted and the foolish could fail to anticipate such a political eventuality. Only such an aristocracy could give cognitive meaning to future political ideals. Only they could animate the restive and elemental masses. They would, in their own time and in response to their own insights, define *democracy* and *socialism*. And, Mussolini concluded, in all probability their socialism would be anti-Marxist and national.[30]

Given the constellation of ideas that had developed since October, 1914, Mussolini's class-orientated socialism had become increasingly diaphanous. It was certainly no longer Marxist. On the eleventh of August, 1918, he changed the subtitle of his paper from "A Socialist Daily" to "A Daily of Combatants and Producers," and in inaugurating the change indicated the designation *socialist* was no longer descriptive of the ideas with which he identified.[31] So many of the categories of what had been orthodox socialism, "class," "class struggle," "surplus value," and "economic determinism," had been either abandoned or so extensively revised that the term *socialism* no longer had cognitive significance.[32] Already in May, 1918, Mussolini had called attention to the hierarchy of productive functions that characterized the productive life of the nation.[33] Neither *proletariat* nor *bourgeoisie* constituted politically meaningful designations. From the vantage point of the nation there were only categories that performed productive functions, and these could be designated *productive classes* to specify one particular role in the system of interlocking roles that constituted national life. It was that unitary life, the life of the nation, which led Mussolini to speak of the "coincidence of interests" that united workers and employers and made possible their collaboration in a program of accelerating overall economic productivity.[34] Thereafter, the program of collaboration between productive categories became a central theme in the formulation of the doctrine of the *Fasci*. Thus, approximately a week after the termination of hostilities, in November, 1918, five months before the birth of the movement that was to become Fascism, Mussolini outlined the economic program he was to make his own. Identified as "National Syndicalism," the program advocated an "economic reconstruction" of the fatherland in which industry and labor would undertake "intense collaboration" in an association of respective energies to realize the highest level of national industrial productivity. The goal of National Syndicalism was to make the nation "more beautiful, more vital, more grand."[35] "This, then," Mussolini maintained, "is the common interest which cancels and suppresses the class struggle: production. . . . For the old political and parasitic socialism, National Syndicalism or productive socialism is substituting itself. . . ."[36] Production must be neither limited nor compromised by special interests.[37] Differences between workers and employers must be arbitrated with respective interests given equal weight before the tribunal of national interest. Thus, a month before the founding of the organization that became the *Partito Nazionale Fascista*, Mussolini reported favorably on the following programmatic proposal of Leon Jouhaux:

a) juridical recognition of syndicalist organizations; b) intervention of these organizations in all labor relations; c) accession to development and control; d) transformation of political administration into economic administration; e) expropriation of the bureaucracy and its substitution by a technical administration: all measures calculated to insure the progressive development of the nation.[38]

These were the programmatic suggestions of "pragmatic National Syndicalism," and they were sufficient, in Mussolini's eyes, to distinguish his economic program from that of "destructive socialism" and the "apolitic and mystic syndicalism of the Sorelian school."

Thus, by March, 1919, when he issued the call for an organization of *Fasci* to "defend the victory," Mussolini had articulated a collection of political, social, and economic conceptions that together constituted a relatively specific doctrine. Three days before the meeting at the Piazza San Sepolcro that saw the birth of Fascism, Mussolini addressed the two thousand workers of Dalmine who, as members of the National Syndicalist *Unione Italiana del Lavoro*, were protesting wage levels and the refusal of employers to recognize their union, but who refused to countenance work stoppage because such strikes adversely affected the national economy.[39] He said,

You have defended your class interests, but you have not forgotten the nation. You have spoken of the people of Italy, not only of your category. . . . In the service of your own immediate interests you might have undertaken a strike in the old manner, the negative and destructive strike; but concerning yourselves with the interests of the people, you have undertaken a positive protest which does not interrupt production. You could not deny the nation for whom you have fought, for whom more than five hundred thousand of our young men died. The nation that has made this sacrifice cannot be denied, because it is a glorious and victorious reality. You are not the poor, the humble and outcast spoken of in the literary rhetoric of socialism; you are producers, and in this capacity you vindicate your right to treat with the industrialists as equals.[40]

These were the ideas he brought to the meeting at the Piazza San Sepolcro where approximately one hundred and forty five men of all political persuasions, from the Futurist F. T. Marinetti to radical revolutionary syndicalist Michele Bianchi, met to found the *Fasci di Combattimento*. There were professionals, industrialists, merchants, and workers among them, with a prevalence of petty-bourgeois elements. In composition, therefore, the founding members of Fascism were of the same class and category provenience as the founders of the Bolshevik Third International that was, at precisely the same time, being founded in Moscow. In both groups there was a heavy representation of journalists, lawyers, and self-employed or unemployed professionals; those individuals generally described as "intellectuals."

The Fascism of San Sepolcro

At the meeting at the Piazza San Sepolcro Mussolini spoke twice, once during the morning hours of March 23, 1919, and the second time during that afternoon. Both speeches were of doctrinal importance and outlined the complex of ideas that were to characterize Fascism throughout its period of initial growth and ultimate succession to power in October, 1922, and that later acquired a broader theoretical perspective and an increasing specificity.

The speech of the afternoon developed characteristically Mussolinian ideas. He insisted on a flexible program because political movements operate on the level of contingencies. Experience with fixed socialist programs counseled the retention of a limited number of guiding postulates that serve to orientate day to day activities, with variable programmatic suggestions which would alter with changed circumstances. For the Fascists, Mussolini advocated but two sustaining realities: *production* and the *nation*. The program for the reorganization of the economy was that of National Syndicalism. National Syndicalism implied the reorganization of the state on syndicalist lines. Mussolini called for the abolition of the Italian Senate and Chamber, and direct representation of the productive categories of the nation. Political representation could not meet the exacting requirements of modern industrial life. He spoke of a proposed technical council of categories representing the productive elements of the nation, a council he called, alternately, a council of corporations. He advocated an active appeal to the laboring masses, supporting their demands for an eight hour work day and advanced social welfare programs. He even advocated support for the workers' aspiration to control industry. Mussolini maintained,

We support these requests because we wish to habituate the working classes to the directive responsibilities of industry, but also to convince the workers that it is not a simple matter to direct a business and a commercial establishment.[41]

All of this was to lead to economic and, ultimately, political democracy. That Mussolini, in his first public statements of specifically Fascist doctrine, should have advanced democracy as an ideal has always been cited, by commentators, as evidence of Mussolini's inconstancy, his lack of serious political commitment. Actually, there is a more generous interpretation. The term *democracy* had, in the Italy of the period, persuasive emotive impact but little cognitive significance. At about the time Mussolini injected the term into his inaugural speech, Pareto was writing: ". . . Democracy is an imprecise term, like many other terms in common usage. . . . There is indeed no hope of devising a strict and precise term for something that is inherently indeterminate and transient."[42] Mussolini was certainly well aware of the inherent vagueness and ambiguity of the term. He had earlier indicated that the term could only be given stipulative meaning by the returning aristocracy of the trenches. In any event, whatever democracy meant to him in 1919, it certainly did not mean simple majority rule. He declared himself "decisively opposed to all forms of dictatorship, from that of the sword to that of the miter cap, from that of money to that of number; we recognize only the dictatorship of will and intelligence."[43] This conviction, coupled with his account of political dynamics given a few paragraphs before, could have left no doubt that whatever else democracy meant at that time to Mussolini it did not mean majority rule, nor even majority initiative. "It is inevitable," he insisted, "that majorities are static, while minorities are dynamic. We wish to be an active minority. . . ."[44] Whatever else this democracy was to be, it was to be the result of minoritarian initiative which would take on the form of a dictatorship of "will and intelligence."

The morning speech was equally instructive. It was there that Mussolini sketched the outlines of Fascist Italy's foreign policy.

Italy was a nation of forty million souls crowded within the confines of 287,000 square kilometers of land surface. One third of that land was mountainous and could not be cultivated. Whatever extra-peninsular territory Italy controlled was largely arid and un-suited for large-scale colonization. On the other hand, he went on to indicate, England, with a population of forty-seven million, dominated a colonial empire of 55 million square kilometers; France, with a population of less than forty million, possessed an empire of 15 million square kilometers. Portugal, Holland, and Belgium possessed equally impressive tracts of land throughout the world. The world, he insisted, was divided into "rich nations and proletarian nations," with the rich desirous of maintaining the *status quo* and the proletarian nations "demanding a place in the world to which they have a right."[45]

Thus, by March, 1919, the general program and strategy of Fascism was apparent. Its theoretical and interpretive formulations were an inheritance from Mussolini's socialist past. In the years that followed the foundation of the *Fasci* until the March on Rome, this was evident in everything Mussolini said and wrote. The world-view he entertained was that with which he had identified as a socialist activist. It was the conception of the world found in the works of Gumplowicz, Pareto, Mosca, Sorel, and Michels. He con-tinued to conceive life as an unremitting struggle filled with conflict and contrast. "Struggle," he maintained, "is the source of all things. . . . Struggle remains forever at the very foundation of human nature as a supreme fatality."[46] If individual men are to prevail in the face of constant and demanding challenge they must organize them-selves in communities of interest and sentiment—and when one speaks of organization one intends hierarchy and leadership. ". . . Men have a diffuse and profound need for discipline, order, and hierarchy."[47] The organization through which intergroup struggle was to be pursued was the nation.

These are the same convictions Mussolini held as a socialist revolutionary. What had altered, as we have seen, was the specific and primary organization. For Mussolini the socialist, the primary organization to which men gave their allegiance was class; for Mussolini the Fascist, the charismatic object of loyalty was the nation. For Fascism, one essential point of reference sufficed: the nation. Everything else followed as a necessary consequence.[48] The nation was an irrepressible historic, physical, and moral fact to which all else was subordinated.[49] It was the union of territorial, material, intellectual, and sentimental interests that persisted through time, into which individuals were born and which survived their passing. It was that social system which was the most viable unit of effective life, a rule-governed context in which functionally defined roles persisted beyond the occupancy by any one person or contemporary collection of persons.[50] The nation was the bearer of the fundamental values of the collectivity.[51] As such, it not only provided for the physical survival of its members but constituted the very foundation of human personality.[52]

Thus the nation fulfilled for Mussolini, as a Fascist, the same functions fulfilled by class for Mussolini as a socialist. As a socialist Mussolini had held that class membership provided the moral structure of individual life. It defined individual duties and responsibilities in the historic and protracted contest between human groups in conflict over material and ideal interests. The myth of the class struggle, understood in its Sorelian sense, imparted the moral significance to the life of individual men. The conception of class struggle constituted the organizing myth of revolutionary syndicalism. After 1915, the conception of the nation performed the same function. A few scant days before the March on Rome and the ascent of Fascism to power, Mussolini maintained,

We have created our myth. The myth is a faith, it is a passion. . . . It is a reality by the fact that it is a goad, a hope, a faith, that it is courage. Our myth is the nation. . . . And to this myth, to this grandeur . . . we subordinate all the rest.[53]

In January of 1922, he had spoken of such subordination in terms of a hierarchy. "Whoever says hierarchies," he argued, "is committed to a scale of human values; whoever says a scale of human values says a scale of human responsibilities and duties, who says hierarchy says discipline."[54]

Nationalism was the organizing or functional myth of Fascism. Upon Fascism's accession to power it became the charter myth of the Regime. The nation was an historic and integral social system composed of a number of subsystems, interconnected by relational and regulative norms, a relatively stable interactive system with subsystems related by regular and recurrent interaction sustained and defined by persistent norms, values expressed in codified law and traditional social discipline in the forms of habit or common sentiment. The nation as such a system incarnates its juridical personality in the state. The state is the ultimate source of authority; it is the ultimate sanction that gives reality to group norms; it is the ultimate repository of force; it is irreducibly sovereign.[55] This is not to say that every historically constituted state so comports itself. The empirical state may fail, in fact, to exercise its sovereignty. Its failure may be the consequence of a number of influences, both material and moral. What threatens, under such circumstances, is the disintegration of the social system into a collection of smaller systems, each governed by a virtual state, an "antistate," which arrogates to itself the defaulted privileges of the sovereign state. Each social element, in such a situation, acts as arbiter in its own interests with an ultimate appeal to force being decisive. Each such collectivity thus becomes a virtual state and exemplifies in fact or in potentia the attributes of the state per se.[56] The result is the disaggregation of what had been the nation into two or more nations in a state of war.

For Mussolini, the state was that repository of force which provides the sanctions necessary for effective group norms. In principle, the state was absolutely sovereign. It might in fact choose not to exercise its prerogatives, but there was no intrinsic or extrinsic limitation to which it was subject. Social life without the state would be impossible. The state provided the necessary conditions. Mussolini's objections to the Marxist thesis of the "withering away of the state" turned upon this conception. The Marxist distinction between the state which governs men and the non-state of the communist future which will govern things was, for Mussolini, devoid of meaning. If fact, he argued, the "governance of things" in the Soviet Union had produced the most elaborate state in history.

Thus by June, 1922, four months before the accession to power, Mussolini had outlined the elements of Fascist doctrine concerning the nation and the state. The nation was conceived to be the people in their totality and the state was the nation's juridical incarnation.[57] By its positive or negative action, the state determined the moral order, the system of hierarchies, the scale of human values into which the individuals, as transient members of the historic social system, were born and lived. In this sense, the state was charged with ultimate moral responsibility. Even religious organizations were subordinate, in principle if not in fact. Religious imperatives could not conflict with secular law; any rules governing religious association could not be incompatible with the interests of the state. Thus, as early as November, 1921, Mussolini characterized the state as an essentially ethical entity. He identified it as *"lo stato etico,"* the "ethical state."[58]

Fascism's Conception of the State

This basically Hegelian, or neo-Hegelian, conception of the state constituted a novel element in developing Fascist doctrine. For a considerable period of time, Mussolini had no specific conception of the state. As a socialist he had grappled with the problem, but there is considerable internal evidence which indicates that his conceptions remained confused and sometimes contradictory. We do know, for example, that for some time Mussolini was influenced by philosophical individualism and its implicit anarchism. He himself indicates that until 1908 he remained under the influence of Nietzsche and Max Stirner.[59] Under their influence he seemed prepared to maintain that the individual, *qua* individual, enjoyed some kind of moral privilege *vis-a-vis* any organized aggregate of men. He seemed to argue that the only law binding upon the individual was a law which the individual laid upon himself. He specifically committed himself to opposing submission to laws having any other origin. Yet, by 1908, he was prepared to admit the real theoretical difficulty in defending such a position. In his essay on Nietzsche, published that year, he was prepared to grant that for Nietzsche the state was a system of "organized oppression at the cost of the individual."[60] But he went on to indicate that Nietzsche's conception of man as a beast of prey necessarily involved a conviction that man as a predatory beast was a denizen of an organized community. Without such a supposition effective struggle would be impossible and no conquest could be secured. He argued that

Above all, a principle of solidarity must govern the relationships of such blond beasts of prey. Even the conquerors obey the dispositions taken up by the collectivity to safeguard the supreme interests of the caste and this can be said to constitute the first limitation upon individual will. . . . The individual cannot, therefore, ever be "unique" in the Stirnerian sense of the word, bowed and vanquished as he is by the inescapable laws of solidarity.[61]

As has been indicated, Mussolini's conception was one which construed man as a quintessentially social animal. While he continued to maintain some form of romantic individualism, his explicit commitment, by 1914, was to the conviction that "only with collectivism is individualism conceivable and realizable."[62] In fact, among his earliest writings there is an interesting and important encomium to Ferdinand Lassalle in which Mussolini outlined a conception of morality and the state surprisingly similar to that with which he identified Fascism in his maturity.

The moral idea which Mussolini applauded at twenty-one was one in which the activity of the individual was governed by the moral concerns for the solidarity of mutual interests and reciprocal obligations of the community of which he was a member. Such a conception involves the notion of a state which is a moral union of individuals.

It is the ultimate integral phase of the evolutionary process of communal life, of the community of blood, place, economic, and intellectual interests. Its function is to conduct the struggle against nature, misery, ignorance, impotence, and slavery of every form in which men find themselves in the state of nature at the commencement of this struggle. The community under the state puts the individual in the circumstances that make it possible for him to attain a sense and a level of life that solitary individuals could never attain.[63]

The state was identified with the moral order that governed the community.

Had this been all Mussolini said on these subjects, interpretation would be a simple matter, but the account would neglect some equally significant statements he made as late as 1920. At the end of 1919, in a period of intense doctrinal reassessment, he once again insisted upon the ontological and implicitly moral priority of the individual. He advocated a loosening of constraints upon the "elementary forces of individuals since outside of the individual no other human reality exists. Why should Stirner not return?"[64] Two weeks later he further maintained:

We have rent every revealed truth, we have spat upon every dogma, rejected every paradise, turned away every charlatan—white, red, or black —who has put in circulation miraculous drugs which promise "happiness" to mankind. We do not believe in programs, schemes, saints, or apostles; above all we do not believe in felicity, salvation, the promised land. We do not believe in a unique solution—be it economic or political or moral —a unilinear solution to the problems of life because . . . life is not linear. . . . We return to the individual. We support everything that exalts and amplifies the individual, that increases his liberty, well-being, and latitude of life. We oppose everything that oppresses and mortifies the individual.[65]

These statements, coupled with his remarks published in April, 1920, leave us with a view of the relationship of the individual and the state which is, *prima facie*, at stark variance with the programmatic doctrine of Fascism as it was to find expression in the official publications of the *Partito Nazionale Fascista*.

In the article of April, 1920, Mussolini, in the course of objecting to state regulations, maintained that his objections did not originate in political objections, nationalism, or utility. He objected to state regulation *per se*. He identified himself as one of a small number of persons in potential revolt against the state, "not against this or that state, but against the state in itself. . . ." He went on to insist,

The state is a tremendous machine that swallows living men and re-gurgitates dead ciphers. . . . This, this is the great malediction that struck mankind during the uncertain beginnings of its history: to create, over the centuries, the state, to find itself overcome, annihilated! . . . Down with the state in all its forms and incarnations. The state of yesterday, today, and tomorrow.[66]

This was the last exasperated expression of the sentimental individualism Mussolini retained from his youth. In November, 1920, he admitted that Fascism had not, as yet, had time to articulate its doctrine but he augured an "elaboration and coordination of its ideas."[67] Fascism as a movement, as an "antiparty," had remained a loose confederation of groups composed of heterogeneous elements united only by a minimal program, but by mid-1920 there was already a movement afoot to organize the *Fasci* into a political party. In order to lay the foundation of the unity required by the anticipated political reorganization, Fascism found itself obliged to specify its position with respect to the critical political concepts of *nation* and *state*."[68] It was during this critical period of doctrinal elaboration that Mussolini probably read, for what might well have been the first time, some of the works of Giovanni Gentile (1875–1944), who was to provide the philosophic rationale for the mature ideology of Fascism. And it was during the meeting of the Third National Congress of Fascists, held in November, 1921, that Mussolini outlined what was to be the Fascist doctrine of the state and identified it with the neo-Hegelian *"stato etico"* of Gentile. Years later he indicated to Yvon de Begnac that he had read Gentile for what was apparently the first time precisely during this period.[69]

Mussolini recognized, in effect, what had transpired. When he addressed the Fascist meeting in Rome organized to found the *Partito Nazionale Fascista,* he admitted that "two Mussolinis" were at war within him—one individualistic and the other disciplined to the Fascism that was the guardian of the nation. Beginning with the insuperable fact of the nation, he argued, he was led inevitably and ineluctably to the state. He was compelled to identify the nation and the state.[70]

Nonetheless, while it can be maintained with some assurance that Mussolini's doctrinal position with respect to the state was significantly influenced, and the recurrent ambiguity in his thought between individualism and collectivism finally overcome, by Gentile's social and political philosophy, there remains a vagueness and an inconsistency in his convictions concerning the nature and function of the state not so easily resolved. In opting for the "ethical state," Mussolini opted for a notion of the state which was essentially, as Gentile recognized, *totalitarian*. The same analysis which made the state absolutely sovereign, the moral embodiment of the national community, also implicitly legitimatized the extension of state control into every aspect of human concern. Nevertheless, throughout this period, Mussolini insisted upon the reduction of the state's obligations to strictly "Manchestrian" agential duties. In May, 1920, he maintained that the state should be reduced to the four functions assigned to it by nineteenth century liberalism: maintenance of the military, public security, taxation, and the administration of justice.[71] The same conviction was reaffirmed in January, 1921.[72] Six months later, in his first speech in the Italian chamber, he repeated the same prescription. He maintained on that occasion,

To save the state surgery is required. . . . [It] is necessary to reduce the state to its purely juridical and political expression. The state provides policemen . . . , well organized justice, an army prepared for every eventuality, and a foreign policy in accord with national requirements. All the rest, including secondary schools, should be restored to the private activity of the individual. If you wish to save the state it is necessary to abolish the collectivist state . . . and return to the Manchestrian state.[73]

In the official Program of the *Partito Nazionale Fascista* of December, 1921, the Party committed itself to a "reduction of the state to its essential functions of a political and juridical order."[74]

At the same time, however, and in the same document, the nation was spoken of as something more than the sum of its living members. It was defined as "the supreme synthesis of all the material and immaterial values of the race," of which the state was the juridical incarnation. All the values of individuals and collective persons (families, communes, corporations,) were to be

promoted, developed and defended within the ambit of the nation, to which they are subordinated. . . . The state must assist in the development of the nation, not monopolizing but promoting every effort calculated to further the ethical, intellectual, religious, artistic, juridical, social, economic, and physiological progress of the national collectivity.

In the effort to indicate the kind of program required to meet such a broad mandate, the Fascists demanded that the state undertake an "organic plan of public works to meet the new economic, technical, and military necessities of the nation," a plan which conceived the completion, reorganization, and electrification of the railway system; the development of hydroelectric power; the expansion of the roads system; as well as the intensification of maritime communication throughout the Mediterranean. Working class and business associations were to be recognized in law as bargaining agents for their members and collective labor contracts would render strikes and lock-outs obsolete. The state would assume responsibility for the administration of such bargaining procedures. The state would maintain "rigid control" of the primary school system with respect to programs and the selection of teaching personnel and their work. The secondary schools and university would be free except for the "control of the state over programs and the spirit of instruction. . . ." At about the same time that the Program of the Party was published, Mussolini announced that Fascism sought to bring discipline and order and a hierarchy to the nation.[75] These were, in fact, obligations no Manchestrian state could discharge.

The conception of the Manchestrian state, with its circumscribed agential functions, is a derivative of contractualism, of the atomistic theory of society. It is anomalous in the context of Mussolini's view of man and society. Mussolini's assessment of man in society remained relatively constant through youth to maturity, from his socialist through his Fascist period. As a youth and as a mature political leader, as a socialist and as a Fascist, Mussolini conceived history as made by an aggressive, resolute, and dedicated minority capable of infusing the inert masses with the motive energy that sustains change. "The masses," for Mussolini, "cannot be the protagonists of history—they are its instrument."[76] He went on, elsewhere, in an echo of Gumplowicz, Mosca, and Michels, to argue that "history has in every case demonstrated that it has always been minorities, exiguous by necessity, that have produced profound revolutions in human society."[77] The masses need the "hero" capable of interpreting their vague and ill-defined aspirations; and the "hero" needs the masses as material to mold.[78] The allusion to the artist and his material pleased Mussolini and he employed the metaphor frequently to exemplify the relationship which obtains between the political leader and the masses. In 1917 he maintained that

the Italian people constitute a mass of precious minerals. It requires smelting, purifying, and working and it is possible that a work of art will result. What is lacking is a government. A man. A man who possesses, as necessary, the delicate touch of an artist and the heavy hand of the warrior.[79]

A few weeks before the March on Rome he said that Fascism has "need of the masses, as an artist has need of raw material to fashion his masterpiece."[80]

Elsewhere, in a restatement of judgments found in Le Bon and Sighele, he argued that

the mass is a herd and as a herd remains subject to instincts and primordial impulses. The mass is without continuity. It is the prey of an elemental dynamism, fragmentary and incoherent. It is matter, in effect, and not spirit.[81]

Spirit finds expression only through an organizing elite, a gifted and select minority capable of channeling the elemental energy of the masses. By the time Mussolini was preparing the Fascist legions for the March on Rome, the implications of this conception had been drawn out. There was an explicit rejection of democracy as it was generally understood. Mussolini anticipated "an 'aristocratic' century—the present—succeeding the last, which was democratic."[82] The last century aspired to a government of many, ideally one which involved everyone. The present century, Mussolini maintained, would see government once again become primarily a minority concern, possibly the concern of a single tribune, a populist leader of men.[83]

Such convictions were fundamentally incompatible with the conception of the state having only peripheral involvement with society via military, public security, taxation, and juridical concerns. Implicit in Mussolini's conception of the state were tutelary, organizational, enterprisory, political, economic, educative, and moral preoccupations that exceeded anything conceived legitimate to the liberal Manchestrian state. The aspiring Fascist elite arrogated to itself responsibilities which made them final arbiters in such a wide range of activities that the state could only be compelled to assume a character essentially distinct from any antecedent state form. This became evident to Fascist theoreticians, including Mussolini himself, and was obvious in everything written during the period prior to the succession to power and the years between 1922 and (at least) 1925. That it was not equally evident to non-Fascists is apparent in the behavior of many political commentators, including liberals such as Benedetto Croce who initially gave Fascism their support. Many such men conceived Fascism as holding forth the prospect of "normalization," the restoration of conditions which obtained before Italy went into the political crisis of the twentieth century. That men could be so mistaken was a consequence of the fact that much of what Mussolini said, during this period, could be construed as a defense of economic and political liberalism. He decried, for example, Lenin's dictatorship and insisted that "we will not accept dictatorship."[84]

Coupled with these seemingly liberal assurances was a positive program for the acceleration of internal industrial development and external economic expansion that could only appeal to bourgeois enterprise. Fascism, rejecting the distributionist preoccupations of socialism, advocated a program of national industrial development. Its focus was productionist. From its very inception as a political movement it operated on the Paretan precept that the fundamental economic problem that faced Italy, as a *proletarian* nation, was the expansion of its industrial capacity rather than redistribution of goods or ownership of the means of production.[85] While Mussolini insisted that the tactical programs of Fascism were under constant revision, were continually transformed and of necessity plastic,[86] he nonetheless maintained that Fascist thought turned on two constants: production and the nation.[87] The nation required rapid industrial expansion and to this end all the productive categories were to collaborate.[88] These strategic directives were advanced on the occasion of the founding of Fascism as a movement, and they remained constant throughout the development of the Party and its accession to power. Thus in June, 1922, Mussolini characterized Fascist syndicalism as national and productivist, and six weeks before the March on Rome he reiterated Fascism's commitment to productivism and the attendant "strict collaboration" between industrial categories.[89]

Conjoined with these sentiments was a commitment to expansionism—political, economic, and moral. "The program of Fascist foreign policy can be given," Mussolini revealed, "in one word: expansionism."[90] The doctrinal slogan which represented this thesis was: "The Mediterranean to the Mediterraneans!"[91]

The theses that Fascist syndicalism and productionism were inseparable and that increased productivity necessitated the abatement of the class struggle to (at worst) episodic encounters, together with the demand that the nation extend its sphere of influence throughout the Mediterranean at the expense of the plutocratic powers,[92] could only exercise a positive influence over Italy's entrepreneurial and commercial classes. The contention that capitalism retained its vitality[93] further reassured them, and Fascism's violent suppression of socialism could only gratify. Within such a context the pronouncement that Fascists sought "to divest the state of all its economic attributes"[94] sounded, to the good bourgeoisie of enervated postwar Italy, like the clarion call for the restoration of nineteenth century economic liberalism with which they traditionally identified.

That Mussolini regularly warned the bourgeoisie that Fascism would not act as a lightning conductor for them, that their special interests would be as readily sacrificed as any in the service of what Fascism understood to be the national interests, that Fascism was essentially antiliberal, did little to dispel their misassessment. What Mussolini was advocating, in fact, was a developmental dictatorship, the reorganization of the nation into "an immense and vigorous army. . . ."[95] Fascism was neither of the Right nor the Left, as those designations have been traditionally understood. It represented neither bourgeois liberalism nor proletarian socialism as such. It was something unique to the twentieth century, a mass-based, elitist movement of solidarity, the meaning of which can be elucidated only following the treatment of the mature ideology of Fascism. But that Fascism was neither a Right wing or Left Wing political movement is indicated by the fact that its doctrine was the result of a confluence of currents of social and political thought that came together from both the Right and the Left. Fascist doctrine was composed of elements matured within the thought of revolutionary syndicalists like Olivetti, Panunzio, Michele Bianchi, and Edmondo Rossoni—elements which proved compatible with the thought of Futurists like Marinetti and nationalists like Dino Grandi and, ultimately, Alfredo Rocco and Corradini. Fascism evinced, in effect, a relatively stable synthetic doctrine appealing to both the radical Left and the radical Right.

The syncretic character of Fascism was reflected in the class and category composition of the Fascist organizations themselves, exemplified in the 1921 analysis provided by the Party Secretary of the membership of the *Partito Nazionale Fascista*. Of the alleged membership of 320,000, an analysis of the class and category derivation of 152,000 members was provided: 23,418 were industrial workers; 36,847 were agricultural workers; 14,989 were employees; 19,783 were students; 7,209 were civil servants or soldiers; 1,506 were merchant seamen. Only 4,269 were characterized as industrialists or employers of labor, 13,879 were merchants or self-employed artisans, and 18,186 were small landowners and/or employers of agricultural contract labor. The Party, as a consequence, had a substantial proletarian character. This general proletarian character was enhanced by the membership of the Fascist Trade Union Congress that, in June, 1922, boasted a membership of 555,000.[96] The working class elements in the Fascist ranks originated, in fact, in the poorest strata of the proletariat.

On the other hand, Fascism attracted an inordinate number of typically middle-class university and secondary school students. These were among the most aggressive and radically nationalist and activist elements. The available statistics indicate that they constituted about fifteen per cent of the active membership of the Party, but contemporary commentators indicate that they exerted an influence far exceeding their numbers. The petty bourgeoisie further provided a significant portion of the cadre of the Fascist squads, and war veterans of diverse class origins provided much of the membership.

Mussolini himself fully exemplified the character of Fascism. His proletarian and petty-bourgeois provenience represented the most substantial constituent components of the movement. His own intellectual development had begun with the vague and sentimental revolutionary socialism that was the common heritage of the Italian agricultural and industrial working classes, and passed into the more sophisticated, but equally revolutionary, syndicalism that effected such an impact on Marxist thought in Italy to finally achieve the synthesis of the social and the national that Sorel held to be the product of Mussolini's peculiar political genius.[97]

In fact, Mussolini's social and political thought reflected rather than anticipated developments. He himself recognized as much on several significant occasions. Pietro Gorgolini's Fascist apologetic, written before Fascism's accession to power and recommended by Mussolini as the best exposition of Fascist doctrine available at that time,[98] indicated as much. Gorgolini alluded to Mussolini's specifically Marxist origins and identified Fascism as a logical development out of Sorelian socialism.[99] As such, Gorgolini rejected the identification of Fascism with specifically bourgeois or proletarian interests.[100] He characterized Fascism as the product of an exiguous minority of men who, having returned from the trenches, had committed themselves to the realization of Italy's greatness, a concern which enjoyed moral priority over the interests of class and category.

Gorgolini's exposition was a competent restatement of Fascist doctrine and was faithful to the position Mussolini had assumed by 1921. Gorgolini insisted that Fascism was a peculiar application of Sorelian syndicalism, an application that had substituted national development for class warfare as the functional myth of social doctrine. The substitution of *nation* as the operative moral and political concept made Fascism unalterably opposed to Marxist socialism, predicated as that socialism was on the priority of class membership. The commitment to the nation had transformed the logic of obligation and had transformed the entire value hierarchy that governed political behavior.[101] This commitment, conjoined with certain factual propositions about social and political dynamics and the role of elites in historical change, as well as the pragmatic orientation of its political program, adequately characterized the developmental dictatorship that Fascism proposed.[102] Fascism was a mass-based movement of solidarity, a movement which advocated the extensive reorganization of the social and economic structure of the state to effect the juridically and politically sustained collaboration of classes and categories in the disciplined service of what was considered to be the real interests of the national community. To this end the state was to assume legislative, executive, enterprisory, and educative responsibilities. The enactment of legislation to effect the juridical recognition of syndicates and employers' associations that would permit the arbitration and mediation of disputes in accordance with the principles of national syndicalism constituted the basis and the first obligation of the social and economic program of Fascism. The enhancement of executive power was equally imperative. The enterprisory functions of the state were advocated in the program manifestoes of the Party and its educative functions were identified with the responsibilities of the "reawakening of the torpid national consciousness," a consciousness natural to man as a social and political animal.

Thus, by the time of its advent to power, Fascism had elaborated the essentials of its own peculiar social and political doctrine.[103] Its historical genesis was fully exemplified in the development of Mussolini's own thought. It was, as Gorgolini made evident, a relatively coherent synthesis of Sorelian, Futurist, and nationalist elements. It was, in general, loosely argued, and its specific tactical programs altered with the political and economic circumstances of Italy in crisis. Its emphases were a function, at any time, of the changed composition of the Party and its leadership. All this having been acknowledged, Fascism nonetheless advanced a social and political doctrine that was as unique, as coherent, and as explicit as any of its competitors on the Italian scene. Mussolini assumed power committed to a constellation of reasoned beliefs, some of which he had developed as a revolutionary syndicalist, others that had developed as a consequence of Italy's experience during World War I, and still others that were the quasi-deductive consequence of the conjunction of those beliefs. Many of the legitimate implications of its original doctrine remained partially interred, to reveal themselves fully only after Fascism's accession to power, when the doctrine went into phased development. This is particularly true with respect to Fascism's conception of the nature and function of the state. The development of Fascist doctrine in the decade following the advent to power was, by and large, devoted to elaborating a consistent conception of the state.

Fascism in Power and the Codification of Doctrine

The years immediately following the March on Rome took on confused features. Mussolini formed a coalition government containing non-Fascist ministers; the Italian parliament was not dissolved although it contained only thirty-five Fascist deputies. The only manifest change obvious to observers was the increased tempo of activity. Formally, the structure of the state and the institutions of the nation remained unaltered. Whatever increased executive power Mussolini deployed was, initially, the consequence of his personal qualities and prestige rather than any substantive constitutional transformation. While it was true that a minority of men, leading disciplined paramilitary bands, had violated the established practices for the legitimate transfer of political power and had seized the machinery of government, Italy was so exhausted by the turmoil that characterized the postwar years that few voices were raised in protest. The monarchy was evidently favorably disposed. The Vatican launched no objection. Giovanni Giolitti, who had dominated Italian politics until 1915, declared that Mussolini's accession to power was the only logical solution to Italy's protracted parliamentary crisis. Antonio Salandra, the former Prime Minister, maintained that Mussolini had every right to assume power, having, in fact, for almost a year constituted the *de facto* government of Italy. Pareto announced that "the March on Rome came at precisely the opportune moment. Any delay would have impaired the effort to arrest the process of degeneration. . . ."[104]

Most of Italy seemed relieved. The accession of Mussolini to power seemed to be another instance of the personal politics that had been a feature of Italian government for over half a century. A forceful leader of men had taken up the reins of government. His exceptional personal qualities seemed to augur the same stability and continuity Italy had enjoyed under previous dynamic leaders. A substantial number of Italians expected, with some apparent justification, a normalization, a re-establishment of political and social equilibrium after the turbulence of the preceding decade. Mussolini had wrested power from the vested ruling class—and yet of the fifteen ministries, only four went to Fascists. The Fascists fared little better in the assignment of under-secretaries. Fifteen were assigned to Fascists, six to members of the Popular Party, three to Liberals, three to Nationals, and three to Democrats. Only the socialists had been systematically excluded. Mussolini showed remarkable deference with respect to the Senate, the respected institution of traditional Italy. The only significant indication that Fascism was not to be a political force in the traditional sense of the word was Mussolini's demand for extraordinary powers for one year to institute the necessary economies of government. The predominantly non-Fascist parliament granted powers with a vote of 215 to 80. But even this enhancement of executive power was not extraconstitutional. Mussolini had won the confidence of the nation, and Parliament had been given a choice between accepting the prevailing national sentiment or, as Mussolini threatened, "vanish."[105] He did indicate the real possibility of significant changes in the electoral process and the abolition of Parliament as it had been constituted. But, with these exceptions, the revolutionary government was surprisingly moderate in its demands.

For those content with the surface appearances, those who could dismiss Mussolini's explicit political and social views, the new government was conceived to be no more than another in the series of coalition governments that had ruled Italy. Only its ascent to power and the political personality of the new *Duce* made it in any sense unique. This complacency was born of an indisposition to take Fascist doctrine seriously. In retrospect, this indisposition is almost inexplicable, for the logic of Fascist commitments was evident. Only a highly selective and nonrepresentative collection of Mussolini's statements could be construed as supporting traditional social and political institutions. Read in context, such statements had stipulative implications. Fascism was a radical social and political movement and required assessment against the traditions out of which it arose and the political convictions of its leaders. In no sense could Fascism be understood to support traditional parliamentary democracy. Fascism entailed a radical reappraisal of the philosophic and theoretical foundations of society and the state and its succession to power could only involve massive alterations in Italy's social and political arrangements.

It was evident that Fascism was predicated on a radical departure from the philosophic and political individualism that provided the core conceptions of liberal and democratic ideology. Its elitism was an immediate surface indication of that fact. More than that, the very essentials of syndicalism and nationalism were fundamentally collectivist both in the philosophic and sociological sense. Fascism was the product of a collectivist tradition. It found its origins in Marxism and in the sociological tradition of Gumplowicz, Pareto, and Michels.

Fascism was born of a philosophic tradition that conceived the individual to be a function of group life. Marx, as one of the foremost spokesmen of this tradition, had understood man to be "by nature . . . a social animal."[106] Out of this essentially theoretical conviction Marx succeeded in deriving normative implications of the following sort: "Man is in the literal sense, a *zoon politikon,* not only a social animal but an animal that can attain individuality only in society."[107] A similar normic model of man was central to the Gumplowiczian tradition which conceived

man as [a social] product, both in body and mind. . . . The social phenomenon is always primary; the thought of the individual and the ethico-social products, such as religion, rights, morals, etc., are derived.[108]

Gumplowicz contended that

the individual is not prior to his group, rather the group is prior to the individual. We are born in a group and we die in it—the group preceded us and will survive us. . . . Aristotle . . . correctly conceived the relationship when he maintained: "the whole is necessarily prior to its parts."[109]

For the syndicalist theoreticians who were to become the first theoreticians of Fascism, this conception of man remained central to their social and political views. Thus Olivetti, having made the transition from proletarian syndicalism to Fascist syndicalism, argued that "society is the necessary presupposition of the individual."[110] He maintained that whatever the individual valued, and whatever was of value in the individual, was a social patrimony. Thought was predicated on language, which was itself a social product and presupposed the rule-governed speech acts which could only be meaningfully conceived in a social context. Speech, and consequently effective thought, presupposed the norms of correct usage, and norms are public and neutral criteria that are social products. The standards the individual employs for the cognitive, moral, and aesthetic governance of his life are social products, derivative products of the cultural community which precedes the individual and survives him. Whatever contribution the individual makes to this collective patrimony is made only within the confines of pre-established norms for truth ascription, normative judgment, and aesthetic appreciation. Human attainments are essentially social and historic products. It is instructive to note that in this context Olivetti had recourse to the German idealist tradition, referring initially to Kant's judgment that man is "by necessity a member of a civil community," and ultimately to the Hegelian conception of society as the expanded, and fundamentally truer, self.[111] In this sense national syndicalism not only increasingly approximated the philosophical posture assumed by Corridonian nationalism (rooted in the same collectivist tradition), but took on neo-Hegelian features which made it compatible with Gentilean idealism. Thus Balbino Giuliano, a Gentilean, publishing his defense of Fascism contemporaneously with that of Olivetti and approximately at the time of Fascism's accession to power, could tender essentially the same arguments in support of man's pre-eminently social nature.[112]

For Giuliano, the development of the individual was a function of a social interaction which presupposed the existence of a rule-governed historic community. Only initially, and as a consequence of the most arid of abstractions, could the individual be conceived as the empirical self, the physical entity that persists for a few score years and then perishes. The self which enjoys substantive moral value is the expanded self that has its origin in an obscure and remote past; its moral substance is rooted in the spiritual community of which it is a constituent but transient member. This truer self speaks the language and thinks the thoughts of a community, having

a life history that reaches into the recesses of the past and antici-
pates an incalculable future. This truer self is the heir of a cultural
patrimony out of which grows the fullness of personality. Whatever
the intrinsic value of the individual, it is the specific and determinate product of a given historical and organic community.
For Fascist syndicalists, nationalists, and Gentilean idealists, that
community is the nation and its sustaining and concrete expression
is the state.

We are nationalists and statists (*statalisti*), affirming the ethicity of the
devotion to the national society and the juridical organization of the
state, because nation and state are not anterior to us and to our individuality, rather they live in our very selves (*nel nostro Io*). . . . Fidelity
to the nation and the state is fidelity to our most profound truth and is
the supreme ethical duty because it is the ultimate necessity of our
spiritual development.[113]

Both Fascist syndicalism and Corridonian nationalism had a
common theoretic origin in the group-orientated sociological tradition of Gumplowicz, Mosca, Pareto, and Michels. What resulted
was a common model of man as a social animal, an explanatory and
theoretical model capable of supporting synthetic knowledge claims.
This natural scientific tradition remained central to Fascist doctrine;
in 1925, Panunzio, who was one of its foremost spokesmen, defined
Fascism as "a political doctrine, that is to say a conception of the
state, which is fundamentally sociological."[114]

But the theoretical model of man advanced by syndicalist and
nationalist theoreticians supported not only cognitive knowledge
claims but normative judgments as well. The conception of man as
a pre-eminently social animal capable of attaining the fullness of
self, humanity, only in a rule-governed social context, deploys a persuasive moral force. The admonition to fulfill oneself is *prima facie*
self-commending. To conceive life in society as the necessary condition of self-realization is to endow society with critical moral
significance. To identify, in some sense, the self with society is to
give society the same moral significance traditionally accorded to
men as spiritual agents. To identify society with the truer self is to
devolve upon it moral privilege. Thus Panunzio, in his *Lo stato di
diritto*, written in 1922, insisted upon the moral primacy of the state

as an ethical entity. The thrust of these conceptions led to a substantial union with the ethical idealism that had enjoyed correlative development in Italy. There was a natural and complementary union of sociological or theoretical and philosophical or normative elements.

The political conceptions advanced by spokesmen of this synthetic and revolutionary doctrine were radically different from those entertained by traditional liberalism. Continental liberalism had identified itself with a belief system, fundamental to which was a specific normic model of man. Man, for the philosophers of liberalism, was conceived as an empirical and individual self, and society was viewed as an aggregate of contracting selves. Society and the state were understood to be completely derivative. The independent and unitary selves which were anterior to society were held to be endowed by nature or nature's God with imprescriptible rights and values, independent of and insulated from society and the state. Among those inalienable rights was liberty. Men were born free, and freedom was understood to signify the absence of restraint. For convenience and security, men could contract to associate themselves in community, to barter some portion of liberty for security. To effect the ends of convenience and security the state was created, but as an agency of restricted purpose its moral significance was negative and contingent. It was conceived as a necessary evil and at its best when it governed least, for all law was restrictive and all restraint was evil. If men could but follow the dictates of reason, law would be entirely superfluous and men could live a life of untrammelled freedom. Society and the state were understood to constitute a continual threat to the native liberties of the individual self, liberties which only the dispersal of state powers into many compartments, each designed to check and balance the other, could insure.

Such convictions supported an initial presumption in favor of the individual's unrestricted activity that any proposed restriction must overcome. The procedural maxim that is its natural corollary is, "All restraint, *qua* restraint, is an evil." Fascism's doctrinal conceptions resulted, on the other hand, in an initial presumption in favor of the law-governed historic community. Individuals are products and not creators of society and the state. Society and the state are the source of the fullness of self, and freedom is activity in conformity to law. As we shall see, when we have occasion to examine the mature political philosophy of Fascism, the activity which the philosophers of liberalism conceived as free was, for Fascists, instinctive or capricious.

For liberalism, society and the state were objects of suspicion and had only contingent moral significance. For Fascism society and the state were the moral substance of man as a human being. Thus, as we have already indicated, pre-Fascist and proto-Fascist syndicalist, nationalist, and Gentilean thought was radically anti-individualist. As early as 1917, Panunzio had fully committed himself to the "organic" as opposed to the "atomistic" and "mechanical" conception of society and the state,[115] a conception which accorded moral privilege to the collectivity, its traditions, and particularly its juridical embodiment in the state, as against the empirical and transient individuals which constituted its membership at any particular time. In this sense Fascism harbored an initial bias in favor of the maintenance of institutions and forms that gave substance to the historic nation and could therefore characterize itself as a "revolutionary conservatism."[116]

All this should have been evident to anyone who took the time to familiarize himself with evolving Fascist doctrine. Had men been familiar with Fascist doctrine, Mussolini's statements concerning the reduction of the state's activities to those proper to it would not have succeeded in generating the complacency that characterized the initiation of the Fascist enterprise. Little more than two months after the March on Rome, Mussolini made clear his intention to create the "Fascist State,"

. . . the single, unitary state, the sole repository of all the history, of the entire future, of all the force of the Italian nation. . . . [The state is] a moral idea which incarnates itself and expresses itself in a system of hierarchies. . . . I intend to re-establish with all the means at my disposal a single national discipline binding upon sect, faction, and party.[117]

From its very inception, Fascism conceived the nation as "the superior synthesis of all the values, material and spiritual," and as such enjoying moral privilege with respect to "individuals, categories, and classes . . . who are instruments that serve the nation. . . ."[118] The interests of individuals, categories, and classes were understood to be legitimate only insofar as they were compatible with the superior interests of the nation. It was clear that Fascists, syndicalists, nationalists, and idealists alike charged the state, as the juridical embodiment of the nation, with the responsibilities of determining the nature and specific objects of national interests at any given time. Mussolini identified the nation and the state.[119] The nation was the sum total of material and spiritual interests of a specific historical community, a community sustained by a prevailing and indomitable sentiment, and the state was its juridical incarnation. The state, as sovereign, had the immediate and mediate responsibility of maintaining the normative order outside of which individual life is meaningless. Society, the historic community, was the matter and the state constituted the form of political life. (As *materia appetit formam,* so *societas appetit status.*) The state, as the legitimate sovereign, was the ultimate repository of force, and as such was charged with sustaining the norms governing individual and collective behavior that make community life possible.[120] Thus, for Fascism, the state was "infinitely superior" to both the individuals and organizations of which the national community was composed. On the first anniversary of the March on Rome, Panunzio described the Fascist state as

a great army, an imposing discipline, a living hierarchy. The military organization of the armed forces is no longer sufficient. United to the armed forces there must be a civilian army that includes functionaries and citizens. . . . Not only soldiers are soldiers and combatants; all the citizens from the most lowly to the highest are soldiers and combatants . . . all are living instruments of that orchestration . . . that is the life of the nation.[121]

These were the characteristics imputed to the state by Fascism from the time of its conception as a political party in November, 1921. Roberto Farinacci, in his history of his period, indicates that the Fascist position *vis-a-vis* the state was finalized only during this period and only with the adoption of Gentile's conception of the "ethical state."[122] Within such a context, allusions to the "Manchestrian state" were simply inappropriate. They conveyed nothing of the implications of the prevailing Fascist conception. They could only deceive. The Fascist doctrine of the state was fundamentally opposed to the liberal "idolatry" that assigned moral, historic, or political priority to the "empiric individual," and consequently opposed to any "inalienable" rights he was conceived to possess.[123]

Fascism had, in effect, "identified society with the nation, the nation with the state, and economic activity with political activity."[124] The state, in turn, was identified with the Party. Fascism, its theorists insisted during the period before Fascism manifested its features as a plebiscitary dictatorship and an explicit totalitarianism, entertained a "total conception of life," with which it would infuse the state. The Party was the bearer of that conception, and the state it would create was to be called a "party-state" (*Stato-Partito*).[125] Its responsibilities were ethical and pedagogic. The Party was charged with the obligation of awakening in the masses the realization of their ultimate real interests, their ultimate identity with the community that constituted their moral substance. These were the arguments articulated during this initial period by theoreticians of the stature of Panunzio, Guido Pighetti, and Massimo Rocca. They responsibly represented Fascist thought, and on the basis of their formulations more confident projections of Fascism's development could be made than any based solely on Fascism's manifest political tactics during the years 1922 through 1924.

Once the logic that sustained, and the content that informed, the rationale of Fascism are reviewed, it is evident that Fascism was, from its very inception, radically opposed to liberalism as a social and political *Weltanschauung*, and to the political democracy which was its foremost political expression. The Fascists themselves never concealed the fact. As we have seen, Mussolini anticipated the beginning of an antiliberal and antidemocratic epoch. Immediately after the March on Rome, he characterized the Fascist revolution, and the Bolshevik revolution as well, as fundamentally antiliberal and antidemocratic.[126] At precisely the same time, Fascist theoreticians were inveighing against liberal institutions. Panunzio, Pighetti, and Olivetti argued that a new form of state was in the process of creation. Panunzio sagely indicated that the existence of the Fascist Militia presaged that Fascism intended to create a state essentially different from the liberal state which was, in principle, forever the prize of numerical majorities. Fascism intended to arm its state with a militia which had pledged its allegiance to a particular party. Fascism thus declared its intention to retain power even, if necessary, in the face of popular opposition. Panunzio pointed to the parallel phenomenon in the revolutionary Soviet Union. The Red Guard was the Leninist analogue of the National Militia of Fascism.[127] They each represented the will to prevail of a political entity unknown before the twentieth century—the unitary party.

Almost immediately following the accession to power, Mussolini officially incorporated the Fascist squads with which he had wrested control of the state from the parliamentary regime into the national armed forces. By January, 1923, the Fascist Militia was an official arm of the state. Edoardo Susmel is correct in indicating that this single act "conferred the sentence of death upon the pre-existing demoliberal state. . . ."[128] No other single act revealed more clearly the implications of Fascism. Fascism never concerned itself, in principle, with electoral majorities. Its concern with majorities was purely tactical. In this regard Mussolini, and Fascism, were brutally frank. Fascism was elitist and Fascist spokesmen never tired of drawing out its practical implications.

. . . [The] masses and elites are indissolubly united in the historic process insofar as the former do not succeed in developing and evolving if not guided and energized by the latter, who [in turn] cannot succeed to dominance if they cannot interpret or anticipate the obscure need and the profound aspirations . . . of the masses.

Progress, in fact, "is the work of a select minority and not of the majority. . . ."[129]

These are simply transliterations of themes found in Oriani, Pareto, Mosca, Sorel, Michels, and a host of other social theorists whose thought Mussolini had made his own years before World War I. Within the context of the nationalism and statism that characterized Fascism by 1921, they constituted the strategic premises of Fascism's totalitarian politics.

The Doctrinal Development of Fascism after 1925

After 1925, as a consequence of a number of circumstances, Fascist doctrine became increasingly standardized; its arguments more tightly developed and its implications more apparent. First and foremost, prior to 1925, Fascism existed in a state of perpetual crisis. After the first impact of the March on Rome, the opposition to Fascism regrouped and undertook a debilitating war of attrition against Mussolini's rule. But more threatening was the disorder that prevailed within the ranks of Fascism itself. Fascism had been a spontaneous and disorderly growth. *Fasci* had organized in all the major cities of North Italy around local popular leaders. These men, while nominally subordinate to the control of the central offices of the movement, were in fact *condottieri* with personal followings. They launched campaigns, quasi-military, organizational, and propagandistic, at their own will and discretion. Any policy decision by Mussolini was likely to be compromised by the independent activity of any or all of the local *ras* (as the local leaders were called). It was with this undisciplined Party that Mussolini seized control of the state. For almost two years thereafter Mussolini continued to promise an end to Fascist violence, and yet the violence persisted. The Party threatened to fragment into factions, and expulsions from its ranks were not uncommon. With the murder of Giacomo Matteotti by Fascists in June, 1924, the entire political situation became critical. For six months, the Fascist government trembled. Finally Mussolini forced the issue. Fascism emerged dominant over the opposition and Mussolini rapidly became absolute master of the Party. On January 3, 1925, after his control over the Party became secure, Mussolini proclaimed that Fascism, and Fascism alone, would rule the nation.[130]

After that date, Fascism could speak without equivocation. Its doctrine could be articulated without qualifications and without tactical reservations; but, as we have seen, this is not to suggest that the doctrine of Fascism had not long since taken on the specific features that were its own. Fascism, from the foundation of the *Partito Nazionale Fascista* in 1921, gravitated around a hard core of concepts that had crystallized into a political doctrine of considerable specificity. In the weeks before the slaying of Matteotti Mussolini could, with justification, maintain that Fascism had a program "based upon a unitary principle, based upon a classic conception of the state," radically different from that of liberalism.[131] After the resolution of the crisis which followed the death of Matteotti, Fascism was free to embark upon a massive program of social revolution, a program accompanied by explicit vindications and anticipated in its doctrinal commitments as early as 1919.[132]

Coupled with these political events was yet another circumstance which conduced to the rapid maturation of Fascist doctrine. Once ensconced in power, Fascism attracted to itself the allegiance of a company of men of substantial intellectual caliber. Immediately upon its advent, Fascism drew upon the services of men of international reputation such as Giovanni Gentile, Corrado Gini, and Roberto Michels. Once Fascism became secure in its rule these men were joined by spokesmen of varied scholarly and scientific disciplines, each contributing in some measure to the finalization of Fascism's doctrinal rationale.

What is interesting and instructive is that irrespective of the diversity of contributions, a collection of themes and concepts remained remarkably persistent and substantially unaltered. Fascist doctrine, after 1921, retained a surprising degree of theme and content persistence. Elements of doctrine were amplified and arguments were reformulated, but given the number of individuals who contributed to its articulation the doctrine remained significantly resistent to substantive alteration. In practice, Fascist social and political ideas took on institutional and technical forms of various kinds, but the supportive rationale which subtended them remained constant. The doctrine, like all social and political doctrines, contained a statement of purposes and arguments understood to sustain those purposes. The doctrine did not contain technical procedures for the realization of ends. The realization of ends was understood to involve a range of problems outside the interest and competence of social and political doctrine. Thus, Mussolini's doctrinal commitment to the propositions that the principal categories of the productive process, capital and labor, receive juridical recognition to meet as equals before the law in order to resolve disputes in a manner compatible with national interests did not contain a specification of the content of the Royal Decree of April 3, 1926, which provided the norms in law for its actuation.

This distinction of ends and means becomes more important when doctrinal commitments are couched in terms that are vague. Under such conditions, applications provide significant content to expressions which have compelling persuasive, but minimal cognitive, force. But even in such cases doctrinal ideals provide an indication of the direction in which legislation will move. A doctrine predicated on a conception of man which conceives each individual as the locus of imprescriptible rights is, of course, less likely to foster legislation restrictive of what liberalism considers individual freedoms. A doctrine which construes individual rights as derivative is, predictably, more disposed to countenance just such legislation. In neither case is any legislation specified, but the possible consequence of doctrinal bias can be anticipated.

In this sense the Fascist Corporative State went through a gradual evolution, what Fascist theoreticians themselves called a "syndical phase" and a "corporative phase," and took on significantly different institutional forms at different times during its existence. Nonetheless, Fascists were to argue that the specific and transient forms which the institutions of the state took on were fully compatible with, and functional expressions of, "ends posed by the state as the fundamental motives of its actions."[133]

The plausibility of this claim can be assessed only by a responsible comparison of authoritative doctrinal goals and the enacted legislation and established institutions presumably calculated to attain them. For the purpose of the present exposition it is only necessary to establish that Fascists understood the relationship of ends to means to be essentially that which is indicated above. Doctrine provided not only broad and programmatic goals, but contained a summary account of the belief system and the grounds of belief; that is to say, a catalogue of essential commitments and at least a preliminary and stenographic presentation of the reasoned judgments construed as supporting beliefs that served to dispel doubts, resolve disputes, and vindicate courses of action.

Thus Fascists identified specific pieces of doctrinal literature as being of major social and political significance. This was true of the

Carta del Lavoro, which was approved by the Fascist Grand Council on April 21, 1927.[134] Similar significance was assigned to the *Dottrina del fascismo,* which appeared over Mussolini's name in 1932.[135] Actually, the significance of such documents was attributable more to their origin than their content. In a hierarchical and authoritarian system, *official* doctrinal statements necessarily possess greater social and political significance than any private formulations, no matter how competent. As a matter of fact, both the *Carta* and the *Dottrina* are highly condensed and elliptical formulations of Fascist doctrine. From the point of view of the rational reconstruction of the historic doctrine of Fascism, the *Carta* is even less than that. It is a collection of pronouncements, a compendious affirmation of "principles."[136] It also provides juridical norms for the formulation and administration of laws governing the relationships between productive categories organized in labor and entrepreneurial syndicates, and the relationship of both to the state. It does not provide a rationale in their support. This can only be afforded by an appeal to more substantial pieces of doctrinal literature.

Any objective review of such doctrinal literature between 1925 and 1943 indicates that Fascism entertained a relatively specific collection of reasoned goals already implicit, if not explicit, in Mussolini's public utterances and published writings up to, and through, 1922. From 1919 until the end of 1924, Mussolini dominated neither the spontaneous organization and development of the *Fasci di combattimento* and the *Partito Nazionale Fascista,* nor their equally spontaneous opinions. The *Fasci* arose spontaneously, and collected heterogeneous elements around a call for the "defense of the national victory," when orthodox Italian socialism called in question the very necessity of involvement in World War I. The very heterogeneity of the constituent elements bred a heterogeneity of opinions that was reflected in the programmatic postures of a movement self-characterized as "problematistic" and "pragmatic."[137] The effort to construct an organization that would host such disparate groups forced the movement to be "antiprejudiced (*antipregiudiziaiole*)." It advertised itself as neither republican nor monarchial, neither Catholic nor anti-Catholic, neither socialist nor anti-socialist.[138] Six months after the *Fasci di combattimento* was formed, Mussolini indicated that it was

a little difficult to define Fascists. They are not republicans, socialists, democrats, conservatives, nor nationalists. They represent a synthesis of all the negations and all the affirmations. . . . While they renounce all the parties, they are their fulfillment.[139]

Whatever this meant, it did indicate that Fascism as an organized force was a mélange of distinct and disparate groups bound together by two irreducible ideals: 1) the nation before and above all else, and 2) a programmatic corollary, the maximization of production. These were the ideal ends with which Mussolini held together the *Fasci* after their inauguration in March, 1919, and they remained constant throughout the subsequent five year period. Whatever he conceived as enhancing the viability of the nation had his approval, and he held the "supreme commandment of the hour" to be production.[140]

Whatever tactical postures nascent Fascism assumed, they were never construed as unalterable. The *Fasci* initially advocated a separation of church and state and a confiscation of church property.[141] This was coupled with a demand for proportional representation in Parliament, the abolition of the Senate, an extension of the vote to women, and the "partial expropriation" of capital through surtaxes and an accelerated inheritance tax.[142] All these tactical programmatic demands were ultimately renounced. Mussolini made clear that such tactical demands were contingent and "would vary in accordance with time and place."[143] Strategy alone was calculated, and resulted in time- and circumstance-conditioned tactics.

It is important to realize that tactics were governed by an overall doctrinal strategy. The partial expropriation of capital was not the consequence of a doctrinal commitment to the Marxist conviction that private capital is an engine for oppression. It was designed to satisfy what Mussolini understood to be the capital requirements of the nation at that particular time. His concern was to maximize production and insure national well-being. If this could be done more effectively without the confiscation of church property and a surcharge on profit, he was prepared to renounce the demand.

At this point the question that immediately suggests itself is: If tactical demands are contingent, how can the observer anticipate with any confidence the course a movement like Fascism will take? The answer is: By having an effective grasp of the doctrinal commitments to which it is wedded. By 1919, Mussolini had identified himself with a constellation of reasonably well-articulated ideas. Those ideas have already been outlined. By 1921, those ideas had become sufficiently precise that a knowledgeable observer weighing them in the context of the prevalent social and political circumstances could predict with some measure of assurance the future features of the projected Fascist state. This is immediately evident in a review of Fascist doctrine after 1925. Its content was a literal restoration of all the critical categories of Mussolini's early social and political convictions. After 1925, Mussolini was no longer trammelled by the necessity to compromise in order to hold together recalcitrant and disparate groups. His hold over the Party was absolute. He no longer had to placate a threatening extra-Party opposition. His ideas reemerged essentially unaltered by the period of forced incubation. After 1925, the doctrine of Fascism was a restatement of the doctrinal elements that Mussolini had made his own during his maturation and his initial leadership of the elements that composed the *Partito Fascista Nazionale*.

Mussolini was remarkably sensitive to the articulation of Fascist doctrine. He read extensively. In the autocratic circumstances he created, he became and remained the direct or mediate arbiter of what was issued as official doctrine. Many of the books issued during the Fascist period bore his introduction and his personal imprimatur. In any event, much of the literature was published under official Fascist auspices—by agencies arrayed with his delegated authority. Final doctrinal authority emanated from Mussolini or men who enjoyed his confidence. Finally, the authors of doctrinal exegesis were sufficiently prudent to search out Mussolini's "definitive" opinions before advancing arguments. Their academic and social positions might very well depend on their orthodoxy. As a result, Fascist doctrine was consistent and reiterative. Whatever disputes were entertained (and there were persistent disputes between an "idealistic" and a "naturalistic" interpretation of the general doctrine and a "political" and a "juridical" interpretation of the state, to cite but two of the most insistent) were undertaken within the guidelines of the more or less specific doctrine. What is essential to acknowledge is that the doctrine was reasonably coherent and specific, and that it was the doctrine with which Mussolini had identified himself since 1921.

By 1927, a number of full-fledged doctrinal expositions of Fascism became available. The theoretical and normative commitments to which these expositions gave expression remained essentially unaltered throughout the Fascist period. What emerged was a systematization: the result of general and rudimentary ideas regularly and consistently applied as a conceptual frame of reference to the interpretation of a body of facts to afford the occasion for the satisfactory explanation of those facts and successful prediction of forthcoming and relevant facts, and consequently a guide to practical orientation.[144] We cannot be concerned with the truth status of the interpretation, the explanation, and the success of such derivative predictions. Our restricted concern is with the systematization itself, the emergent social and political philosophy which attained maturity with the fully explicit synthesis of Gentilean idealism and Fascist political doctrine that took place in 1932. Here the focus of attention will be directed to a summary outline of Fascism's mature social and political doctrine. Whether it achieved the rigor which would qualify it as social and political philosophy is an academic question. The distinction between the mature social and political doctrine and Gentile's idealism is introduced here only for ease of exposition. Fascism, after 1921, was essentially compatible with Gentile's "Actualism," largely because of historic and intellectual circumstances. Gentilean idealists, nationalists, and national syndicalists all accepted a common core of doctrinal elements—and by 1921 Mussolini himself had introduced Gentile's conception of the *stato etico* into Fascist doctrine. The differences that obtained were the consequence of the evident sociological biases of nationalism and national syndicalism.[145] Gentile's analysis was irreducibly normative and philosophical. The conclusions arrived at were, nonetheless, essentially compatible. The differences will be specified in the treatment of Gentile's contribution to Fascist ideology.

The Mature Doctrine of Fascism   Fascist theorists, repeating one of Mussolini's convictions, maintained that every social and political doctrine revolved around a specific conception of man and society.[146] If this is true, Fascism's doctrine gravitated around a normic conception of man and society which Fascist theoreticians themselves variously characterized as "organic," "solidaristic," or "communalistic" in order to distinguish it from the liberal conception to which Fascism was intransigently opposed.

Before the advent of Fascism, both syndicalists and nationalists referred to their general conception of man and society as "organic"; that is to say, society was understood to constitute a system, an integrated network of recurrent norm-governed interpersonal behavior patterns, comprehensive and differentiated enough to be self-sufficient with respect to the functional requirements of its members, and capable of long-term persistence.[147] The individual was understood to be a functioning component of a self-regulating social system. He was conceived as a determinate person only insofar as he assumed functions within the structure of relations which preceded his role occupancy and which would persist beyond it.[148]

For Fascists to speak of a social system, of integration, of norm governance, and of pattern persistence implied the existence of a central and sovereign agency of control and regulation: the state. Thus, in one of the early systematizations of Fascist doctrine, Giovanni Corso could maintain that "society, law, and state are inseparable notions. . . . The one is intrinsic to the other."[149] In 1935, Stefano Raguso insisted that even the "simplest community of men is inconceivable unless sustained by an active principle of organization [and] . . . this principle of organization . . . consists . . . in the subordination to a sovereign, political power."[150]

This relationship had already been systematized in 1927 by Corrado Gini (1884–1965), who was a member of the commission studying constitutional reform after Fascism's accession to power. He described society as "a system normally found in evolutionary or devolutionary equilibrium possessed of the capacity of self-conservation and re-equilibrization" which finds its highest expression in the modern state, since the normal conditions of [such] an organism are characterized by a *consensus* among its parts such that the interests of each are tempered by, and founded in, the common advantage of the organism. . . . [Such] a consensus is not attained without a central regulatory power . . . [that] conciliates the interests of the majority or the generality of the existing generation with the superior interests of the future life of the nation. . . . The notion of national interest as superior to the interests of the majority and even of the totality of citizens accords itself well with the organicistic conception of society. The organism has vital and evident requirements that transcend the present and to which present interests must frequently be sacrificed.[151]

Gini's exposition was, initially, that of a sociologist. He was articulating theoretical propositions which claimed explanatory and predictive capacity. But the normative and specifically political implications were obvious. Once society was described as an organism, the collectivity, the organized whole, became the focus of value; and the individual, as a constituent part of the whole, was a locus of value only as he contributed to the maintenance of the whole. In a specifically political context, therefore, Gini argued:

The liberal theory assumes that society consists of an aggregate of individuals who must look after their own interests and it regards the state as an emanation of the individual wills intended to eliminate the conflicts between the interests of individuals. The nationalistic theory, on the contrary, views society as a true and distinct organism of a rank superior to that of the individuals who compose it, an organism endowed with a life of its own and with interests of its own. These interests result from the coordination of the desires for the time being of the current generation together with the interests of all the future generations which are to constitute the future life of the nation. Often enough these are in harmony one with the other, but occasionally the interests of future generations are opposed to those of the present generation, and in any case they may differ notably, if not in direction, at least in intensity. The agency destined to give effect to these higher interests of society is the state, sacrificing, wherever necessary, the interests of the individual and operating in opposition to the will of the present generation.[152]

Gini's statement is a reformulation of an account provided by Alfredo Rocco (1875–1935), the Fascist Minister of Justice, in 1925.

Rocco identified the social and political views of Fascism as an "integral doctrine of sociality." Rocco maintained that

Man lives and must live in society. A human being outside the pale of society is an inconceivable thing—a non-man. . . . [Society, in turn], is a fraction of the human species endowed with unity of organization for the attainment of the peculiar ends of the species. . . . Fascism replaces therefore the old atomistic and mechanical theory which was at the basis of the liberal and democratic doctrines with an organic and historic concept. When I say organic I do not wish to convey the impression that I consider society as an organism in the manner of the so-called "organic theories of the state"; but rather to indicate that the social groups as fractions of the species receive thereby a life and scope which transcend the scope and life of the individuals identifying themselves with the history and finalities of the uninterrupted series of generations. . . . The important thing is to ascertain that this organic concept of the state gives to society a continuous life over and beyond the existence of the several individuals. The relations therefore between the state and citizens are completely reversed by the Fascist doctrine. Instead of the liberal-democratic formula, "society for the individual," we have, "individuals for society" with this difference however: that while the liberal doctrines eliminated society, Fascism does not submerge the individual in the social group. It subordinates him, but does not eliminate him. . . . For Fascism, society is the end, individuals the means, and its whole life consists in using individuals as instruments for its social ends. . . . The fundamental problem of society in the old doctrines is the question of the rights of individuals. . . . Fascism on the other hand faces squarely the problem of the right of the state and the duty of individuals. Individual rights are only recognized in so far as they are implied in the rights of the state.[153]

Rocco's account received the explicit endorsement of Mussolini, and the related set of propositions which constituted its substance appeared and reappeared in Fascist doctrinal statements throughout the Fascist period.[154] Rocco's statement is clearly an effort at political vindication for Fascist policies. Gini's account has putative cognitive intention. Gini is maintaining that an adequate account of human behavior must refer to the roles and status of individuals. The concepts of role and status are unintelligible unless their activity is understood within the context of institutions, subsystems that require patterned interpersonal responses. Such re-

sponses are diagnostic of some specific aspect of extant organizational or societal forms. Any compelling account of man's behavior
must refer to such irreducibly social facts.[155] References to goal-
directed and goal-organized behavior summarize persistent patterns
of behavior; the observational meaning of such statements are un-
packed to deliver a conjunction of statements concerning the behavior of a number of individuals. But the regular relationships
which evidently obtain between individuals can only be explained
by references to the norms which establish their appropriateness or
inappropriateness. It is evident that even Rocco so conceives the
analysis. He speaks of the social group, "pervaded by spiritual influences": the unity of language, of culture, of religion, of tradition,
of customs, and of law, all of which are norm governed and provide the minimum essential to the pattern maintenance which defines "society."[156]

Thus far the references to the nation have been peripheral to
the reconstruction of Fascist doctrine. A similar analysis could be
provided for any social group, any organized collectivity. In fact,
we have seen that just such an account was inherited by Fascism
from the sociological tradition which effectively began with Gumplowicz. Gini cites Gumplowicz as being prominent among the
predecessors of organicism.[157] Organicism as an analytic and explanatory technique was not object specific, that is to say the objections to methodological individualism did not entail reference to
any specific organized group, race, class, sect, caste, or nation as
the privileged unit of analysis. If the orthodox Marxist analysis were
correct, class would constitute the effective unit of analysis. Fascist
theoreticians, for reasons other than their methodological bias, opted
for the nation as the primary object of contemporary analysis. Since
their theoretical account had obvious normative implications, the
nation became the object of loyalty.

As we have seen, the radical syndicalists were among the first
to make the analytic and theoretic shift from class to nation as the
unit of analysis. Olivetti described syndicalism as "the philosophy
of association," predicated on the empirical generalization that human existence was impossible outside the confines of some "ordered
association" of similars.[158] The central issue became: What similarities are sufficient to maintain a viable association? Once those

similarities were identified, the unit of analysis could be identified.

Arturo Labriola (1873–1959), one of the founders of syndicalism in Italy, argued that experience had indicated that class sentiment was largely artificial, that class interests alone had proved incapable of generating and sustaining group building dispositions. "There is no doubt," he insisted, "that national sentiment and ethnic sentiment are much more spontaneous and potent."[159] As early as 1911, he had indicated that the sentiment of nationality was a product of group life spent within the confines of a norm- and rule-governed association far more extensive and more charged with emotion than class membership.[160] This analysis was pursued by Fascist theoreticians and the objective grounds of "similarity," the factors which conduced to group maintenance and persistence, were finally specified as common territorial origins, common descent, common customs and usages, common culture, a language spoken in common, and common history and a common system of laws.[161] These were the objective grounds upon which the sentiment of nationality rested. In his introductory lectures in political sociology at the University of Rome, in 1927, Michels so specified them.[162] As we have indicated, Mussolini had made such an analysis his own before 1919.

Fascist theorists conceived man a group animal possessed of natural dispositions which conduced to the maintenance of organized community life. As we shall indicate (in Chapter 6), they were to argue that man shares with all social animals a sense of territoriality and a disposition to identify with a restricted community of similars. The similarities which sustain group cohesion vary in time and place, but in general some feature of high social visibility provides the initial ground for identification. Possessed of these dispositional characteristics, men are always found in groups of restricted compass. It is not an accident that Michels should be a spokesman for these conceptions. He was a lineal descendant of the tradition of Gumplowicz, Pareto, and Mosca, characterizing man in essentially the same way and identifying the same group-building factors isolated by his antecedents. Similarly, Enzio Maria Olivetti, the son of A. O. Olivetti, in a book which received Mussolini's endorsement,[163] traced these doctrinal elements to the "anti-individualistic sociological tradition" popular in antebellum Italy,[164] an evident allusion to those men in the Gumplowiczian tradition. Carlo Costamagna, in one of the most mature expressions of Fascist doctrine, gives clear evidence of his dependence not only upon Pareto and Mosca, but of familiarity with the work of Gumplowicz as well.[165]

Fascist doctrine inherited these conceptions from the sociological traditions of prewar Italy, but it was the conception of the state, which became central to Fascist thought only in 1921, which gave Fascism a specific and determinate character of its own. Thus, Fascists indicated that while the people, sustained by the group building sentiments to which we have alluded, constitute the content of the state, the state is formally defined by its political and juridical functions. Fascists held that, technically speaking, any form of ordered, autonomous associated life was animated by a state.[166] The state is "any society or community of men held together by a political nexus."[167] The formal element in the state is its sovereign political and juridical power. The state "is the creator of an order, through the medium of law, or norms, that reduces all the component entities to unity and coordinates all activities to a common end."[168] The state is the ultimate repository of force to which all order must, in the final analysis, appeal for regulative sanction. Fascist theorists like Panunzio recognized that organized associations within the state had the capacity to issue rules and regulations governing their collective membership, but they held that such rules and regulations were effective only if they were directly or indirectly sanctioned by the state.[169] That is, it was recognized that association would follow interests, real or fancied, that provided the grounds of identification among men. The imposing rise of economic organizations, specifically the syndicates, was ample evidence of that historic reality. Sects, clubs, cooperatives, cultural associations—all constituted interest-fostered, rule-governed associations within the state. All were autonomous insofar as they were capable of governing their own internal organization by the promulgation of procedural and substantive rules. The state might not, for whatever reasons, exercise its sovereign right over them. Organizations might continue to function on the strength of their own capacity to sanction their members. Nonetheless, Fascists insisted, the state is the sole and ultimate source of imperative sanction since the state has the *exclusive* right to the regulation of the use of force. In effect, Fascism rejected the thesis that there was any limit, in principle, to the state's political and juridical sovereignty. The state was "integral," "totalitarian." Fascism conceived no interest—economic, educational, religious, or cultural—as falling outside its purview. There was, consequently, no *private* as distinct from *public* interest.[170] This idea found doctrinal expression in Mussolini's aphorism: "Everything within the state, nothing outside the state, and nothing against the state."[171]

If the term *community* has as its reference a number of individuals whose behavior is governed by a normative order, and if the state provides the ultimate sanction that sustains that order, the state is then understood to constitute an underlying and essential social reality that is coextensive and coterminous with, and logically prior to, the community. If that community is a nation—a community having a common history and culture, that manifests itself in shared, stable, and habitual preferences and priorities that permit members to share more intimately with each other a wider range of communication than with outsiders—then the nation and the state are, in some critical sense, conflated. In speaking of the state *per se* one refers to the normative order, and in speaking of the nation one speaks of the collection of living individuals whose behavior exemplifies that order.

These conceptions find stenographic expression in the *Carta del Lavoro* as:

The . . . nation is an organism having ends, life and potentialities superior in power and duration to the individuals, taken singly or collectively, composing it. It is a moral, political and economic entity which finds its integral realization in the Fascist State.[172]

The state, consequently, assumes the responsibility for maintaining the moral order that provides the continuity of the historic community that is the nation.[173]

In the document that became the basis for the mature ideology of Fascism, Mussolini summarizes these doctrinal conceptions in the following manner:

The keystone of Fascist doctrine is the conception of the state, of its essence, of its tasks, of its ends. For Fascism, the state is an absolute before which individuals are relative. Individuals and groups are "conceivable" insofar as they are within the state. The liberal state does not direct the interaction and the material and spiritual development of the collectivity, but restricts itself to registering the results; the Fascist state has a consciousness of its own, a will of its own, and for this reason it is identified as an "ethical" state. In 1929 . . . I indicated: "For Fascism, the state is not the night watchman preoccupied only with the personal security of citizens; still less is it an organization for purely material ends, to guarantee a certain well-being and a relatively peaceful social order, for in such case only an administrative council would be necessary. Nor is the state a purely political creation without contact with material and complex reality of individuals and peoples. The state, as Fascism conceives and actuates it, is a spiritual and moral fact, because it renders concrete the political, juridical, and economic organization of the nation and that organization is, in its origin and its development, a manifestation of the spirit. The state is the guarantor of internal and external security, but it is also the custodian and the vehicle of transmission of the spirit of the people as it has been elaborated throughout the centuries in language, custom, and faith. The state is not only the present but it is also the past and above all the future. It is the state that transcends the brevity of individual life and represents the immanent consciousness of the nation. The form in which the state represents itself changes, but its necessity remains. It is the state that educates citizens to civic virtue, rendering them conscious of their mission; that calls them to unity, harmonizing their interests in justice; that transmits their achievements in science, arts, law and human solidarity; that lifts men from the elementary life in tribes to the highest expression of human power that is empire, entrusting to the ages the names of those who died for its integrity or in obedience to its laws. . . ."[174]

This conception of the state as the moral substance of the nation and the individual, as the tutor of civic virtue, as the immanent conscience of the community and the preformed moral order in which the individual finds his truest self, is the recognizable transliteration of the moral conceptions of Georges Sorel. For Sorel, the agency of moral regeneration, in an age grown flaccid, was the syndicate, the working class organized in the service of the social revolution. The syndicate was governed by a moral order which established the form and content of individual obligations, obligations which provided the grounds for moral ascription, obligations calculated to govern the lives of heroes. Such lives would be lives of dedication and sacrifice in the service of an ideal. The pursuit of the ideal was to be undertaken with a singleness of purpose that required the challenge of violence as the test of commitment.

All these elements survived in Mussolini's mature social and political conceptions. What changed was the object of loyalty; class gave way to nation.[175] The struggle which provided the occasion for commitment was the struggle between nations rather than classes. The test of violence was provided by the revolutionary ascent to power and by war, that ultimate test of heroism and sacrifice. The nation was the vehicle of moral regeneration. The nation, as an ideal to be attained, was the organizing myth of the Fascist revolution and the charter myth of the Regime.[176]

Fascist theorists never succeeded in developing a fully convincing account of myth as it was employed in Fascist doctrine. Although the literature devoted to the concept was abundant, surprisingly little of it met the most elementary requirements of intellectual rigor. This was recognized by the best of the Fascist theoreticians themselves.[177] Certain characterizations can, however, be specified. It is clear that the concept originated with Sorel and Pareto. In this respect it is unfortunate that commentators have failed to take Fascists seriously when they identified the concept with that advanced by these social thinkers. Pareto clearly indicated that "social doctrine . . . if it is to have any influence, has to take the form of a 'myth.' "[178]

Fascists, in general, understood the myth to have imperative and exhortatory functions. Its language is the language of advocacy. As such its prescriptions and proscriptions are never the consequence of demonstration, its conclusions never the necessary consequence of inferences validly derived from any finite set of descriptive propositions. Myths are, in the Paretan sense, nonlogical products; they are essentially moral arguments and as such fall outside the domain of what Pareto, and the Fascists after him, characterized as logico-experimental reasoning. It is in this sense that myths constitute a distinct class of concerns. They rest inextricably on sentiments—attitudes that, while influenced by reasoning, are never their deductive consequence. Every myth rests on an attitudinal bias and every argument which concludes with an exhortation or delivers a normative judgment rests inextricably on an irreducible sentiment. In every argument having moral import there are words having a self-recommending quality. It is this quality which provides those arguments the capacity for negotiating between descriptive and normative propositions. One must, in any such discussion, presuppose a positive bias with respect to some general value, be it personal or collective survival, freedom, democracy, order self-fulfillment, glory, or profit (and so forth), before any argument can be joined. Thus Mussolini argued that before a convincing argument can be tendered for policy, one is compelled to assume that one's audience shares a sentiment favoring some admittedly vague but compelling values.[179] The implications of a value can be specified by increasingly precise definition and reasons can be advanced in its support, but the value must enjoy a given initial persuasive force before discussion can be meaningfully undertaken.[180] Thus, for example, in order to establish the moral primacy of the nation it is necessary to assume that one shares with one's interlocutor a positive sentiment favoring the fulfillment of the self. Argument then has the requisite foothold. One can then argue, employing descriptive and analytic propositions, that fulfillment of the self in any meaningful sense is impossible outside a well-ordered community of men, that language and thought, essential to the fulfillment of the self, is psychologically if not logically inconceivable outside the norm-governed speech relations that obtain only in communion with language users. These arguments, conjoined with descriptive propositions concerning the necessary conditions for the maintenance of pattern persistence and social organization, can conduce to judgments ascribing value to the state as the agency charged with the obligation of fostering and defending the normative order of the community. By virtue of this consideration—the inextricable necessity of assuming shared sentiment as a presupposition of meaningful discourse—social and political argument assumes a character that distinguishes it from arguments in the domain of science. Social and political arguments are inescapably nonlogical. By dint of such arguments a hierarchy of values is advanced for assigning obligations and making ascriptions of praise and blame. One has engendered a moral system. If the state acts as guardian of that system it is identified as "ethical." If the system is predicated on a central core of commitments to which all other commitments are subordinate, that core is identified as the *myth* of the system. The central myth of Fascism was the nation.

Mussolini, and Fascist theorists in general, maintained that every political system was animated, implicitly or explicitly, by an organizing and, under appropriate circumstances, a charter myth.[181] Thus, Oscar di Giamberardino maintained that "every social and political theory . . . has as its foundation a particular manner of conceiving man in his individuality and in his relationship with his kind. . . ."[182] It is such a conception of man, a conception formulated in deceptively descriptive terms, that issues in normative prescriptive and proscriptive judgments. Such a conception is a myth, not because it is untrue, but because a theoretical account *per se* is incapable of taking on the normative character requisite to social and political advocacy. Politics employs the language of advocacy predicated on the basis of shared sentiment, and consequently employs arguments intrinsically distinct from those of science which, ideally, is value-free.

This was the general manner of conceiving the political myth to be found in the best of Fascist theoretical literature. As such the analysis was, with some modification, Paretan and Sorelian. Like those accounts it harbored special difficulties. Both Canepa and Costamagna, for example, speak of the sentiment upon which political argument is predicated in terms of "intuitions" and "faith." In this sense, such sentiments have an irreducible quality very similar to Pareto's "residues" and Sorel's "intuitions." All such terms are vague and their immediate implication is that "intuitions," "faith," and "residues" are incorrigible. They are simply given. Although Fascists regularly *argued* in support of their own specific political myth, the use of terms like "intuition" and "faith" suggests a commitment insulated from any reasoned discourse. The further implication is that any difference in sentiment, understood as a "faith" or an incorrigible "intuition," could only be resolved by recourse to violence. This disability found expression in the writings of Fascist "mystics," who insisted upon a transrational accreditation of their knowledge claims.[183] Should their contention be accepted as true, there could be no rational way by virtue of which differences could be resolved. Opponents could only be treated as though they fell into two exhaustive categories: (1) those incorrigibly ignorant, and (2) those who were perverse. The former must remain forever under the tutelage of the enlightened and the latter are the legitimate objects of punishment.

There is some evidence, as we have indicated, that Mussolini himself did not entertain transrationalist presumptions. Mussolini was an anti-intellectualist, in the sense we have specified, but there is no evidence, and some counterevidence, that he was a transrationalist. Nonetheless, these issues were not definitively resolved during the Fascist period and, as we shall see, infected Fascist ideology even in its most substantial form.

Once the fundamental conceptions of Fascist doctrine are understood, the remainder of its rationale reveals itself as a restatement of those elements with which Mussolini identified in his youth. Most of those elements took on the form of descriptive and quasi-theoretical propositions concerned with the nature of man, singly and in collection. Most of them have become familiar to us in the literature devoted to the exposition of Fascist doctrine.

Man is essentially a social animal. As such, he is disposed to identify with a community of limited compass. This identification involves a developmental process commencing in earliest childhood, at which time norms are inculcated and the child inured to responsible social life. Hence Fascism's insistence upon the political organization of the young. The on-going process of socialization is largely effected by mimetism and suggestion. Hence Fascism's insistence upon the need for ritual and ceremony. In fact, Fascists argued that the moral life of the majority of individuals never matured beyond these stages; their values and preferences are never more than the reflection of those prevalent within the community with which they identify. Hence the Fascist insistence upon the responsibility of the state to control the media of communication so that the average citizen is exposed to a carefully controlled environment.

The Fascist assessment of man was far from flattering. Mussolini was quite graphic in his negative appraisal.[184] Left to their own devices, men succumb to their stupidities and their basest impulses. Only in an atmosphere of high moral tension, under the insistent goad of a demanding ideal and the discipline required for its realization, can men hope to transcend themselves. Such circumstances can only obtain under the disciplined control of a rigorously self-selected elite capable of imposing its will upon the elemental energies of the masses. Hence the Fascist insistence upon the unitary, hierarchical, and disciplined Party. The Party was to assume tutelary, educative, and moral obligations that were to create *homines novi*, living a new life in a new style and temper.[185]

Finally, if the masses are essentially inert, capable of providing only elemental energy in the service of directed change, any conception of popular sovereignty would be hazardous in principle. With the rejection of popular sovereignty, the abandonment of popular and uncontrolled elections follows. Fascism opted for a plebiscitary Bonapartism and such a system was compatible with its doctrinal convictions and its proto-Fascist traditions. The elite initiates change and then, after every technique for creating popular consensus has been employed, a plebiscite is undertaken, not to legitimize the change but to more effectively mobilize the masses in its service. Fascism was a mass-based movement of solidarity and it was far from indifferent to the masses. It recognized the introduction of the masses into the realm of political life to be one of the most novel features of the twentieth century. Its intention was to control the masses; to create, on the basis of a value consensus, a unified mass movement of support for the policies of the dirigent elite. It conceived the nation in terms of a vast army, capable of dedication, heroism, and ultimate victory only if competently marshalled and directed by a political elite.

It is difficult not to hear in all this the echo of the social and political convictions of the young Mussolini. The same themes recur, the same analyses are pursued, the same arguments are advanced, and the arguments are supported by the same appeals. The difference resides in their increasing systematization. Late in the Fascist period they were given what was perhaps their clearest and most uncompromising expression in Carlo Costamagna's *Dottrina del fascismo*. Fascism's rationale, he maintained, rested upon three fundamental conceptual considerations: the political formula, the minoritarian political class which sought its actuation, and the political mass through which it was effected.[186] All were considerations that occupied Mussolini in his youth. For, while the term *political formula* was borrowed from Mosca, Costamagna proceeded to identify it with the Paretan and Sorelian *myth*. His analysis of the function of myth was essentially that of the young Mussolini. The political formula, Costamagna maintained, was a stenographic and sometimes elliptical formula which expressed the ultimate moral basis upon which the legitimation of the power of a political class rests. Recognition, on the part of the political mass, of the legitimacy of rule entails the moral obligation of obedience to rule. Moreover, the political formula provides the hierarchy of values which order the moral universe of the individual. The political formula provides the content of imperatives and their normative force as well. In terms of the doctrinal language of Fascism, the nation was construed to be the real and ultimate source of all that was valuable and valued in the individual. The nation was understood to be essentially a norm-governed community. The state was the ultimate source of sanction which, in making the norms operative, made the nation a reality. In this fashion the state and the nation are identified with the expression *"stato-nazione."* Since the normative system is the constitutive moral substance of the people that constitute the content of the nation-state, the state and the people are identified with the expression *"stato-popolo."* Since the prevailing normative system is the product of a series of creative acts on the part of historic political elites, and the contemporary political elite is charged with the responsibility of sustaining and perpetuating that system and educating the masses to its responsibilities, that elite organized in a unitary party and that system can be identified with the expression *"stato-partito."* What results is a convenient set of substitutions that permits the nation to be identified with the state, the people and the party. This, in essence, is what Fascism meant by an "integral political system," or *totalitarianism.* In effect, what was implied was an identification of the ultimate real interests of the nation, the state, the party, and the individual, however divergent their apparent interests. Since the state and the party were effectively identified with the will of one man, Mussolini, he was, via the substitutions above indicated, identified with the nation. It was this identification which characterized Mussolini's leadership as "charismatic"; the Duce was conceived as the "living and active incarnation" of the nation.[187] This conception of charisma entered official

Fascist doctrine, for Michels identified the Regime as "charismatic government," and the official Party manual of 1936 maintained that "the 'charismatic' theory of the national society has found, in reality its first full realization in Fascism."[188] The Duce was Head of the Government and Prime Minister, originator of decree-laws, effective head of all the military, political, and economic institutions of the Regime, Commander of the National Militia, Head of the Grand Council of Fascism, Grand Marshall of the armed forces of the nation—and the physical embodiment of the nation.

The Fascist Synthesis

Fascist doctrine was largely Mussolini's own product. Some of its elements were vital constituents of Mussolini's social and political thought as early as 1904 (when he was twenty-one). As he himself indicated, however, those elements had themselves been constituents of other political and intellectual traditions.[189] The three principal doctrinal sources of the Fascist synthesis were, as we have seen, the antiparliamentarian sociological tradition of Gumplowicz, Mosca, and Pareto, the radical syndicalist tradition of Sorel, and the nationalist tradition of Corradini. A common provenience and a constellation of historic circumstances brought these traditions together in Fascism. What was lacking was a principle of unity, a concept which would articulate these elements into a defensible rationale. That unifying concept was the Gentilean notion of the state; and with its adoption, Fascism became the first frank totalitarian movement of the twentieth century.

The capstone of Fascist totalitarianism was the conception of the state. The doctrine of Fascism rests upon the moral priority of the nation and the state as its moral substance against which all other values are relative. Since this is the case, we have not dealt with the varying and various institutions through which the integration of the economy was effected.[190] The institutional structure of the Corporative State is far less significant than the hierarchy of values which provided its rationale. Fascists early made it plain that they would use whatever methods proved effective in their effort to integrate the economic, intellectual, and political life of the nation into one infrangible unity.[191]

The rationale calculated to support the entire system was expressed at various levels of sophistication. Its most mature expression is found in the works of Giovanni Gentile, who contributed to Fascist ideology the critical conception of the "ethical state." It is to Gentile, therefore, that one must have recourse for the social and political philosophy of Fascism in its most convincing and competent formulation. It is to his work we will now turn our attention.

CHAPTER FIVE

The Social and Political Philosophy of Fascism

ANY ATTEMPT at the reconstruction of Fascist social and political philosophy is beset by a number of considerations, at least two of which must be responsibly considered before exposition can begin. The first concern turns on the issue of whether Fascism had any specifically philosophical pretensions. It has been so frequently reiterated that Fascism was anti-intellectual, and consequently anti-philosophical, that such statements are accepted as truisms.[1] While such judgments are not entirely unfounded, much of the historical truth is sacrificed in their unqualified acceptance. A distinction must be made, as has already been suggested, between anti-intellectualism and the simple rejection of reasoned argument. Anti-intellectualism itself represents a system of thought. Mussolini and nascent Fascism early identified themselves with just such a system of thought when they took up pragmatism, as it was understood in Italy. Papini, whom we have seen exercised considerable influence on the development of Mussolini's thought, had been among the first to level the charge of "intellectualism" against philosophy. He understood the indictment to mean that philosophy, in attempting to force reality—the immediately given and urgent facts—into a Procrustean bed of abstract categories and concepts, had rendered itself sterile. Papini renounced the search for transempirical universals and advocated a return to particulars, to action in the world of men and things.[2] Prezzolini, equally influential in the development of Mussolini's thought, argued in a book reviewed by Mussolini in 1909 that Sorel's syndicalism had accomplished just that. Revolutionary syndicalism, as pragmatic activism, eschewed the intellectualism which sought to reduce the world to *a priori* categories and abstract universals. Syndicalism enjoined a responsible concern for contemporary men and their real and insistent problems. This did not mean, as Prezzolini indicated, that men should not reason concerning those problems, or that they should not employ the imagal trial and error techniques that characterize intelligence.[3] It meant the employment of a method that commenced with problems to be solved, problems which beset men as real beings in a real context. We have suggested that this was the manner in which Mussolini construed the relationship of reason to reality and that he therefore opted for a form of pragmatism that made the need for action the energy source for systematic thought, and made effective action the test of meaning and truth. However difficult this position may be to defend, it cannot be characterized as simply irrational, and it is antiphilosophical in only the special sense of assuming a special philosophical position *vis-a-vis* philosophy in general.

Reason was understood by those of pragmatic persuasion as instrumental in resolving real problems that beset mankind. The motives for acts were variously characterized as sentiments and needs. That a man chose to live rather than to die was understood as a sentiment; once the sentiment was given, reason was employed to safeguard and further survival. In this sense Italian pragmatism conceived action and will as precedent to reason (in a manner not unlike the Humean analysis).[4] The test of truth was instrumental efficacy—the ability to fulfill expectations.[5]

Italian pragmatism went into rapid eclipse in the years immediately preceding and following World War I. Papini and Prezzolini, for example, quickly went over to idealism as it had articulated itself in Italy since the turn of the century.[6] Ugo Spirito, in a volume written after World War II, traced the course Italian philosophy had taken from the commencement of the twentieth century. It began with an acritical positivism; rapidly transformed itself into pragmatism,[7] voluntarism, and relativism; to give way, immediately before World War I, to the neo-idealism of Croce and Gentile.[8] This is, as we have seen, essentially the course pursued by Mussolini himself. Beginning with the positivism of his early (1904) essay, *L'uomo e la divinità*, Mussolini developed through a period of emphatic pragmatism that continued from 1909 until 1921, thence into the relativism of the brief essay, "Relativismo e fascismo,"[9] to conclude, a few weeks later, in neo-idealism.[10]

That there was continuity in this process is suggested by the fact that the development was general rather than individual. Some of the most aggressive thinkers in Italy, including many of the radical and avant-garde intellectuals, had followed the same course. This is particularly true of the radical syndicalists, notably Arturo Labriola and A. O. Olivetti. Mussolini, in fact, reflected rather than anticipated the general current. In general, it can be argued that neo-idealism integrated much of what it considered viable in pragmatism and relativism, and the transition from one to the other to neo-idealism need not constitute evidence of fecklessness, but might equally well constitute an indication of development.[11]

Moreover, there was substantial political and tactical reason for making such a transition. Neo-idealism early identified itself with the nationalist currents in Italy. Syndicalism, in turn, had gradually absorbed neo-idealist elements. When Fascism found itself with a union of nationalist and syndicalist elements, neo-idealism constituted a common matrix in which all could find a place. Finally, it was the neo-idealist conception of the "*stato etico*" which united the maturing political commitments of Fascism into a defensible coherency.

The above considerations suggest (1) that although Fascist theoreticians remained confirmed anti-intellectualists,[12] they were not characteristically opposed to reasoning *per se* and, consequently, took the development of their social and political thought seriously, and (2) that neo-idealism, in some form, became fundamental to the system. The next section will be devoted to a closer examination of these claims.

Fascism and Philosophy For the purpose of analysis, a stipulative definition of *ideology* was offered which suggested that an ideology involved (1) an implicit or explicit value system, accompanied by (2) a relatively coherent system of generalizations about nature, society, and man, to which a group appeals to justify the issuance of social and political directive, prescriptions, and proscriptions, as well as (3) the formal and informal directives, prescriptions, and proscriptions themselves.[13] Historically, this definition accords well with distinctions made in practice by Fascist theoreticians. While there is considerable overlap between the constituents of Fascist ideology, a distinction can be made between the reasoned value system that subtends the more general doctrine and the doctrine itself. The former is properly the province of social and political philosophy. Speculative social and political philosophy provides the reasoned arguments in support of the values upon which doctrine ultimately rests. A mature ideology involves an explicit, argued commitment to a system of values about the "true ends of human existence" (a speculative social and political philosophy) that prompts the more or less systematic marshalling of facts and convictions about society and its organization (a doctrine) in the service of a practical social action program (prescriptive and proscriptive guides for behavior).

In 1908, as a young socialist theoretician, Mussolini identified what we have termed *ideology* as a "complete, harmonious and synthetic doctrine," one composed of three elements: ideal, doctrinal, and practical.[14] A quarter of a century later the *Dottrina del fascismo* argued that Fascist practice could not be understood without an appreciation of its conception of life—and that its conception of life, possessed of an ideal or philosophic content, found expression in a doctrine which was contingent, correlative to the exigencies of time and place.[15]

Mussolini seemed to have consistently maintained the distinction. In 1926 he had identified a ". . . zone reserved . . . to the meditation of the supreme ends of life . . . [which leads] inevitably to philosophy [which] . . . alone can illuminate science and lead it to the terrain of the universal idea."[16] Furthermore, he regularly made appeal to doctrine for the premises which subtend legislation, to refer the doctrine, in turn, to the ultimate values upon which it rested.[17] Thus, while he did indicate that the first *Fasci d'azione rivoluzionaria* of 1915 had no "specific doctrinal plan," having arisen out of the urgent need for action, he did insist that the intimations and anticipations of the *Fasci Italiani di Combattimento* of 1919 ultimately provided the foundation for an independent and self-sufficient system of political thought.[18]

In February, 1922, having made the transition to neo-idealism, Mussolini briefly reviewed the political developments in Italy since the beginning of the century. He indicated that

the political process was accompanied by a philosophical development: if it is true that matter remained for a century on the altars, today it is spirit that has taken its place. . . . When one says that God returns, one intends to say that the values of the spirit are returning.[19]

He thereafter regularly spoke of political systems as systems of values.[20] In 1932, the *Dottrina del fascismo* maintained that every political conception of the state must be fundamentally

. . . a conception of life: a philosophy or an intuition, a system of ideas that pursues a logical construction or collects itself in a vision or a faith, but always, at least virtually, an organic conception of the world. . . .[21]

Fascist theoreticians regularly reiterated these contentions. Canepa, in his systematic explication of Fascist doctrine, maintained that "not only Fascist doctrine, but all doctrines have at their base a given number of fundamental values."[22] He therefore distinguished social and political philosophy from other related and unrelated concerns by virtue of its normative character. He understood it to be qualitatively different from science because science is essentially amoral. Science is concerned with the ordering of phenomena by means of regularity analyses that ideally provide general laws that serve to increase predictive confidence and control. The "mature" or "exact" sciences have been remarkably successful in so ordering experience. The "immature" sciences of sociology, psychology, and all their attendant subsidiary disciplines have been less successful, but are nonetheless animated by the same purpose and the same lack of normative concern. They are concerned with nature, whether physical or human, as it is—not as it should be.[23]

Science thus provides an effective means of control and prediction. Probability assessments concerning specific courses of action can be made once a determination of the initial conditions and the regularities under which the phenomena under scrutiny can be subsumed has been undertaken. Such knowledge is essential to the attainment of ends, but it does not pretend to inform us what ends to choose. The choice of ends is the consequence of the exercise of significant choice which is a function of a system of values entertained by an individual or group, and a system of values rests tacitly or explicitly on a working theory of the "true ends of human existence." Where the commitment is explicit we legitimately speak of "moral philosophy," and where the commitment is implicit we might speak of "sentiment," or "attitudinal bias." Where such commitments function in a social and political context, providing the conceptual framework for the marshalling of facts, we speak of social and political philosophy in its familiar meaning. Such a systematically related set of arguments, based on a specific value hierarchy, was characterized by Canepa as a *sistema di dottrina*. Panunzio, in a similar appraisal, drew the distinction between the "'theoretical' substance of Fascism," and its "practical, active, more immediate, one might say more physical, mechanical side."[24] Luigi Volpicelli spoke of the "political values" of Fascism that remained constant throughout the course of its variable and contingent practice.[25] Elsewhere, in focusing on this same distinction, Volpicelli maintained that Fascism had clarified ". . . its own thought, its own philosophy, its own conception of values that are implicit in its revolutionary activities."[26]

Characteristically, doctrine entertains only implicit values. Values determine the range and relevance of factual material that doctrine will incorporate into its arguments, but the specific statement and reasoned defence of values is the distinguishing species trait of social and political philosophy.

Fascism's origins in anti-intellectualist traditions from pragmatism to neo-idealism led Fascist theoreticians to distinguish the rationale of Fascism from philosophy as it was "commonly understood."[27] Thus, Mussolini rejected philosophical systems that were "arbitrary mental constructions," as "arid, sterile, and antiproductive."[28] But the rejection of "preconceived doctrines,"[29] "dogmas,"[30] "ideological" or "mystical sublimations,"[31] could not be understood to entail a renunciation of the critical and systematic elaboration of a specifically Fascist social and political philosophy.[32]

In 1929, when Mussolini addressed the Seventh National Congress of Philosophy in Rome, he contended that it was necessary to philosophize (*fare della filosofia*); that the professional philosophers attending the Congress should not be surprised at his participation in their enterprise for he found their themes not only intrinsically interesting but essential "from the point of view of doctrine, which serves to animate the practical orientations of every-day activity."[33] In 1921, he charged philosophy with the obligation "of furnishing the brain with doctrines and solid convictions [that would] not . . . disarm action, but . . . strengthen it to render it more sapient."[34]

There is thus considerable evidence that thinking Fascists took the philosophical enterprise seriously. M. Marchello spoke of the "technical" doctrinal elaboration of "Fascist philosophical ideas" as the "central problem" of Fascist culture, while Gentile spoke of the necessity of rendering the political philosophy of Fascism clear and consistent, internally coherent, and defensible in the contest with opponents.[35] By 1935, the Library of the Italian Chamber of Deputies contained approximately ten thousand volumes devoted to Fascism in general, and over two thousand dealing specifically with its doctrine.[36] The enormous bulk of such material can only be offered as evidence of interest in the area; it does not testify to the quality of the product. As a matter of fact, Canepa dryly noted that "an imposing percentage" of such doctrinal material was "less than mediocre," composed as it was of books that were "imbecile, botched, confused . . . without seriousness or conviction."[37] Nonetheless, it is evident that by 1930 there was a serious concern for systematical ideological elaboration.

Giovanni Gentile and the Philosophy of Fascism

By 1921, Fascism had evolved a central core of concepts and theoretical commitments that distinguished it from alternate doctrinal systems. By 1927, its doctrine had been elaborated into a relatively coherent system. By 1930, Mussolini had apparently become convinced that Fascism required an explicit argued defense of its value system; in other words, a statement of its social and political philosophy. This statement was forthcoming in the *Dottrina del fascismo,* which appeared under the heading *"Fascismo"* in the appropriate place in the *Enciclopedia Italiana.*

The *Dottrina,* which appeared in 1932, was divided into two parts. One was entitled "Fundamental Ideas," and the other "Political and Social Doctrine." Both appeared over the name of Mussolini. Actually, Mussolini wrote only the latter. Giovanni Gentile was the author of the "Fundamental Ideas."[38] Mussolini chose him to be Fascism's philosophical spokesman, for the entire essay, including the philosophical portion written by Gentile, became the basis of the official philosophy of Fascism.[39] It was published over the objections of the Vatican, which recognized in it the principles of Actualism, the philosophy of Gentile, against which the Roman Catholic Church had inveighed for years.

During the Fascist period, the actual author of the "Fundamental Ideas" was never officially acknowledged and many Fascist thinkers resisted the association of the philosophy of Fascism with Gentile's Actualism.[40] With the recognition of Gentile as its author, such reservations are difficult to defend. The "Fundamental Ideas" are patently Actualist. Their author was the founder of Actualism and identified himself as a Fascist.[41] He conceived the Fascist State to be the embodiment of his principles.[42] In its service, he labored as its most renowned theorist, as a public administrator, as a member of the Fascist Grand Council and the fundamental Committee on Constitutional Reform; and as its protagonist, he was assassinated on the fifteenth of April, 1944. Mussolini himself reviewed Gentile's philosophical statement before its official publication and approved it even against the objections of powerful forces in Italy. Moreover, Actualism was compatible with whatever explicit *philosophical* postures Mussolini assumed after 1921.

There is a strong possibility that Mussolini had read something of Gentile's as early as 1908. In a conversation with Yvon De Begnac, Mussolini indicated that he could not say to what extent Gentile's ideas had influenced him during this early period, implying that he had read or heard of Gentile's ideas prior to that time.[43] That he had heard of Gentile is almost certain. Gentile's early essay on Marx was highly regarded among revolutionary syndicalists, and Arturo Labriola's interpretation of Marx's thought rests heavily on Gentile's account.[44] As we shall indicate, Gentile's ideas were relatively well known in socialist circles in general. Gentile's influence extended beyond the syndicalists, and by 1914, as has been indicated, both Prezzolini and Papini had come to accept some form of neo-idealism. With the outbreak of World War I, Gentile was among those academicians who actively called for intervention.[45] When the nationalists Francesco Coppola and Alfredo Rocco (later to become the Fascist Minister of Justice) founded the journal, *Politica*, in December, 1918, Gentile contributed to its first number. Gentile thus exercised considerable influence over those nationalist and syndicalist elements that most readily gravitated into the orbit of Fascism.[46] By 1921, Gentile was reasonably well known in the revolutionary, interventionist, and nationalist circles in which Mussolini was active.

In conversations with De Begnac, Mussolini provided a brief and essentially accurate account of his intellectual development. He indicated that he gradually disabused himself of the positivism of Roberto Ardigò, to take up a form of pragmatism and activism found in the works of Papini.[47] The traumatic experiences of World War I, he maintained, seemed to antiquate all these ideas. Papini and Sorel seemed to belong to a by-gone epoch. "It was Gentile," Mussolini went on to insist, "who prepared the road for those—like me—who wished to take it."[48] He indicated that the firm commitment to some form of neo-idealism was taken up in 1921. This was the time immediately prior to the organization of the *Partito Nazionale Fascista*, when he wrote to Michele Bianchi that Fascism required, on pain of extinction, a body of doctrine which he did not hesitate to call "the philosophy of Fascism."[49]

Mussolini, as has been suggested, entertained neo-idealist elements even before his break with official socialism. Benedetto Croce has indicated as much in his intellectual history of Italy devoted to this period.[50] But it was only in November, 1921, that Mussolini identified the theoretically crucial Fascist conception of the state with that of Gentile's *"stato etico."* In December of that year, before the Chamber, he made an explicit confession of neo-idealist commitment. Thus, while he maintained sharp reservations concerning the "metaphysics and lyricism" of neo-idealism,[51] it is clear that he harbored a qualified acceptance of some form of idealist epistemology and, more explicitly, some form of ethical idealism.[52]

Mussolini's relationship with Gentile prior to Gentile's appointment as Mussolini's Minister of Education in 1922 appears therefore, to have been more than casual.[53] Harris is probably wrong in suggesting that Mussolini's choice of Gentile as Minister was governed by "a coincidence of nomenclature," in that Gentile had founded the *Fascio di Educazione Nazionale,* a name which approximated Fascism.[54] The use of the name *"Fascio"* was far too common in Italy to weigh in any serious judgment. Mussolini had certainly heard of Gentile's work prior to 1922, and there is internal evidence that Mussolini had read at least parts of Gentile's *Teoria generale dello spirito come atto puro* before that time.[55] Mussolini's identification of the Fascist conception of the state with Gentile's *"stato etico"* certainly suggests more than casual familiarity with Gentile's thought. For the purposes of exposition, however, the most important consideration is the judgment of De Begnac, who claims that Gentile's Actualism served to explicate some, if not all, of the fundamental belief system of Fascism.[56] After 1922, Mussolini's (and consequently Fascism's) statements of the conceived relationship between the state, constituent associations, and individuals are almost always consistent with Gentile's views and Gentile's views were compatible with Fascist doctrine as it had developed. By 1922, nationalists of Gentilean persuasion, like Balbino Giuliano (who was later Minister of National Education) and Giuseppe Bottai (who became Minister of Corporations), had become principal Fascist theoreticians; even the thought of Alfredo Rocco, a Corradinian nationalist, advanced doctrinal views that in Harris' judgment, amounted "almost to a complete coincidence" with those of Gentile.[57]

It can be said with some confidence, therefore, that Gentile's Actualism was the final theoretical supplement to Fascism as a system of social and political thought. The currents of antiparliamentarianism, revolutionary syndicalism, and nationalism had merged with Actualism to produce the ideology of Fascism. Whatever philosophical and doctrinal disputes agitated Fascism thereafter (and there were many) were conducted within a system of thought that provided the rationale for the charter myth of the Regime.

Gentile was, in fact, by his own and by Mussolini's choosing, the philosopher of Fascism.

Fascism and Actualism   To identify Actualism as the philosophic rationale of Fascism is not to equate Fascism with Actualism. Fascist ideology included a doctrine, the essentials of which had been organized into a relatively well integrated system before 1921. Some implicit values obviously governed the collection of descriptive and theoretical propositions with which it identified; that Mussolini, and Fascism, harbored some values is clearly evident. The collection of relevant facts and their articulation into doctrine is determined by the values explicit or implicit in the system. Only determinate ends to be attained permit criteria for selection and a determination of relevance.[58] Thus, as early as 1904 (when he was twenty-one), Mussolini maintained: "Our morality says to man: behave in accordance with your conscience and fulfill oneself as man [*sii uomo*]!"[59] Forty years later, in his final apologetic for Fascism, Gentile wrote: "In seeking to define the moral law [it can be] expressed as strictly as possible in the admonition: fulfill oneself as man [*sii uomo*]."[60]

Such admonitions obviously have imperative, but little cognitive, force. To paraphrase Aristotle, such propositions are generally admitted, but obscure. It would be difficult to conceive of anyone seriously advocating that men fulfill themselves as anything other than man, but what it means for man to fulfill himself as man requires considerable elaboration. The commitment to the fulfillment of man as a value functions initially as nothing more than a certificate of rectitude and can count as initial evidence that its proponent is prepared to enter into intelligent dialogue. Once such an unobjectionable and porous sentiment is expressed, any definitional, descriptive and theoretical elaborations undertaken to impart it cognitive significance become the occasion for intelligent dispute. As these elaborations become more specific, the criteria for selection and relevance become increasingly evident. The system of thought articulates itself in an elaborate and complicated dialectical process.

It was in this general capacity that Actualism served Fascism.

By and large, it was left to Gentile to identify and explicate the fundamental values of Fascism and to undertake their reasoned defense. It was his account which appeared and reappeared in the most mature expressions of Fascist ideology, but this is not to say that Fascism was Actualism. Actualism was, in a critical sense, compatible with, and provided the reasoned arguments in support of, the essential values which subtended Fascism as a social and political system, but it would be anachronistic to identify the two. Fascism had, by the time of its association with Actualism, already developed a relatively mature doctrinal system, a collection of descriptive and theoretical commitments which had already given it a distinguishable and relatively stable character of its own. In this sense, Fascism contained Actualism, yet remained distinct from it. There is no evidence, for example, that Fascism ever identified with the metaphysics and epistemology of Actualism. There is no indication that the more esoteric and systematic doctrines of Actualism exercised any influence on Fascist thought. The elements of Actualism that Fascism absorbed were only those calculated to explicate implicit values and integrate its ideological constituents into a unified system. Those elements were almost exclusively those concerned with Gentile's conception of man and his corollary considerations devoted to political life in general and the nature of the state specifically.[61] These are the elements found in the "Fundamental Ideas" of the *Dottrina* and they became the essential nucleus of the belief system of Fascism.[62]

Gentile and the Fascist Conception of Man and Man's Freedom

Central to the tightly written formulations of the "Fundamental Ideas" is a conception of man, a normative conception which imparts ethical significance to Fascism's pronouncements concerning the state and the nation.[63] As a normative conception it is qualitatively distinct from those descriptive and theoretical propositions with which the sociological tradition from Gumplowicz to Michels provided Fascist doctrine. Such propositions had clear normative implications, but they remained tacit within the context of the disciplines whose product they were. Thus, while Gumplowicz conceived man as an essentially social animal, the conception was formulated for essentially explanatory and predictive purposes. Gentile's conception of man as a social animal[64] was developed because of its ethical significance. Both rejected the "individualistic" or "atomistic" conception of man central to the world view of classical liberalism, and both advanced essentially the same reasons for its rejection. Both conceived methodological individualism incapable of providing significant insight into some of the most imposing features of man's life in society. For the behavioral scientist those features were man's manifest behaviors. For Gentile they were his ethical comportment.

For Gentile indefeasible difficulties beset liberal political philosophy because the state and society are conceived as somehow antagonistic to the "self" or the "true individuality" of men.[65] The philosophers of classical liberalism contended that every law was an evil and all government a potential evil because they conceived law and governance a constraint on liberty and every constraint on liberty a moral infraction. For them, *liberty* meant essentially nothing more than the absence of constraint. So conceived, liberty was radically incompatible with law. Within such a conception, the absence of law was understood to afford the maximum formal occasions for freedom to act. According to Locke, the complete absence of law would leave men in "a state of perfect freedom to order their actions and dispose of their possessions and persons as they think fit. . . ."

Paradoxically, such theorists proceed to argue that a certain minimum of this antagonistic constraint is the *sine qua non* of the full development of freedom, without which human life is at best "nasty, brutish and short." According to the contractualist thesis, the "free individual" upon entering society is compelled to surrender some measure of his liberty to secure elementary rights. The initial issue, Gentile argued, is whether there is any effective liberty without the security of elementary right. Without freedom from violence, plunder, and death, without freedom from circumstances which render each the enemy of all and everyone the enemy of everyone else, is it at all meaningful to speak of freedom and liberty? Outside of society, the putative "natural freedom" of individuals to order their actions and dispose of their possessions and persons as they think fit diminishes conspicuously in factual significance.

We are faced, Gentile contended, with a singular circumstance: liberty (made significant by the acquisition of essential elementary rights) is enhanced, as it were, by subtraction, which suggests that "liberty" is not all of a piece, like a bolt of cloth, but rather something like a plant that flourishes only with judicious pruning. If the analogy is appropriate, the pruning could hardly be conceived as destructive of liberty. Restraints which foster the increased *effective* freedom of the individual, by insulating him from arbitrary and unpredictable violence and hindrance by affording him certain securities, cannot seriously be deprecated as antagonistic to liberty. The paradox, Gentile suggested arose out of the mistaken conception that the claims of "others" upon the "self" were destructive of the individual's liberty, to the neglect of the alternative thesis that the recognition of mutual claims enhances rather than diminishes effective freedom.

According to Gentile, the notion that man exists in perfect freedom anterior or exterior to society is simply a fiction.[66] Insofar as man is outside the organization of society with its system of reciprocal rules and obligations, he has no significant freedom. Outside of society man would be the subject of nature, not its master. He would be the enemy of all and friend of none. He would be threatened by persons and things alike. His would be a state of abject dependence. There would be no freedom, no security, for each man would be exposed to the open wrongs of every enemy. There would be no assurance of life, much less of liberty. The freedom that man is supposed to barter away in part upon entering society, in order to secure the remainder, has no real existence. It is, according to Gentile, an imaginary possession which then, by an imaginary transfer, is conveyed to society.

Gentile objected that only if the *individual* is conceived in a wholly abstract manner could such a notion arise at all.[67] So conceived, individuality, the peculiar genius and completeness of life, is not nourished and fostered by the rule-governed relations and obligations arising in society, but is ensconced in the recesses of an innermost particular self,[68] to be cherished in that recess, safe from the buffetings of a threatening external natural and social world. The only possible outcome of such a conviction was the kind of speculative and pious anarchism[69] that characterized nineteenth century liberal thought. The egocentric recluse, Thoreau, was taken to be the model of the fully developed self. Society was held to be the father of monotony and uniformity, the moral enemy of "human nature."

Gentile argued that freedom *from* violence and depredation was one of the *necessary conditions* of substantial freedom. Furthermore, the rule-governed association of men was not only a necessary condition for freedom, but *freedom could be meaningfully understood only as rule-governed behavior*. Ethical idealists have long argued that the concept of man as a rational animal implicitly entails a recognition that man is a social animal. Reasoning necessarily appeals to inter-subjective rules governing truth ascription and moral assessment. Reason is the name given to the rule-governed enterprise that involves all men who seek to establish truth and vindicate moral decisions. This can only be accomplished by appeals to criteria that prescind from personal interest, that are public and neutral, that are essentially social products. The establishment of truth status and the vindication of moral decisions involve socially established criteria, criteria that ideally withstand the scrutiny of the "universal power of reason that belongs alike to gods and men; to the dead, the living, and the still unborn."[70] That which binds all men together is their humanity expressed in rule-governed reason—in thought. Outside that spiritual communion they are animals without a conception of truth or morality and without the semblance of freedom. Thus Gentile maintained that the "human individual is not an atom. Immanent in the concept of an individual is the concept of society. . . . Man is, in an absolute sense, a political animal."[71] Man, as a spiritual agent, is an essentially social animal who finds freedom only in a rule-governed association with other men.

Consequently, for Gentile, it is thinking which uniquely characterizes men. Since thinking involves rule-governed language behavior and must be "social" in that sense, Gentile's model of man is normic in that it offers not only a collection of descriptive propositions characterizing what man *is*, but also a recommendation concerning what man *should be.* "Scrutinizing the content of the moral law," Gentile argued, ". . . one provides the most rigorous concept in the admonition: render yourself human. But for clarity's sake it is preferable to say . . . Think."[72] Man cannot judge ". . . according to his own private bias but as a man possessing the faculty of judgment that is common and proper to all men—the universal power of reason. . . . For at the root of the 'I' there is a 'We.' The community to which an individual belongs is the basis of his spiritual existence. . . ."[73] Whether the concern is with truth or morality, the standards of correct thought and behavior arise only in a rule-governed association of persons which provides the individual with "an internal law to which his every word, his every action must conform at the moment of utterance or performance."[74] There is no rule without a standard by virtue of which correctness or incorrectness could be applied and no standard for the followers of rules unless there are those whose assessments provide the necessary conditions for the ascriptions *correct* and *incorrect.*

Language is the essential and indissoluble link between men. As such it is a paradigm of social interrelations. If thought is man's essence, and language its expression, man can attain true humanity only in spiritual union with his fellows. Gentile finds the conception of man outside society not only an historical and empirical fiction, but literally senseless. An individual outside society would either be a god or an animal.[75] Man, to be truly man, must respond to the imperious voice of reason, the voice of the spiritual community in which reason can be said to manifest itself. To reason is to show oneself disposed to submit to the procedural rules required by the concept rule-following. Ideally, reasoning is understood to be universal, but Gentile argued that the reasoning of men is always conditioned by historic circumstances. It is conditioned by the historic language of the spiritual community of which the empiric individual is a member. It is conditioned by the morality of that community. It is conditioned by the technical circumstances in which it is pursued. Ideally, all reasoning prescinds from personal and local limitations, but such reasoning is an aspiration, a moral ideal. In reality, our thinking is always circumscribed by the brute facts of the world in which we live. Our actual thinking takes place in specific communities, in given familial, associational, and national circumstances.

Gentile argued that even science, for example, although *ideally* universal, is in fact always historically particular and national. The ascription *true* to specific scientific formulations always involves consideration of a determinate set of necessary conditions such as falsifiability (i.e., some determinate empirical operation can either confirm or infirm the subject proposition), relevance (i.e., the theoretical proposition answers the original question or is relevant to such a question), and predictive power (i.e., such a proposition would reveal that specific matters of fact would prove to be the case which were not known to be the case when the original proposition was formulated). But these considerations are not *sufficient* for truth ascription. At least one other consideration bears upon such an assessment, and that is the compatibility of the proposed proposition with a body of propositions having moral or cultural character. "Scientific criteria" alone do not determine the acceptance of a scientific proposition. The fitness of a proposition, or set of propositions, articulated as a theory to support desirable conduct of citizens or, more accurately, to support moral behavior, has always served as a consideration in scientific truth ascription. For Gentile, such an understanding is essential to the appreciation of science as a *national* enterprise.[76] Only if science is regarded either as a collection of facts or as a picture of some pre-existing objective reality could the conviction that science is independent of all moral and political considerations arise. Gentile, however, held that science is an instrument that serves to provide men with predictive competence in the service of ideal ends. Science, moreover, as an instrument, consists of a system of propositions and the operational definitions of its terms, and is governed by criteria for truth ascription. These criteria include simplicity, agreement with common sense, *and* fitness for supporting desirable human conduct. Thus it is not only the case that science is instrumental activity undertaken to realize some ideal end. A scientist must at some point in his enterprise validate—that is, accept or reject—a proffered hypothesis. But since no scientific proposition is ever exhaustively verified, the scientist is required to tender a judgment of sufficiency; he must, at some point, make a value judgment on the question of whether the evidence to support a scientific proposition is sufficiently strong to warrant a truth ascription. When such an ascription is made will depend upon the importance, in the ethical sense, of making such an ascription, and this is inevitably influenced by moral, political, religious, and possibly aesthetic considerations. In effect, Gentile insisted, science can never be absolutely independent of the national culture in which it flourishes.[77] In this sense, Gentile's conceptions were irreducibly historical and national. The pursuit of truth and morality was a dialectical and historical process conducted within the confines of a national community.

The individual is born into a national association, a complex system of interrelated rule-systems including civil and criminal codes, rules governing truth ascription in science, inculpation and exculpation in moral conduct and aesthetic judgment, and political order. These rule systems give continuity and identity to the individual's actions. His actions are rational, and hence not impulsive or instinctive, when the community of which he is a member can fathom the *point* of them—that is, when his actions are in conformity with rules. Since only actions which are rational and meaningful can be *chosen*, only rational acts are free. If freedom is acting in accordance with rules, then the meaning of freedom is logically dependent on a social context. That context, for Gentile, is the historical nation-state, which is the "[moral] substance of our human personality. . . . [The] state and the nation [are] intrinsic to and native to our very being insofar as the universal will of the state is coextensive with our concrete and actual ethical personality."[78]

Freedom as Rule-Governed Behavior

Freedom finds expression in action *chosen* because it conforms to explicitly or implicitly formulated rules. Reflex or instinctive action is not free because it is not chosen. Random or capricious action is not free because it does not conform to rules. Since reflex or instinctive action is not free, it is not subject to inculpation or exculpation. If random or capricious action is judged immoral, it is because we assume that the agent behaved in such a manner in willful violation of his understanding of established rules. Only the agent's explicit exposition of the *reasons* governing what we felt to be his random or capricious behavior could justify his behavior or infirm our judgment concerning his guilt. Gentile is arguing that action in clear conformity with socially established rules is never questioned because such actions satisfy traditional norms. We never ask someone why one speaks the language correctly, why one persists in driving within the speed limit, or why one accepts a scientific proposition when it conforms to accepted criteria for admissibility. Nor do we consider one's actions "coerced" when one acts in conformity to rules. One exemplifies what we mean by a free agent. One has chosen to behave in a certain way and we see the point of it. It is when one behaves otherwise that we question the behavior. We ask him to justify his actions as exemplifying rule-governed conduct. When a neologism is coined, reasons are given in its support. When someone speeds in traffic, he delivers reasons for the violation of rules, and those reasons appeal to intersubjective criteria—a set of socially acceptable values which the agent believes reveal the point of his conduct (e.g., a man who speeds in traffic to bring an injured child to a doctor expects that the point of his conduct will be apparent to a traffic officer who stops him). Apparent departures from rule-following conduct are justified only when they are revealed to be instances of such socially responsible conduct. If one fails to convince us of the legitimacy of his appeal, we charge him with moral or intellectual perversity.

Codified law is sanctioned by its rationality, its transparency—that is to say, the point of it.[79] Gentile argued that rules are vindicated only by indicating their function in the development of man as a free, moral, and rational agent. The submission to the rules governing language enhances the development of man as a personality. Submission to the rules governing morality and science has the same effect. Each rule system receives its sanction from the moral imperative: render oneself human, *sii uomo.*[80] Society can compel conformity to rule and law because they are understood to be conducive to this end. There is thus, in Gentile's system, an initial presumption in favor of tradition, rule, and law. Tradition, rule, and law are not initially required to justify themselves.[81] Those agents who choose to violate them are required to justify their infractions. Their justifications can appeal to changed conditions which require alterations in tradition, rule, or law, or they can demonstrate that a tradition, rule, or law impairs self-development. But in any event change must be justified before a communal court of appeals, before a court which follows the pre-established rules that license reasoning. Such procedures are always social. The individual who chooses a free and justifiable course of action never transcends the community, the *We* of which he is a member. That community has

a determinate historical existence having form: language and custom, institutions and laws, traditions and moral principles, memories and hopes. For man [such a community] is the nation; having a concrete personality, it is the state.[82]

Thus, for Gentile, a "person" is conceived as a complex whole, an ensemble of relations exemplified in communications of intelligence and law, without which a person cannot be said to be other than a material thing. A human person can never exist or be understood apart from the communal life which his essence requires. Society is the unity of the universal and the particular, and constitutes a whole which is greater than its immediate parts. Society is a rule-governed association which gives meaning to the parts which compose it at any particular time. The state is the effective will of the community, that sovereign source of sanction that is the ultimate support of the rule of law. In principle there is no law, rule, or custom that is outside its scope. Society and the state, for Gentile and for Fascist ethicists in general, had, therefore, a logical, factual, and moral priority over the individuals of whom it was composed.[83] This conception accords an ethical priority to the rule-governed association outside of which humanity is impossible and outside of which significant freedom is inconceivable. It rests on a normic model of man as a rule-following animal and tenders an initial presumption in favor of the obedience of rules and the rule-governed community.[84] Violation of established law, disobedience of rules, thoughtless or willful neglect of responsibility always demands an accounting. Consequently, Fascist ethicists interpret the liberal, individualist principle "all restraint, qua restraint, is an evil," with its initial presumption in favor of an individual with "reasons," "rights," and "freedoms" peculiar to himself and independent of society, as not only mistaken, but profoundly immoral —a consequence, Fascists insist, of liberalism's radically egoistic model of man.

Gentile maintains that the individual who seeks to absent himself from rules and obligations laid upon him by positive law and social sanction in the historic national community is morally required to justify his abstention. This follows from Gentile's understanding of man. Man is conceived to be free only in the sense that his choices are rational and rationality is understood to necessarily entail conditions which make rule-following possible. Thus, the existence of rule-governed associations in which those preconditions are realized is logically prior to the individual who accedes to rationality and morality only within their confines. The community therefore enjoys a moral privilege, for its rules make cognitive and moral choice possible, and only choice can make man what he is and should be. The disposition to violate social rules and codified law and absent oneself from one's obligations demands an accounting. Such a formal, or procedural, maxim does not function as a premise in a deductive argument that would permit us to decide whether any given justification is adequate, but it does indicate where the responsibility for justification lies. Outside the strict confines of social and political philosophy, such a recommendation fosters a *doctrinal bias* in favor of the collectivity.

Central to Gentile's social and political philosophy is a recommended definition of man supported by analytic and factual argument. His recommended definition provides an initial presumption in favor of the collectivity, over and against the individual, as a focus of interest and privilege. Totalitarian systems, predicated on the priority of the collectivity rather than the individual, tend, as a consequence, to develop structuralist, functionalist, and organicistic conceptions of society. The nation is conceived as an organic or functional whole in which individuals find their place, in which they "define" themselves. The state is understood to be the express will of such an organic whole, representing the will of the whole people as distinct from the immediate and empirical will of the individuals composing it.[85] Such a will transcends in scope and interest the will of individuals, classes, or categories. It is a will which includes the express will of antecedent individuals, classes, or categories (the logical presupposition of *established* rules), and must attempt to assess the interests of the future collectivity (establishing the rules which will provide the basis for future choice).

Gentile, therefore, sees no necessary conflict between freedom and the obedience to the rules and laws of a given national community.[86] Rational laws and rules constrain only the momentary and immediate will. The hindrance to impulse is not a limitation of liberty; it is the necessary condition for the effective operation of the particular individual's true or rational will. It is a discipline required by the very conception of freedom. Rules and law are given; they are the preformed moral realm into which the individual is born. As aspects of the moral realm, rule-systems must be continually scrutinized, reassessed, and modified, but the system in its entirety cannot, at any one time, he rejected. The very logic of judgment requires that the critic would have to accept some, in fact much, of the pre-established rules (the rules of language, of truth ascription, of value ascription, and so forth). In this sense, Gentile and other Fascist ethicists were traditionalist and conservative. Man commences his rational and moral life as the denizen of a specific historic community.[87] He rejects aspects of that community's prescriptions and proscriptions only when armed with sufficient reason. Man in the mythical state of nature, devoid of the rule-system governing human association, is a man devoid of human contacts, devoid of language,[88] thought, and morality; devoid not only of freedom, and hence morality, but of humanity itself. As men increase the complexity of their law-governed relations they correspondingly increase their humanity and their freedom. Society is the discipline which affords true liberty because it constitutes the material and logical prerequisites of reason without which there can be no humanity, much less freedom. As such, society speaks with authority and demands discipline.[89] It is the authority and the discipline which man, as a true person, would lay upon himself.[90] It is his rational will made concrete. In its concrete actuality that embodied will is the historic state.[91]

The state not only protects the individual's life and property, but it is also the medium of transmission of funded knowledge, traditions, rules, and laws—the spiritual patrimony that makes man what he is. There cannot be, consequently, any consistent appeal to rights or freedoms apart from the state, for every such appeal must be couched in terms of reasons which appeal to the socially established rules and values licensing such reasoning. The claimant is not arguing that he possesses rights or freedoms apart from the community and its embodiment in the state. What he is arguing is that the historical, determinate state is not the *ideal* state.[92] The claimant is advancing a virtual, or ideal, state against the existing state. The appeal he is making is not to anything apart from the state, but to a state which he conceives would more adequately embody the collective will. Thus Gentile, and Fascist theorists in general, argued that rights and freedoms cannot be conceived apart from the state.[93] Any alternative course, i.e., conceiving individuals possessed of "inalienable" or "natural" rights, courts paradox and confusion. If men are understood to possess a "natural right" to "life, liberty and the pursuit of happiness," it would be strange that the state can, in fact, oblige individual men to lay down their lives in the defense of the community, imprison individual men for infractions of social rules, and define the legitimate happiness that men can pursue. None of these "inalienable" rights are inalienable. They are concessions made by the state.[94]

Gentile and Fascist Totalitarianism

The logic of Gentile's rationale requires (irrespective of qualifications[95]) that the *individual,* the *people,* the *party,* the *nation,* and the *state* be, in some sense, substitution instances of each other. Thus Gentile held that "the state is the very personality of the individual," while being at the same time the "will of the nation."[96] The Party, in turn, he argued, "ceases to be *a* party . . . and as an organization of the great majority of the nation or of the politically significant masses of the Italian people becomes the nation. . . ."[97] The individual, the Party, the people, the nation, and the state constitute an historic rule-governed moral association in which ultimate individual and collective interests conflate. In some sense the individual *is* the collectivity as people, nation, or state.[98] By virtue of this rationale, Fascist theorists could argue that "in Fascist ethics the end of society is identical with that of man;

the same reason that affords norms for individual life provides norms for social life. . . ."[99] In Gentile's words,

The human individual is not an atom. Immanent in the concept of an individual is the concept of society. . . . Only this identity can account for the necessary and intrinsic relation between the two terms of the synthesis which requires that the concept of one term must involve the concept of the other. . . . I hope that the importance of this concept will escape no one, for in my judgment it is the keystone of the great edifice of human society.[100]

Political philosophers have long recognized the legitimacy of public restraint applied to the momentary zeal of individuals when it might involve the individual's own injury. The right to restrain individual action is sanctioned by the restraining agencies acting to effect what is understood to be the *real* will of the individuals involved. Those agencies compel the individual to act as he would act were his will not temporarily clouded by enthusiasm or passion.[101] This real will, essential to the real or ultimate interests of the individual, is understood to be occasionally at variance with the individual's immediate impulse. The state has the moral right to act in the name of that will in restraining the individual. Conjoined with the conviction that a minority can speak for that real will, such an analysis produces the rationale of Fascism. On such occasions the will of the state as expressed by a minority is understood to be identical with the real will of the individual. That minority represents the real will of the individual—identical with his own were his reason not distracted.[102] At certain critical junctures in the life of the nation that universal will can find itself "incarnated and revealed in a few or a single individual. . . ."[103]

Such a will can manifest the real will of an entire people divested of the contingencies of class and category—a will which attempts to express the real and ultimate will of the entire spiritual community. The minority of men who express this will as leaders of a particular historic community speak for their nation and for their epoch.[104] They are possessed of the "political genius" which commands the assent of the common rational will. They not only resolve the concrete problems of a given time and place but are inspired by a view of life which invokes the assent of the masses.

This view of life is expressed in an appropriate "political formula" which expresses the "will of a political elite."[105]

This was the social and political philosophy which Gentile brought to Fascism. In it the nationalism and statism of Fascism found argued defense. In it elitism and anti-individualism were provided their rationale. It afforded the portentous logic of substitutions which conceived the individual, people, party, nation, and state as a single moral entity having but one constellation of *ultimate* interests. It was the first, and perhaps only, explicit argued defense of the charismatic totalitarianism of the twentieth century. It was this social and political philosophy to which Gentile gave expression in the "Fundamental Ideas" of the *Dottrina*.

Man, as Fascism conceives him [*L'uomo del fascismo*], is an individual who is at once nation and fatherland, the moral law which binds . . . individuals and generations. . . . [to] an objective will that transcends the particular individual and elevates him to conscious membership in a spiritual community. . . . Fascism is an historical conception in which man is not what he is, except as a function of the spiritual process in which he participates, in his family and social group, in the nation and history. . . . Hence the great value of tradition in memories, in language, in rules of social life. Outside of history man is nothing. . . . Liberalism negated the state in the interests of the particular individual; Fascism reaffirms the state as the true reality of the individual. And if liberty is to be attributed to real man, and not to that abstraction of individualistic liberalism, Fascism is for liberty. It is for the only liberty that can be a serious thing, the liberty of the state and the individual in the state, since for the Fascist all is in the state and nothing human or spiritual exists, or much less has value, outside the state. In this sense, Fascism is totalitarian and the Fascist State, the synthesis and unity of all values, interprets, develops, and gives power to every aspect of the life of the people. . . . Grouped in accordance with their several interests, individuals are classes; they are trade unions according to their several economic activities; but they are first and foremost the state. The state is not therefore a mere aggregate, the sum of individuals composing the majority . . . [but] a people conceived . . . qualitatively, not quantitatively, as the idea that is more powerful because more moral, more coherent, truer; but manifests itself in the people as the consciousness and will of the minority, if not, indeed, of one. [This] idea tends to realize itself in the consciousness and will of all. . . . The nation as state is an ethical reality. . . .[106]

By 1932, Fascism had thus made explicit its social and political philosophy, and it was to this social and political philosophy that Fascist legislation and Fascist policy made ultimate recourse. The doctrinal principles of the organismic conception of the nation, class collaboration, the unitary party, and totalitarianism find support in the justificatory arguments marshalled in the social and political philosophy of Giovanni Gentile.

Gentile and Fascist Criticism: The Concept of Consent

If Gentile provided Fascism its rationale, he also provided its conscience. This was evident throughout the Fascist period and frequently made him the object of bitter Fascist criticism. This was so much so that at the time of his assassination rumor had it that he was killed by Fascist "intransigents." This was not the case, but it does indicate the intensity of anti-Gentilean opposition among some Fascist elements. Gentile was, in fact, subject to Fascist criticism throughout his twenty years of activity as a Fascist apologist. Theoreticians of the first rank, like Panunzio and Costamagna, remained his critics throughout the entire period.

There are a number of substantial philosophical criticisms of Actualism as a system of thought, and it cannot be our purpose here to review, analyze, rebut, or corroborate such accounts.[107] Our present concern is Fascism, and Actualism is dealt with only as the rationale of Fascism. Since this is the case, the discussion here will be restricted almost exclusively to Fascist criticisms of Actualism, for such criticism is the most instructive for our purposes. It tells us a great deal about Fascism.

Most Fascist criticism turned on what was considered to be Gentile's excessive rationalism. Costamagna, one of the most mature of the Fascist critics, directed his criticism against the "formalism" and "intellectualism" that characterized neo-idealism,[108] because he felt that "rational thought" could not provide the ultimate basis for action. This criticism is at once curious and vague. Gentile certainly admitted that reason, as such, could not provide the grounds for action. He argued that a "myth," a "faith in a moral reality," was the ultimate motive force of spiritual life and he never hesitated to call Actualism and Fascism fundamentally "religious" belief systems, inveighing against those "intellectualistic" systems which sundered "thought from action, science from life, the brain from the heart and theory from practice. . . ."[109] He regularly alluded to the "sentiment" which was the initial evidence of a spiritual communion, the love of family, religion, and fatherland.[110] Sentiment, for Gentile as well as Mussolini was "prior to thought and the basis of it."[111] But sentiment was not self-confirming. Sentiment was the initial moment of spiritual life, but reason that manifested itself in positive action was its test. This was true of Actualism, and it was also true of Gentile's social and political views. Gentile insisted that if the state were to have moral worth it must not be only an empirical fact. As a fact the state and the order it maintains constitute a pre-formed moral world into which the moral agent is simply thrust. It assumes moral significance only when the individual is *persuaded* or persuades himself that the state is *his* state. Only then does the state become a moral reality for the individual. The individual *consents* to rule and thereby lays the laws upon himself.[112] Gentile maintained,

The government . . . makes the laws and sees to their observance; and the governed, in order to be governed, presuppose its activity. And in the abstract such is the case. But just as positive law is negated in actual ethical action, so every opposition between the government and the governed is abolished with the consent of the latter, without which the government cannot prevail. This consent can be spontaneous or coerced. And the morality of the state, through which the government exercises its authority, requires a maximum of spontaneity and a minimum of coercion. . . .[113]

"Persuasion" and "consent" are terms that can only be appropriately applied in contexts where intellectual freedom obtains. Men are persuaded to consent without coercion only by good reasons. Gentile maintained,

For us a man is human only when we believe we can influence him through speech, which appeals to reason, which is the privilege of human beings, and to those sentiments which, as the prerogative of man, are characterized as human, which together seem to be the base upon which reason founds itself.[114]

Thus persuasion, for Gentile, involved an appeal to reason and human sentiment. Sentiment, as we have suggested, is the initial impulse of spiritual life. Spiritual life is not "the natural life, simply instinctive, but it is life governed by thought. . . [for] man is a thinking being."[115] Thus Gentile felt that the citizen could be convinced that the state constituted the essence of his moral personality. Gentile maintained that even the delinquent could be brought to the realization that the historically constituted state exists as it does "for good reasons."[116] The state, he insisted, is not the result of individual caprice, nor the effect of a combination of arbitrary actions, the state is reason, in which we participate through reflection.[117] The process by virtue of which the individual is made to perceive the essential rationality of the state and by which he is brought to consent to rule is long and vexatious. Gentile insisted,

The human world is filled with children and he who lacks patience and disdains the nonsense he hears spoken all around him . . . can swing his mace. But to what effect? One does not teach nor disseminate the truth in such fashion; the kingdom of the spirit that we would construct remains forever faulted.[118]

It is evident that such a conception would prove tedious to a revolutionary movement of solidarity, a movement that aspired to national consensus. In his most consistent arguments, Gentile conceived that consensus as the product of reasoned dialogue, not the artifact of a monopoly of information and propaganda media. In 1925, when he was actively concerned with educational reform in Italy, he advocated the organization of Fascist universities which would act as nuclei from which the new political conceptions would gradually radiate. He foresaw the conquest of Fascist thought as a gradual process that would genuinely win the hearts and minds of the Italian people while at the same time respecting those who could not, in honesty, adhere to the new Regime.[119] It was the same doctrine he advocated in 1943 with his commitment to toleration. He denounced dogma and the attempt to mechanically impose conformity upon men.[120] He opposed the intolerance that was the consequence of a knowledge claim that was not "rationally acquired," but was conceived as licensed by an "immediate gift of grace," an "unsought illumination." These were the convictions which inspired Gentile's notion of "cultural imperialism," the triumph of Fascist ideas without the military conquest of a single square kilometer of foreign soil. Expansion, Gentile argued, is the natural thrust of the vital spirit. But its conquests are spiritual. No true conquest can result from violence or the imposition of an unreasoning dogma. Violence is, at best, a defense against those we no longer can acknowledge as rational. Dogma is the refuge of the unthinking and obtuse.

These convictions could only generate resistance on the part of many Fascists. The most immediate response was to deny the sovereignty of reason. Thus, Costamagna's objections to Gentile became a counterclaim which made truth the result of an "inspiration," which pretended to a "metarational and metaphilosophical" source of knowledge.[121] Such inspiration was intransigent in the face of opposition. A distinction could be drawn, as Gentile indicated, between the "elect" and the "damned." The state would no longer have a pedagogical function, but would assume the guise of a disciplinarian. Individuals could no longer be convinced that the state was the proper object of loyalty because it constituted the very moral substance of the self. The state would be conceived an end in itself, obliged to compel individuals to sacrifice for ends extrinsic to themselves. "[It] is necessary," Costamagna argued, "to advance an end extrinsic to the individual and therefore to impose a 'national order.' That end is determined by the magistracy of a 'spiritual intuition.'"[122]

Possessed of privileged truths, those who act in the capacity of the state can *command* obedience. Their knowledge claims, which legitimize their rule, are certified by references to "intuitions" and "inspiration," forever insulated against scrutiny and refutation. Such a system aspires to produce a population inured to obedience and disciplined to obligations it can never really understand.

The most emphatic expression of this kind of mysticism is found in the works of Julius Evola. He appealed to government by the *Wise*, those possessed of a "sacred wisdom," that comes about as a consequence of "interior transformation"; a wisdom that defies thought and speech, that "cannot be taught by books or in universities or transmitted through words. . . ."[123] He anticipated a caste of rulers, a hierarchy of power, which possessed this occult, irrefutable, and incommunicable wisdom.

Evola remained an implacable opponent of Gentile throughout the Fascist period and, since he survived the war, has continued his shrill polemic against his defunct opponent.[124] His significance is that he represented this kind of opposition to Gentile's interpretation of Fascism. In all probability, this mysticism had its origins in the intuitionism that found its way into syndicalism through Sorel and Bergson. This current of transrationalism was present in Fascism and infected the thought of men as capable as Costamagna. The advantages of transrationalism are obvious, and there were many Fascists prepared to opt for such an epistemology in order to provide the legitimation of minority rule.

There is no evidence that Mussolini ever tendered transrational knowledge claims. His personal position in this respect was not incompatible with that of Gentile. The distinction between them originated in the fact that Mussolini had articulated a fairly consistent set of descriptive and theoretical propositions concerning man in general that necessarily influenced his conception of the relationship between the governors and the governed. In 1924, he delivered a candid appraisal of man as he understood him. Man, Mussolini insisted, is a creature driven by his crassest impulses, more addicted to material goods than to his own kin. Driven by his egoism, man has an inherent disposition to avoid obligations, disobey the laws, and avoid service to his community. Under the influence of these unrestrained impulses society tends to disintegrate. It is left to government to "educate his passions, his egoisms, his interests to a scope of a general order that almost always transcends those of the individual. . . ."[125] Under such circumstances there can be no government which is exclusively consensual. "There are few —heroes and saints—prepared to sacrifice their immediate selves on the altar of the state. All the rest remain in a state of potential rebellion against the state."[126] Twenty years later, in his private reflections after the coup of 1943, Mussolini maintained that of the three aspects of the soul that Plato attributed to men, the masses "lacked the highest, the intellective."[127] They possessed the vegetative and sensitive faculties, but lacked the requisite for true self-governance.

Fascism came to Actualism already possessed of a stable collection of such judgments concerning man and society. These judgments were essentially those of Mussolini as he had formulated them from his own experience and the prevailing descriptive and theoretical literature of his time. That experience and that literature tended to create in him a pervasive pessimism concerning mankind taken individually or collectively. He shared this pessimism with Gumplowicz, Pareto, Mosca, Sorel, and Michels. His prior assessment could only influence his overt conduct and his appraisal of the realism of Actualism's moral aspirations. Any practical judgment which serves as a guide to conduct will be the quasi-deductive consequence of the antecedent normative and synthetic judgments which constitute its grounds. In Mussolini's case, Gentile's moral ideals could very well have functioned as an ideal limit toward which men aspire but, conjoined with the radical perversity and egoism of men, those ideals could only produce a conception of government conceived more in the guise of a disciplinarian than a teacher.

It is clear that for Gentile the state was essentially a teacher,[128] while for Mussolini the state was essentially a disciplinarian. For Mussolini the restoration of "principles and values" could only be the consequence of restoring the lost virtues of "devotion and discipline."[129] For Gentile, the principal tasks of the state were pedagogical: to elicit consensus through persuasion. For Mussolini the task was the inculcation of civic virtue, that "temperance" recommended by Plato which produces in ordinary men the recognition that they must be ruled.[130] The techniques for inculcating such moral virtue (in the Aristotelean sense) were essentially non-rational appeals that took on the characteristic forms of ritual and ceremony, imitation and habit, and the constant reiteration of elemental myths—truths formulated with the simplicity and elegance calculated to capture the popular imagination. Ideally, such myths should be true, summary, and elliptical expressions of complex truths that, fully articulated, are too difficult for the popular mind. Thus, there were at least two conceptions of *myth* in Fascist social and political thought: (1) myth as a systematic collection of propositions subtended by one or more normative commitments, providing the initial criteria of relevance and the impulse for articulation (i.e., the individual must accede to some primitive and initial values if any social and political discussion is to gain a foothold); and (2) myth as a stenographic account of a more elaborate social and political conception, prepared specifically to induce the general masses to obedience (an organizing or charter myth). Fascist theorists move freely between these two interpretations.

A third conception of *myth* was the one advanced by the transrationalists. For them, a myth was in some sense truer than true, the product of privileged insight that defied explication by reason. This third interpretation was that of theoreticians such as Evola, and seems to have been clearly rejected by Mussolini, however convenient it might have been.[131] He specifically renounced that mysticism which advanced truth claims won without recourse to reason,[132] but this conception of the myth, nonetheless, made its regular appearance in Fascist apologetics. Mario Palmieri expressed it in the following manner:

Vainly we strive through observation, experimentation, analysis, logic, to reach the core of being. The highest truths are hidden from us. Only that magic flash of a moment of supreme intuition, that flash which renders for an instant man akin to God, can reveal the Truth. And we shall never know the ecstasy of that moment. The supreme gifts of synthesis, intuition, revelation, are denied to us; they belong rightly to the hero and to none other.[133]

Clearly, this is at odds with Gentile's political philosophy if it is offered as a rationale for political obedience. For Gentile, no man can be morally compelled to obedience by another man's mystic intuition of *Truth*. Truth, and the political form in which it finds expression, is the product of each man's growing spiritual insight, a process eminently individual and pre-eminently rational (though governed by social norms). Thus, Palmieri's suggestion that the "first principle of the Fascist conduct of life rests upon a mystic belief of the oneness of all living beings . . ."[134] is a poor rendering of Gentile's argument that the fullness of self requires a recognition that extrapersonal relations with things, but primarily with other persons, constitute elements of the truer and expanded self.

Gentile and Fascist Criticism: The Rationale of Dictatorship

Gentile provided Fascism with its most coherent and defensible normative rationale. His moral imperative, *sii uomo!* enjoys the evident advantage of being *prima facie* self-recommending. The admonition to fulfill oneself is an obligation which commends itself to the individual without argument. It serves as a normative premise that, conjoined with analytic and descriptive propositions, permits the issuance of prescriptions and proscriptions. Even Gentile's opponents, when developing a defense of Fascism's normative principles, had recourse to Gentilean arguments. Costamagna maintained,

. . . [For] Fascism the state, insofar as it answers the positive and practical exigencies of organization, is the indispensable condition for the development . . . of the individual personality and the maintenance of moral institutions within the human community.

The state is understood to possess ethical character because

it provides the necessary, if not sufficient, conditions for the existence and development of the moral personality of the individual. . . . [It] conforms to the natural end of man, that of actuating his essential personality. . . .[135]

Standard Fascist apologetics iterated and reiterated variations of Gentile's arguments. One representative account read:

The state is conceived as the universal ethical will, as the creative foundation of law, as educator of the spirit, the soul of the individual's soul. . . . The individual discovers his personality in the nation. . . . In such a supreme vision, the individual incarnates and confounds himself in the nation, recognizing as liberty the harmony of the ideal which is that of the individual and the . . . nation.[136]

The hierarchy of values that characterized Fascist thought rested on the self-recommending admonition to fulfill oneself. A set of propositions, both definitional and descriptive, specified the conditions for such fulfillment. Among them, the proposition that man is, by nature, a social animal led to a commitment to the nation as the most viable contemporary human association and to the state as its organizing will, the preformed moral order which provides the elemental spiritual substance of the self. Ideally, all men must be awakened to the reasoned awareness of the moral identity of individual and collective interests. But since Fascism came to ethical idealism already convinced of the essential moral and intellectual frailty of man,[137] the role of nonrational appeals and compulsion became imposing. Man, outside the firm and directive tutelage of an inspired and enlightened elite, remains debased, caught up in the trammels of material and sensual concerns. Only an aristocracy of will and intelligence can discipline the refractory masses to moral purposes that transcend the circle of their immediate concerns. Such an aristocracy habituates the masses to virtue which they could never otherwise attain.

All of this followed the account already found in Oriani's *La rivolta ideale*, that Mussolini, as a youth, found so "magnificent," and that he later identified as having nourished Fascism.[138] Oriani maintained,

Man is so constituted that truth, when it cannot arise from the core of his spirit, enters from without and descends upon him; man sees and repeats without understanding; he imitates, habituates himself to doing that which others would have persuaded him to do. Mimetism is the law of education for inferiors.[139]

This conception, consonant with the entire tradition (from Gumplowicz to Sorel) in which Mussolini matured, remained constant in Fascist social and political thought. The state was to habituate the masses to virtue. In general, without the discipline of the state men are incapable of attaining the sublimity of true spirituality. Left to their own devices, the masses gravitate toward the meanest mediocrity, driven by passion, suggestibility, and egotism.[140] Uneducated to political life, divested of the "order and guidance of the state and a government," mankind takes on that "chaotic, anarchic and amoral form" characteristic of the masses.[141] At best, Mussolini argued, "the people are that part of the nation that does not know what it wants . . . [that is] incapable of governing itself."[142]

Like all arguments in social and political philosophy, the vindications offered by Fascists were composed of normative and descriptive propositions. The admonition to fulfill oneself is the affirmation

232

of a value. The strength of such an affirmation is that it is self-recommending. Conjoined with factual propositions about the character of man, the implications of such an admonition became increasingly evident. To satisfy the normative requirements of the obligations they imposed upon themselves and the nation, Fascists insisted upon an *epistemarchy,* the rule of an exiguous aristocracy of intelligence and will, the "sublime warriors" sought by Sorel.[143] Thus, in 1938, Pietro Ubaldi identified the task of Fascism as "the creation of a new humanity," the *homines novi* of Sorel. But the accomplishment of such a task required a real awareness of the "laws of collective psychology," which indicate that

. . . the response of the majority stabilizes itself not at the level of the collective mean, but at that of the most inferior. The problem is psychological, not mathematical: majority opinion cannot constitute the criterion of truth; such opinion is its debasement. Social life requires the tutelage of the less developed by the more highly developed, in order to indicate to them the path to follow. The majority cannot understand, select, and decide the best course; it can only follow. . . . To govern, certain special qualities and gifts are necessary: an inclusive vision, a profound intuition, a supreme will, rectitude, and sacrifice, qualities possessed only by the exceptional, never by the mass. The exceptional must be lifted above the mass in order to elevate them. The people . . . have need of education. . . . These are the laws of nature. The collective mind is akin to that of a minor, unconscious of the ultimate goals, which only a leader can envision. He that is possessed of that vision has the responsibility of imposing that vision upon those who are unseeing. It is obvious that, for a child, certain ends must be imposed upon him, even with force if necessary, should his ignorance make this necessary.[144]

It was this collection of descriptive generalizations that Fascists advanced as justification for the series of enactments that transformed the parliamentary regime of Italy into a dictatorship. Beginning with the extension of the powers and prerogatives of the executive that made him responsible only to the King, through the enabling legislation of 1926 that gave the executive the power to issue decree-laws and the total integration of the productive categories of the nation beneath what Fascists themselves called "the dictatorial power which occupies the vertex of the Fascist Regime," Fascism exemplified its social and political convictions in manifest practice.[145] The power of issuing legislation was transferred from pre-revolutionary legislative channels to the Head of the Government. After 1928, the selection of members of the modified Chamber of Deputies was the result of a mixed system of popular nomination and Party confirmation and, finally, plebiscitary approval of a "national list." In no serious sense could Fascism be considered a regime of popular representation, if the term is understood in the manner common to parliamentary political systems. Throughout the corporative structure and the modified Chamber, a system evolved which was referred to, by Francesco Paoloni and Panunzio, as "representation without elections." Representatives of the various associations, productive categories, or noneconomic groups were generally hierarchically designated. Their function, moreover, was markedly different from that understood to obtain in parliamentary systems. W. Cesarini Sforza described the orthodox system as one in which representatives of local and special interests sought to capture the state as an executive political arm of their category or class interests. If it proved impossible to dominate the state alone they would enter into combination with representatives of other interests in order to effect control. It was not the will of the nation which found expression, but the will of a particular group or constellation of groups of vested interests. Fascism, on the other hand, Cesarini Sforza insisted, organized the new Chamber as a place in which the "organs of the state effect their will, not as representatives of the people, but as organs of the state—that is the integral and unitary realization of the will of the nation."[146]

If men were, in fact, creatures who responded to their most immediate material interests rather than any ultimate collective interests, and if they made mimetic response to example and positive response to suggestion in situations of high moral tension, then it was the responsibility of men cognizant of higher and ultimate considerations to provide media for the expression of their material concerns (the corporative structure), but only within circumstances which would insure effective control. Control would be effected by constant appeal to sentiment, to collective empathy, to the fundamental ethnocentric disposition of man as a group animal in a climate of high emotive tension. The alternative would be to leave the masses to the manipulation of divergent party and local influence, with each faction employing its own nonrational techniques to create faction and dissension within the body politic. Factitious distinctions of class, category, and sect would threaten the viability of the nation in a world of intense national competition.

For Fascists, local, economic, or confessional concerns could never be permitted to constitute the primary focus of the individual's life. Regular ceremony and ritual, mass demonstrations, the donning of the black-shirt (which obliterated class and category distinctions) were all calculated to generate a group-sustaining empathy that would unite the individual in what Mussolini called a new "collective sense of life," the "beauty of a life lived in communion."[147]

Thus, Mussolini and the Fascists sought to give substance to the neo-idealist conviction that the individual, the people, the nation, the party, and the state could be conceived, in a real sense, to be substitution instances of each other. For Gentile, the substitutions were negotiated by *convincing* the individual that he was, in the profoundest sense of self, his people, nation, party, and state. For Fascism, the identification was effected by *nonlogical, emotive appeals,* since man in general was the product of influences that were fundamentally nonrational. These convictions were fully manifested in the social and political thought of Mussolini while still a socialist theoretician, and they remained constant throughout his political life.[148] Just such conviction made Fascists unalterably opposed to political democracy. A multiparty situation merely permitted a number of demagogues to manipulate the nonrational sentiments of the masses to create dissidence in the state and weaken it before real and potential international competition.

In a unitary party situation the directive elite is in a position to manipulate man's group-building susceptibilities in the service of the collective interests. Those individuals capable of assuming leadership roles in the elite can be identified by their superiors in the variety of organizations in which the young and the old, the male and the female, individuals of all classes, categories, and sects are organized. They can be elevated to the ranks of the strategic elites to become the executive, enterprisory, and educative aristocracy of the future. Thus, while the popular consensus upon which the Regime rested was understood to be an artifact of the almost complete propaganda and educational monopoly enjoyed by the state and the Party apparatus, the state and the Party were ideally understood to represent the superior intelligence and the select moral qualities of the nation. Fascists generally argued that possession of such qualities was initially certified by successful revolution. This is the only operational meaning that can be given to the statement that the *Duce* was "sent by Providence." Once installed in power, regard for the continued viability of the system insures a persistent and objective selection of qualified personnel to continually replenish the ranks of the strategic and directive elite.

That the Fascist experiment was a failure is now a matter of history. That it failed was recognized by Mussolini himself.[149] The reasons for its failure are, of course, far too complex and obscure to permit adequate assessment here. The present concern is to indicate that Fascist political policy followed Fascist doctrinal and philosophical commitments with remarkable consistency. That Fascism was not Actualism was a consequence of Fascism's anterior doctrinal commitments. Those commitments were commitments to a select set of factual propositions, the truth or falsity of which could be determined by the normal verification procedures of science. Those commitments, conjoined with the initial values of Actualism, produced the rationale for dictatorship. The institutional character of that dictatorship is not our immediate concern.[150] Only one feature of Fascist rule need occupy us here—the tendency for the hierarchical system of Fascism to devolve into one of personal rule. Because responsibility and power were hierarchical, there was a tendency for initiative to emanate exclusively from the apex of the system and for subordinates to simply lapse into apathy or imitation. Thus, Fascists accurately described the Fascist government as one not of "popular determination," but one of "popular adherence," one in which the "principle of authority" was gradually inculcated in the masses via the educational and propaganda media in the possession of the state, but only "according to the political directives issued by the Head of the Government."[151] Panunzio, whose life for half a century was a life of Fascist thought, could correctly identify "the center and motor" of the entire system as "the Head of the Government."[152]

The "cult of the hero" became a characteristic feature of the system. The "cult of personality," of charismatic or pseudocharismatic leadership, now recognized as diagnostic of totalitarian systems, received its first doctrinal rationale in Fascism. Since, according to Fascist theorists, the masses represent only elemental energies capable of being mobilized for whatever purpose, the function of directive leadership becomes critical. The tradition out of which Fascism grew insisted that the masses required leadership, and Fascist theoreticians maintained that

the slow ascent of humanity has always been marked by the appearance of a dominating and guiding hero. Every forward movement has been accomplished first by an individual, behind whom there followed, adoring or trembling, the unknowing masses. . . . The need of the masses to bow before a unique personality having a face and a name, possessed of a dominating spirit . . . arises from needs innate in man from antiquity.[153]

This is little more than a restatement of Michels' political sociology, a reformulation of Le Bon and Sorel. Michels chose to call this type of leadership "charismatic," to provide substance to a category available in Max Weber's typology that advanced a distinction between "traditional" or dynastic leadership and the "rational-legal" leadership that prevailed in parliamentary regimes.[154] Since Weber employed the term *charismatic* for leaders possessed of a putative divine mandate, the term *pseudocharismatic* has been suggested to better identify totalitarian leaders.[155] Totalitarian dictators, of whom Mussolini was the paradigm, rest their rule on nonrational emotional appeals that are legitimized in rational terms. Such leadership is understood to be a defensible and rational necessity, given the truth of a collection of descriptive propositions about man and social life. Submission to such rule is initially spontaneous, but is latterly reinforced by the control of mass communications and propaganda.

In Fascist Italy the result was an identification of Mussolini with the state and consequently with the nation. The popular cry, *"Tu sei l'Italia"* ("You are Italy"), was a rendering of this identification implicit in Fascist doctrine from the time of the formal founding of the *Partito Nazionale Fascista*. For Gentile, such an identification was possible only when the national leader was the embodiment of the universal rational will. For Fascists, the identification was the result of nonrational appeals that trafficked on the natural disposition of men to identify with a community of limited compass and a man as a symbol of that community. For Gentile, rational will was the basis of political consent and allegiance; for Fascists, group sentiment. However the identification was interpreted, it meant that the leader would assume imposing obligations, for he was the responsible and directive will of the national community.

Through the twenty years of Fascist rule, Mussolini assumed more and more personal responsibility and the remaining agencies of the state atrophied. The process was exemplified by the history of the Grand Council of Fascism itself. The Grand Council met, in its consultative capacity, 139 times in the first decade of Fascist rule. From 1932 until the coup of 1943 it met only 47 times. A similar process can be documented for almost every state and Party agency. The system succumbed to a fatal torpor.[156] When Mussolini was deposed, in the coup of July, 1943, the system was not even capable of impulsive resistance. Bottai, one of Mussolini's closest collaborators, wrote a fitting epitaph to the experiment. "It is not enough to act upon the 'masses.' It is necessary to act upon men and among men."

Bottai was a Gentilean and, like Gentile, he maintained that only reasoned conviction could win abiding allegiance. The minimal requirement was a cadre of *convinced* Fascists, men whose will was buttressed by reasoned commitment. During its twenty year experiment, Fascism had produced only the semblance of commitment. Sentiment and intuition are extremely volatile. Neither can be the basis of an enduring system. Under pressure, sentiments conflict and the black shirt is easily exchanged for the red bandana. Mussolini himself was stupefied by the rapidity with which all traces of allegiance to Fascism vanished.[157]

In September, 1943, when he called for a Fascist restoration in the North of Italy, one of the few notables of prewar Fascism to publicly announce his adherence to the *Partito Fascista Repubblicano* was Giovanni Gentile. In November, Gentile met with Mussolini and Mussolini spoke of the resistance to Actualism on the part of "intransigents" in the Party. Gentile spoke of the necessity for the "pacification of hearts," with evident allusions to his doctrine of toleration, developed in his final volume, *Genesi e struttura della società*, just completed in September. On November 26th he accepted an appointment as President of the Italian Academy. Throughout this period he called for a renunciation of vengeance and violence in order that the moral and sentimental unity of the nation could be restored.[158] He was preoccupied with the Florentine provincial leaders in the effort to intervene in behalf of those arrested on suspicion of political subversion. It was on the return from one such mission, on April 15, 1944, that he was met at the entrance to his residence by two men. One of them inquired whether he was Professor Giovanni Gentile. On receiving an affirmative reply the men fired a volley of pistol shots at close range. Gentile died instantly. The Fascists immediately imprisoned three anti-Fascist university professors by way of reprisal, but Gentile's family argued successfully for their release. Gentile was buried beside the bones of Michelangelo and Machiavelli.

Actualism and the Proto-Fascist Sociological Tradition

The tension between Actualism as an ethical idealism and Fascist doctrine as a product of a naturalistic and sociological tradition persisted throughout the Fascist period. Gentile maintained that the nationalistic elements in Fascism were wedded to a form of naturalism to which they were prepared to sacrifice significant ethical values.[159] These nationalists conceived the nation as a natural product of shared group-building sentiments rather than a willed conviction in a common destiny. The nationalists, conversely, insisted that Gentile's thought was too "abstract" and "intellectualistic" to be effective. They demanded an increasing "realism." A. C. Puchetti's *Il fascismo scientifico* was an early statement of this view. Panunzio, Costamagna, Gini, and Corradini were essentially of the opinion that Fascism, as a system of thought, was fundamentally sociological. Nino Tripodi, also of this persuasion, held that the values that subtended Fascism could be explicated as "traditional autochthonous values" held by the historic community that was the Italian nation.[160] These were "constant" sentiments endemic to Italian life. These were the "natural bases" upon which policy, if it were to be realistic, must rest. In effect, these men entertained a form of naturalistic ethics that conceived moral imperatives to be the consequence of an argument composed of descriptive propositions. Such an effort was obviously doomed to failure, but it did produce a detailed and self-conscious explication of nationhood and the relationship understood to obtain between men and society.

This process of explication was accelerated by the continental advent of National Socialism, with its naturalistic racism. The result was the articulation of Fascist racism, a confluence of the sociological elements inherent in Fascism, its nationalism, and the biologism that was, at least in part, the consequence of its association with National Socialism. It was a development in Fascist social and political thought which left Gentile distressed, Mussolini no little embarrassed, and commentators on Fascist thought very much confused.

The final expression assumed by Fascist social and political thought was an attempted synthesis of neo-idealist and naturalistic elements in its racial doctrine. The synthesis, as we shall see, was not fully successful. It did, however, produce a relatively sophisticated system of thought, features of which have appeared and reappeared in the totalitarian and quasitotalitarian political environments of our own time.

CHAPTER SIX

Final Doctrinal Developments: Racism

WITH few exceptions, Fascism as an ideological phenomenon has been cavalierly assessed. The last decade of its intellectual development is almost completely uncharted. Yet this period includes the articulation of Fascist racism and the rationale for the "socialization" of the ephemeral Social Republic of Salò. Both are essential for an adequate appraisal of paradigmatic Fascism. The first, Fascist racism, makes evident the continuity that underlay Fascist thought; the second reveals the radicalism implicit in its totalitarianism.

Of the two doctrinal developments, Fascist racism remains almost entirely misunderstood not only in Anglo-American literature, but in world literature as well. Italians equipped to deal with this feature of Fascism have, for a variety of reasons, been ill-disposed to tender an adequate appraisal. Since the termination of World War II, Italian literature has been unremittingly polemical. Any sustained effort at objectivity tends to be interpreted as "apologetic" and subject to formal and informal sanction. Still more inhibiting has been a pervasive embarrassment on the part of Italians with respect to the whole catastrophic Fascist experiment. Italians have, in general, been content to treat the entire period as an historic anomaly, as though the political events of a quarter century of Italian history had been the exclusive product of one man's whimsy. More recently, in the neo-Fascist apologetics that have begun to make regular appearance, there has been a tendency to dismiss Fascist racism as an aberrancy, an excrescence for which National Socialist influence was solely responsible.[1] The result has been a confluence of anti-Fascist and neo-Fascist opinion that simply dismisses Fascist racism as a serious object of ideological concern. At best, anti-Fascists cite Fascist racism as evidence that Fascism had no firm doctrinal commitments and that its postures, at any specific juncture, were a function of its immediate political interests. Neo-Fascists, when they do not maintain an embarrassed silence in its regard, treat Fascist racism as an ideological encumbrance, an inessential appurtenance. The best of recent scholarship, as we have already indicated, tends to be confused. Fascism is understood to have resisted National Socialist racism initially, then to have succumbed to Hitler's blandishments and accepted his racism "*in toto.*"[2] There are, of course, singular exceptions. Renzo De Felice's recent *Storia degli ebrei italiani sotto il fascismo*[3] treats the phenomenon of Fascist racism with requisite care and detachment, but focusses attention primarily on the Jewish question, and the general question of Fascist racism is treated only peripherally. There is, then, no substantive treatment of Fascist racism and consequently no adequate exposition of its genesis and character. The following account is intended to serve as a corrective and a supplement to that now available in the literature. It is intended to reveal the logic (the term understood in its extended rather than its formal sense) of Fascist racism.

The Ideological Context

Fascist ideology was a relative stable compound of diverse intellectual constituents, a proto-Fascist sociological tradition with an emphatic nationalist interpretation conjoined with a form of neo-Hegelian idealism that had already matured in Italy before the organization of the first *Fasci*. Both constituents retained a relative independence even after the maturation of Fascism as an ideology. Olivetti, Panunzio, Gini, and Corradini, for example, representatives of the first tradition, lived well into, or survived, the Fascist period and were among its foremost spokesmen. Gentile, as spokesman for the second, was assassinated in 1944. Ugo Spirito, his student and a prominent Fascist intellectual, survived the war.

Spokesmen of the first tradition always resisted what they understood to be the efforts of Actualism to monopolize Fascist ideology. They insisted that Fascism, as a pragmatic political system, must give constant evidence of its concern for contemporary political issues rather than preoccupy itself with "abstract" or "philosophical" lucubrations. They tended to be more "scientistic," to conceive politics as an applied science concerned with the regularities that govern the behavior of men in association. They sought to explain, predict, and control collective human behavior by isolating the determinate variables that influenced conduct. Long before Fascism developed as an ideology, Panunzio, Olivetti, Corradini, and Mussolini had conceived collective human behavior to be governed by interests and sentiments: interests which defined societal goals and norms, and sentiments which identified the individual with his kinship, his territorial and traditional community—a community of men united by a pervasive sense of identity. For the nationalists, that association was the rule-governed national community, a community sufficiently comprehensive and diverse to satisfy the functional needs of its members from its own resources. That community was sustained by the natural disposition of men, as well as all social animals, to aggregate in preferred associations—assemblages typically ethnocentric.

The idealists, in turn, resisted what they considered simplistic and "naturalistic" interpretations of what they conceived to be essentially moral phenomena. They conceived obligation to the community to be the consequence of willed commitment, and they interpreted the system of patterned interpersonal expectations that obtained within the nation as the result of the assumption of moral enjoinments and proscriptions. Their analysis employed normative language rather than the language of social science.

Mature Fascism tended to construe both as compatible with its broad interpretation of social dynamics. The masses, inert and pliable, were motivated by sentiments and a vague recognition of interests. The members of the responsible and strategic elite were governed by willed and reasoned conviction. They mobilized the passive masses to their purpose through the employment of ritual, symbolism, and slogan. Those of "naturalistic" persuasion tended to conceive consensus as the consequence of endogenous and exogenous natural factors. The idealists tended to conceive consensus as the product of normative commitment and moral contagion. Fascists conceived pattern maintenance in society to be a function of elite superordination and mass compliance. Fascists, as an elite, sought to vindicate their dominance by moral argument, and effect it by exploiting the suggestibility of the masses. In this sense they had proceeded beyond the analysis of Gumplowicz, Pareto, Mosca, Sorel, and Michels. Governance had moral as well as natural dimensions. Elite rule was licensed, ultimately, by moral argument. Mass compliance was affected by suggestion, by the moral contagion and imitation spoken of by Sighele and Le Bon, by the deployment of appropriate political formulae and political and social myths.

That Fascism thus represented a relatively stable synthesis of two currents of pre-Fascist thought did not preclude the periodic re-emergence of one at the expense of the other. A residual tension between them remained throughout the Fascist period. After 1938, that tension mounted under the influence of National Socialism. By 1944, only Mussolini's personal influence obviated an open rupture between the two. After the death of Gentile (1944), and with Mussolini the hostage of National Socialist Germany, Fascism became responsible for the final tragic and shameful excesses of racism in Italy.

The Background and Genesis of Fascist Racism

The interpretation of the racist postures of Fascism as a simple aping of National Socialism is simplistic and only partially true. The extent of its truth can be judged only after the concept *Fascist racism* is explicated with some measure of specificity. Today, the expression *racism* has only pejorative use and no recognizable cognitive reference. Contemporary usage is almost exclusively emotive, associating Fascist racism with any and all discriminatory practices directed against any distinguishable group. Thus, the Ku Klux Klan is spoken of as advocating Fascist racism. South Africa is spoken of as Fascist because it discriminates on the basis of racial classification. At its worst, the expression Fascist racism is used to cover any and all the practices of both Fascist Italy and National Socialist Germany.

Such usage is manifestly uninformative and painfully privative. Not every form of racism is the preamble to genocide. Certainly contemporary analysts would distinguish the "antiracist racism" of Senghor's myth of Negritude from the racism of National Socialist Germany, and no cognitive purpose is served by identifying the racism of South Africa with that of National Socialist Germany. For our purposes, the identification of Fascist racism with the racism of Hitler's Germany is particularly to be deplored. In its long history, racism has had and will continue to have a multiplicity of forms, and any responsible treatment must accommodate all of them. In other words, a taxonomy which includes a graded series of categories will be more adequate for an assessment of racism than would be any dichotomous distinction between Fascist racism and nonracism or antiracism. Racism, understood as any system of propositions concerned with collective or individual human behavior that employs racial provenience or phenotypic racial traits as significant explanatory variables, is at least as old as Aristotle's *Physiognomonica*.

Understood in this sense, racism was always a minor theme in the body of proto-Fascist and Fascist thought. In the mid-'thirties it became more emphatic and, by 1940, it occupied a prominent place in Fascist doctrinal and ideological literature.

In the late 'thirties, when Fascism frankly characterized itself as "racist," it pointed to this earlier tradition in order to defend itself against the charge of mimicry. It was to this tradition that Mussolini alluded, in 1938, in his reply to critics. "I spoke of the Aryan race in 1921," Mussolini affirmed on that occasion, "and after that always of race. Once or twice I spoke of *stirpe,* alluding, as was evident, to race."[4] In this way, Mussolini sought to document the ancestry of Italian racism, an ancestry subsequently reasserted in standard Fascist apologetics.[5]

In a certain sense Mussolini's claim was justified, but in order to explicate in just what sense it was justified some indication of the nature of Fascist racism during the period in question must be undertaken. It will become evident that the racism of this early period was essentially a benign product of Italian and non-Italian proto-Fascist thought.

The speech to which Mussolini referred in the effort to document early Fascist racism was a speech delivered in Bologna on April 3, 1921, in which he maintained that "Fascism was born . . . out of a profound, perennial need of this our Aryan and Mediterranean race (*stirpe*)." On that same occasion, he went on to indicate that Fascism had dedicated itself to making forty million Italians a "great family," united in "one single pride of race." Fascism sought to impart to Italians a sense of "racial solidarity (*la solidarietà della stirpe*)."[6] Still earlier, in 1918, Mussolini had employed racial categories for explanatory purposes. He characterized the "Latin race" as "feeling the beauty of personal audacity, the fascination of danger, and possessed of the taste for adventure."[7]

After 1921, the term *race* appeared regularly in Mussolini's speeches. In 1923, he spoke of the flower of the race that collected around the standards of Fascism, of Fascism as the prodigy of the race, as the historic product of an old but ever youthful race, and of Rome as the living heart of the race.[8] In 1924 and 1925, he spoke of Fascism as the ineluctible response of the race to the exigencies of the time.[9] In 1926, he insisted that the Genoese belonged to "a race that had created its fortune under difficult circumstances . . . a race that had evinced sublime heroism throughout history. . . ."[10] Throughout this period he insisted that Fascism preoccupy itself with the well-being of the race.

From 1918 through the first decade of Fascist rule, Mussolini had regular recourse to such locutions. Viewed in retrospect, taken out of historic context and sorted out of his voluminous writings and speeches, such references suggest far more than that with which they can be objectively credited. The contexts in which they appear are exhortative, distinguished more by their emotive character than by their cognitive force. If the term race has minimal specific intention in English, it has even less in the Italy of the period. The term had broad connotation but little explicit denotation. Michels, for example, writing in 1924, spoke of the phenomena associated with "race or, to speak . . . more precisely, people or nation."[11]

The treatment of "race," "people," and "nation" as substitution instances of each other was commonplace in the Italian and nationalist literature of the period. The publications of F. T. Marinetti, the founder of the nationalistic Futurists and an intimate of Mussolini during this early period of Fascist doctrinal elaboration, provide ample documentation of such usage. The term race abounded in the work of Marinetti,[12] and appears to have been the immediate source of Mussolini's inspiration. Mussolini's identification of the "Latin race" with the qualities of audacity and a taste for adventure, for example, was taken directly from the Futurist manifestoes of the period, in which Italians were conceived as possessed of a "will to conquest and adventure."[13] Similarly, Mussolini's exhortation to "racial pride" found its source in Futurist invocations. At least as early as March, 1919, two years before Mussolini's appeal, Marinetti had deprecated those peoples devoid of "racial pride."[14] Even earlier, in April, 1915, the Futurist Guglielmo Jannelli had maintained that Italians needed "racial pride."[15]

It is important to establish that this "race pride" was understood as "a new *national consciousness*."[16] The identification between "pride of race" and the "Italian national consciousness" was made specific in the Futurist treatment of *coscienza nazionale* as synonymous with *il prestigio della nostra razza* (the prestige of our race). Similarly, the treatment of expressions such as "our race," "the Italian race," "Italian blood," and "Italian people" establishes their semantic equivalence.[17] Thus, when two years later Mussolini referred to "racial solidarity," he rendered the expression specific by identifying it with "a union of free spirits in the Italian nation."[18]

Mussolini's use of the term *Aryan* to identify Italians during this early period was no more ominous than was his use of the term race. The term Aryan was in common usage in Italy and was used to refer to any of a number of peoples who spoke one of the related languages designated as Indoeuropean.[19] In 1903, Giuseppe Sergi had published his *Arii in Europa e in Asia,* which had been anticipated eight years before by his volume devoted to the Mediterranean branch of the Aryan race, *Origine e diffusione della stirpe mediterranea.* Vilfredo Pareto, in his *Trattato di sociologia generale* (1916), made frequent reference to the Aryan race and its Mediterranean branch.[20]

Mussolini's use of "Aryan" and "Mediterranean" in such a context can hardly be used to document a racism of the virulent sort with which the world is now familiar. There can be little serious doubt that the racism manifested by Fascism in its formative years was hardly more than a euphoric nationalism. The expression "our race" was uniformly understood to denote Italians (as distinct from Frenchmen or Englishmen), irrespective or anthropometric traits. In 1923, Mussolini said,

. . . before I love the French, the English, the Hottentots, I love Italians. That is to say I love those of my own race, those that speak my language, that share my customs, that share with me the same history.[21]

Fascist racism of this period was thus devoid of specifically *biological* intention. There was no suggestion that the conjectured admirable traits of the Latin race were hereditary and static. Marinetti and Mussolini both maintained that Italians could be, and had been, corrupted by inept governments, by false philosophies, by clericalism and egotism. The appeal was to the *will* of Italians rather than their genes—to their heroism rather than their heredity. Fascism, like Futurism and nationalism, was concerned with the *nation,* understood as a social aggregate with moral, cultural, and historic continuity.[22]

Fascism's programs throughout its first decade of power were calculated to improve the quantity and quality of the population of Italy. The programs were essentially demographic and euthenic in character, devoted to efforts to increase the birth-rate of Italy, provide more adequate pre- and post-natal care, institute inoculation programs to combat infectious diseases, drain malarial swamps, reduce the incidence of tuberculosis, and further popular athletics and sports.[23] These programs were already foreshadowed in the Futurist manifestoes of the period immediately prior to and during World War I.

During the years of World War II, in a discussion with Bruno Spampanato, Mussolini characterized his racism as follows:

I have occupied myself with racism since 1922, but a racism of my own. The health, the conservation of the race, its betterment, the struggle against tuberculosis, [the advocacy of] mass sport, children to camps— that was racism as I understood it. But there was also a moral racism that I advocated, the pride in belonging to this millennarian race born between the snows of the Alps and the fire of Etna. Our racism with respect to the outside world? The elevation of Italian prestige, of the genius of our civilization. . . .[24]

In so identifying his racism Mussolini specifically referred to this period between 1922 and 1932, when Fascist racism was essentially Fascist nationalism.

There are, however, some qualifications which must be appended to this account. An accurate representation of the development of Fascist racism would be incomplete if some indication of the divergent elements present in this early period was not given. Even as early as the prefascist nationalist writings of Oriani there was a suggestion of *biologism* in the concept of race. Oriani, for example, contrary to the subsequent Fascist practice, drew a distinction between race and nationality. He conceived races to be the first order of distinction among men, and nationality a second and more restricted distinction. He maintained that

. . . there is certainly an individuality in race that maintains itself against all geographic and historic counterinfluences: each race has an original consciousness and thought. . . . Race is therefore the first moment in the individuality of a people. . . . Every people preserves the essential character of its own race; all of a people's posterior creations are inspired by the race's primitive conceptions, beyond the confines of which no people can issue. . . . One can leave one's nation, but it is impossible to transcend the confines of race; a white can never be a Negro or a Mongoloid; a difference remains in the simplest depths of the heart, on the most impersonal heights of thought.[25]

Such sentiments were contained in the volume characterized by Mussolini as "magnificent" when he was still a revolutionary socialist (in 1909), and republished, with an introduction by Mussolini, in 1943. Mussolini himself, furthermore, continued to emphasize the historic, cultural, and political significance of the major races of mankind. In 1928, in his introduction to a monograph by Richard Korherr, Mussolini spoke of the peril posed by the "colored races" as a consequence of their higher fertility rate. He warned of the "innundation of the entire white race, the race of the Occident, by the races of color. . . ." As symptomatic of the threat he cited the restiveness of the Negroes in New York's Harlem.[26]

The entire nationalist and Futurist movement had also tended to an ambiguous and half-articulated anti-Semitism. Oriani had tendered vague objections against the Jews in Italy, and the Jews constituted for Corradini the "negation of Italy's new Roman consciousness. . . ."[27] But anti-Semitism remained a secondary and accessory concern for the nationalists, whose principal efforts were devoted to rekindling the spirit of Italian patriotism. The secondary and accessory concerns nonetheless found an echo in the words of Mussolini, and in June, 1919, he charged that

. . . the great Jewish bankers of London and New York, bound by the chains of races to those of Moscow and Budapest, are taking revenge against the Aryan race that condemned them to dispersion for centuries. In Russia, eighty per cent of the leaders of the Soviets are Jews; in Budapest seventeen of the twenty-two people's commissars are Jews. . . . World finance is in the hands of the Jews and he who holds a people's purse directs its politics. Behind the puppets of Paris are [Jews] . . . who possess the same blood as the oppressors of Petersburg and Budapest. Race does not betray itself.[28]

Again, in the service of historical accuracy, Mussolini's utterances must be placed in context. They are no more singular than similar utterances which were commonplace in nationalist and syndicalist circles. Georges Sorel, for example, had been a quite vociferous anti-Semite. Sorel charged the Jews with being economic parasites, destructive social critics, and inveterate opponents of French nationalism. On the theoretical level, however, anti-Semitism remained for Sorel a "private, minor motif, existing in large measure apart from the foundations of his philosophy or sociology."[29]

Mussolini's anti-Semitism during this period was of similar order. Placed in the context of nationalist, Futurist, and syndicalist statements, and against the background of the sometimes virulent anti-Semitic pronouncements of the Catholic Church around the turn of the century, Mussolini's remarks appear quite bland and unimposing. He made no similar allusions to the Jews during nor after this period and, in 1929, as well as in his conversations with Ludwig in 1932, he denied that there was or would be anti-Semitism in Italy.[30]

Some of Mussolini's intimate associates during this early period were Jews and his first official biographer was the Jewess Margherita

Sarfatti.[31] Mussolini's position during this period, considered in contemporary context and objectively weighed, seemed adequately assessed by De Felice:

For many, many years, Mussolini could not be considered an anti-Semite. Until 1937, the idea of an official anti-Semitism was completely alien to him. The Jews of Italy enjoyed, under Fascism, neither more nor less of the same "liberty" enjoyed by other Italians. Persecuted Jews from abroad found in him, if not a protector, a political leader who frequently rendered assistance and opened the doors of Italy to them, unlike—it is necessary to remember—many heads of state.[32]

Nonetheless, Mussolini entertained a certain diffidence with respect to the Jews. He had forbidden his daughter to marry a Jew,[33] and he was ill-disposed, as were all emphatic nationalists, to all those who appeared cosmopolitan, international—who in one fashion or another maintained contacts and commitments which transcended the confines of the nation.

There were, then, in nationalism, syndicalism, and Futurism—all of which were ultimately absorbed into Fascism—elements which in retrospect appear ominous. It was for this reason that the nationalism of Corradini, and of the nationalists in general, remained suspect to Gentile. He felt that the nationalists were not fully cognizant of the logic of their own position. They tended to treat the nation as though it were something given, as a presupposition, an extrinsic material or biological reality to which one submitted, rather than an inward ideal to be won and against which the historic nation and its embodied will in the state were to be measured.[34]

Gentile resisted any collective ascriptions of praise or blame whether applied to nations, races, or peoples. Gentile denounced Fichte's assertion of the essential superiority of the German people, just as he would reject Futurist pronouncements about the "indisputable creative genius of the Italian race."[35] Gentile held such postures to be simple prejudice which it was a moral obligation to overcome.[36] The circumstances surrounding World War I and the postwar period did mollify Gentile considerably, and he wrote a very accommodating article on Oriani that was published in the nationalist press.[37] Nonetheless, he remained forever suspicious of any form of nationalism predicated on any sort of naturalism and biologism, particularly if its adherents were given to making ascriptions of collective superiority and inferiority. There is no evidence to indicate that Gentile ever changed his position.

For a variety of reasons, Gentile, like Mussolini, entered into increasing rapprochement with the nationalists.[38] Ultimately idealists, nationalists, and Futurists united in Fascism. Futurism was all but absorbed in Fascism,[39] but the nationalist elements were more enduring and ultimately became the loci of theoretical tension.

In the decade following its accession to power, Fascism was occupied with articulating its ideology. Race constituted but a minor preoccupation. The "Fundamental Ideas" of the *Dottrina* of 1932 contained but a single pertinent reference to race and, that was to dismiss it as the material foundation of the nation. This is not to say, however, that Fascism had not already formulated a reasonably specific racial doctrine.

The Racial Doctrine of Fascism

By 1930, Fascism had developed a synoptic theory of race which related the state, the nation, and the race to each other in a collection of propositions that pretended to coherence and explanatory significance. By that year, Fascist race theory had found academic expression in the work of Corrado Gini, particularly in his *Nascita, evoluzione e morte delle nazioni.* After 1930, Fascist race theory matured in a relatively coherent manner. The theoretical tensions that accumulated around its central concepts are the identifiable consequence of the impact of National Socialist racial theory and Fascist Italy's efforts to provide it some accommodation. Independent of those excrescences there was a specific Fascist racial theory, with which Mussolini identified himself, that persisted throughout the Fascist period.

Fascist racial theory developed along the lines of antecedent theoretical and ideological commitments. The theoretical commitments were those of a Gumplowiczian and post-Gumplowiczian sociological tradition. The anterior ideological commitments were those made to nationalism and statism.

As we have seen, nationalism was the critical focus in the doctrinal orientation of Italian Fascism. National sentiment was conceived as the arbiter of class and local antagonism.[40] A new economic system was to be animated by the sentiment of national solidarity. Out of a new consciousness of national purpose, a vital sense of dedication was to arise.[41] Fascism conceived itself as transforming the

. . . sovereignty of an amorphous people . . . into the sovereignty of an organic people . . . a true political revolution and at the same time a social revolution, creator of a strong national society intimately and necessarily characterized by solidarity.[42]

National sentiment was conceived as a natural, positive disposition on the part of an aggregate of men to place general interest before immediate private interest[43]—an expression of man's essentially social or associative nature[44]—a disposition expressed and reinforced in resistance against outgroups.[45] Out of these and related emotional forces an *ethos* was to be articulated that would integrate the various social and productive components into a viable organic unity convinced of its collective historical and cultural destiny.[46] The will of such a community was understood to manifest itself in the state. It was into this antecedent conceptual scheme that the concept of race had to be synthesized.

The scientific materials which the Italian academic community provided for the resultant synthesis included a conception of race as a dynamic constant, the ultimate product of geographic and social isolation[47] and attendant inbreeding, natural and artificial selection, and genetic mutation.[48] Within such a conception each anthropological race was understood to be the end product of a long historical process, a function of protracted inbreeding, differential birth rate, selection, and genetic variation. Any inbreeding community was understood to constitute a race in formation—its degree of uniformity of type a function of the length of its isolation, the intensity of selection it had undergone under specific environmental circumstances, the size of the breeding population, and the reproductive rate of its constituent groups[49]—all of which were determined in large part by *political* circumstances.

In Fascist theoretical accounts these notions were advanced in the affirmation that "long established nations . . . can solidify themselves into races, becoming new races. . . ."[50]

It is to be understood that the "new races" . . . are *nations solidified into races,* that is to say, politico-cultural entities, solidified through time and intermarriage into a unity of blood derived from a harmonious and stable fusion of several "old races". . . .[51]

It was argued that at any given time an anthropological race is a statistical abstraction, the consequence of the investigator's having established a polar, or ideal, type that affords sorting criteria used to delimit a unit series. Every population will show natural variability, and the degree of variability will depend upon a variety of exogenous and endogenous factors.[52] In evolutionary time the major geographic races (*razze grandi*) develop relatively uniform local variations (*razze piccole*). No race appears fully developed in history. Each is the product of *politically established social isolation,* selective influences, and breeding practices which tend to stabilize specific types in specific ecological niches. Race formation is thus understood to be a dynamic and historic *political* process. As soon as a local variation begins to expand because it is possessed of some trait of high survival value and/or increased fertility, it is subjected to environmental conditions and genetic factors which tend to introduce variations, marking it off from its parent-type. Anthropological races, then, were understood to be abstract entities, the result of the anthropologist's efforts to bring order into the abundance of data available to him.[53] Such abstractions have heuristic and didactic value, but their use obscured the political and dynamic dimension of the biological process of raciation. Any less dynamic conception of race tends to identify "pure races" with the abstract characteristics of the anthropologist's polar type. Actually, few individuals in nature are possessed of all the traits (even if the number of such traits is limited) which are used as sorting criteria to identify races. Most individuals within a geographic race show a mixture of traits attributable to two or more local races. The natural variability of populations is further complicated by variations produced by environmental factors. Fascist theoreticians indicated that the environment could influence cephallic index, stature, and pigmentation.[54] In a breeding population the size of Italy, characterized by small in-breeding pockets, subject to a diversity of environmental influences, an anthropometrically uniform population could not be expected to obtain, and yet such variability was not unequivocal evidence of racial hybridization.

Within the context of such a dynamic view, the nation could be conceived as a "race cradle," a politically defined endogamous breeding circle whose sovereign independence and internal mobility would tend to relate all constituent members to a common gene pool that, given sufficient time, would produce a relatively distinct type, a "new race" (*una razza nuova*), in a "unity of blood."[55] In this context the nation was understood to constitute the political vehicle of a race in formation. The state, as the conscious will of the nation could, through its legislative enactments limiting citizenship and establishing regulations governing marriage, through a concerted demographic and eugenic program, through its emigration and immigration policies, act as the ultimate arbiter of what the race was to become.[56] It can express, in law, the will of the nation that aspires to become a viable and relatively homogeneous race. The ideal the state fosters accelerates the process of specific race formation. The state defends the integrity of the race in formation, protecting its elements, selecting its constituent members, and guarding its territorial confines.

Every nation is distinguished by the diverse components which constitute its breeding population. In each nation, various elements of "old" race types are united (the products of antecedent breeding communities: hordal, tribal, or city-state).[57] Fascist theoreticians advanced such a conception as a rationale for speaking of an "Italian race," an historic breeding community which they contended was relatively isolated and endogamous for a thousand years.[58] Similarly, they spoke of a "British race," a "Japanese race," and even, on occasion, of a "North American type."[59] Every nation was conceived as a race at one or another state in its development.

A nation composed of harmonious, assimilable components was understood to display inherent viability, a common sense of purpose and destiny; one composed of disparate groups of markedly diverse racial type was conceived as an artificial agglomeration devoid of a sense of common interest. Such a nation would tend to disaggregate under minimal internal or external pressure.[60] Such heterogeneously constituted communities, it was argued, tend to fragment into ethnic or racial enclaves which do not identify with the general community. These come to constitute nuclei of ir- redentist, racist, or local "nationalist" agitation.[61] A nation, on the other hand, composed of *related* "old races" (not distinguishable by traits of high social visibility) tends to coalesce, to gradually pro- duce a political community bound together by innumerable ties of blood relationship until ultimately, under ideal conditions, a new anthropological race emerges. It becomes a race "purified," a racial fusion stabilized in time.[62]

Fascist theorists thus explicated the concept *race* by making a politically defined *population* its referent. Rather than the taxonomic or morphological conception of race, Fascist theoreticians advanced a notion of "natio-races," politically defined breeding circles, ani- mated through the legislative enactments and the pedagogical activities of the state to produce the breeding communities for ideal racial types. The ideal type for Fascism was conceived as "Nordo- Aryan." In general, the Italians were to be classified among the family of people identified as Aryan. These peoples were under- stood to include elements of various European "old races," fused into a stable and harmonious "new race."[63] The Nordic ideal was conceived as a *tactical* device which was to foster a strictly Euro- pean orientation. The designation *Mediterranean*, while technically correct, suggested to Fascists a politically inadmissible affiliation with Semites. The relationship with Nordic Europe was essentially spiritual or cultural, rather than morphological.[64]

This conception of race constitutes the core of Fascism's specific racial doctrine. It conceived *race* as coextensive and coterminous (for all intents and purposes) with *nation*, and provided the theo- retical substructure of Mussolinian convictions advanced as early as 1917. That such a relationship should obtain is not surprising—nor does it require that Mussolini be understood to have entertained such theoretical convictions as early as the March on Rome. That Mussolini's use of the term race should be compatible with Fascist doctrine as it developed throughout the last decade of Fascist rule only requires recognition of the fact that the dynamic conception which conceived the term race as having a *politically defined population* as its referent is found, in fact, in the works of Ludwig

Gumplowicz, whose works exercised enormous influence on Italian syndicalist thought during the period of Mussolini's maturation.

Gumplowicz had tendered a stipulative definition of race which made it the logical equivalent of "ethnic and social group," or "heterogeneous social element," an equivalence which conceived every socially or politically isolated group as a race in formation. Social and political isolation was the consequence of man's natural disposition, as a social and political animal, to aggregate in preferred and self-regarding associations. Such associations evinced a syndrome of in-group preferences and out-group avoidances which defined effective breeding circles (*Blutsgemeinschaften*). Such conceptions and their attendant rationale passed into Italian literature and were echoed in Pareto's *Corso*. Pareto recognized the then standard taxonomic definition of race and suggested that use of the term be specifically restricted to that intention. He suggested the use of the term "ethnic group" (*etnia*) to refer to politically defined social elements.[65] Italian academicians during the Fascist period recognized just such a distinction and accepted the proposed terminological distinction but insisted, with Gumplowicz, that the relationship between racial and ethnic entities was not mutually exclusive. The ethnic group, under specific conditions, could develop into a relatively homogeneous population genetically distinct from allopatric populations, and at that point would qualify as an anthropological race in the restricted sense of the term. Thus, Mario Canella distinguished between protomorphic, archimorphic, and neomorphic races—races at various stages of progressive development.[66] The nation constituted a breeding circle, a race in formation. It was this Gumplowiczian concept which passed directly into Fascist doctrinal literature. Nicola Pende, one of Fascism's foremost race theorists, developed precisely this Gumplowiczian conception as the basis of the Fascist conception of race.[67] It was a conception already mature in Gini's work (published in 1930).[68] Gini was familiar with the work of Gumplowicz and cites his *Rassenkampf* and his *Die sociologische Staatsidee* in his notes.[69] Gini, furthermore, specifically supervised Canella's work and his (and Gumplowicz's) influence is evident throughout.[70]

The continuity of Gumplowiczian elements in Fascist race

theory can be still more adequately documented by tracing this continuity in the influence of Sir Arthur Keith, the English anthropologist, on Fascist academicians and ideologues. As early as 1919, Keith had advanced a Gumplowiczian populationist conception of race and argued that nations constituted political vehicles for race formation.[71] Renato Biasutti, in his monumental *Razze e popoli della terra* (1941), similarly spoke of the nation as

an anthropological reality, not only the locus of a particular conglomerate of racial elements, but as a distinct locus of phenomena of fusion and harmonization which as such stimulates the formation of new [racial] forms.[72]

The nation was a specific anthropological and biological reality defined in terms of politically restricted gene-flow. He and Canella proceeded to identify this conception with the work of Sir Arthur Keith.[73]

Outside of specific academic circles, Fascist doctrinal literature employed these concepts to relate race, ethnic group, people, and nation. Race was a classificatory concept and could be employed to identify races in formation. Races at various stages of development were politically defined historic ethnic communities or peoples. A single people within a specific polity constituted a nation. Under optimum conditions "people," "race," and "nation" denoted the same class of individuals. The concept of race was thus employed to refer to biological, but not exclusively anthropological, entities.[74] Guido Landra, one of Fascist Italy's race theorists, identified such use in the works of Georges Montandon, an active French collaborator on the Fascist doctrinal journal *Difesa della razza*.[75] Montandon, in turn, indicated that the conception that "taxonomic races arise out of national, social and political formations" was advanced by "English authors," an evident allusion to the well-known theoretical works published by Keith.[76] Keith, of course, did not conceal the historic origins of these conceptions. Particularly in his postwar publications, Keith documented his intellectual debt to Ludwig Gumplowicz.[77]

Such essentially Gumplowiczian conceptions permitted Fascist theoreticians to assimilate racism into totalitarian nationalism. By virtue of such conceptions, the critical unit of analysis remained the historic national community. The politically constituted rule-governed national community could remain the object of primary loyalty and the repository of values. In such guise, Fascist race theory was radically different from that of National Socialism. National Socialists ultimately espoused a consistent racism and explicitly and implicitly abandoned nationalism.[78] *Race,* understood in a strict morphological sense, could not have the nation as its referent. In general, National Socialist theorists tended to maintain a static taxonomic conception of race and specifically rejected Gumplowicz' alternate dynamic interpretation as "typically Jewish."[79]

Among the last books Mussolini is known to have read was one devoted to the exposition of the thought of Gobineau, the nineteenth century French taxonomic racist so much admired in National Socialist Germany. Mussolini carefully noted the passages in the book that documented Gobineau's objections to nationalism.[80] Like the majority of Fascist theoreticians, Mussolini recognized that biological determinism conjoined with a strict taxonomic classification of human races was antithetical to any nationalism. Fascist race theory developed out of the sociological traditions of proto-Fascism and disported literally all the conceptions first fully articulated by Ludwig Gumplowicz in the last quarter of the nineteenth century. As such, Fascist race theory was radically different from that of National Socialism.

How closely the Fascist theory of raciation followed that of Gumplowicz is indicated by the critical role played by the concept "ethnocentrism" in the explanatory accounts advanced by academicians in Fascist Italy. Canella makes specific reference to that constellation of ethnocentric dispositional behaviors identified by Gumplowicz. For both men, all social aggregates employ an inventory of ideal types, a positive in-group and a negative out-group image. Such images provide fixed points in the catalogue of moral obligations. Through them, individuals come to identify with a specific reference community. That community constitutes not only the preformed moral universe in which the individual matures to responsibility, but also conditions him to favor individuals from his own community, a preference that constitutes the precondition for endogamy and differential raciation.[81] The process by which such dispositions are fostered and maintained involves all the inter-personal and intrapsychic mechanisms identified by Gumplowicz, Le Bon, and Sighele. Accounts similar to that provided by Canella are found in the works of Gini, Biasutti, Pende, Landra, and Alfredo Niceforo, and they document the essential continuity of Fascist thought from the proto-Fascist conceptions of Gumplowicz, Mosca, Pareto, Sorel, and Michels through the doctrinal and theoretical accounts advanced in the final ideological expressions of the Regime.

The Impact of National Socialist Racism

Extraneous to this continu-ity were conceptions of racial superiority and in-feriority and the pointless, inept and morally indefensible anti-Semitism that Mussolini intro-duced in 1938. The insinuation of these indigestible elements into Fascist race theory was only part of the price Mussolini was to pay for the "Pact of Steel." It was all the more shameful because Hitler had never made the alliance with Italy contingent upon such espousals. Mussolini apparently felt that the introduction of such material into the ideological system of Fascism would reduce the psychological distance that separated the people of Fascist Italy from those of National Socialist Germany. If that was his intention, there is no evidence that he succeeded, and some considerable evidence that he did not. Not only did the Italian population not rise to the demands of these doctrinal curiosities, but these ex-traneous materials created enormous tensions within the ideological system of Fascism.

This is not to say that some form of anti-Semitism might not have developed out of Fascist nationalism. At least one element in the Fascist armory of abuses directed against the Jews might be considered "native" to Fascism. One of the principal arguments used against the Jews was that employed by Paolo Orano, an old-line revolutionary syndicalist and an intimate of Mussolini from the prefascist period.[82] He maintained that in a totalitarian and solidarist community there was no place for self-regarding sects. In effect, what Orano demanded was that the Jewish community lose its special identity and assimilate itself into the totalitarian society. As early as 1922, Michels had alluded to the possibility that Fascist nationalism might precipitate just such a confrontation with the Jewish residents of Italy.[83]

Totalitarianism, with its tutelary, pedagogical, and solidarist pretensions, seeks to monopolize the loyalty of its citizenry. It tends to seek exclusive control over the education of the young and employs every device to dissipate any conflicting loyalties its citizens might entertain. In Fascist Italy this tendency was exemplified in the protracted and acrimonious struggle between the Regime and the Church. That the Jewish community, quite independent of any influence from the North, might similarly have been the victim of Fascism's drive for monolithic solidarity is quite possible but, given the small number of resident Jews in Italy, not probable.[84]

The best representatives of Fascism, the idealists like Gentile and Spirito as well as those in the syndicalist and juridical tradition like Panunzio and Costamagna, continued to resist the anti-Semitism that the association with National Socialist Germany brought in its train. All recognized the inestimable debt that Fascism owed to the scholarship of men of Jewish provenience like Ludwig Gumplowicz, Roberto Michels, and Angelo Oliviero Olivetti.

Throughout this period, Fascist race theory continued to react to the influence of National Socialist race theory as it exercised more and more influence upon Fascist doctrine. With the advent of Hitler to power in 1932, Fascist doctrine was compelled to relate itself to National Socialist doctrine. Between the years 1932 and 1938, the increasing rapprochement with National Socialist Germany forced an intensive and probing reconsideration of Fascist racial theory. In 1938 Fascist Italy published the *Manifesto del razzismo italiano* in an effort to codify its official position with respect to the race question. Like all doctrinal statements the *Manifesto* was elliptical and stenographic, but it did document the influence of extraneous pressures that were being felt by the theoreticians of Fascism.

The years between 1932 and 1938 evidence significant changes in Fascist *attitude* rather than substantial changes in Fascist *analysis* with regard to National Socialist race theory. The initial encounters between Fascism and National Socialist race theory immediately after 1932 were made with studied reserve and were characterized by hostility. The Fascist objections to National Socialist theory were made in the tradition of the young Mussolini, who as early as 1911 mocked the racial speculations of Arthur de Gobineau, Ludwig Woltmann, Houston Stewart Chamberlain, and Vacher de Lapouge, all of whom were to figure prominently as precursors of National Socialist "Nordicism."[85] In 1912, Mussolini again mocked simplistic racial interpretations of history.[86] Years later, as head of the Fascist state, he repeated his objections.[87] Mussolini's statements were sufficiently explicit to render misunderstanding impossible. As late as 1942, Aldo Capasso could still insist that

Benito Mussolini, a youth, but already an acute journalist and student, early perceived the weaknesses of the simplisms [of Gobineau, Lapouge, Woltmann, etc.] and exposed their excesses to corrosive irony.[88]

Fascist Italy never simply aped National Socialist race theory.

As has already been suggested, Fascist objections to the race theory emanating from the North rested not only on appeals to authority, but were substantive as well. National Socialist race theory was, in its various and varied half-official expressions, materialist,[89] sometimes theosophical,[90] and almost always anti-Christian and anti-Roman.[91] To a movement fundamentally idealist in philosophical orientation, animated by the myth of Rome Eternal, and that had but a few years before concluded the Lateran Pact of Concord with the Roman Church, such postures were less than endearing. To these disabilities was added, particularly during the early period of National Socialist ascendancy, a disposition on the part of German theorists to equate "Nordics" (understood to designate persons possessed of a specific constellation of observable physical traits) with the unique "culture creators" of history. The cultural eminence of the Greece and Rome of antiquity was traced to the presence in their respective populations of persons of Nordic provenience. The culture of the Middle Ages was created by Nordics, and even the Italian Renaissance was understood to be the consequence of the infusion of "Nordic vitality." Alfred Rosenberg, the principal ideologue of National Socialist racism, had gone so far as to suggest that since Fascism had its origins in the industrial North of Italy it was somehow the product of Nordic genes![92] Since Italy, a land of predominantly Alpine and Mediterranean inhabitants, could boast of but little "Nordic blood," such theses were hardly calculated to generate much enthusiasm.

In 1933, Gaetano Mosca wrote his scathing critique of biological and taxonomic racism. Some commentators have interpreted his critique as exemplifying an "act of courage" in defiance of Fascist racism,[93] when as a matter of fact it was nothing more than the articulation of what was all but universal Fascist opinion at that time. In 1934, Giovanni Selvi, writing in the official Fascist theoretical journal, *Gerarchia*, insisted that National Socialist racism was "scientifically unfounded, contradictory and simplistic."[94] That same year, Giuseppe Bianchini characterized National Socialist racism as a threat to civilization.[95] In 1936, again in *Gerarchia*, José Gomez de Teràn dismissed National Socialist racism as "a pseudo-scientific and mystic lyricism."[96]

Mosca's criticisms of the static race theory of National Socialism were no more searching nor scathing than that which appeared in the official publications of the *Partito Nazionale Fascista*. Mussolini's own criticisms were similarly arch. In 1934, he pointed out that science "does not guarantee the 'purity' of anyone's blood," and that the "new 'civilizers' from the North might well have unrecognized relatives even within the walls of Tel Aviv."[97] Such remarks, conjoined with his assessment of racism made to Emil Ludwig in 1932, indicate that he was far from identifying himself with National Socialist racism.[98]

From 1933 through 1936, with the exception of a few non-representative journals, the Fascist and non-Fascist press of Italy indicated that a gulf separated the two regimes on the race question. In the first months of 1936, Gentile insisted that the "Italian ideal" was not a "sordid racism," but was "intelligently universal and human."[99] After 1936, the increasingly intimate rapprochement with National Socialist Germany moderated the tone, but did not alter the substance, of Fascist criticism. The criticisms of static and morphological racism appear in the definitive ideological work by Antonio Canepa in 1937, in the official *Gerarchia* in 1938, in Luigi Franzi's expository work published by the Istituto Nazionale di Cultura Fascista in 1939, in the revised edition of Carlo Costamagna's *Dottrina del Fascismo* in 1940, in Enzo Leoni's exposition of Fascist racism in 1941, and in Aldo Capasso's work in 1942.[100] Fascism *never* identified itself with National Socialist racial theories.

Only in 1937 was there an attempt on the part of a minority of Fascist theoreticians to read National Socialist racist literature with sympathy. Giulio Cogni's *Razzismo*,[101] published in that year, constituted such an attempt. How impossible it was to attempt a synthesis of National Socialist and Fascist racism was made painfully evident by Cogni's effort.

The book was largely a paraphrase of Rosenberg's *Mythus des 20. Jahrhunderts,* supplemented by elements distilled from the works of Hans Guenther (who was otherwise regularly and roundly criticized by Fascist theoreticians[102]). As an inevitable consequence, the expression "Nordic blood" (*il sangue Nordico*) abounded in Cogni's text. Since there were but few identifiable Nordics in Italy, the tactical disadvantages of such a theory were immediately apparent. Later Fascist commentators were more emphatic in highlighting this shortcoming. Franzi, in 1939, indicated that if National Socialist race theory understood a Nordic to be a person characterized by a specific constellation of morphological traits (tall, dolichocephalic, slender, blue-eyed, and blond), then only twelve per cent of the Swedish population, the most Nordic of populations, could pass muster as Nordics.[103] If a strict anthropological definition of "Nordic" were maintained, it threatened to make the racist movement an esoteric sect rather than a revolutionary force. This had been evident at the time of Cogni's exposition and he had been quick to indicate that "Nordic blood" was not to be understood to refer to persons having specific physical traits. Cogni insisted.

Nordic blood, for those *not* informed concerning Nordic theories, means simply and exclusively Germanic blood or, at least, the blood of blond peoples that live in the north. Nothing could be more imprecise—at least if one lifts oneself above the foolishness of popular publications and German enthusiasts to the level of theoretical works of racists who know what they are about.[104]

He went on to indicate that some "enthusiasts" had insisted that "superiority" could be identified with certain physical traits of nordicity. But this was an aberrancy (*fissazione mentale*), a foolishness of physical anthropologists.[105] He rejected the attempt to correlate physical traits with a rank order of spiritual values.

Cogni insisted that Nordicism could not be understood as a strictly anthropological concept. He identified the term *Nordic* with the less specific *Aryan* (at the time when theorists in National Socialist Germany were proceeding from the vague and ambiguous linguistic term *Aryan* to the more anthropologically specific term *Nordic*) and then proceeded to identify Aryan with certain "spiritual attributes." He argued:

Nordic, Aryan, in the true sense, is not confined to this or that racial particularity: it is not defined within the confines of flesh and intellect. . . . Aryan is equivalent to genius, profound mystery of the spirit. . . .[106]

While he went on to qualify this identity, the concept remained essentially "mystical," a "racial theosophy" which found similar expression in the works of Julius Evola.[107]

This "spiritual" interpretation of Nordicism was the last and only serious attempt to synthesize National Socialist race theories into the body of Fascist thought,[108] and it is interesting that it could only be accomplished at the expense of its cognitive content. In 1938, under the auspices of the Ministero della Cultura Popolare, Fascist academicians were assembled to organize the elements of Fascist race theory into one official and coherent exposition of interrelated theses. The document which resulted was the Fascist racial *Manifesto* (see Appendix A). Before its issuance it was reviewed and probably edited by Mussolini himself.[109]

The Manifesto of Fascist Racism   Perhaps the most striking feature of the Fascist *Manifesto* was the rejection, in principle, of any *a priori* ascription of superiority or inferiority to any given race. The tactical and theoretical grounds for such a reservation are not far to seek. On the doctrinal level, Fascism had committed itself to the primacy of politics, of political organization as the decisive factor in historical development,[110] and to nationalism as its most consistent expression. Since Europe was composed of a variety of minor races[111] any national complex could not be coextensive with any particular taxonomic race.[112] Every European nation was a mixture of several such races. To characterize one of those races as superior would be to threaten the integrity of the nation with the creation of *castes*, individuals assigned to each as a consequence of possessing a syndrome of metric and nonmetric physical traits.[113] Such a threat to the integrity of the nation was perceived by Fascists as particularly ominous.[114] Landra, one of the architects of the *Manifesto*, contended,

It is pernicious to divide a people into various races on the basis of a typology that uses certain somatic characteristics as sorting criteria, particularly when the different types are to be assigned diverse ranks in a hierarchical scale.[115]

To attempt to assess the merits of individuals by employing an index of physical traits threatened to create a nation of closed castes, laying, furthermore, the foundation of a "racist internationalism," akin to the "class internationalism" of Marxism, which cut across national boundaries.[116]

Furthermore, the conception that the measure of an individual's worth was his particular biological heredity ran counter to Fascism's philosophy of ethical voluntarism and personal heroism. Fascist theoreticians were explicit in their rejection of "biological materialism and determinism."[117] Nor were the objections simply determined by anterior philosophical commitments. As late as 1940, Costamagna rested his reservations on the paucity of compelling scientific evidence certifying the simple heritability of psychic traits as well as the modest experimental data correlating racial physical with racial mental traits.[118] Capasso further argued that, even granting some measure of biological determinism, individual variability made a commitment to the slogan *Race is Destiny* unwarranted.[119] He went on to contend that the multiplicity of types which entered into the modern European had so confounded the particulate hereditary materiels that the ascription of specific mental traits to any given individual, whatever his physical attributes, was impossible.[120] Similar disclaimers were entered by more academic commentators throughout the final Fascist period.[121] The tendency to emphasize the distinction between somatotype and psychological traits was emphatic in the work of Giovanni Marro.[122]

Fascist racism distinguished itself from its northern counterpart, as we have seen, in maintaining an essentially historicist, political, and dynamic interpretation against the antihistorical, biological, and essentially static orientation of National Socialist theories. Much of the race theory formulated by National Socialist theoreticians conceived race in an essentially traditional manner, defining race as a taxonomic entity, membership in which was determined by possession of a constellation of heritable biological traits. World history was conceived in terms of the interaction of such static biological and racial types (Nordic, Mediterranean, Alpine, and so forth) that were differentially endowed, each race having its own patrimony of mental and physical attributes. History was understood to be no more than the account of contacts between such racially diverse groups, their progressive intermixture, and the subsequent degeneration of the superior (*Entnordung*).[123] The political task of the age was to reconstitute the lost "purity" of the superior stock and subsequently to provide a propitious environment for its maintenance.

Mussolini had earlier inveighed against such simplisms and in September, 1940, in a conversation with Yvon de Begnac, he maintained, "Races exist. . . . This is irrepressible fact. There are neither superior nor inferior races. One should not indulge, especially in this area, in materialist interpretations."[124] He had intimated as much to Ludwig in 1932[125] and in 1939 recommended an article written by Mario Missiroli which argued:

Biological diversity does not authorize, in science, a scale of values by virtue of which races can be classified as "superior" or "inferior." One can only legitimately speak of "different" races.[126]

To construe history as the struggle of anthropologically defined races was conceived a gross oversimplification. Such a conception seemed to rest on the conviction that discrete races of men were uniformly endowed with determinate and enduring traits which could only be altered by racial mixture. Fascist theoreticians had early objected to such conjectures on empirical grounds even before the advent of National Socialism in Germany. Demographers in Fascist Italy had indicated that even if a given group were possessed of a specific trait, physical or mental, such a trait would be found distributed among the population in a normal distribution curve; that is, it would find most emphatic expression among some few individuals, minimal expression among some few others, and the majority would possess the trait to a degree approximating the mean. There was individual variability in the possession of each specific group trait (except fixed traits). Given the normal variability in the possession of traits and the diversity of reproductive rate among groups in the population, each generation would display group traits transmitted by only some of the individuals of the preceding generation. Should differential reproduction characterize special segments of the breeding population collected at one or the other end of the distribution curve, the traits which characterized the entire group would change, sometimes with astonishing rapidity, over a relatively brief time without interracial hybridization.[127] In such a case, race would not be an historical constant, but an historical product, a function of dynamic demographic processes and the normal distribution of traits in the subject population. Fascist theorists were quick to emphasize these and similar theoretical considerations in the defense of a concept of race that included inherent variability and collective genetic "drift."[128] Such commitments provided support not only for Fascism's general dynamic and developmental orientation but defended the "racial integrity" of the nation. Metric and nonmetric variability in the population did not need to be conceived as *prima facie* evidence of extensive racial hybridization.[129] Local variations could be understood as the consequence of local breeding practices and special selective factors. The threat of dividing the Fascist nation into racial castes was obviated[130] and the attempt to restore lost "racial purity" was rejected as a serious political concern.[131]

The reservations advanced by Fascist theoreticians were directed primarily against facets of National Socialist race theory which threatened the integrity of their system. On the philosophic level, Fascists were committed to concepts of individual initiative and moral responsibility which they found threatened by notions of biological determinism; on the doctrinal level, their commitment to the primacy of politics was threatened by the biological interpretation of history; on the tactical level, their allegiance to the unity of the nation and the substantive dignity and equality of its constituent members was compromised by a system of racial classification that threatened to divide Italians along racial lines, ascribing superiority to some and inferiority to others on the basis of select physical traits. Out of such considerations Fascist theoreticians were charged with the responsibility of constructing a coherent racial theory which accorded itself with the philosophical and doctrinal concepts and tactical exigencies of Fascism as well as available scientific evidence.

Fascism's racial doctrine was, therefore, a relatively consistent application of an identifiable collection of core conceptions that were its patrimony from a proto-Fascist past. Nonetheless, Fascism's rapprochement with National Socialism was not without its influence. Thus, while the *Manifesto* insisted that "to say that human races exist is not to say, *a priori,* that there exist superior and inferior human races, but only that different human races exist," almost every academician involved in the formulation of the *Manifesto* went on record as defending the specific thesis of Negro biological inferiority.[132] Hardly an issue of the doctrinal journal, *Difesa della Razza,* appeared without an article supporting such a thesis. Although there were, as has been indicated, dissenting voices among academicians and Fascist theoreticians themselves,[133] the general tendency was to conceive the Negroid races as in some substantial sense biologically inferior. As long as the question was a factual one, the empirical data cited by Fascist theoreticians making the claim could be interpreted in at least two ways: Negroid deficiencies in test performance, for example, could be interpreted as evidence of natural, genetic inferiority or environmental deprivation; statistical differences in cerebral morphology and cranial capacity could be interpreted as indicative of reduced intellectual proficiency or any explicit causal relationship could be denied. Both interpretations of the data were tendered at one time or another by Italian experimental scientists before and during the Fascist period. If some Fascist theoreticians opted for one rather than the other alternative, it could only be for reasons other than scientific.

We have suggested that the earliest of the Italian nationalists entertained a vague and, at that time, theoretically unimportant sense of racial difference. Oriani had spoken of the "irreducible differences" between the Caucasoid and the Negroid races. And Mussolini had spoken of the threat of the "colored races." The increasing preoccuption with race, provoked by the advent of National Socialism in Germany, necessitated a painful probing in this area.

Whether Fascism, left to its own devices, would have developed a conviction in the invidious genetic differences between the major races of mankind is difficult to determine. The antimiscegenation legislation passed by the Fascist Regime after the conquest of Abyssinia was motivated exclusively by Mussolini's concern for "Italian prestige" rather than the protection of the biological patrimony of Italians.[134] Mussolini felt that Italian males, driven by what he called their "irresistible sexual hunger," were undermining Italy's stature in the eyes of indigenous natives by indiscriminately consorting with native women. Mussolini's concerns, apparently, did not even attain the doctrinal level. They were essentially, if not exclusively, political or tactical considerations. In 1938, when he reviewed this legislation, the justification he tendered turned on the "lack of racial dignity" on the part of Italians that diminished their stature as "bearers of civilization" in the eyes of the autochthonous population.[135] He made no recourse to notions of racial superiority as such. In 1940, as we have indicated, he rejected the ascription of "superior" and "inferior" when it was made to the races of man. Mussolini seemed more concerned, in the tradition of the early Futurists and nationalists, with fashioning Italians into a Nietzsechean "race of masters"[136]—confident carriers of Italy's civilizing influence—than in making a case for Italian or Caucasoid biological superiority. The peril Mussolini saw in the colored races was political, not biological.

Fascist ideologues, faced with the evident necessity of integrating Mussolini's tactical legislation into a doctrinal system that would satisfy the National Socialists, with whom contact became more and more intimate, resolved their difficulties by a half-hearted biologism. At this point the racial doctrine became internally inconsistent and in important respects at variance with the Actualist philosophy with which Mussolini himself had identified Fascism. Under the influence of National Socialism biologism, a minor theme in nationalist literature became a major threat to the coherence of Fascist ideology.

Because of this increased tension, the *Manifesto* harbored a number of intrinsic difficulties. The first thesis of the *Manifesto*, for example, defined race as a "material reality" by virtue of which "masses of men" could be identified with physical and psychological traits that are heritable. While standard taxonomists might object to the inclusion of psychic characteristics in the classification of races, many classical anthropologists had, certainly up until that time, included such characteristics among the heritable racial traits. For the purposes of immanent criticisms we can grant their inclusion. Such a definition of geographic and minor races (geographic races would include the Caucasoid, Negroid, and Mongoloid races; the minor races would include such races as the Nordic, Alpine, and Mediterranean races) would be consistent with standard taxonomies. The fourth thesis, however, introduces the concept *Aryan* into the discussion. Aryan does not have a specific biological or anthropological referent. It is by-and-large a linguistic and cultural term referring to a family of peoples which spoke an Aryan or Indo-European language and were carriers of some features of Aryan culture. As we have seen, Fascist theoreticians held the Aryans to have been a mixture of European minor races possessed of a variety of physical traits.[137] Similarly, the "Italian race" referred to by the sixth thesis was a race similarly possessed of a wide variety of physical traits, diverse in stature, cephalic index, pigmentation, and constitution. Such a race no longer accords with the static *anthropological* and *morphological* definition of race advanced in the first thesis. The definition had, in the body of the *Manifesto,* not too subtly changed from a classical anthropological to a populationist definition. The "Italian race" referred to in the sixth thesis is a political community identified as *a breeding circle,* an incipient or perhaps mesodiacritic race, the members of which give evidence of a wide range of physical traits. Any similarity of "psychic" traits in such a community could be *adequately* interpreted as the consequence of cultural conditioning. Yet many Fascist theoreticians came to conceive the "Italian race" as given evidence of *specific* and *hereditary* psychic characteristics peculiar to itself.[138] Giovanni Marro specifically redefined the concept of race in order to justify just such a commitment. He argued:

By race we mean a human group that shares in common an harmonious complex of endowments and spiritual tendencies, constituents of a specific mental entity—a group that has as a formative substratum an historic past, a patrimony transmitted through generations, that directs and polarizes that which is intrinsic to the individual and the collectivity.[139]

Hereditary morphological traits were reduced to a second rank order in classification making "intrinsic spiritual traits" primary.[140] Canella maintained:

An Italian of Nordic or Dalonordic type is none the less always an Italian, quite different from a Scandinavian or a Hollander; a French Mediterranean cannot have the same mentality as an English or Spanish Mediterranean; the character of an Ukrainian Alpine cannot be that of a Bavarian or Umbrian Alpine, and so forth.[141]

These uniformly Italian "spiritual traits" were somehow conceived as "biopsychic," heritable.[142] The only evidence, of course, for their heritability was the historic and cultural continuity of the "Italian people." Such evidence, discursive and speculative, lends itself to a number of alternative interpretations, the most immediate being that of induced continuity, the transmission of cultural traits through formal and informal learning, through suggestion and developmental identification. What is important to note is that the *Manifesto*, in the course of the discussion, ambiguously employed two different and vaguely defined conceptions of race. Fascist theoreticians, cognizant of the definition of race which correlated the physical traits of minor races (pigmentation, stature, and cephalic index) with psychic traits (whatever they might be), proceeded to deny such correlations in their exposition. To defend the spiritual unity of Italians, Caspasso denied that an Italian possessed of a Mediterranean physiognomy invariably possessed a specific Mediterranean mentality or that one possessed of Nordic physical traits was inevitably possessed of a Nordic mentality.[143] No Italian could be assigned specific mental traits on the basis of his physical appearance. The contention was that physical traits were much less plastic than psychological traits and repeated the elements of the "old" or anthropological races of which the "new" Italian race was composed. And yet the Italian race possessed a "magnificent and coherent psychological unity."[144] "In mysterious ways," he goes on, "[the Italian] character is determined by its given racial composition rather than by environmental influences."[145]

The interpretation commonly given would be that while a great deal is as yet unknown concerning human learning, there is no necessity to introduce *mysteries* in the attempt to explain cultural continuity. There can be little doubt that while a specific hereditary potential is a necessary condition of cultural assimilation, heredity does not, in itself, provide the necessary and sufficient condition for the production and/or assimilation of a *particular* culture.

The synthesis of the classical anthropological and populationist conceptions of race is *not* successfully effected in the *Manifesto*. This confusion, and others which abound in the *Manifesto* and in the writings of Fascist theoreticians attempting its explication, can reasonably be interpreted as the consequence of tensions arising from anterior doctrinal and immediate tactical considerations. The primary concern of Fascist theoreticians was to protect the unity of the nation. Any conception of race that threatened that unity was inadmissible. The morphological or classical anthropological conception of race, employed as the National Socialists were disposed to employ it, constituted just a threat. Landra, in his lecture at the University of Berlin, in 1939, focused on these specific difficulties.[146] The classification of citizens into categories hierarchically ranked in accordance with taxonomic criteria would divide Italy into a multiplicity of races and racial hybrids, each possessed of diverse intrinsic value. The unity of the nation would be irretrievably lost. To avoid such an eventuality, a populationist interpretation of race was introduced in the very body of the *Manifesto* that had advanced, in its opening paragraphs, a morphological conception. This apparent discrepancy was bridged by conceiving nations as "protomorphic" or "adiacritic" races, i.e., races in the process of formation. Anthropological or pandiacritic races were understood to be the historic product of protracted selection and genetic isolation.[147] The Italian nation, defined as a politically circumscribed breeding community, was then ascribed certain uniform psychic traits which would animate the population with a sense of common destiny and collective worth. That these common traits were conceived as *heritable* by many Fascist theorists was probably the consequence of Fascism's acquiesence to National Socialist biologism (and the resurgence of nationalist biologism). The political association of National Socialist Germany and Fascist Italy required some substantial unity in orientation. It would have been tactically unpolitic to reject biologism out of hand. It was reinterpreted by Fascists (not without theoretical tension) so that it did not constitute a threat to the integrity of the nation. By 1938, a substantial number of lesser Fascist theorists attempted a synthesis of biological racism and nationalism which committed them to notions which assigned certain mental traits to specific communities of men. The geographic races of man, characterized by a constellation of metric and non-metric physical traits, were purportedly possessed of correlative psychic traits. This was true of minor races as well (constituent components of geographic races). But the European races had mingled on the European continent and produced various breeding communities of varying size and extent. Some racial hybridization between local races was admitted. But each population, because of protracted inbreeding, was developing a "new race" that, given sufficient time and suitable conditions, would produce a morphological race possessed of uniform anthropological characteristics. But such a process could only involve imposing periods of time. The immediate unity of the nation must be sustained by a sense of common destiny. This sense of common destiny was predicated on the existence of common psychic traits which, in ways mysterious, were understood as shared by all Italians in a manner which physical traits were not. These shared psychic traits could not be admitted as the consequence of a shared history and culture because Fascism had, by that time, encumbered itself with anti-Semitic and anti-miscegenation legislation (the heritage, in the former case, of the traffic with National Socialism) that could only be vindicated by an appeal to biological determinism of some sort.

The attempt to meet all the demands of the situation forced Fascist theoreticians to assume postures which could hardly be consistently defended. Psychic traits were at one time less plastic than physical traits (to support the legislation directed against Italo-Jewish "miscegenation")[148] and at other times psychic traits were more plastic than physical traits (to support the homogeneity of the Italian nation in the face of the evident physical variability of its population).[149] Races were, on the one hand, defined in terms of groups of men commonly possessed of similar physical and psychic traits (to justify the legislation against miscegenation between Italians and non-European races) and on the other as "stable" hybrids of two or more anthropological races (to defend the equality of all Italians irrespective of heterogeneity of race). The term *Nordic* was used on some occasions to identify a given race possessed of certain shared physical and mental traits, and on other occasions to mean a cultural orientation. There was a renunciation of the doctrine of racial superiority and inferiority on the one hand (to protect the integrity of Italians of Nordic, Mediterranean, Alpine, Dinaric, or hybrid derivation), and yet, on the other hand, there was a proscription against the marriage of Italians to non-Europeans, presumably predicated on the superiority of European biological heritage.

Fascist theoreticians, Mussolini among them, favored a populationist definition of race (the "new races" of which they spoke). Though such a definition makes the concept of race compatible with nationalism (since the nation is conceived as a politically defined breeding community, the material base for the development of a race), the concept does not lend itself unequivocally to ascriptions of uniform and hereditary psychic traits to such a community (they were spoken of as heritable spiritual *tendencies*). If psychic traits are heritable, then they must vary as physical traits vary. This would be true if race were to be understood in purely biological terms. If psychic traits are inherited in conformity to the Mendelian laws of genetic transmission, one would expect the psychic traits of a given population to vary as physical traits vary. Consequently, any observed sense of common purpose, common culture, and common destiny would only be conceived as induced rather than inherited.

The difficulties evident in the *Manifesto* become imposing when the ninth thesis, devoted to the Jews, is considered. The ninth thesis was intended to provide a doctrinal justification for the *ad hoc* anti-Jewish legislation promulgated by the Regime in 1938. That anti-Semitism was an extraneous encumbrance on Fascist ideology becomes obvious when one considers the enormous confusion which surrounded the issue.

The ninth thesis of the *Manifesto* maintains that "the Jews do not belong to the Aryan race." But the Aryan race was admittedly a collection of minor anthropological races including Nordics, Dalonordics, Alpines, Mediterraneans, Dinarics, and Baltics, united by a tenuous unity of related languages and cultural derivatives.[150] Canella, in his discussion of the Jewish "race," indicated that,

. . . the Jews do not constitute an anthropological race, but rather a mixture, in various measure, of the most disparate racial elements: primarily Arabs and Assyrioids, then Egyptians, Ethiopians, Mediterraneans, Negroids, Baltics, Alpines, Nordics, and so forth. . . .[151]

The Jews, as a group, therefore, contained at least some elements of the same minor races of which the Aryans were composed.

While there were some anthropologists in Italy and some Fascist apologists[152] who maintained that the Jews constituted an identifiable physical type, the vast majority of Italian scholars agreed with Canella that "the so-called Jewish race . . . cannot be considered a true race . . . but a mixture of heterogeneous racial elements."[153] Whatever distinctions were to be made could not be made on the basis of any reasonably strict anthropological criteria. The best that could be offered to vindicate anti-Semitic legislation was the suggestion that while the Jews did

. . . not constitute a race in the strict anthropological sense, they constitute a very compact ethnic group . . . and manifest a *forma mentis* so typical that it would be legitimate to consider them, even if it be with some reservations, as a "psychological" race.[154]

Whatever their "somatic type," they displayed "mental and moral traits which, in general, characterize them."[155]

Again, the arguments took a form similar to those developed for the "psychological unity" of the "Italian race." Whatever unity existed was the cultural and historic unity of an association of men living under a cultural system having significant elements of historic continuity. Again, an adequate explanation of such a continuity did not require race (understood in any strictly biological sense) as an explanatory variable. The Jews did not evidence any more strictly anthropological homogeneity than did the Italians or the Aryans. The customs and traditions and institutions of Jews, Italians, and Aryans each displayed some sort of continuity. To explain this continuity by making appeal to some hereditary substance was a surrender to a biological simplism of an indefensible sort. Italian scholars themselves were uncomfortable with the purported explanation, and as late as 1943 still admonished racist enthusiasts that

. . . it has not always been the case that investigators have taken precise account of the enormous difficulties of various sorts that face a truly scientific study of racial psychic traits. . . . It remains to be determined how much, in all this, can be considered truly innate and hereditary and how much, instead, is the effect of environmental factors.[156]

The doctrinal attempts to provide a rationale for anti-Semitic legislation introduced to curry favor with National Socialist Germany were almost uniformly inept. They were attempts to graft on to the neo-idealism of Fascist philosophy the imported cuttings of a mystical and biological racism. That such an attempt was made was the consequence of the increasingly intimate alliance with, and ultimate dependence upon, National Socialist Germany. In discussions with Ciano, Mussolini indicated that he was convinced that the "theories of Rosenberg" could not, under any circumstances, survive the war.[157] To Spampanato he further confided:

The *Manifesto on Race* could have been avoided. It is a scientific abstruseness of certain scholars and journalists, a German text translated into bad Italian. It is a long way from anything I have said, written, or signed in fact. I suggest you look at the back issues of *Il Popolo d'Italia*. I have always considered the Italian people an admirable product of diverse ethnic fusions on the basis of a geographic, economic, and especially spiritual unity. It has been the spirit which has put our culture on the by-ways of the world.[158]

The attempt to incorporate biological racism into Fascism revealed the extent of the differences which separated Fascism as a mature ideology from National Socialism. The political alliance with National Socialist Germany, furthermore, provoked the development of a biologism latent in the writings of some nationalists. They sought to make race the principal repository of value, thereby threatening to subvert Fascism's entire rationale. Mussolini, apparently surrendering to what he conceived to be the political necessities generated by the alliance with National Socialist Germany, had neither the will nor the disposition to control the situation. The alliance with Germany was of prime political importance and in its service Mussolini permitted the ideological coherence of Fascism to be, in considerable measure, compromised. The

277

gradual growth of German influence in this sphere of doctrinal elaboration was completely inimical to Fascist idealism. Gentile, for example, had befriended Jewish scholars driven from Germany and had even assisted some of them to escape from Italy when anti-Semitic persecutions began.[159] He was among the few men in Fascist Italy who remained assiduously aloof from anti-Semitism and who, at considerable personal risk, ventured to manifest his objections by paying public homage to his Jewish teacher Alessandro D'Ancona in 1941, when the anti-Semitic campaign was well under way.[160]

There is little doubt concerning Mussolini's personal convictions. Mussolini's personal relationship with Jews evidenced little systematic bias. His friendship with Angelica Balabanoff and Margherita Sarfatti was intimate and enduring. Aldo Finzi was a member of Mussolini's first cabinet and Guido Jung was his Minister of Finance for many years. There were Jews present at the foundation of the Fascist Party in March, 1919, and Jews served in many leading positions in the state. In 1941, Mussolini himself indicated that he "could not forget that four of the seven founders of Italian nationalism were Jews."[161] He had personally interceded with Hitler on behalf of Henri Bergson and had "Aryanized" a number of Italian Jews for valor. Long after the promulgation of Fascist anti-Semitic legislation Jews continued to occupy important official and unofficial positions in Italy.[162]

Mussolini's anti-Jewish attitude was dictated not by theoretical but almost solely by tactical, i.e., political, considerations. Like most nationalists he did oppose political Zionism because of its threat of dual loyalties. He was suspicious of any community within the body politic which maintained exclusive institutions. But by the middle of 1936, Mussolini felt that the Jewish issue had become one of singular political importance because of Hitler's intransigence. Mussolini had attempted, in 1933, to convince Hitler that state anti-Semitism was dangerous and that while

. . . every regime has not only the right but the duty to eliminate from posts of command elements in which it does not have complete trust, it is not necessary, in fact it can be disastrous, to make a question of race—Semitism and Aryanism—that which is simply a measure of defense. . . .[163]

278

When he failed to convince Hitler, he decided to accommodate the National Socialists by introducing anti-Semitic legislation in Italy as evidence of his good faith. He conceived it an offering calculated to solidify the Italo-German alliance.

There is no doubt that Mussolini's decision to introduce . . . state anti-Semitism into Italy was determined, essentially, by the conviction that it was necessary to eliminate every marked difference in the politics of the two regimes in order to render the Italo-German alliance infrangible.[164]

It is not the purpose here to pursue the character of Fascist anti-Semitic legislation. For the purposes of perspective, it is only necessary to indicate that Fascist anti-Semitism "had its own specific characteristics and could absolutely not be put on the same level as that of Germany, nor that of its other satellites, including Vichy France."[165] Fascist anti-Semitism was tactical—and a certain measure of bad conscience seems to have attended anti-Jewish measures. There is ample evidence that well into 1943, Italian officials (with Mussolini's connivance) systematically obstructed National Socialist attempts to transport Jews out of Fascist occupied territory.[166] Rosenberg lamented that Mussolini had protected Jews, and the Fascist "intransigents" denounced him to Goebbels for entertaining "injudicious tolerance" for Jews and Freemasons.[167] An anti-Semitism which singled out individuals for discrimination solely on the basis of their membership in a putative biological community was incompatible with the social and political values with which Mussolini had identified Fascism. The attempts to provide a doctrinal rationale created serious theoretical tensions in the systematic ideology of Fascism. Discriminatory racial legislation could be most convincingly vindicated by an appeal to collective biological values—group superiority or inferiority. And yet Mario Missiroli, in the article on the race issue specifically recommended by Mussolini, maintained that

. . . the highest spiritual values are a conquest of conscience, the consequence of effort and perpetual choice and, as such, are not determined by natural fact, for should such be the case nature would subordinate spirit, which would be manifestly contrary to the ethics of Fascism, founded as it is upon the absolute and incontestible supremacy of the will and moral responsibility.[168]

Such a position left no room for the notions of biological determinism that would most effectively vindicate the proscriptive legislation levelled against the Jews of Italy. Such legislation required some doctrine of collective guilt. Giovanni Preziosi, perhaps Fascist Italy's only consistent anti-Semite, had accordingly argued that "whoever possesses a drop of Jewish blood possesses a solidarity with the race,"[169] as warrant for legislation directed against Jews. Only some conviction of biological determinism could provide the legitimation for such discrimination.

By the time of the instauration in the North in 1943, two Fascist factions had polarized. Fascism had split along lines of cleavage that followed the race question. The Fascist intransigents openly renounced Gentile[170] and advocated the reconstruction of Fascist philosophy on the basis of National Socialist biologism. For a time Preziosi, an intimate of Alfred Rosenberg and a vocal critic of Mussolini,[171] had been considered by the National Socialists as the successor to Mussolini.[172] His opposition to Gentile was so violent that it was first believed that Gentile's assassination had been the work of his faction. The intransigent opposition had been so vociferous that Gentile had at first refused to participate in the Fascist republican government founded in 1943. Only a personal appeal by Mussolini convinced him to assume the presidency of the Italian Academy.[173]

The assassination of Gentile in April, 1944, profoundly affected Mussolini. It was only with Gentile's death that Mussolini acceded to National Socialist pressure and appointed Preziosi, whom he found "repulsive," Inspector General for Race.[174] This marked the last and most tragic phase of anti-Semitism in Fascist Italy.

As late as 1941, Mussolini personally deplored the excesses of anti-Semitic propaganda.[175] But in a regime like that of Fascism, he had to bear responsibility for the particularly vile character that propaganda had assumed as early as 1938. By 1943, Mussolini himself was making ready reference to the "Judeo-Masonic-Bolsheviks" of France, to "Jewish capitalism," to "Masonic-Judaic intrigues," to Americans as the "levy of Israel," an "Israel that wants its integral, spiteful vengeance" undertaken in accordance with its "Talmudic doctrine."[176]

For all that, anti-Semitism never figured in those documents which could be conceived as composing Mussolini's political testament. In his conversations with Maddalena Mollier in March, 1945, and with the Prefect Nicoletti and the journalist Cabella in April, 1945, immediately before his death, Mussolini made no reference at all to the Jewish question. It would seem that he did not feel that it was an essential concern for Fascism. His overall position seems to have been one of diffidence concerning organized Jewry, particularly political Zionism. The public position assumed by international Jewish groups, particularly during the Ethiopian campaign, seems to have aggravated his diffidence. But the ultimate determinant, which made anti-Semitism state policy in Fascist Italy, was the alliance with National Socialist Germany.

The Fascist doctrine on race was a relatively coherent and specific body of propositions which developed out of core conceptions inherited from a pre- and proto-Fascist sociological tradition. Its critical elements can be traced back to Gumplowicz—and in its specifically Fascist forms was consonant with the totalitarian nationalism of Fascist ideology. The increasingly intimate relationship with National Socialist Germany provoked theoretical tensions within the doctrinal system and precipitated a growth of accessory elements to be found in Fascism's nationalist tradition. Minor anti-Semitic themes became exaggerated under National Socialist influences and peripheral biological concerns pressed themselves to the forefront. National Socialist racism was radically incompatible with nationalism, and as a consequence the attempt to accommodate the elements of static and taxonomic elements created serious difficulties for Fascism's doctrinal system.

In retrospect, it is possible to reconstruct a specifically Fascist racial doctrine with a fair degree of specificity. Until 1938, that doctrine existed without the encumbrances of National Socialist elements. Only then did the accretions which resulted from Fascist Italy's traffic with National Socialist Germany begin to weigh down Fascist ideology. All the major ideologues of Fascism, including Mussolini and Gentile, recognized the disabilities that resulted.

In effect, Fascist racial doctrine was, in itself, significantly different from that of National Socialism. The effort to make the one compatible with the other created enormous problems for Fascism and never succeeded in convincing the National Socialists that Fascist racism was serious. To observers outside both systems of thought, the conviction has prevailed that Fascism had no racial doctrine—that it either mimicked National Socialism or simply made *ad hoc* pronouncements on such matters. Neither interpretation is true. There was a specifically Fascist doctrine of race, but it was subsequently contaminated by elements introduced through contact with National Socialism. Both the indigenous Fascist racial doctrine and the extraneous elements which collected around it can now be identified with some certainty.

Fascist racism was an endogenous growth, the product of early Fascist commitments. It was but one expression of the totalitarian nationalism that became the core of Fascist doctrine after 1918, an expression not incompatible with the fully articulated ideology as it manifested itself by 1932.

CHAPTER SEVEN

Final Doctrinal Developments: Socialization

THE FINAL phase of Fascist development took place in a context of national tragedy. Italian soil was invaded by one of the most powerful combinations of military force in world history. On July 25 and 26, 1943, a palace coup deposed Mussolini. During the last week of July, all of August, and the first week of September, he was held under house arrest on the Island of Ponza, then on the Island of La Maddelena off Sardinia, finally, on the Gran Sasso. On September 8, the Italian radio announced the unconditional capitulation of the Badoglio government to the Allies. The King and Badoglio then fled Rome to ensconce themselves behind the Allied lines in southern Italy while the German army occupied Rome. The Italian army, shorn of leadership and beset by conflicting orders, disintegrated, and 600,000 disarmed Italian soldiers were deported to concentration camps in Germany. German military units occupied all the major strategic points on the peninsula and German aircraft wreaked havoc on the Italian naval units that had been ordered to surrender at Allied ports. Allied aircraft, in turn, began an indiscriminate saturation bombing of Italian cities. Italians were defeated enemy nationals to the Allies and traitors to the Germans.

Among Italians, political activists had organized the Committee of National Liberation. The C.L.N. became the nucleus of anti-Fascist partisan bands throughout the nation, a development that gave impetus to the savage fratricidal war that ravaged Italy for Fascism's final six hundred days. In turn, small Fascist units began to reorganize after the initial stupor of the Fascist debacle had dissipated itself. Some of the Fascist hierarchy had repaired to Germany to solicit Hitler's support for a resurgent Fascist provisional government to rule the truncated peninsula. A few hours after the announcement of the surrender by the Badoglio government, Italian radios picked up the notes of the Fascist hymn "Giovinezza" and Alessandro Pavolini implored Italian soldiers to resist the Royal order of surrender, in the name of a newly constituted Fascist national government.

On September 12, a German glider detachment, under the orders of the German Commando Otto Skorzeny, landed at the Campo Imperiale at the Gran Sasso and liberated Mussolini (four Italian airmen had made a previous attempt and were shot for their trouble). After a harrowing flight from the Gran Sasso, Mussolini was shuttled to a Heinkel aircraft at the airfield of Pratica di Mare, flown to Vienna, and flown from there to Munich where he met his family for the first time since his arrest in July. On September 14, he was flown to Hitler's headquarters where the two dictators greeted each other with what Goebbels described as exceptional cordiality and friendship. For two hours the two men were closeted together.

All the evidence available indicates that Mussolini was at that time physically debilitated and emotionally exhausted. The German physician who examined him shortly after his liberation described him as "a very ailing man, who has bravely borne atrocious pain for nearly four years." Mussolini was overcome by the extent of the tragedy that had befallen Italy and he was convinced that Fascism, as a political movement, had been definitively defeated.[1] In the end, it was only Hitler's threat to unleash on Italy the vengeance threatened in his speech of September 10 that compelled Mussolini to attempt a restoration of Fascist government. Mussolini met with a small group of Fascists at Rastenburg in order to prepare the new government.

The Germans insisted that the new government be instituted with dispatch. That such a government would be politically effective was never seriously entertained. Goebbels maintained, in a judgment that was apparently that of the German rulers in general:

Fascism seems . . . to show no political strength whatever. We must now proceed very coolly and realistically in all these matters. We must use Fascism as far as possible, but of course must not expect the impossible. In the Fuehrer's calculation, Italy used to be a factor of power. That is no longer the case. . . . Italy has abdicated as a people and as a nation. That's in accordance with the law of nature and the principles of justice in historical development.[2]

Mussolini himself conceived the new government primarily as a buffer against German vengeance, and second as a vehicle for the "pacification of Italian hearts," an effort to reduce the fratricidal animosities that threatened civil war.

Hitler, however, insisted that the Fascists mete out punishments to the "traitors of Fascism," beginning with the members of the Grand Council of Fascism whose vote on the night of July 25, 1943, threw the Regime into the crisis which gave the King the opportunity to dismiss Mussolini. Hitler was horrified to find that Mussolini entertained no such intention. Goebbels reported that

the Fuehrer expected that the first thing the Duce would do would be to wreak full vengeance on his betrayers. But he gave no such indication, and thereby showed his real limitations. He is not a revolutionary like the Fuehrer or Stalin. He is so bound to his own Italian people that he lacks the broad qualities of a world-wide revolutionary and insurrectionist.[3]

Even Franco Martinelli, who can hardly be charged with philo-Fascism, after having surveyed the available evidence, reported that "vengeance had no attraction for [Mussolini]. He was motivated, rather, by a desire to rescue the nation from ultimate ruin, to save that which could be saved."[4] Carlo Silvestri, an anti-Fascist throughout his adult life, insisted that Mussolini's intention was to "diminish the tragic consequences of the situation and to humanize the unbridled passions [unleashed by the circumstances]."[5]

To serve these ends, Mussolini strove to reconstitute the Italian army and internal security forces in order to see to it that Italians rather than Germans would deal with Italians, and that the sovereignty and territorial integrity of the nation would be defended by Italian forces. Furthermore, he made genuine efforts to placate the anti-Fascist opposition. He maintained that he sought a government of national unity in which the entire range of political opinion might find expression. Both efforts, that of reconstituting the armed forces of the nation and that of abating fratricidal passions, were to prove signal failures.

Italian units fought throughout the remainder of the war, some in special units under German command, some, under *Condottieri* like Valerio Borghese, undertaking acts of heroism and sacrifice. But an effective Italian army was never reconstituted. The Germans remained dubious of Italian commitment and did everything possible to frustrate Mussolini's efforts.[6] The attempt to preclude civil war was equally ineffectual. By the time of the convocation in November of the first congress of the newly reorganized *Partito Fascista Repubblicano*, individual acts of violence and terrorism by both sides had exacerbated the situation. During the Fascist Congress at Verona the assembled members were greeted with the announcement of the assassination of Iginio Ghisellini, the Fascist *Federale* of Ferrara. A punitive squad of Fascists left Verona immediately for Ferrara and there summarily executed eleven hostages. Thereafter, there was a doleful repetition of ambuscades and the execution of hostages that savaged Italy for the remainder of the war. The mutual brutality spared no one. It was in the course of this savagery that Gentile was assassinated on April 15, 1944.

Conjoined with his effort to reconstruct a national army and pacify the fratricidal passion of the Italian people was one further enterprise upon which Mussolini embarked during the final days of Fascism: the socialization of the Italian economy. It is this final doctrinal development that concerns us here. It was the final expression of Mussolini's social and political thought and revealed, in Fascism's final hours, the ideals that animated the first national totalitarianism of the twentieth century.

The Social Conceptions
of Republican Fascism

From the moment Mussolini reappeared on the Italian scene he made it clear that he intended to restore a state that would be "national and social in the most profound sense," a Fascist state returned to its doctrinal "origins," a state that would finally eliminate plutocratic traces and make labor, in all its forms, its "infrangible basis."[7] During the first meeting of the Council of Ministers of the new Republic, he insisted that the state should possess

a pronounced social content in order to resolve the social question (at least in its most urgent aspects), in order to establish the place, the function, the responsibility of labor in a national and truly modern society.[8]

He ordered the fusion of the various syndical confederations into a single General Confederation of Labor "within the compass and in the climate of the Party, which will infuse it with its own revolutionary force."

In November, 1943, the newly constituted Fascist Republican Party, which by that time numbered 250,000 adherents, issued its Program Manifesto (See Appendix B). Because a Constituent Assembly was never held in the besieged Republic, the Program Manifesto was, in effect, the Constitution of the Republic of Salò. It was the work of Pavolini, who was *de facto* Secretary of the Party, and of Nicola Bombacci, a former socialist deputy and communist who had been one of the young Mussolini's socialist associates. It was Mussolini himself, however, who inspired the document and he reviewed it before presenting it to the Fascist Congress, where it was accepted by acclamation.[9] Over half of the Manifesto was devoted to the social question—to Fascist socialization.

The Manifesto repeated Mussolini's intention to make the "basis of the Social Republic . . . manual, technical and intellectual labor in every form." While it guaranteed private property it insisted that private property would not be permitted to "undermine the physical and moral personality . . . through exploitation." Furthermore, every economic activity which transcended strictly

287

private interests, affecting the community through its scope or function, was conceived as falling within the state's sphere of interest. Public utilities and war industries were to be state administered through governmental or paragovernmental agencies. Throughout industry, whether state, semi-state, or private, the labor force would elect representatives to managerial collegia which would direct each enterprise and provide for local and regional wage scales and profit sharing. In agriculture, where private initiative failed to satisfy state criteria for efficient use, land was to be expropriated and allotted to those who could work it effectively or, according to the circumstances, transformed into cooperative or state farms. Artisans and small scale producers would continue to operate as private entrepreneurs but only within the confines of state quantity and quality controls and constrained by fixed price scales. Every worker was to be automatically enrolled in his category syndicate in one Confederation which would include all workers and technical and professional personnel, with the exclusion of owners who were not themselves entrepreneurial directors or technicians. All the social legislation of the antecedent Fascist period was to be retained, with the Labor Charter of 1927 recognized as the initial point of the contemporary evolution. National minimal wages were to be established and workers were to gradually accede to domiciliary ownership when the sum of the rent paid for their housing covered the capital and interest involved. Payment in rent would thereby establish a title of purchase.

This was the program of renascent Fascism, and its emphatic socialist content was obvious to all, both friend and foe alike. At the fifth meeting of the Council of Ministers in January, 1944, Mussolini laid down the "Fundamental Premises for the Creation of a New Structure for the Italian Economy."[10] It was announced that

the state, on the basis of the ninth declaration of the Labor Charter and the programmatic postulates of the first report of the *Partito Fascista Repubblicano* of Verona, assumes the direct management of those industries that control sectors vital to the economic and political independence of the nation, including those enterprises that furnish primary materials and energy and other indispensable services for the development of the economic life of the nation.[11]

Expropriation was to be compensated by the issuance of negotiable, transferable, and interest-bearing certificates.

Coupled with the state ownership of these key sectors of the economy was a general process of "socialization." State-owned industries were to be administered by a managerial council elected by all the working personnel of each individual enterprise. The elected council was to deliberate and render decisions concerning all the questions inherent in the development of the concern's production within the ambit of "a unitary national plan determined by the competent organs of the Italian Social Republic."

In private enterprises, based on share capital, a collegial council was to be formed of labor representatives—workers, clerks, and technicians—equal in number to those representatives elected by an assembly of shareholders. In those industries owned by individuals employing fifty or more persons, a managerial council of workers, clerks, and technicians, composed of at least three members, was to be established.

Each enterprise was to have a director. In nationalized industries this director was nominated by the state. In private industries the director would be the owner of the industry himself or someone nominated by the managerial council. The director of each industry would be politically and juridically responsible to the state for the maintenance of production and for discipline. In each industry, public or private, the managerial council, elected by the collective labor force, would deliberate concerning internal regulations and whatever controversies might arise from their implementation. The profits of private industry were not to exceed limits to be annually specified by the state in conformity with the economic requirements of the productive community as a whole. Should profits exceed the maximum established, surplus profit was to be shared by the labor force of the particular industry and the state. The funds received by the state would be applied to social welfare programs.

On February 12, 1944, the Republican Council of Ministers met to implement the "Fundamental Premises."[12] On the 13th it was announced that all enterprises based upon share capital exceeding one million lire or employing at least one hundred workers were to be socialized. Each such enterprise would operate under the management of (a) an assembly, (b) an administrative or managerial council, (c) a syndical collegium, and (d) a director. The assembly, composed of the entire body of employees and the share holders of the enterprise, each category having an equal number of votes, would elect an administrative council and a syndical collegium. The administrative council would be composed of representatives of labor and capital in equal number. The collegium would be composed of representatives of labor. The director of the enterprise was to be elected by the assembly and appointed by the council.

In industries not covered by the antecedent regulations, an administrative council was to be organized composed of an equal number of representatives from labor and from capital. In enterprises owned by individuals in which the capital invested did not exceed one million lire, or in which those employed numbered less than one hundred, a managerial council was to be constituted composed of at least three members elected from among the workers, white collar workers, and technicians. The election of representatives to the administrative or managerial councils, the syndical collegia, and the director was to involve all employees in each enterprise and was to be by secret ballot.

Angelo Tarchi was appointed Minister of Corporations and charged with the responsibility of overcoming the obstacles that Mussolini was advised would be thrown in the path of socialization by the "intriguing plutocracy in Italy."[13] The Minister also had the authority to intervene in cases where any industrial establishment, in his opinion, gave rise to "any serious misgiving." Furthermore, since the directors of each enterprise were politically and juridically responsible to the state, the state retained ultimate control over the economy.

The Resistance to Fascist Socialization

The foregoing constituted the outline of the new structure of an integral Fascist economy. In the deliberation before the announcement by the Council of Ministers on February 13, 1944, Mussolini advised the German authorities of his plan for massive economic reform. Needless to say the Germans, who were responsible to Hitler for the maintenance of discipline and productivity in Italy, resisted in the fear that Italian industry would suffer under the impact of such legislation. Dr. Rudolf Rahn, a senior member of the German staff in Italy, approached Mussolini directly and reported to Berlin that the proposed reconstruction of Italian economy was the work of Mussolini himself. He also indicated that Italian capitalists had approached General Leyhers of the German military staff and asked for his intercession in resisting the Fascist program. Rahn further indicated that he had fully discussed the program with Mussolini, and Mussolini had firmly opposed any modification of the legislation designed to finally break the capitalist resistance to Fascism. Mussolini charged the large capitalists not only with undermining the Fascist Regime, but also with actively supporting the C.N.L. and the communist partisans who had begun to appear in increasing numbers throughout the North. Mussolini argued that the nationalization of key sectors of the economy and socialization of the larger individual enterprises was long overdue and that the state-owned and government-controlled industries had had a long record of superiority over the capitalist enterprises of Italy. Mussolini's measures, Rahn reported, were directed chiefly against the industrialists and factory owners "who were for the most part typical representatives of high finance," who invariably put private interests before the interests of the nation.[14]

Irrespective of Hitler's and Rahn's passive support, the German officials in Italy continued to obstruct the implementation of the decrees on socialization. Coupled with German obstruction was the resistance of socialist and communist organizers among the diffident and apathetic Italian working class. In a curious collaboration between the Germans, Italian capitalists, and the socialist and communist elements in Italy, Fascism's desperate efforts to divest the capitalist class of its economic base were regularly impeded. Tarchi noted with bitterness that the industrialists made common cause not only with the German authorities, but with the socialist and communist "secret action committees" as well, in order to obstruct the Fascist legislation on socialization. The conspiracy against nationalization and socialization effectively postponed any serious efforts to implement the legislation throughout the Spring of 1944. Nonetheless, Mussolini decided to try to override German opposition by unilaterally ordering implementation on June 30. General Leyers of the military staff immediately insisted that certain firms be "protected" against the new Fascist legislation. Nonetheless, during the remaining ten months of the Fascist Republic about seventy industrial establishments were socialized. Most of the establishments effected were those that the Germans felt were nonessential to the war effort, principally those involved in publishing books and newspapers. Preliminaries to socialization were undertaken, nevertheless, in paper pulp, graphic arts, consumer produce, and chemical industries. Industrial combines such as Alfa Romeo, Dalmine, Motomeccaniche, Burgo, Fiat, Montecatini, Acciaierie e Ferriere Lombarde, Puricelli, and Olivetti were effected. But Mussolini was obstructed by massive resistance on the part of the combined forces of German officialdom, Italian capitalism, and the communist and socialist action committees, as well as the general indifference of the working class. It was this curious combination of forces that faulted the final efforts to achieve a Fascist socialism.

Fascist Socialism

Commentators have assessed this final development of Fascist doctrine as another instance of Mussolini's incomprehensible changes in course—another instance of his doctrinal gymnastics. It has also been conceived as a simple ploy, characteristic of Mussolini's personal politics, calculated to gull the working class.[15] Neither interpretation is adequate.

The first is no interpretation at all. It requires a negative proof that Mussolini's thought displayed no continuity, that socialization, as a program, had no antecedents in Mussolini's thought or in Fascist doctrine. The second interpretation is manifestly unconvincing. Mussolini was well aware that whatever security the Fascist Republic enjoyed was afforded by German bayonets. If he had wished only to remain in power (the motive, presumably, for wanting to gull the working class), he did not have to consider duping Italians; the German Army would assure him tenure.

Mussolini was sufficiently astute to realize that Italians, in general, entertained little enthusiasm for his reborn Fascism. Whatever evidence is available indicates that Mussolini's Republic was designed as a social and political legacy to the Italy that would survive the war—an Italy that Mussolini realized would be an Italy without Mussolini. In January, 1945, four months before his death, Mussolini appointed Giuseppe Spinelli as Minister of Labor and charged him with the responsibility of planting the soil of Italy with "social mines."[16] Mussolini anticipated that the process of socialization would proceed to the point where it could not be reversed by the returning monarchists and industrialists. Mussolini hoped that Fascism would bequeath to post-war Italy a socialized economy.

Socialization was, in fact, the product of a maturation of trends already implicit in the earliest Fascist formulations. The trend that matured into socialization was already manifest by the time of the Second Convention of Syndical and Corporative Studies, held in Ferrara in May, 1932. Its substance was provided by the persistent *socialist* and *anti-bourgeois* biases of radical national syndicalism conjoined with the totalitarian pretensions of neo-idealism. Its spokesman at the Convention was Ugo Spirito, one of the most prominent students of Giovanni Gentile.

Spirito delivered a communication at the Convention, "Individuo e stato nell'economia corporativa,"[17] that revealed the course Fascist thought was taking after seven years of secure power. Because of the nature of the communication, Spirito had submitted it to Mussolini for approval before he delivered it. He had taken this precaution on the suggestion of Gentile, who had also read and approved the statement.[18]

It is clear from Spirito's communication that Fascism, while explicit in its criticism of some of the central concepts of Marxist socialism, nevertheless recognized certain of its positive values. Spirito conceived the corporativism of Fascism, as it had evolved to that point, as *transitional:* a transitory hybrid form that would ultimately divest itself of residual capitalist elements to become an "integral corporativism" in which private property would no longer constitute loci of particular interests independent of, and conceivably opposed to, the interests of the state.[19] He anticipated the Fascist revolution as traversing diverse stages. A new social and economic order could not be substituted overnight in a complex industrial nation without courting chaos. Fascism was a conservative revolution, but a revolution nonetheless. In so characterizing the

293

Fascist revolution, Spirito echoed judgments made by Mussolini throughout his political career. In 1919, Mussolini insisted that "a political revolution can be made in twenty-four hours, but one does not subvert a nation's economy, which is part of the world economic system, in twenty-four hours. This is not to say that Fascism will constitute itself a 'body guard' of the bourgeoisie. . . ."[20] In discussing the economic transformation of society, Mussolini maintained that any massive economic reform required in anticipation "a profound preliminary elaboration of institutions and social consciousness."[21] In 1944, he confided to Rahn, "I have always been extremely cautious about economic matters . . . and have expounded the view before now that whereas surgical methods may often be applicable to politics, where economics are concerned medical or even homeopathic methods should be applied."[22]

At the commencement of the Fascist enterprise these sentiments were conjoined with the conviction that capitalism, as a mode of production, still retained the vitality required by the productionist program of Italian nationalism.[23] It was only in November, 1933, that Mussolini became convinced that the crisis that had beset capitalism for four years was not a crisis *within* the system, but a crisis *of* the system. It was on that occasion that he spoke of "the complete organic and totalitarian regulation of production," a "regulated" and "controlled" economy—a "burial" of capitalism.[24]

The first Fascist attempts to intervene in the Italian economy had in fact, been effected long before by the Convention of the Palazzo Chigi and the Pact signed at the Palazzo Vidoni, in 1925 and early 1926. The Pact of the Palazzo Vidoni provided for a recognition by the Confederation of Industry of the Confederation of Corporations for Labor as the sole bargaining agent for Italians workers. The agreement provided the basis for the collective contracts which were to govern the relations between capital and labor throughout the next decade. At the time the agreement was considered (even by informed American analysts) a significant victory for the Fascist working class syndicates. Edmondo Rossoni, leader of the Fascist syndicates, considered the individual factory commissions that prevailed at that time, a hold-over from the socialist factory occupation movement of 1920, pliant instruments in the hands of employers and ineffectual in collective bargaining. In their place the syndicates had received national recognition for a unitary Confederation which, juridically, could meet the industrialists' Confederation of Industry on an equal footing. Furthermore, the recognition of collective contracts which were compulsory augured the extensive involvement of the state in the economy of the nation. Rossoni conceived the Pact as a step in the direction of the integralist totalitarian state.[25] However overly optimistic Rossoni's analysis proved with respect to the benefits it would bring the working class, the Pact was, as later events were to reveal, the first step in the direction of totalitarian control of the economy. In any event, the Pact was certainly not universally welcomed by the entrepreneurial class.[26]

From that point on Fascist social and economic legislation became increasingly tutelary and interventionist. The Law of April 3, and the by-laws of July 1, 1926, marked further inroads by the Fascist state into the Italian economy. In 1927, the Labor Charter was made a juridical norm governing the relations between capital and labor. Though the seventh declaration of the Charter maintained that "the corporate state considers that private enterprise in the sphere of production is the most effective and useful instrument in the interests of the nation," the ninth indicated that state intervention would make itself manifest when "private initiative is lacking or insufficient." More significant still was the contention that "in view of the fact that the private organization of production is a function of national concern, the organizer of the enterprise is responsible to the state. . . ." Giuseppe Bottai in his commentary on the Charter, made painfully clear, at the very time of its promulgation, the intentions of this final clause.

Because the functions of the private merchant and industrialist are functions of national concern, they are obliged to execute them *in conformity with the national interest* and in the direction of production they are *responsible before the state*.[27]

Irrespective of the euphoric statements of Fascist apologists throughout the period before World War II, responsible Fascists recognized that the existing machinery of class and category conciliation instituted by the Regime did not *resolve* the social problem.[28] Fascist syndicalists, for example, regularly complained of violation of contractual obligations on the part of entrepreneurs.[29] The fact is that knowledgeable Fascists recognized that the machinery of conciliation constructed by the state could not effectively resolve the disparity between productive classes. Mussolini ultimately made this fact public. In January, 1944, he wrote that twenty years of experience had taught Fascists that

the state . . . could not limit itself to the functions of mediation between classes because the substantially greater force the capitalist classes were capable of deploying rendered inoperative the juridical equality upon which parity was predicated. This superior force . . . permitted the capitalist classes to dominate, and turn to their own advantage, every action by the state. . . .[30]

In any event, by 1930 it was evident that Fascism, for its own purposes, would have to evolve institutions and techniques to restrict the independent power of the possessing classes. This was to be effected not only to render the state truly sovereign, but also to defend those socialist values that Fascist syndicalists and neo-idealists had never abjured. Even Corradini had insisted that Fascism meant to "transcend socialism, not to disperse it, not to destroy its accomplishments." He went on to say,

It is necessary to make such an affirmation. . . . It is fundamental; it is an essentially Fascist affirmation. Between Fascism and socialism there is an historic connection, that is to say an historic continuity. . . . Fascism transcends socialism, but garners the good fruit of socialist efforts and in accordance with its own laws . . . this work will continue.[31]

By the time Spirito delivered his communication at the Convention of 1932, these sentiments had united with neo-idealist totalitarian aspirations. The result was variously identified as "Fascist communism," "Fascist Bolshevism" or "Fascist socialism."

Spirito was concerned with what he called the "internal logic" of the Fascist revolution. This "logic" was predicated on the Actualist conviction that a "speculative identity" obtained between the individual and the state. "The first thesis," he insisted years later, "[was] the identification of the individual and the state."[32] This was precisely how Gentile construed the analysis. In commenting on

Spirito's communication, in 1932, he maintained that it turned on the ultimate identity of the two terms *individual* and *state*. [33] In effect, what the identification accomplished was to nullify the distinction, long entertained by liberals of all persuasion, between individual and collective interests, private and public concerns. Approximately a year later, in speaking on corporativist legislation, Mussolini announced that its "fundamental premises" were:

There are no economic matters which only affect private or individual interests. From the day when man resigned or adapted himself to life in common with his fellow beings, not a single one of his actions begins, develops, or is concluded in him alone, but has repercussions that go beyond his person.[34]

The fundamental philosophical premise of the liberal economic and political order, the distinction between self-regarding and other-regarding acts, was rejected, In effect, *all* acts were public acts and *all* interests were public interests.

The hub of Spirito's analysis turned on the tendency of Fascist corporativism, as it was then constituted, to recreate particular loci of special interests that rendered impossible the identification of individual, class, and category interests with the state. Industrial establishments had expanded enormously on anonymous capital— shares distributed throughout the possessing class who themselves did not participate directly in the enterprise. The workers identified themselves with syndicates that served their immediate wage interests and were effectively excluded from direct participation in management. The managers of such enterprises were often marginal, identifying neither with capital nor with labor. Each class and category pursued distinct and often antithetical interests and the state functioned in the capacity of a mediator, attempting to reconcile opposing interests. What was lacking was an effective identity of interests.

Spirito insisted that such circumstances could only characterize a transition to an economic system that would synthesize interests, a social order in which every individual, category, and class would identify with the collective well-being. This could only be accomplished by transcending the duality that beset transitional corporativism. Corporativism as it was then constituted was composed of a confederation of industrial organizations representing capitalist interests, and a confederation of workers' syndicates. A radical identity of interests could only be accomplished by instituting a single and integral corporation that would abolish the distinction between entrepreneur and worker. Spirito maintained that this could only be achieved by making each enterprise the property of all participant workers. Workers would then become owners. Their efforts would be rewarded not only by wages but also by profit increments on their capital holdings. They would then participate directly in the industrial process by selecting a managerial staff for their individual enterprises. Production would then take place within the confines of a "unitary and national economic program," with the national corporative councils transformed from organs of class conciliation into the directive organs of production.[35] Corporativism would then become technical, organic, rational, and totalitarian.

Spirito advocated a unified and national economic program, the direct participation of workers in the management and direction of industry, the elimination of the institutional distinction between classes, and the subsequent abolition of classes themselves.[36] He recognized his programmatic proposals as socialist, as a form of national socialism. He maintained

One does a disservice to Fascism in conceiving it antithetical to Bolshevism, as one might oppose good and evil or truth and error. . . . If today the energies of the political orientation [of our time] find expression in Fascism and Bolshevism, it is clear that the future belongs not to that regime which negates the other, but that which, of the two, has shown itself capable of incorporating and transcending the other in a more advanced form. . . . Fascism has the responsibility to make manifest the fact that it represents a constructive force that moves in the vanguard of history and leaves behind, after having absorbed them, socialism and Bolshevism.[37]

Throughout the next two years Spirito published a series of articles in standard theoretical journals of the Regime devoted to explicating what the neo-idealists and syndicalists held to be the revolutionary exigencies that faced Fascist corporativism. In 1934, he focused on a problem with which Fascist syndicalists had remained preoccupied—the participation of labor in the management of enterprise. While insisting on the necessity of national organization of labor in industrial syndicates, Spirito maintained that it was also necessary to institute factory committees that "would directly participate in the direction of the individual enterprise."[38]

Thus, by 1934, radical Fascists had outlined what they conceived to be the "integral corporativism" always implicit in Fascism. It was not difficult to reconstruct such intentions from the programmatic suggestions advanced by the Party as early as 1921. Most Fascists had accepted the necessity of compromise with the forces operative in the Italian environment immediately after the March on Rome, but after a dozen years in power, and after eight years of secure political monopoly, syndicalists and neo-idealists were becoming increasingly restive.

In the years following Spirito's communication and the emphatic reappearance of anticapitalist elements in Mussolini's public statements, sympathetic foreign commentators anticipated the advent of a specifically "non-Marxist socialism" in Fascist Italy. Pierre Drieu la Rochelle, Marcel Deat, and Mihail Manoilesco spoke of a Fascist "neo-socialism," and of Fascist corporativism as it was then constituted, as an "intermediary form" designed to ultimately eradicate the last traces of capitalism.[39]

In 1934, Mussolini reiterated that capitalism, as an economic system, was no longer viable. Fascist economy was to be based not on individual profit but on collective interests. Reorganization was to rest on the premise of "self-discipline of production entrusted to producers," a programmatic proposal which referred not only to industrialists and employers but to workers as well. Mussolini insisted,

It means that the workers must enter more and more intimately into the productive process and share its necessary discipline. . . . If the past century was the century of capitalist power, the twentieth century is the century of the power and glory of labor.[40]

That same year, Mussolini outlined a plan of cooperation with the socialist Emilio Caldara and the socialist publication *Il Lavoro*, which was permitted to continue publication throughout this period. A significant number of socialists collected around the Fascist standard and even Arturo Labriola, the revolutionary syndicalist with whom Mussolini had collaborated as a youth in Switzerland, returned from expatriation during this period.[41]

Beginning with this period, planning agencies began to make their appearance in Fascist Italy. The corporative institutions had begun essentially as agencies calculated to meet divergent class and category interests, but they gradually began to take on advisory and planning functions. They began to meet with more frequency in order to formulate plans for the development and coordination of national development for their respective productive categories. There was a gradual concentration of economic talent in the technical offices of the Ministry of Corporations, in the National Research Council, and ultimately in the Permanent Price Control Committee of the Fascist Party. In 1936, Mussolini announced a "plan" for the autarchic development of the Italian economy.[42] Mussolini spoke of the nationalization of key sectors of the economy and of the necessity of divesting those sectors of industry of their *de jure* immunity, an immunity they had already *de facto* lost. He spoke of indirect, but effective, control of other sectors of the economy, and contended that under the system as it was developing the

workers [would be] collaborators in the enterprise on the same footing as the purveyors of capital and the technical directors. . . . Under the Fascist Regime labor, in its manifold forms, becomes the gauge for the social and national utility of individuals and groups. . . . The economic changes I have described, and this innovation in the political constitutional field, will realize in full the fundamental postulates acclaimed by the Fascist revolution seventeen years ago at the meeting in Piazza San Sepolcro.[43]

In 1937, Mussolini reviewed the extensive measure of state involvement in extractive and productive industries.[44] He also indicated that banks had been given the status of institutions of public law and that their policies were to an ever increasing degree directed by the Ministry of Finance, the Ministry of Corporations, and the Fascist Party itself. Credit institutions fell increasingly under the aegis of government fiat, and the control of credit institutions provided the Fascist state with its most effective device for controlling the economy. Through such control, Italian credits abroad fell under the supervision of the Undersecretariat for Credit and Exchange, which consequently controlled the flow of Italian imports and exports.

The consequence of these developments was not difficult to anticipate. H. Arthur Steiner indicated, in 1938,

Needless to remark, the propertied classes in Italy have lost much of whatever enthusiasm they may have had for Mussolini's Fascism. This is one of the reasons why Mussolini tends to look to the working classes for support, one of the explanations of a more intelligent labor policy.[45]

As a matter of fact, Steiner had transposed cause for effect. Mussolini's syndicalist and totalitarian aspirations had been contained by the compromises required by the political and economic situation that prevailed upon his accession to power. The period immediately following the accession of Fascism to power found the established socialist parties unalterably opposed to Mussolini. He had garnered support from sections of the industrial bourgeoisie in his protracted and savage struggle with the socialists, who had opposed Italy's entrance into World War I and who continued to oppose the national syndicalists after the war. The first Fascist bands were composed of war veterans who, irrespective of their syndicalist persuasions, were nationalists. They were supported, in no small measure, by industrialist and propertied elements panicked by socialist and communist successes in the immediate postwar period. The monarchy, to a significant extent involved with conservative and large landholding sections of the titled upper middle classes, had permitted the Fascists to assume political control. Confined by all these forces, Mussolini had tempered the original Fascist demands. As Fascism secured its control it found itself harboring within its own ranks many of those conservative and capitalist elements that had given the movement critical support in its bid for power. Within the Party itself, factions collected around these well-entrenched and politically powerful interests. Behind its monolithic facade and its factitious consensus, all these forces deployed their energies and jockeyed for increased control of the state apparatus and influence in the Party itself.

Revolutionary Fascism and the "Dyarchic" System

In November, 1943, two months after the instauration of the Republic of Salò, Mussolini characterized the first two decades of Fascist rule as encumbered by compromise.[46] He revealed the fact that his totalitarian state had been anything but totalitarian in practice. He described the two decades of Fascist power as rule by a "dyarchy." "The grand bourgeoisie, industrialists, land holders, financiers, in order not to expose themselves directly, marched behind the royal coat of arms."[47] For two decades Italy had been ruled by a dual government, a traditional and conservative coalition collected behind the monarchy and a revolutionary counter-elite within the Party organization. The duality of rulership was evidenced in a system of parallel institutions: the traditional Council of Ministers, the product of the prerevolutionary Italian *Statuto,* and the Grand Council of Fascism, the creation of the Fascist revolution; the traditional army, which pledged allegiance to the Royal House, and the Fascist Militia, which took its oath to Mussolini. The traditional police forces were responsible to the monarchy; the Fascist Party had its own Party police. Fascism had its hymns, salutes, and rituals; the monarchy retained its traditional hymns, salutes, and ceremonies.

Mussolini insisted that within this *de facto* dual state, "plutocratic elements and sections of the clergy" pursued their particular interests and exercised their parochial influence to the impediment of Fascist purposes.[48] "Specific industrial and financial groups," united behind the monarchy, had conducted a "sordid and implacable struggle" against the social and economic policies of revolutionary Fascism.[49] Behind the monarchy all the forces of reactionary capitalism had aligned themselves.[50] In effect, Mussolini argued, Fascism had been betrayed by the grand bourgeoisie that had leagued itself with the monarchy throughout the twenty years of Fascist rule.[51]

Certainly by the time of the outbreak of World War II, important strata of the industrial and financial bourgeoisie viewed the Fascist experiment with more than considerable diffidence. As early as 1931, reports began filling the files of the Fascist secret police which indicated that while the possessing and capitalist classes had welcomed the advent of Fascism and the Duce as the savior of order and society and the defender of Italy against Bolshevism, now the situation had altered. The Duce is today more popular among the working classes than among the capitalist bourgeoisie. . . . The bourgeoisie complains that "Mussolini is slowly, sweetly and silently, moving in the direction of a form of Bolshevism." In effect, there is a reaction of class egoism against the vanguard politics of the corporative state.[52]

As though to bear out such reports, the first act of the Badoglio government after the King's dismissal of Mussolini was to dismantle the entire institutional apparatus of the corporative state. It was evident that strategic elements among the Italian economic and military elite found Mussolini's corporativism particularly inhibiting, not so much because of what it had accomplished, since Mussolini was often more than accommodating in his dealings with the possessing classes, but because of the threat to privilege and control that corporativism harbored. Socialization was not Fascism's simple reflex response to defeat and humiliation. Mussolini had already outlined a program of socialization that was essentially that of the Social Republic as early as 1938. At that time, he had made clear his commitment to the essentials of the program revealed in Spirito's communication before the Convention of Ferrara in 1932.[53] In 1941, he repeated the same programmatic outline of Fascist socialization to Ermanno Amicucci, who was then in the Ministry of Corporations.[54] These were intimations well calculated to generate diffidence among the industrial and traditional aristocracy.

The internal development of Fascism was as clear after 1932 as was its potential threat to the industrial, financial, and large land-holding middle classes. In 1935, when the final phase of Fascist development began, Panunzio insisted that "the working class . . . assume the management of production within the compass of the corporative economy" of the nation, a feature of Fascist socialization anticipated three years before by Spirito as "integral corporativism" and that Panunzio identified as "integral syndicalism."[55] At about the same time the official journal of the Party, although insisting that classes no longer effectively existed in the totalitarian state, confided that the "bourgeoisie still seeks to maintain itself as the 'ruling class'. . . ."[56]

The Fascist Conception of Property   In 1939, the Confederazione
Fascista dei Lavoratori
dell'Agricoltura published
an elaborate exposition of
the "Fascist Conception of Private Property." What became manifestly evident was the fact that Fascist thought was inextricably wedded to radical national syndicalist and neo-idealist conceptions. The
central and recurrent theme was that articulated by Bottai in 1927:
while ownership of the means of production were to remain in
private hands in Fascist Italy, responsibility for the maintenance and
orderly development of production in the interests of the collectivity
was a responsibility owed to the state. Salvatore Gatti insisted that
the conception of private property's responsibilities to the Fascist
state effectively distinguished Fascism from liberalism. In effect
such responsibilities, in his judgment, eclipsed the individualistic
and atomistic conception of private property. "Within the Fascist
conception, [the interests] of society are no longer conceived to be
antithetical to, in opposition to those of, the individual."[57] The
sustaining logic of the neo-idealist conviction of the ultimate identity
of the particular with the universal was applied to the juridical conception of private property.

Property implied, for Fascists, a juridical order, and such an
order implied the existence and superintendence of the state.
Property can exist only when an aggregate of men are governed by
a sovereign order. The attempt to distinguish the "rights" of
property, as though such rights were antecedent to, and independent
of, the state was conceived as a singularly bourgeois rationalization,
the inheritance of the French Revolution—and radically mistaken.
Property logically and existentially depends upon the existence of
a sustaining normative order. As a consequence, rights are derivative
and entail obligations to that order which subtends them. Obligations are defined, and rights are contingently assigned by the state,
the articulate and ultimate will of the organized collective.[58]

Private property is sanctioned and guaranteed not as a consequence of
any natural rights on the part of the individual, not on the basis of some
pretended inviolability of any such putative right conceived as absolute,
but only insofar as the institution of private property evidences its

304

utility, fulfills an instrumental function in the productive process, in the interests of the nation. . . .[59]

For Panunzio, this constituted the "social conception of property of the Fascist Regime."[60]

The liberal conception of private property as a right that enjoys procedural privilege with respect to public law was conceived to be the analytic consequence of the liberal conception of liberty, an abstract conception which construed liberty negatively as the absence of state interference.[61] Such a conception of property made the rights of property extrinsic and independent of the state. The state, consequently, was not uniquely sovereign. The state exercised agential police functions in the service of the protection of individual private property. The opposing Fascist conception argued that property can only exist in a rule-governed context, in an order sustained by the ultimate sanctions which are the prerogative of the truly sovereign state. Property can only be understood to be a social and juridical derivative sustained by the pacific coexistence of subjects within the sovereign state.[62] Because of its derivative and instrumental character, property was conceived to be subject to collective discipline. Thus, though the Fascist conception of property refused to countenance collective possession as such, individual ownership rights were understood to be strictly subordinate to collective discipline. It was not the individual ownership of property that concerned Fascists, but its subordination to collective control. Property was understood to perform social functions rather than to manifest individual rights.[63] It was clear that the conception of property as a social function was broad enough to include socialization of the means of production, should that be required by the national interests as interpreted by the state.[64]

While there was clearly resistance to Spirito's original proposal to render the means of production the collective property of the Fascist corporations, there was an equally clear recognition that the social conception of property could and, in fact, was leading to an increased direct involvement of labor, the ultimate source of property, in the management and administration of industry, in an unequivocal anticipation of the legislation on socialization promulgated during the Fascist Social Republic.[65] That labor would assume the prerogatives of management, share in its responsibilities, and enjoy its attendant profits, was anticipated.

If labor, like language, is inconceivable outside a normative and rule-governed social context, property, which is the real product of labor in common, must display all the features of sociality. Property must perform social functions and all forms of labor must be intrinsically and responsibly involved in the productive process. Interests must be united in a rule-governed collective enterprise. This could be done, ran arguments that were variations upon and an explication of themes presented by Spirito at the Ferrara conference of 1932, only if property was conceived as a social product responsible to the collectivity that is its necessary foundation, and if labor were intimately and responsibly drawn into the management and shared in the rewards of the national industrial enterprise.

By the time of Fascist Italy's involvement in World War II, therefore, the lines of contest between Fascists and their conservative opponents were clearly drawn. Fascism was manifestly committed to the realization of a non-Marxist national socialism clearly implied in its first doctrinal formulations. The ensuing military struggle did nothing to abate the ferocity of the internal revolutionary struggle going on within the Fascist state. Panunzio, writing in the official Party journal in 1940, insisted that the war then in progress could not obscure the fact that a "vertical war, a social and economic war, continued unabated. . . . The antithesis is one and one alone, and it obtains between two terms: plutocracy and labor. The triumph will be that of labor alone."[66]

The End of Compromise and the Advent of Fascist Socialism

With the catastrophe of 1943, the monarchy fell away and took up its position with the victorious anti-Fascist allied armies. The Badoglio government stripped the economy of the corporativist institutions erected during the Fascist period and the Fascist Party was abolished. When Mussolini reappeared after his liberation by the Germans, only those elements of Fascism surfaced that had associated themselves with the revolutionary syndicalism and neo-idealism of Mussolini's initial program. Their presence was exemplified by Nicola Bombacci, the radical socialist and sometimes communist, and Giovanni Gentile, the author of Actualism, both of whom became chief among Mussolini's counselors. Mussolini himself, before he knew who would collect around the standards of the new Fascist Republican Party, committed himself to the realization of the original sydicalist and neo-idealist program of Fascism. His original intention was to call his new republic the Italian *Socialist* Republic. Ultimately what resulted was identified as the Italian *Social* Republic—which nonetheless advertised itself as the vehicle of an Italian socialism, a national socialism. "Socialization," Mussolini maintained, "is nothing other than the humane and Italian realization of everything that is capable of being achieved of socialism. . . . The capitulation of September signified the liquidation of the bourgeoisie as a ruling class."[67] "The Republic of the Italian Workers," he continued, "is the decisive realization of all those postulates which, for forty years, were inscribed on the banners of socialist movements."[68]

In March, 1945, a month before his death, he told Ivanoe Fossani that he had been and remained a socialist. He maintained,

The charge of incoherence [made against me] was without foundation. My conduct has always been rectilinear in the sense of looking always at the substance of things and not at their form. I adapted myself, with socialist intentions (*socialisticamente*), to reality.[69]

No less creditable a witness than Cesare Rossi, long an anti-Fascist, indicated that Mussolini remained transfixed, throughout his entire political life, by socialism.[70]

On the twenty-first anniversary of the March on Rome, in the tragic days of the Republic, Pavolini announced,

By order of the Duce, in a closed Party meeting, the programmatic directives concerning the most important state problems and those concerning the developments with respect to labor were specified. They can be characterized, I have no hestitancy in saying, most appropriately as socialist rather than social.[71]

Several days later Ferdinando Mezzasoma, Minister of Propaganda for the Social Republic, maintained that the Republic was based on the "true socialism" that Mussolini had never renounced.[72]

These doctrinal developments were not without effect. A not inconsiderable group of socialists collected around the standards of the new Republic and as late as November, 1944, Mussolini took the initiative in releasing the socialist Corrado Bonfantini in an effort to bridge the distance that separated Fascists and the more orthodox socialists. Piero Pisenti, the Minister of Justice, conceived the differences between Fascists and socialists to be purely "formal," and negotiated with Gabriele Vigorelli and Bonfantini to effect a collaboration between socialists and Fascists that would attempt to realize the programmatic goals of Fascist socialism.[73] In fact, however, the socialists had already organized themselves behind the forces in the South and the efforts came to naught.

With the eclipse of the Social Republic, among the first acts of the Committee of National Liberation, all but dominated by socialists and communists, was the abrogation of the decrees on socialization. The proclamation of April 25, 1945, read,

Considering the antinational objectives of the Fascist decrees on "socialization" with which the so-called Fascist republican government attempted to dupe the working classes of occupied Italy into serving and collaborating with the invader [and] . . . in order to secure . . . the continuity and reinforcement of productive activity in the spirit of effective national solidarity, [the C.N.L.] decrees that [such legislation] . . . is hereby abrogated.[74]

It was a curious justification. For whatever reason, Fascism had passed legislation that could provide significant leverage to the industrial proletariat in their contest with Italy's possessing classes. Socialization had provided for syndical collegia and managerial committees that had the *de jure* right to significantly influence the entire productive enterprise of the nation. All that would have been necessary to obviate the "antinational objectives" of the legislation on socialization would have been the election of representative socialist or communist factory collegia and committees. Instead, the laws themselves were abrogated and the control over Italy's productive enterprise was returned to its capitalist owners. Today that control remains securely in the hands of those same owners. The advantage afforded socialists by the legislation on socialization was sacrificed in the "national interest"—an interest for which Fascism, by its own admission, had compromised its syndicalist and national socialist aspirations for more than a generation.

Gentile and the Criticism of Classical Marxism

That the recrudescence of Fascist socialism was neither casual nor simply a tactical artifice is indicated by the course of Gentile's thought throughout the period of Fascist ascendancy, from 1925 until 1943. More suggestive still is the fact that Gentile began his intellectual labors with significant Marx studies, published in 1897 and 1899 when he was in his early twenties.

Gentile, who was eight years Mussolini's senior, published his *Una critica del materialismo storico* four years before Mussolini's first published article in 1901. The *Critica* was a short but responsible criticism of Marxism's theory of history. It was a youthful work, neither particularly original nor giving evidence of a very extensive inquiry into available Marxist literature. The theses advanced were not fully coherent, nor was the analysis devoted to primary source material. The second essay, *La filosofia della prassi*, published two years later when Gentile was twenty-four was, on the other hand, a genuinely original piece of work. Based largely on his knowledge of the classical German philosophical tradition, Gentile's reconstruction of the thought of the young Marx has withstood the test of time. Even the relatively recent publication of the philosophical work of the young Marx, the *Economic Philosophic Manuscripts of 1844*, and the full text of the *German Ideology* of 1845, has left Gentile's interpretation among the best available. Only the most recent analyses equal it in insight and merit.[75]

The *Critica*, however, is valuable because it indicates the nature of Gentile's reservations about Marxism as a science of history. Gentile focused his attention on the prevailing socialist interpretation of historical materialism, which held that Marxism provided a science of history, a collection of natural laws governing men in association, by virtue of which relatively specific predictions concerning the future course of society could be forthcoming. He quoted Antonio Labriola to illustrate the predictive pretensions of classical Marxism.

The advent of communism is not a postulate that turns on a criticism [of prevailing society], nor a goal freely chosen; its advent is rather the result of an immanent process of history. . . . We are compelled to recognize . . . in the present course of things a necessity that transcends our every sympathy and our every subjective acquiesence.[76]

Labriola conceived historical materialism as a scientific account of the course history would take, the demonstrative proof of the inevitable social revolution immanent in the very process of social life itself.

It was against such contentions that Gentile leveled his primary objections. He denied that men could simply "discover" natural *or* social laws. He held that such a view, although prevalent and common-sensical, was fundamentally mistaken. Men do not simply contemplate facts and observe laws. Facts emerge only within the context of some one or another perspective, a perspective that provides the sorting criteria for what are to constitute facts. Neither physicists nor historians simply observe random and indiscriminate occurrences. They have, in effect, selective vision. They have decided upon criteria of relevance and significance. They have criteria governing the admissibility of descriptive propositions advanced as true. Moreover, such synthetic propositions are collected together in systematic relationships, in valid argument forms. These forms require a commitment to consistency and an intersubjectively established system of transformation rules. In other words, for Gentile, explanations and predictions are forthcoming only when men, possessed of values, purposes, and intentions turn these to account in the empirical world. A world without men harbors no facts, is characterized by no laws—for only men's values characterize occurrences as relevant and significant, and only the commitment to consistency permits the application of the rules of inference to be applied to the world.

In effect, Gentile argued that every science rests on some set of tacit or express values. Men pursue physics because they would control their environment to render their lives more secure and their future predictable. Facts manifest themselves as relevant to those purposes. The criteria for admissibility of propositions as true in the formalized sciences rest on the acceptance of the axioms from which they commence. The entire enterprise involves an implicit commitment to consistency as a value.

What was true for every science was certainly true for history. He insisted,

History conceived as something external and independent of men has neither significance nor laws. It is always men who see a significance in history, moving in accordance to laws. It is always men, in short, who make history and the laws govern it.[77]

Gentile's objection to historical materialism was a special case of his general objection of positivism. A decade later, Mussolini raised the same objection and, as a consequence, made the transition from positivism to pragmatism.

Gentile's argument was more than a simple rejection of historic fatalism *or* economic determinism. He was not charging the Marxists with simplemindedness in their analysis of the human factor in the process of history. He recognized that the Marxists understood that men made history in the uninspired sense that men must do something in order that history should have something to record. Instead, he was arguing that any knowledge enterprise intrinsically involves some antecedent commitment to values express or implied. Every knowledge enterprise necessarily involves the commitment to consistency and truth, the willingness to concede that self-contradiction is stultifying and that ascriptions of truth require something more than subjective conviction. He argued that classical Marxism misunderstood the knowledge enterprise. Human values could not be explained by historical materialism because historical materialism as an attempt to explain and predict was itself part of the human knowledge enterprise and as such rested upon some set of implicit human values. Any proffered explanation of human values necessarily implies some antecedent values. This is the substance of Gentile's reservations concerning positivism in general and historical materialism in particular.[78]

These reservations were more profound and certainly more explicit than any raised by Mussolini himself. But some of the implications of Gentile's position were essentially those of Mussolini. If every human enterprise, including the knowledge enterprise, requires commitment to some set of explicit or implicit values there is no such thing as *pure* or *value-free* science. But more than that, even when science is effectively pursued, and its underlying values not subject to question, any collection of its true descriptive and analytic statements does not provide the antecedents for a deductive conclusion which has prescriptive force. Again, some statement of value or values must enter into the antecedent to permit the licit transit from the antecedent to a conclusion which involves advocacy.[79]

Gentile went on to insist that historical materialism need not be interpreted in the positivistic manner characteristic of the orthodox socialism of the time. He held that the positivistic interpretation was largely the product of Engels' efforts and did not necessarily represent the thought of Marx. Gentile held that a more convincing interpretation of historical materialism could be given in terms of an Hegelian account, an interpretation more faithful to the philosophical orientation of the young Marx. Gentile argued that the young Marx had opposed that form of materialism that made men simple observers in a world of natural processes. Marx, he argued, conceived men *participants,* in quite the Hegelian sense. Men were participants in a dialectical and developmental process, in a world historical process that both influenced and was influenced by the activity of men. Within the context of such an interpretation of total immanence, any effort to accord primacy to some set of abstract variables, economic, material, or moral, was to court paradox and miss the entire point of the Hegelian dialectic.

Certainly Marx's arguments *could* be narrowly construed. Marx's arguments were almost always elliptical and because of their synoptic and stenographic character Marx often seemed to argue that all of man's conceptual or ideological products could be exhaustively explained by reference to the material productive forces and the productive relations in which the productive process was conducted. He seemed to argue that ideological variables, philosophy, morality, arts, and perhaps even science could be understood to be dependent variables and the productive forces and productive relations the independent or explanatory variables. This was how many early Marxists interpreted historical materialism. It was this interpretation that Sorel, Croce, and Gentile (for partially similar and partially different reasons) resisted. Gentile insisted that such an interpretation would violate Marx's clear intention. In *La filosofia della prassi*, Gentile maintained that Marx had argued that

the materialistic doctrine concerning the changing of circumstances and education forgets that circumstances are changed by men and that the educator himself must be educated. . . . The coincidence of the changing of circumstances and of human activity or self-changing can only be comprehended and rationally understood as revolutionary practice.[80]

Gentile interpreted Marx to mean that men make their own history in a substantial sense, that the variables abstractly identified as economic and material and those characterized as ethical or philosophical were related in an immanent and dialectical manner in what we would today call an interdependency relationship.[81]

There is considerable substance in Gentile's interpretation. Certainly, since the publication of much of Marx's writings that were unavailable to Gentile, there has been a gradual accumulation of evidence that such an alternate interpretation of classical Marxism is possible. Orthodox Marxists have argued that Marx's *German Ideology* supports an interpretation of strict economic determinism by citing instances where Marx speaks of "the phantoms formed in the human brain" as "sublimates of their material life process . . .," and "civil society" and "social intercourse" as "determined by the existing productive forces . . .," and where he speaks of explaining "all the different theoretical products and forms of consciousness, religion, philosophy, ethics, etc., etc.," by referring to the "real process of production, starting out from the material production of life itself . . ."[82] But Gentile could cite as counterinstances places where Marx refers to "individuals" as being themselves "instruments of production."[83]

If individuals are themselves instruments of production, it would seem that they and their thoughts and aspirations could hardly be conceived as derivative of a more primary process going on in the productive base of society, a base which includes the instruments of production. It would seem that the activity of individuals, and the motives that initiate such activities, would be as fundamental as the productive process itself, for they would be, by definition, part of that process. In fact, we have seen that Mussolini used a similar argument to support his own neo-idealist and voluntarist interpretation of historical materialism. Mussolini indicated that Marx had insisted that "of all the instruments of production, the greatest productive power is the revolutionary class itself."[84]

If individuals and the revolutionary class are themselves productive forces, then any dichotomy between primary productive and derived "ideological" variables is faulted. The relationship between them must be one of interdependence. In this sense, Gentile's interpretation was one with that of Pareto, Mosca, Michels, and Mussolini. It was voluntaristic in the sense that it provided for the operation, within the historical process, of human will and commitment, of human *praxis*. It was not specifically anti-Marxist, unless one accepted as legitimate only that interpretation offered by a specific school of Marx scholars. Neither Sorel, Michels, nor Mussolini conceived themselves, when they offered this alternative interpretation, as anti-Marxist. Neither, in fact, did Gentile. He welcomed the Marxist efforts as an attempt, in positivistic guise, to reintroduce the truths of Hegelianism.[85]

It is obvious that Gentile found in Marx all the elements of an essentially Hegelian world view. The normic model of man which subtended Marx's views was Hegelian. "The ego [the empirical self] . . . is real only as an element in a collective, in a society, as a term in social relations, which gradually render the self more concrete."[86] This was an Hegelian, a Marxian, and a Gentilean conception of the relationship between the individual and the collectivity. It was a conception of the relationship between the individual and his social group shared by sociologists in the Gumplowiczian tradition from Mosca to Michels, and was also found in the early writings of Mussolini. Outside of history, outside of the community in which he labors and lives, the individual is nothing.

Marx, Gentile maintained, correctly

opposed himself to that nominalistic intuition that conceived society only in terms of individuals who can enter into [contractual] accord, but who nonetheless always remain intrinsically independent of one another. . . . [Marx] correctly observed that such an interpretation was an abstraction, that society was primary and that individuals exist only as parts organically related to the whole.[87]

The individual was an individual only insofar as he was social, political. For Marx, this was expressed in the epigram which maintained that the human essence is "the ensemble of social relations."

The conception of the individual as intrinsically related to his historic, cultural, and economic community is a conception which Gentile retained throughout his life. In his final apologetic for Fascism, Gentile insisted that "at the root of the 'I' is a 'We.' The community to which an individual belongs is the basis of his spiritual existence. . . ."[88] We have seen that this conception remained central to Actualism, and it is found clearly stated for the first time in Gentile's essays on Marx. Not only is the conception clearly articulated, but it is identified with the basic philosophical predispositions of Marx. What Gentile was to call the "speculative identification of the individual with his community," was central to Actualism and to Marxism alike.[89] In this sense Gentile, like Mussolini, was never an anti-Marxist. In fact, in his introduction to the new edition of his essays on Marx in 1937, at the height of Fascism's political power, Gentile indicated that those essays contained the "first germs" of his own mature social and political philosophy.[90]

Gentile and Fascist Socialism

But more than the common normic model of man, Gentile's account indicates that he shared with Marx certain critical elements that were to mature into the "humanism of labor" that sought realization in the Fascist Republic of Salò. Since the empirical individual became a person only in the relationships he established with his peers in an historically and socioculturally defined community, labor, in all its forms, was understood to be intrinsically valuable. The individual creates himself in labor, and that, for Gentile, constituted the moral significance of activity.[91] Man is what he does and consequently everything he does is of moral import. This was a conviction that Gentile never abandoned, and it is found in all his published works throughout the period of Fascist rule. In the *Preliminari allo studio del fanciullo* published in 1922, and in all the subsequent editions throughout the Fascist period, labor was identified as "that universal human activity" which serves the "supreme end of human existence": self realization.[92] A similar account of labor is found in *Guerra e fede,* published in 1919, and in almost every major piece of literature published by Gentile for a quarter of a century.[93] In the *Genesi e struttura della società,* this conception matured into the following account:

To the humanism of culture, which was indeed a glorious step in the liberation of man, there succeeds today or will succeed tomorrow the humanism of labor. For the creation of great industry and the advance of the worker onto the great stage of history have profoundly modified the modern conception of culture. The word used to mean intellectual culture and especially art and literature; it left out of account the vast segment of humanity who do not raise their eyes toward the free horizons of the higher culture, but labor at the foundations of human culture. There at the foundation man is in contact with nature, and *labors* on it; but he labors *as a man,* he is aware of what he is doing, aware of himself and of the world in which he is incorporated. . . . It was necessary, therefore, that the conception of human culture appropriate to literary and philosophical humanism should be extended to embrace every form of activity in which man labors to create his humanity. It was necessary that the high dignity which man by taking thought had discovered in thought itself should be accorded to the "worker" also. It was necessary that thinkers, scientists, and artists should join hands with the workers in this consciousness of the universal dignity of humanity.

There is no doubt that the social changes and the parallel socialist movements of the nineteenth century have created this new humanism, the actual organization of which in concrete political terms is the task and the concern of our century. The state can no longer be thought of as the state of the citizen (or of the man and the citizen) as in the days of the French Revolution; it is and it should be the state of the *workers,* separated as they are by their different interests into the natural categories that are gradually becoming established. . . . The real man, the man who counts, is the man who works, and whose worth is measured by his work. For it is indeed true that value is labor; and a man's worth is to be measured according to the quantity and quality of his work.[94]

This was the rationale offered by Gentile in his final apologetic for the Fascist Workers' State, the Republic of Salò. It was a maturation of elements already contained in Gentile's first essays on Marxism. It exemplified Gentile's consistent attitude toward orthodox socialism. In Gentile's first Fascist polemic he insisted that a distinction be made between the various forms of socialism that had developed during the early part of the twentieth century.[95] Fascism opposed specific theoretical commitments made by some of the official socialist organizations. Fascism denied, for example, that the class struggle was the ultimate conflict that characterized historical development. Fascism rejected, furthermore, the materialism and the determinism many theoreticians identified with socialism. It rejected the anti-national biases of socialist internationalism. But Fascism itself was a variant of Sorelian syndicalism which advertized itself as a voluntaristic, neo-idealist and elitist socialism. This current of socialist thought neither Fascism nor Gentile ever rejected. "Fascism," Gentile insisted, "as a consequence of its Marxian and Sorelian patrimony . . . conjoined with the influence of contemporary Italian idealism, through which Fascist thought attained maturity, conceives philosophy as *praxis*."[96]

In so characterizing Fascism, Gentile harkened back to the tradition of which he was a part. Among his first published writings was his essay, *La filosofia della prassi* (*The Philosophy of Praxis*). He had interpreted Marx and historical materialism in a neo-Hegelian sense. He saw Marx's emphasis on *praxis* as a commitment to a form of voluntarism and neo-idealism, an interpretation which he shared with the young Mussolini and many of the revolutionary syndicalists and pragmatists who constituted the social and political intellectual *avant garde* in Italy during the first two decades of the twentieth century.

Like all representative Fascist intellectuals, Gentile's assessment of socialism was thus never simply negative. As early as 1919 he insisted that socialism was a "vital, healthy, and salutary force in [Italian] political life."[97] In the mid-'thirties, when the Second Convention of Syndical and Corporative Studies sparked the protracted and acerbacious discussion of "Fascist socialism," Gentile calmly asserted that "in principle, the socialists were correct in opposing capitalism as an economic system."[98] In this he merely

317

echoed Spirito, whose communication had provoked the confrontation between the conservative and the revolutionary Fascist factions.
In fact, he said no more than Mussolini had said. Gentile's appraisal
of socialism as a social and political movement was not substantially
different at any point from that offered by Mussolini in his
formative years.

There is no direct evidence that Mussolini was familiar with
Gentile's early work on Marx or Marxian socialism, but Gentile's
work was well known among the revolutionary syndicalists with
whom the young Mussolini was intimately involved. Arturo
Labriola, one of the young Mussolini's first mentors and collaborators, was very much under the influence of Gentile's essays.
Labriola's interpretation of Marx's works show the unmistakable
influence of Gentile's voluntaristic and neo-idealist influence.
Labriola specifically cited Gentile's essays in his volume, *Marx
nell'economia e come teorico del socialismo,* published in 1908, and
his account of Marx's philosophy is fully consistent with that advanced by Gentile. Moreover, Gentile's essays were known to Croce
and Sorel so that his ideas were current among socialist theoreticians
throughout Mussolini's formative years. How well known Gentile's
essays were is indicated by the fact that Lenin himself recommended
them as a "noteworthy" contribution to the theoretical literature
devoted to Marxist studies.[99]

Gentile's ideas were therefore relatively well known in the
socialist circles in which Mussolini was active during the period
antecedent to the development of Fascism. In fact, Gentilean
idealism followed a trajectory parallel to that of Mussolini's social
and political thought. Initially, Gentile's reservations concerning
Marxism as it was then understood were essentially those shared by
Mussolini and the revolutionary syndicalists. What stood between
the syndicalists and the neo-idealists was the class bias of syndicalism. When the syndicalists took up nationalism as a normative point
of departure the differences between neo-idealism and national
syndicalism became insubstantial. By 1921, Mussolini could identify
himself with Gentilean neo-idealism and the firm outlines of Fascist
doctrine revealed themselves. Fascism always conceived itself as
a progressive and neo-idealist variant of socialism—and in the years
between 1930 and the outbreak of World War II came to be so

conceived by its conservative camp followers. It was during this period that many of the socialist syndicalists who had been alienated by Fascism's tactical anti-socialism became reconciled with Fascism. Arturo Labriola, who had gone into exile, returned to "proletarian Italy" to cast his lot with Fascism; it was Labriola, as a socialist and a syndicalist, who maintained, after the defeat of Fascism, that "the corporative organization was already socialist and it should not have been surrendered so easily."[100]

During the 'thirties the course Fascism was taking was evidenced in the writings of the syndicalists and the neo-idealists. The debate that followed the discussions at Ferrara in 1932 made abundantly clear Fascism's totalitarian socialist intentions. The right to private property was to be conceived as a contingent, not an absolute right. The national economy was to be governed by an integrated and centralized programmatic plan. The working class was to be gradually drawn into industrial management and labor was to be made the basis of the state in the sense that a man's worth, or the worth of any productive category, was to be judged by its contribution to national well-being.[101] This development had become so manifest that when Gentile spoke in the defense of Fascism, in 1943, before the July coup that deposed Mussolini, he spoke categorically of a Fascist "order . . . based on the principle that the sole and ultimate source of value was labor: that human labor is the realization of spiritual life in the totality of its economic and ethical interests."[102] He went on to indicate that "whoever speaks of communism in Italy today is an impatient corporativist," clearly implying that Fascist Italy had the full intention of ultimately realizing a variant of socialism appropriate to its national circumstances.[103]

That Fascist socialism was neither an aberrancy nor a political tactic is indicated not only by the evidence of a maturing current of neo-socialist social and political thought, but also by the fact that while Gentile was completely cut off from organized Fascism, during the interregnum that followed Mussolini's ouster in July, 1943, until his reappearance in September, 1943, he composed the rationale for the neo-socialism of Salò. It was during this brief period that he wrote his final Fascist apologetic, *Genesi e struttura della società*. This book, written when Gentile had no contact with

Mussolini or the Fascist hierarchy, contains phrases, whole passages, that appear in Mussolini's first statements about the intentions of the renascent Fascist movement. Mussolini, having seen neither Gentile nor his work in the interim, spoke of the Fascist Workers' State and the State of Labor, employing expressions to be found in Gentile's vindication of the neo-socialist "humanism of labor."

There is no explicit evidence that Mussolini *ever* read Gentile's final work. It was published only after the defeat of Fascism and the death of Mussolini. And yet, the document contains the rationale for Fascist socialism, the radicalization of corporativism. Gentile was, of course, one of Mussolini's principal confidants during Fascism's final period.[104] So fully had neo-idealism assimilated to itself the neo-socialist and national syndicalist sentiments of Mussolini that the counsel of Bombacci, the socialist and communist, and Gentile, the neo-Hegelian, were conceived as fully compatible.

Mussolini had begun his political career as a Sorelian syndicalist. As such, his Marxism was already independent and unorthodox. Certainly his emphases and his analyses were distinct from those of the orthodox European socialism expressed by the various social democratic parties. Mussolini, like Sorel, conceived of revolution in essentially moral terms. The working class was itself, and in its totality, the vehicle of moral regeneration. The individual was identified with his class, and his class was for him the ultimate source of obligation and value. Without his class membership the individual could not constitute himself a person in the moral sense. It was class membership and the class struggle that provided orientation, that provided the basis for moral ascription and normative evaluation, that afforded the individual the moral substance of his life. The class, of course, had its dirigent elite, an exiguous minority charged with the obligation of dominance. The outbreak of World War I forced the reorientation of proletarian syndicalism; what emerged was a national syndicalism. The nation assumed the role of the charismatic object of loyalty. Italy became a "proletarian nation"; identification with *this* community provided the moral substance of personality. At this point Sorelian syndicalism entered into its enduring rapprochement with Gentilean neo-idealism. There was between them an essential compatibility of analyses and moral conviction. The nation would realize the socialist and syndicalist aspirations of proletarian syndicalism and the moral purpose of neo-idealism. For fifteen years Fascism, by its own admission, compromised its intentions by attempting to effect a synthesis of antithetical non-Fascist elements. The result was a compromise state, what Mussolini called a "dyarchy." The conservative opposition to Fascism collected around the monarchy. Large scale financial and industrial interests, allied with the land-holding aristocracy, employed both the Church and the monarchy to frustrate the revolutionary totalitarianism of Fascism. Only the surgical separation of the monarchy and the instauration of the Fascist Republic in the North permitted the realization of the Fascist social program. The result, the Fascists insisted, was a national socialism, the fulfillment of Sorelian ideals within a national context. Gentile's "humanism of labor," which found political expression in the Fascist Workers' State, was the embodiment of the Sorelian ideals of Fascism.[105]

Totalitarian Socialism

Fascist totalitarianism was predicated on what Gentile termed the "speculative identity of the individual and the state."[106] The ultimate interests of the individual and the interests of the collectivity organized as the state were understood to be fully compatible. To make evident this radical compatibility was the pedagogical responsibility of the revolutionary elite organized as a unitary party. It was obvious that, given such a conviction, Fascism could not be content only to mediate between special interests operative within the confines of the politically organized nation. Fascism would have to reconstruct society until no distinction remained between public and private interest, between collective and individual interest. This was the principal thrust of Spirito's contribution at the Convention of Ferrara, in 1932. Fascists correctly conceived the distinction between public and private, collective and individual, as part of the heritage of classical liberalism with its individualistic and pluralistic conception of society. The neo-idealists and radical syndicalists never ceased their systematic resistence to these conceptions. Both the idealists and the syndicalists were heirs to a collectivistic and anti-individualistic tradition which had developed in Germany and Austria as neo-Hegelianism and Gumplowiczian-inspired sociology.

This collectivism and anti-individualistic tradition took on a radical totalitarian form in Fascist Italy, a form exemplified in the logic of substitutions that constituted the core of the charter myth legitimizing the Regime. Through a series of substitutions, the individual was identified with the nation, the nation with the state, the state with the party, and the party with the party leader. If such identifications were to be something more than empty sophistry, the Regime was charged with the responsibility of creating the institutions and machinery that would absorb the life activities of each individual, each class and productive category, each regional and strata interest, into the state.

The machinery employed by the Fascist Regime to implement this program is now part of the institutional history of Mussolini's Italy. Outside of the party structure itself, workers and entrepreneurs were organized in state-sponsored syndicates and confederations. After working hours the working class was under the constant tutelage of the elaborate Dopolavoro and "leisure-time" organizations. The young men of the nation were organized into the Balilla and the Avanguardisti, and the girls were organized into corresponding groups. Conjoined to these were a host of cultural and university organizations designed to preclude the possibility of any influence that might counter Fascist efforts calculated to inculcate in all citizens of whatever age or class provenience the secular ideology of the Party.

Fascism aspired to a complete identification of the individual and the collective will. It was this identification that was the very cornerstone of Fascist social and political thought. Central to Fascist ideology was a conception succinctly expressed by Gentile in his final work:

The human individual is not an atom. Immanent in the concept of an individual is the concept of society. . . . Only this identity can account for the necessary and intrinsic relation between the two terms of the synthesis, which requires that the concept of one term must involve the concept of the other. . . . I hope that the importance of this concept will escape no one, for in my judgment it is the keystone of the great edifice of human society.[107]

For Fascists, an identity obtained between the terms *individual* and *state*. Thus, Gentile could maintain that "the state is the very personality of the individual," and at the same time is the unitary will of the nation.[108] This was a thesis he had already propounded in his *I fondamenti della filosofia del diritto,* published in 1916. In this sense, he was a Fascist before the advent of Fascism.[109] The conclusions to which this argument led were evident in *La riforma dell'educazione,* published three years before the March on Rome. Gentile maintained,

In the way of conclusion, it may be said that I, as a citizen, have indeed a will of my own; but that upon further investigation my will is found to coincide exactly with the will of the state, and I want anything only insofar as the state wants me to want it. . . . Since the nation, as the state, is of the essence and nature of our very being, it is evident that the universal will of the state is identical [*tutt'uno*] with our concrete and actual ethical personality.[110]

This was the argument regularly exploited by Fascist intellectuals throughout the Fascist period. In his defense of Fascist socialism in 1932, Spirito argued,

The individual must finally become aware that in the process of conquering his true liberty he cannot stop at intermediate and hybrid forms. . . . He must seek and find an absolute identity between his own goal and that of the state . . . because private and public are the same thing. . . .[111]

In 1942, Gerardo Pannese rendered this in epigrammatic form: "In Fascist ethics the end of society is identical with that of man. . . ."[112] In the official *Dottrina* it was expressed in the following manner:

Man, as Fascism conceives him, is an individual who is at once nation and fatherland. . . . Fascism is an historical conception in which man is not what he is except as a function of the spiritual process in which he participates. . . . Liberalism negated the state in the interests of the particular individual; Fascism reaffirms the state as the true reality of the individual. . . .[113]

The individual might initially conceive his interests as distinct from, even opposed to, those of the state. The Fascists argued that such interests must, in some ultimate sense, be fully compatible. In the last analysis, what the individual wills is what the state wills. This constitutes the cognitive substance of Fascism's redefinition of *liberty* and *democracy*. When Fascists spoke of liberty and democracy, they qualified their reference with an antecedent *true*. The use of such a qualifier is clear indication that a redefinition of terms had taken place. The qualifier *true* was immediate evidence that the cognitive meaning of the terms *liberty* and *democracy* had altered. The *true* liberty and and democracy advocated by Fascism was the liberty and democracy of totalitarianism: the identification of the individual with his primary collectivity, the nation organized into the state.

To achieve this identification was recognized as an enormous pedagogical and institutional task. It required systematic inculcation of a set of normative principles. To this end, Fascists frankly and openly employed all the techniques of moral suasion and mimetic and emotive suggestion. They exploited the suggestibility of the masses by employing techniques long familiar to social psychologists, techniques summarily outlined by Le Bon and Sighele. In an atmosphere of high emotional salience they sought to instill in their subjects the conviction that they, the Italian nation, the Fascist Party, and the Duce were, in some profound sense, one. The will of one was the will of all. This would constitute the factitious democratic consensus that would support the Regime. This would legitimate the plebiscitary and "participatory" dictatorship of Mussolini. This would provide the substance and the rationale of charismatic leadership, as Fascism came to understand it. Its rationale was not religious, it was philosophical. Mussolini ruled not under a mandate from God, but as the putative embodiment of the "ultimate" common will.

It is within this context that the meaning of Fascist socialization is to be assessed. The defining characteristic of Fascism was its totalitarianism.[114] That the Party failed to create a totalitarian society was the consequence of a number of historic and economic considerations that need not detain us. Its intentions, almost from its first appearance as a political force, were manifestly clear. Every individual, every faction, every political or economic interest was to be assimilated to the national purpose as conceived by the Party and its leadership. Those interests that resisted being mustered to that purpose were conceived as "antinational" and "antisocial." Gentile's resistance to the much heralded Concordat between the Fascist state and the Papal See was based primarily on his adamant refusal to conceive the possibility that the state could surrender any of its sovereignty to *any* special interest, secular or religious. In fact, the Lateran accords proved to be only the opening signal for a protracted struggle between Fascism and the Catholic Church.[115] At best, the Concordat was a compromise, and after the initial enthusiasm for what was considered a significant diplomatic accomplishment had abated, thinking Fascists recognized it as such. Although they learned to accommodate each other, the Catholic Church remained an indigestible element in the Fascist totalitarian state.

More urgent than the struggle with the Church was the fact that the Italian economy as Fascism inherited it permitted special interests to collect around private property to such an extent that entire classes and productive categories remained characterized by distinct and special interests. The working class remained preoccupied with conditions of labor and remuneration while the propertied classes concerned themselves with maintaining an attractive profit and income structure. Such interests made the various interest groups resistent to the totalitarian aspirations of Fascism. What was in the interests of labor was not in the interests of capital and what was in the interests of the state need not be in the interests, however construed, of either. As a consequence, Fascist theoreticians made increasingly emphatic the need for harmonizing interests by undermining the ability of private property to act as loci of private interests. Spirito, for this reason and with this intention, was one of the most forceful opponents of private property as an institution. He argued that private property fostered the development of special and divisive interests in what aspired to be a totalitarian and monolithic society. This was the argument Spirito specifically advanced in a communication before the Third International Hegelian Congress, held in Rome in 1933.[116]

The most consistent and articulate Fascists recognized that private property and capitalism as an economic system obstructed the totalitarian goals of Fascism. Within the confines of capitalism as a productive system, they argued, labor took no intrinsic interest in the economic enterprise of the nation because workers were forced to remain preoccupied with their precarious standard of living. Since labor's standard of living was a function of its ability to command higher and higher wages, its interests were parochial, special, distinct from those of the nation in its entirety.

These were the considerations that led Fascist theoreticians to advocate a massive curb on private property and an increasing involvement of labor in the management and direction of industry. These were the considerations behind the creation of syndical collegia, management committees, and profit-sharing programs. At one stroke, socialization would break the resistance of the propertied classes and involve labor in the industrial enterprise. Interests would conflate and the Fascist state would assume the totalitarian unity to which Fascism had always aspired.

Fascist socialization was conceived as the culmination of Fascist corporativism. It was to resolve the duality between capital and labor that had too long obstructed the total unity of the Fascist state.[117] It was clear that within the unity of the new Fascist National Labor State the involvement of labor in the industrial enterprise, through elected representatives, was to be effected within the confines of a national plan controlled by the technical agencies of the Party. The direct responsibility of the directors of the several enterprises to the state insured Party control. The Fascist Republic was thus to remain totalitarian, subject to the tutelary, pedagogical, and enterprisory control of the unitary party.[118] The liberty which Fascism continued to advertise was the liberty central to Gentile's neo-Hegelian conception of the identity of the individual and the collective will, the unity of private and public interests. Fascism continued to advocate "individual liberty and class liberty, but only that constructive liberty within the confines of the state. . . ."[119] Any other liberty would be unreal, capricious. The state remained, for Mussolini, the ultimate arbiter of the national will. It was the concrete expression of national life, the ultimate repository of value, the moral substance of the ethical personality of each individual.[120] The individual was the state, and the state was Italy, and Italy was Fascism, and Mussolini was all of them. Such a series of substitutions constitutes the sustaining logic of charismatic totalitarian socialism.[121]

It is obvious that the self-criticism and the tolerance of divergent opinion which the Fascist Republic permitted was only to be conducted within the restrictive confines established by the unitary party. Mussolini was painfully specific in this regard even in the final months of the Social Republic. He maintained,

In these latter days let us speak clearly. Those who accept our program . . . can work with us, either inside or outside our ranks. . . . Further than this one cannot, one should not, go—out of respect to our dead, out of consideration for the responsible solidarity with the Fascists of the invaded regions, out of consideration for our own personal dignity. And beyond that we will not go.[122]

For all of his tactical shifts of emphasis in the chaos of the final months of the Social Republic, Mussolini never surrendered the totalitarian pretensions of Fascism. He conceived Fascism to be a totalitarian national socialism, the only socialism viable in the twentieth century. Given his conviction, born in his young manhood, that every society is governed by an organizing minority, that the masses have an ineluctible need for leadership, this was the only conceivable conclusion to which his social and political thought could come.

This was Mussolini's final social and political conception—a national socialism that harbored all the transmuted elements of the revolutionary syndicalism of his youth, fused with the nationalism that was the product of the crisis of World War I. Neo-idealism was the solvent of both.

For Mussolini, the nation was the ethnocentric community in which men effectively organized themselves, as moral agents, to compete in the modern world. At its best, and in its most consistent expression, Fascist racism served this conception of the nation as the ultimate object of loyalty. Mussolini's socialism, in turn, was predicated on the effective identification of the individual, his sect, his category, and his class with his nation. Socialization constituted Mussolini's final effort to effect that identification by eliminating loci of special interests. Sustaining the political and social system that was to realize this vision of society was a charter myth and an ideology, an argued system of beliefs about man and the world animated by specific normative convictions. The descriptive propositions concerning man and the world derive in large part from the sociological tradition with which Mussolini was familiar. The normative convictions were essentially those of Gentile's neo-idealism. The synthesis of the two was neither fully one nor the other. It was the ideology of Fascism. Still harboring these convictions, Mussolini fell before the guns of political assassins on the afternoon of April 28, 1945, three months before his sixty-second birthday.

CHAPTER EIGHT

The Totalitarian Epoch

THE DEATH of Mussolini marked the end of the Fascist experiment on the Italian peninsula. For some, the defeat of the Axis Powers marked the end of a specific Fascist Era, a discrete period of world history now gratefully traversed, safely relegated to books that preoccupy themselves with the dead and painful past.

And yet the years that followed the termination of hostilities failed to bring with them the burgeoning of freedom, international harmony, and collective well-being that seemed to be so much the aspiration of the united "antifascist" powers. It rapidly became evident that the fulfillment of the hopes that lighted the way of the world throughout the dark and dreadful years of world conflict was not to be the simple consequence of the defeat of international "fascism." Soon the suspicion was abroad that if World War II marked the end of an era, that era was only a phase of a broader, more complex, and perhaps more threatening epoch: the epoch of totalitarianism.

Totalitarianism of the Right and of the Left

The failure on the part of some of the most astute political analysts of our time to anticipate the political developments that followed the termination of hostilities after the second global conflict of our century was at least partly the consequence of the prevailing disposition to construe the relationship between "Marxism" and "Fascism" (however it was understood or misunderstood) as unilinear, each occupying the extreme of a continuum from "left" to "right," from "extreme liberalism" to "authoritarianism." Under the influence of this pervasive conviction, item scales were constructed by social scientists to reflect this unilinearity—with "extreme liberal," i.e., "Marxist," views the furthest removed from extreme "fascist" views. If the Marxists sinned, they were understood to sin on the side of virtue. In effect, experimental psychologists accepted critical auxiliary assumptions characteristic of Marxist interpretations of contemporary political movements. Marxists of all and sundry persuasions have insisted that Marxism and its variants have all been, in some radical sense, "democratic." Fascism, in whatever forms it took (and Marxist commentators have included in the class of fascist movements political systems as varied as the plebiscitary dictatorship of Louis Napoleon and reformist "social democracy"[1]), was conceived as fundamentally "antidemocratic." As a consequence, social scientists constructed pattern variable schemata which pretended to distinguish between the two in terms, for example, of "universalism" and "particularism," "equality" and "ascription." "Left Wing movements" were "universalistic and equalitarian," hence democratic in some real sense, while "right-wing movements" were "particularistic and ascriptive," hence fundamentally antidemocratic.[2]

The empirical studies conducted in the effort to identify "fascists" experimentally were governed by such auxiliary assumptions. The result was an artifact of those assumptions. In the study of "potential fascists," that is, the "authoritarian personalities" so extensively studied in the United States immediately following the War, the research was conducted on the basis of an extremely unsophisticated conception of a Right/Left continuum expressed in terms of American political clichés that ultilized the familiar vocabulary of Marxist and quasi-Marxist analyses.[3]

It soon became apparent, however, that

Fascism and Bolshevism, only a few decades ago thought of as worlds apart, have now been recognized increasingly as sharing many very important features. Their common hostility towards civil liberties, political democracy, their common antipathy for parliamentary institutions, individualism, private enterprise, their image of the political world as a struggle between morally irreconcilable forces, their belief that all their opponents are secretly leagued against them and their own predilection for secrecy, their conviction that all forms of power are in a hostile world concentrated in a few hands and their own aspirations for concentrated and total power—all these showed that the two extremes had much in common.[4]

The high hopes that animated the entire "antifascist" consortium throughout World War II foundered on the fact that the contemporary variants of Marxism were not radically democratic, but were instead essentially totalitarian political systems as much opposed to parliamentary democracy as was paradigmatic Fascism. The typology employed to classify the various contending political systems before the War was fundamentally mistaken. Marxism-Leninism and the subsequent variants that proliferated after the termination of hostilities shared more features with paradigmatic Fascism than they did or do with liberalism and the parliamentary democracy which is its characteristic political expression. The gradual recognition of this fact has led experimental scientists and political analysts to search out a more responsible and informative classificatory system through which investigation of their domain of inquiry could be pursued more effectively.

If political behavior is a function of psychologically genotypic personality dispositions operating within a special sociopolitical context, and Left Wing and Right Wing radicals display analogous political behavior, one would expect their psychologically genotypic personality profiles, as revealed in diagnostic test performance, to display similarities. During the last decade experimental psychologists have attempted to construct item scales and conduct research that would confirm such an intuitive experimental hypothesis. There is no *probative* evidence that such similarities do, in fact, obtain.

H. J. Eysenck's analysis of T. Coulter's study of 1953,[5] for example, affirming such a similarity, has been subjected to searching criticism.[6] M. Rokeach, on the other hand, employing a scale calculated to measure the subject's disposition to conceive the world in closed categories, in terms of a "dogma," does, however, suggest that extreme attitudes of either the Left or the Right are alternative phenotypic manifestations of the same personality dispositions.[7] I. A. Taylor's studies, in turn, provide empirical evidence to support the thesis that suggests that the underlying personality dispositions of both Left and Right Wing radicals are similar in significant respects.[8] More recently H. McClosky and J. Schaar have provided further evidence that radical beliefs, either of the Left or Right, share critical similarities.[9]

Such studies provide presumptive evidence that advocates of radical ideologies share certain psychologically genotypic dispositional traits. The fact that the sample populations tested represent local communists, rather than communists from one of the established communist communities, and that the "fascists" available for testing are similarly of local provenience and are frequently selected or self-selected on the basis of a curious list of political opinions that bear little resemblance to the political commitments of paradigmatic fascists, weakens the probative force of such findings. Nonetheless such findings, together with the descriptive evidence available from a careful scrutiny of political opinions expressed by representative Marxists or their contemporary variants, and fascist spokesmen and whatever living representatives of paradigmatic Fascism remain, affords a good presumptive case for the existence of an underlying similarity of personality structure subtending radical political orientation, whether it be of Left or Right Wing provenience.

The presumptive case supports the conviction that both fascism and the variants of Marxism that today receive so much attention constitute species of a single genus: totalitarianism. Had Anglo-American political commentators not been under the pervasive influence of Marxist or quasi-Marxist analyses, this would have been evident long before the advent of World War II. Such astute observers as Ely Halevy and Franz Borkenau indicated as much. Halevy argued that although Russian socialism had developed out of the democratic and anti-statist tradition of classical Marxism, it had quickly begun to assume the elitist, authoritarian, nationalist, and statist features of Fascism until he could maintain that "Bolshevism is, literally, a 'fascism.' "[10] Borkenau, in turn, went so far as to suggest that Bolshevism was a "conscious and intentional imitation of Fascism. . . ."[11]

That such was the case should have been evident before the War—had Anglo-American analysts taken the trouble to treat Fascism as a serious political movement and inform themselves of its ideological commitments. The fact is that both paradigmatic Fascism and contemporary Marxism are rooted in the same ideological traditions and share some critical normative convictions. Mussolini was a well-informed and convinced Marxist. His ultimate political convictions represent a reform of classical Marxism in the direction of a restoration of its Hegelian elements. Gentile, a neo-Hegelian, construed Marxism as a variant of Hegelianism and Fascism as its most consistent contemporary expression. Leninism, like Fascism, is heir to a similar patrimony that reveals itself, for example, in the conceptions of the relation between the individual and society and in the isomorphic arguments that provide vindications for their respective totalitarian political practices.

Classical Marxism and the Totalitarian Ethic

That similar arguments subtend both Marxism and Fascism is revealed in even the most elementary analysis of the normative arguments tendered by Marx himself. Marx, even in his earliest manuscripts, was concerned with formulating a *theoretical* conception of man. His original conception was a vague "model" of man as a social being, a descriptive frame of reference simpler in obvious ways from the being it was understood to represent. As a model, it was calculated to afford a parsimonious account of, and facilitate insight into, the more complex and elusive real being. In his *Economic and Philosophic Manuscripts* of 1844, this model was reduced to stenographic formulations, and the relationship between the individual and "social-being" was regularly reduced to one of identity. "The individual *is* the *social-being*. His life . . . *is* . . . an expression and confirmation of social life. Man's individual and species life (*Gattungsleben*) are not different. . . ."[12]

Framed in such a manner, the model becomes an analytic conceptual schema and is recognizable as an Hegelian inheritance. It was the common heritage of almost all the Left Wing Hegelians of the period. Moses Hess, himself such an Hegelian, and a mentor of both Marx and Engels, identified this model as that of "modern German philosophy." "The individual . . . according to contemporary German philosophy," Hess indicated, "*is* the species, the totality, humanity. . . ."[13] This vague and ambiguous conception remained central to Marx's theoretical accounts. "Man," Marx contended, "*is* the human world, the state, society," and the human essence was understood to be no more than "the *ensemble* of social relations."[14]

Such a conceptual bias produced in Marx a conviction that a "real science" of society could only be established by making "the social relationship of 'man to man' the basic principle of . . . theory,"[15] and that relationship was construed to be, in some sense, an identity. The theory which sought to explicate this relationship drew inferences from a set of descriptive propositions which could be taken as premises. The propositions which so served were understood to be broad empirical generalizations capable of generating theorems of increasing specificity which themselves were subject to empirical confirmation and disconfirmation. The theory was expressed in terms of very broad (and consequently vague) sequential laws which conceived determinate changes in the productive forces generating changes in the division of labor in society that in turn entailed alterations in productive relations. The ordering of the constituent propositions indicated the implications of the conceptual model by providing an inventory of determinants, directing the strategy of research and explanation by isolating the prime variables. Variables were identified as belonging to the productive forces, the relations of production, the superstructural or class interests—to specify only the most prominent categories. Changes in variables belonging to one or another category were related in a law-like manner, indicating the direction in which variables influenced each other. The theory established the cognitive implications of the initial definitional schema.

Marx defended his use of his theoretical scheme and the initial definition of man with which he had begun with standard arguments. The notion of man he advanced, he argued, was (1) intuitively more tenable than the mechanistic and atomistic conception of "bourgeois" social theory; (2) it had specific empirical referents and consequently could generate a variety of verification studies; and (3) it provided a more parsimonious account of the range of phenomena under scrutiny.[16] All of this can be said in the language of contemporary theory construction in the social sciences. But social science is ideally concerned with the formulation and issuance of "if-then," or "theoretical," propositions, descriptive or explanatory accounts systematically relating recurrent phenomena for purposes of prediction and control. It does not conceive the issuance of imperatives, or the identification of ideals toward which men should aspire, to be among its legitimate concerns. Marx's analysis, on the other hand, characteristically delivered itself of conclusions unmistakably normative and couched in the language of advocacy rather than empirical assessment. His analysis led to "the doctrine that man is the supreme being for man . . .," and ended "with the categorical imperative to overthrow all those conditions in which man is an abased, enslaved, abandoned, contemptible being. . . ."[17] Marx's prose, particularly of this early period is charged with imperative force. "Man is the highest being for man,"[18] an evident value, is conjoined with the injunction, "One must rekindle in the hearts of . . . men their human self-consciousness, freedom. Only this sentiment . . . can make out of a society a community of men devoted to their supreme ends. . . ."[19]

Thus, Marx's model of man supported normative conclusions as well as discharging scientific or purely descriptive functions. What is of interest in the present context is that one and the same theoretical model could serve in such diverse capacities. The initial conception employed was, in fact, "normic," in the sense that as a theoretical model having a *prima facie* descriptive character it also possessed normative force capable of providing support for imperatives.

Marx's theoretical account of man identified him, as an individual, with his society, with the human macrosphere, or with the *ensemble* of social relations which constitute society and/or the macrosphere. The individual man, Marx argued, is neither a particular thing nor a being possessed of an abstract essence. Man, Marx seemed to argue, is an existence which *is* social activity, a variable in an interactive context.

The cognitive meaning of such formulations is obscure enough, but such formulations have the species traits of definitional, empirical, or theoretical propositions. They support normative conclusions because implicit in such an account is at least one proposition rich with normative force. The emotive features which even elementary analysis reveals make manifest how it is possible for Marx to negotiate the transition from presumably descriptive propositions to normative results.

The procedure reveals its traces in a variety of places, not only in Marx's earlier writings but in his mature work as well. Thus, in the notes Marx wrote for his *Contribution to the Critique of Political Economy,* he contended, as we have seen, that "Man is in the most literal sense a *zoon politikon,* not merely a social animal, *but an animal which can develop into an individual only in society.*"[20]

Cognitively, this appears to be little more than an implication of the vague putative identity relationship conceived to subsist between the individual and his society. But such an implication has "vectoral force"—it not only describes or defines but it tacitly *recommends*. The implication has persuasive force. To identify the conditions necessary for the realization of individuality entails, *psychologically,* a recommendation to support and foster them. One *ought* to defend and foster the conditions requisite to such fulfillment.

Marx's recommended definition of man, defended by appeals to its theoretical fruitfulness when expanded, its confirmability and parsimoniousness when applied in the empirical domain, has emotive implications that permit the transition from cognitive premises to normative conclusions. Marx's definition has the dual characteristics of a condensed theoretical proposition that can function in an articulated social science theory and that can serve as a normative ideal as well. Men *should* fulfill themselves and if man, in some unspecified sense, *is* society, *is* the ensemble of social relations—if society is the necessary ground of individuation—then society and macrosocial relations have at least an instrumental and, by virtue of the identity relation, an intrinsic value. Fulfillment *means* the un-alienated identity of the individual and his productive community. This seems to be one of the implications of saying that man's essence *is* an *ensemble* of social relations, of saying that man *is* the human world, the state, and society. "What is to be avoided above all," Marx argued, "is the re-establishing of 'Society' as an abstraction *vis-à-vis* the individual. . . . Man, much as he may . . . be a *particular* individual . . . is just as much the *totality*. . . ."[21] A relationship so conceived is taken to support normative conclusions —and Marx's ethics takes on an empirical or naturalistic character.

This conception of man was central to the "humanism" of the Left Wing Hegelians. For Moses Hess, it meant that "Only as a *social being* is the human being *truly* and *really alive*,"[22] and Marx could maintain ". . . my *own* existence *is* social activity. . . . My *general* consciousness is only the *theoretical* shape of that of which the *living* shape is the real community, the social fabric, although at the present day *general* consciousness (*Gattungsbewusstsein*) is an abstraction from real life and as such antagonistically confronts it."[23]

By identifying the individual with a "totality" (whether it be society or the state) one can, by a series of not too complicated substitutions, *demonstrate* that without society the individual is not *truly* an individual, not *truly* human; and, further, that the interests of the "totality" and the individual must ultimately coincide. Thus the justificatory arguments for normative judgments succeed in taking on a quasi-demonstrative character and have implications for social and political conduct.

As a consequence Marx's purpose, the resolution of the social contradictions which compromised what he called the "unity of human essence. . . . *the practical identity of man with man*,"[24] could muster formal as well as empirical or theoretical warrant in its support as well as provide the rationale for political conduct. In this sense, Marx's arguments are curiously Hegelian in character and implication, and the "individuality," "fulfillment," and "freedom," promised are Hegelian "individuality," "fulfillment," and "freedom," *the unity of the particular with the universal.* It is the harmonizing of the ego with its otherness. The "human emancipation" that constitutes Marx's explicit moral ideal during his early revolutionary activity is understood to be a "genuine and harmonious species life . . .,"[25] which was to find expression (in the *Communist Manifesto*) in the search for "an association in which the free development of each is the condition for the free development of all."[26]

Marx negotiates the is/ought hiatus by harnessing the implicit recommendation contained in the seemingly descriptive and definitional propositions that identify (in some unspecified sense) the individual with his social macrosphere. If man *is* his society, a disharmonious, contradictory, and debased society can only engender a disharmonious, contradictory, and debased individual. Marx's conception of alienation is, in fact, predicated on this putative identity relationship. To become a fully human being, harmonizing existence and essence, the harmonious identity of the particular with the universal must be restored. This harmony of ultimate interests is the condition of the "development of human powers as such," that Marx, in his maturity, made the "end in itself."[27]

Contemporary Marxists seem at least intuitively aware of the nature of the argument advanced by Marx. While the normic model of man advanced by Marx is defended by appeals to theoretical fruitfulness, empirical confirmation, and descriptive parsimony, it is recognized that the model serves more than theoretical and descriptive purposes. Once it identified the locus of *fulfillment* and *freedom*, moral judgments were able to gain a foothold. Fulfillment and freedom recommend themselves as self-evident values. Marx's normic conception is recognized as providing the foundation for Marxist ethics and Marxist political activity.

Thus, Adam Schaff can argue that "the propositions of socialist humanism and its precepts . . . flow from the theory of historical materialism, and in particular [from] the specific understanding of the individual as a social product—as a product of 'the totality of social relations.' . . ."[28] Schaff is sufficiently well informed to know that no conjunction of descriptive propositions can ever provide the ultimate basis for ethical conclusions. Among the set of propositions from which a normative judgment derives there must be some element of value. Schaff therefore does not pretend to offer a demonstration but makes recourse to metaphor and speaks of socialist ethics "flowing" from the Marxist theory of history.

This transition from descriptive to normative domains is possible only because individuality, freedom, and fulfillment are *defined*, by Marx, in terms of social relations. Apart from social relations there is, strictly speaking, no individuality, no personality, no humanity. If one accepts such a definition (actually a redefinition, for it was formulated to counter the prevailing "bourgeois" atomistic definition of man), a reasonably specific set of values (psychologically) follow. What would one oppose to Marx's account? Depersonalization, inhumanity, slavery, or debasement as values? Marx's initial definition (advanced in descriptive guise) identifying the individual and society mobilizes sufficient commendatory force to deliver the ethical conclusions that remained central to the Marxian enterprise throughout the life of its founder and that now provide the legitimizing rationale for Leninist political conduct.

Ethical arguments emanating from the Marxist countries regularly traffic on such a "logic." A seemingly descriptive account of man's "essence" is identified with the totality of social relations; what results is the prescriptive ideal of a "human society" or a "social humanity."[29] Thus, what Marx referred to as the "supreme end" for man, his fulfillment and freedom, the full development of his personality,[30] is only possible within the harmonious and intricate network of socialist social relations realized in harmoniously integrated social collectives of varying form, function, and extent. The perfection of man, the fulfillment of the self, requires the perfection of the relations and institutions of the society in which he lives. Society is man's essence; the more perfect society, the more perfect man. Thus, Marxist ethics conceives a substantive identity between collective and individual interests. Marxist philosophers therefore characterize the distinguishing trait of Marxist ethics to be the resolution of what "bourgeois" ethics held to be the inevitable antagonism between the individual and society.[31] Thus, the central achievement of Marxist ethics is understood to reside in "harmonizing the private interest of the individual with collective or social interest."[32] As a matter of fact, this putative harmony is the analytic consequence of defining man's essence as the totality of social relations.

The identification of the individual with any aggregate of men (the society or the state) accomplishes a variety of tasks. The most important for our purposes here is to effectively empty the concept *freedom* of any descriptive content. Freedom has, in the West, been traditionally defined in terms of the absence of social and legal obstruction to the individual's freedom of action. Once the individual is, in some fundamental sense, identified with his collectivity, restraint and absence of restraint lose their descriptive significance and freedom cannot be non-vacuously characterized. Once such an identification is accomplished, the individual who is constrained by his collectivity is only *seemingly* constrained. Since the collectivity is his greater self, by submitting to its demands he answers a law he has, in some sense, laid upon himself. He remains, according to this rationale—the empirical constraint notwithstanding—the autonomous moral agent who freely acts to obey his truer self. Freedom and constraint conflate and the instances of the one are no longer distinguishable from instances of the other. There remains only seeming freedom (acts undertaken which conflict with the interests of the collectivity) and real freedom (acts undertaken which harmonize with the interests of the collectivity).

Thus Soviet moral philosophers have argued, "A correctly understood personal interest is an interest that is always compatible with collective goals,"[33] which is a reformulation of the judgment made by Engels in 1845: "In communist society . . . the interests of individuals do not conflict, but are identical. . . . Public interests no longer differ from the interests of each individual."[34] Such judgments rest on a putative identity relationship between the individual and his community and provide the charter myth for the totalitarian rule of the single party.

Only as long as freedom is negatively construed as the absence of collective restraint imposed on the individual's freedom to act in his own interest is a real distinction between freedom and constraint, between private and public interest, possible. As long as freedom is so understood, a free act is one undertaken by the individual as a self-directed activity, motivated by self-regarding interests and personal motives. Any conflict of interest between the individual and his collectivity can then be squarely faced and mediated by an appeal to the respective merits of the individual versus the collective interest in each particular confrontation. The most generous interpretation of Mill's first principle, "All restraint, *qua* restraint, is an evil," is that which interprets it as a formal or procedural maxim that requires that any restraint imposed by public power upon the individual's freely chosen activity be justified by public, neutral, and relevant reasons.[35] It does not necessarily imply that freedom of individual action is valuable in and of itself, but it does advance an initial presumption in favor of the individual's freedom to act, which must be overcome. Given the individual's vulnerability to society, his intrinsic powerlessness against any organized collective or unorganized aggregate, such an initial presumption has much to recommend it. It merely means that the burden of justifying restraint imposed upon the individual rests upon the stronger public power. It means that the individual's defenses against collective demands, at best never very imposing, are not further undermined by requiring that *he* justify to the community every non-conformist act he undertakes. He cannot be required to show that his every act is compatible with collective interests without a recognition that what will result, in all probability, will be a community with a high conformity index. This stultifying eventuality seems to be anticipated by Soviet philosophers with satisfaction. "People are cultivating the habit of framing their actions," we are told, "in accordance with the demands and opinions of the collective."[36] Elsewhere, one of the corollaries of such a view is expressed as: "The community of interests, the social, political, and ideological unity of men in socialist society provides the foundation for complete personal happiness."[37]

Marx effectively exposed the shortcomings of the arguments advanced by "bourgeois" philosophers in support of the "atomic conception of man." He correctly recognized that the case for psychological individualism was unconvincing. There was no empirical warrant for the characterization of man as an atom and of society as an aggregate of atoms. Marx's alternate conception of man enjoyed a more compelling empirical warrant; it could, with suitable sematic and syntactical specification, support instructive verification studies. And yet Marx's conception of man led to an interpretation of individual rights and freedoms as *derivative,* and consequently advanced a *prima facie* presumption in favor of the interests of the collectivity as exemplifying the true or more profound freedom of the individual. Contemporary Soviet Marxists draw out the implications of this procedural presumption in a variety of contentions:

To learn to live in a collective means to regard oneself an integral part of it and always to remain true to the guiding principle of collectivism: one for all and all for one. When people take their stand by this rule, they harmoniously blend their personal interests with those of the community. . . . Building a new society, therefore, implies that personal interests coincide with those of the community . . . creative endeavor adorns the collective and its members and is no longer an expression of the subordination of personal to communal interests, but their *confluence*. . . . Whoever violates the collective's rules, lets down or even shames his comrades, is in for heavy criticism. . . . Private life is the sphere in which a person lives when he is not engaged in productive or public activities, that is to say, the part of his life that he sets apart for himself. Is this the purely personal affair of everyone? No, a person's private life is inextricably bound up with public affairs. . . .[38]

And furthermore:

When the social interest is lifted to the level of the principal interest of the personality, then there can be no renunciation of personal interests as the enemies of Marxism contend, rather personal interest thereby finds its highest fulfillment. . . . The new, communist ethics declares: Think above all of social interests, conceive them as your own most important interest and you enhance thereby the collective as well as your own personal well-being.[39]

All of these contentions could be made compatible with arguments that construe the collective and the individual interests *substantially compatible,* though recognizing the distinction between them. And it is true that some Marxists argue in such fashion.[40] But the more ominous contention is that there obtains, in some obscure sense, an *identity* of interests between the personal and the social interests. And it is this contention that gives moral priority and control privilege to the collective and its self-selected representatives as against the individual. Lenin, in the tradition of classical Marxism and under the direct influence of Hegel, seemed to argue such an identification with the claim that "the individual *is* the *universal.* . . . Consequently the opposites (the individual is opposed to the universal) are identical. . . . Every individual is (in one way or another) a universal."[41]

It is this sort of persuasive definition that permits Leninists to speak of a unitary collective will, as it finds expression in the will of the party, as being in the interests of all classes, strata, and individuals in the population.[42] If "the individual is an ensemble of determinate social relations," it is possible to argue that he is but a "part of a greater, encompassing social whole," which, because of a single pattern of social relations governing the activities of all, evinces a single and coherent will.[43] Such a unitary will represents the will of all and finds expression in the will of the single party.

This kind of argument provides the rationale for the logic of substitutions that make the will of the party the will of the proletariat, and that makes the will of the proletariat the will of the Soviet people, and that makes the will of the Soviet people the ultimate will of humanity. All that is necessary to complete the legitimation of totalitarian dictatorship is the recognition that the will of a single man is in some manner identical with the will of the party. Under the rigors of such a system of identifications any activity which is incompatible with the collective will as it finds expression in the periodic programmatic statements of the party, in its leader, and in the laws of the state is *prima facie* the product of ignorance or perversity. When faced by deviation of whatever sort, one must either educate (the increasing emphasis in the Soviet Union even today on the tutelary and pedagogical responsibilities of the ideological agencies of the party) or punish (the "Builders of Communism" are admonished to be unrelenting in their opposition to the "enemies of the people").

Though it is perhaps an exaggeration to say, "In the ideal totalitarian state 'everything that is not compulsory is forbidden,' "[44] there is an evident tendency in a totalitarian system to move in just such a direction. Soviet legal development is characterized by a conscious extension of law to cover the most intimate and personal relations.[45] It is the logic of identities, a heritage of classical Marxism, that subtends such developments in the total or administered state. It is the logic of identities that permits one man or a select group of men to speak in the name of the interests of all. It is the unified and harmonious will, the exemplification of the identity of all with all, that institutionalizes anxiety, for under such circumstances the individual who deviates from collective norms (as they find varied and changing expression in the determinations of the unitary party) can only expect to be accounted a fool or a criminal.

Thanks to the identification of public and individual interests, the individual who pursues his own concerns can expect to be apprized either as one who cannot assess his true interests—a fool—or as one who chooses to be antisocial—a criminal. It is interesting to note that the identity relationship between the individual and his community permits transit only in one direction. The collective interests are the individual's true interests. But should the individual attempt to argue that because there obtains an identity of interests between the individual and his collectivity everything the individual does must be in the collective interests, he is immediately characterized as "petty-bourgeois," a defender of "outworn and moribund views which are incompatible with the essence of [the] socialist order."[46]

One of the critical arguments in the armory used to vindicate totalitarian systems is the logic of substitutions that permits the identification of the individual with some critical specific collectivity. Such an identification is central to Marx's normative system and is clearly an Hegelian inheritance. The same argument, as we have seen, is fundamental to the social and political philosophy of Gentile and found expression in representative Fascist vindications. Ugo Spirito confirmed that Gentile's Fascist rationale was "inspired by the Marxist dialectic," which took "its point of departure from the identification of the individual and the state. . . ."[47]

Classical Marxism follows essentially the same logic as Hegelianism and provides the same occasion for the convenient substitution of leader, party, state, nation, class, and individual interests as does paradigmatic Fascism. In both systems all interests are conceived as harmonized, the analytic consequence of conceiving a "speculative" identity to obtain between the individual and his collective. It is the logic of substitutions that licenses the rule of the minoritarian unitary party and its leader. It is the leader and the party that speak in the ultimate interests of all. Since the ultimate interests of all are identical, only one representation of those interests can be true. The unitary party and its leader assume all the pedagogical, enterprisory, and tutelary roles that have come to characterize the totalitarian political party.

The charter arguments that vindicate the rule of the unitary party, whether of the Left or Right are essentially the same. Marxist "humanism" and Fascist "humanism of labor" share the same species traits, revealed in the similarity of arguments mustered in their defense and the similarity of content that gives them descriptive substance. They originate in the Hegelianism which is their ultimate historic source.

Leninism and Fascism as Totalitarianisms

If a particular constellation of genotypic political attitudes (the existence of which is suggested by the results obtained by a variety of test vehicles) manifests itself in overt commitment to radical political organizations that advocate a totalitarianism of either the Left or Right, and if an analysis of the ideological vindications of such political movements reveal a substantial similarity in justificatory argument, all that remains in order to deliver a compelling presumptive argument for the identification of the diverse variants of contemporary Marxism as members of a genus which includes paradigmatic Fascism is to indicate the pervasive similarities in institutional structure of such political systems. The institutional features of Left and Right Wing totalitarian systems do, in fact, reveal a surprising similarity, a fact not lost upon Fascist commentators even during periods of the most exacerbated political contest with Marxist movements.

As early as 1933, Mussolini, himself, indicated his awareness of the gradual convergence between Soviet totalitarianism and his own. By 1938, he was prepared to suggest that the process of phased involution of the Leninist system had produced an involuntary and inconsistent fascism. As early as 1934, Fascist theoreticians could contend that "in the course of its development the Russian revolution has gradually given evidence of fully abandoning Marxist postulates and of a gradual, if surreptitious acceptance of certain fundamental political principles that characterize Fascism."[48]

While such judgments were relatively common among non-Marxist and Fascist commentators, they were not unknown among knowledgeable Marxists. Leon Trotsky, for example, maintained that "Stalinism and Fascism, in spite of a deep difference in social foundations, are symmetrical phenomena. In many of their features they show a deadly similarity."[49]

Those similarities include a commitment to national development and/or reconstruction under a highly centralized and authoritarian party elite, a restoration of the authority of the state, an effective program of class and category collaboration within the confines of a national economic plan, exclusive and systematic training of the youth of the nation in conformity with a secular ideology characterized by a relatively specific constellation of exclusive social and political beliefs, a unitary party monopoly of the means of coercion and communication, and leadership by charismatic or pseudocharismatic leaders charged with enormous responsibilities and endowed with prodigious powers. In all cases the totalitarian state assumes pedagogical, enterprisory, and tutelary functions unknown in traditional parliamentary regimes.

The convergence of Leninist systems toward that of the paradigmatic Fascist model has been gradual. Fascists were, in fact, well aware of the gradual involution of Leninism as a political system and saw in the process the evidence that Fascism constituted the ideal type of the political system of the twentieth century. To most effectively outline the process of involution that has revealed the essenially totalitarian and inconsistent fascist features of contemporary Leninism, it is only necessary to briefly retrace the history of Marxism as a social and political ideology.

The Involution of Leninism

Classical Marxism evolved out of a body of thought first articulated in the early 1840's. As young men in their twenties, both Marx and Engels committed themselves to a secular humanism that resolved to "overthrow all those conditions in which man is an abased, enslaved, abandoned, contemptible being. . . ."[50] They sought to "rekindle in the hearts of . . . men their human self-consciousness, freedom. Only this sentiment . . . can make out of a society a community of men devoted to their supreme ends. . . ."[51]

The elements of this humanism persisted into Marx's maturity and reappear in the manuscript on which he was working when death came to him in 1883. Such elements deploy emotive force but little cognitive meaning unless they are conjoined with definitional,

346

descriptive, and theoretical elaborations. It is to these statemental components that one must direct his attention, for they sketch the implications of stated values and as they are modified or abandoned the value commitments themselves necessarily undergo alteration. They are, in effect, redefined.

Marx dedicated himself to the liberation of man, what he called in his youth "universal human emancipation." As a substantive and critical thinker he could not be content with simple advocacy. He sought to specify programmatic goals and effectively implement desired change. In order to accomplish his purposes he was forced to come to grips with the reality of the environment in which he found himself. To discharge this latter responsibility he assumed all the obligations of a social theorist. He was obliged to articulate a social theory that met all the minimal scientific requirements of consistency and truth—to generate a theory that would deliver effective control and predictive power. What he produced was later identified by Engels as the "materialist conception of history." The fundamental explanatory proposition of that conception was that "in every historical epoch, the prevailing mode of economic production and exchange, and the social organization necessarily following from it, form the basis upon which is built up, and from which alone can be explained, the political and intellectual history of that epoch. . . ."[52]

What this meant (without entering into a variety of legitimate qualifications) was that human political, social, and intellectual history is a superstructural or derivative product of activity in the economic substructure of society. Economic variables are privileged or primary variables. They are independent, while all others are dependent variables. Political, social, and intellectual behaviors are explicable only in terms of economic variables. Thus, while both Marx and Engels contended that "the history of all hitherto existing society is the history of class struggles," it was evident that class struggle is "nothing but the reflex, in thought of [the] conflict" between "new productive forces" and the prevailing "mode of using them."[53] The intellectual, political, and social history of any epoch is to be explained only via relationships which obtain in the economic base of society. Marx insisted,

We set out from real, active men, and on the basis of their real life process we demonstrate the development of the ideological reflexes and echoes of this life process. The phantoms formed in the human brain are . . . necessarily sublimates of their material life process . . . all of ideology . . . thus no longer retain[s] the semblance of independence . . . men developing their material productive and their material intercourse alter . . . their thinking. . . . Life is not determined by consciousness, but consciousness by life.[54]

Politics, art, religion, ethics, consciousness itself, are completely "absorbed" by economics.[55]

Given this theoretical interpretation, and having discovered what they held to be the "laws of social development" in unrestricted generalizations about the productive processes relating men in association, Marx and Engels conceived themselves equipped to tender predictions about the future course of collective human behavior. As Marx maintained that he had discovered those economic laws of society "working with iron necessity toward inevitable results," those "immanent laws" that "beget with the inexorability of a law of nature" specific and specifiable consequences, both he and Engels could predict social change with the certainty of "a mathematical or mechanical demonstration."[56]

Such predictions were predicated on the thesis that consciousness was an "efflux," an "echo" of material conditions obtaining in the economic base. Possessed of an awareness of the economic circumstances governing the life of the working class, both Marx and Engels felt confident in predicting a "spontaneous" revolutionary consciousness among the proletariat.[57] The proletariat, for both Marx and Engels, was understood as "misery conscious of its spiritual and physical misery," driven to revolution by the very circumstances which obtained in the productive substructure of society itself.[58] Revolution was assured independently of any political party or leadership.[59] The decline of wages below the subsistence minimum, a process made inevitable by the tendencies operating within the productive processes of capitalism itself, supplied the conditions that rendered revolution a predictable necessity.[60] "The majority of the proletariat . . . has no other choice than to starve or to rebel."[61]

Since the necessary and sufficient conditions for revolution obtain only in the advanced capitalist countries, revolution involves the "immense majority" of men who have been reduced by mature capitalism to the status of proletarians. The Communist revolution, as Marx and Engels conceived it, was therefore a "self-conscious, independent movement of the immense majority, in the interests of the immense majority."[62] It was a manifestly democratic movement —the product of the moving forces of history itself. Both Marx and Engels were convinced that political movements reflected the "given economic situation" of any historical period. Consequently, they argued that the proletarian revolution was the active response of the vast majority of men proletarianized by the processes of production prevalent in mature capitalist countries. The political expression of mass emiseration was mass revolution. Past revolutions had been undertaken by exiguous minorities leading restive and unconscious masses. The proletarian revolution, on the other hand, was conceived by Marx and Engels as a vast, conscious, and independent movement by a knowledgeable majority. The movement is "instinctive, spontaneous, irrepressible." "The time of surprise attacks," Engels insisted, "of revolutions carried through by small conscious minorities at the head of unconscious masses, is past."[63]

A vast majority of men, driven below the level of subsistence by dysfunctional productive relations that maldistributed the enormous productivity of capitalist society, would seize the apparatus of production to administer it in the service of the majority. The state, which had been the coercive executive arm of oppressing classes throughout history, would simply wither away and in its place would arise an administration that would concern itself with the "mere superintendence of production."[64] The governance of men would be transformed into a democratic administration of things. The "dictatorship of the proletariat" was not to be a dictatorship in any significant sense of the word. The model of that "dictatorship" for both Marx and Engels was the Paris Commune of 1871. The Commune provided for universal suffrage; representatives were endowed with only severely restricted agential powers and always subject to referendum and recall.[65] "Nothing," Marx insisted, "could be more foreign to the spirit of the Commune than to supersede universal suffrage by hierarchic investiture."[66]

This, then, was the body of theoretical propositions that classical Marxism advanced to support its normative injunctions. Men could overcome alienation and accede to universal emancipation because the very logic of history conspired in their service. Mature capitalism had generated the necessary and sufficient conditions for a majoritarian liberating revolution. The vast majority of thinking men were driven to seize the productive apparatus of advanced capitalism to administer it democratically in their own conscious interest. The theory and the normative commitment of classical Marxism were thus essentially congruent.

With the advent of the twentieth century, however, Marxism entered into crisis. The recurrent predictions of imminent revolution in the advanced capitalist countries went unfulfilled. The proletariat failed to develop the consciousness requisite to revolution. In 1868, Engels lamented that the proletariat of England had succeeded in developing only a "bourgeois consciousness."[67] Marx voiced the same misgivings in 1870.[68] The dependency relationship between revolutionary consciousness and "objective conditions" could no longer be advanced with the assurance required by the theory.

It is clear that although the theoretical propositions of Marx and Engels were formulated in vague and ambiguous language, Marxism was committed to the conviction that revolutionary consciousness was derivative of more fundamental processes in society. The production of revolutionary consciousness was inevitable, and it would affect the vast majority of men working under advanced capitalist conditions. That vast majority would be driven to rebellion and would seize the technological apparatus and plant provided by capitalism itself upon which to erect the social structure of socialism. An elaborate productive base, conjoined with socialist consciousness, both of them products of capitalism itself, would produce the socialist society which was the conscious desire of the vast majority of men—an outcome that would satisfy the normative aspirations of classical Marxism.

Unfortunately for classical Marxism, the proletarian majority whom they had charged with this historic mission failed to develop the requisite consciousness. Revolutionary sentiment developed in those areas of the world under objective conditions which did not accord themselves with the requirements of the theory. Lenin found himself in circumstances in which a restive revolutionary sentiment mobilized itself outside the advanced capitalist countries. He had the painful choice of either attempting to harness that revolutionary ardor behind the further development of capitalism, hoping that capitalism would, as classical Marxism suggested, eventually develop the requisite consciousness among the working-class, or he could modify classical Marxism and seek to generate the motive consciousness among the elemental masses independent of, and if necessary contrary to, objective conditions. He opted for the latter alternative. Lenin insisted that consciousness must be *brought* to the working masses, now no longer simply the proletarian majority of which classical Marxism spoke, but a coalition of the peasant masses and the proletarian minority of Czarist Russia. Lenin rejected the thesis of spontaneous revolutionary consciousness. He denied that the revolution must wait until the vast majority of men had developed the "spontaneous" and "instinctive" consciousness of their real interests. In 1901, Lenin maintained that

. . . the "ideologist" is worthy of the name only when he precedes the spontaneous movement, points out the road, and is able ahead of all others to solve all the theoretical, political, tactical, and organizational questions which the "material elements" of the movement spontaneously encounter. . . .[69]

He argued further that the "spontaneous awakening of the masses" must be led by "ideologists" sufficiently "trained theoretically to be proof against all vacillations. . . ." The revolution demands "a strong and centralized organization of revolutionaries" who would provide the minoritarian "conscious element" necessary to direct the "spontaneous element."[70] What Lenin proposed was a minority "vanguard party" of professional revolutionaries whose will would offset the deficiencies of world history.

In Italy, at almost the same time, Mussolini was arguing almost the same thesis. Socialism, Mussolini maintained, was failing because it had not taken cognizance of the critical role played in revolution by effective political and insurrectionary elites. It was in 1904 that Mussolini rejected the deterministic thesis that revolution was the necessary and spontaneous product of capitalist economic conditions. He opted instead for a thesis which would restore to history the "creative will of determinate and determining men" who could leave the imprint of their influence on things and institutions and who would direct historical and political events in a determinate direction. Such men would constitute a minoritarian "socialist vanguard" and bring to the elemental energy of the majority a consciousness of historic purpose.

Thus, at approximately the same time, in two different locales, both Lenin and Mussolini, as socialist theoreticians and political leaders, introduced substantive modifications into the loose theoretical structure of classical Marxism. Their modifications were essentially the same. They were both elitists and voluntarists. They conceived the majority as the fodder, rather than the conscious agents, of social revolution. This is the essence of the modified socialism that animated their political activities. They both conceived the socialist party as a centralized, hierarchically integrated elite of professional revolutionaries charged with the responsibilities of history which classical Marxism had originally devolved upon the vast majority of thinking proletarians. Both Mussolini and Lenin led revolutionary movements in economically backward environments. Both drew their support, in large measure, from restive non-proletarian masses which Marx had always conceived to be essentially reactionary—that is, devoid of serious historical significance.

By 1902, Lenin understood the revolutionary consciousness of the masses to be a product not of the economic processes characteristic of capitalism, but of the active intercession of declassed bourgeois intellectuals. Such men, among whom Lenin numbered Marx and Engels as well as himself, were charged with the responsibility of making the masses conscious of their real rather than their immediate interests. Without the intercession of such men, Lenin argued, the masses could achieve only a "trade union mentality," an addiction to their primitive and immediate interests. Only the theoretical elite could divine the real and ultimate interests of the masses and thus act in the name of history. The revolution was not to be made by the vast majority of self-conscious and knowledgeable men as an automatic process, but by an aggressive elite mobilizing the elemental masses in the name of the ultimate interests of man. This was the sustaining logic of both the Bolshevik revolution of 1917 and the Fascist revolution of 1922. In both cases a minority of men, leading paramilitary bands, seized the state machinery in the name of their vision of society. Both revolutions were hierarchically led minoritarian revolutions. Both mobilized the restive energies of the masses in the service of a revolution guided by the insights of a man, or a small assembly of men, charged with the responsibility of lifting the consciousness of the masses to the level of their vision of social and political truth. The political organizations led by both men were not orthodox political parties; they represented movements of solidarity, movements charged with infusing the masses with a belief system. Both movements jealously defended the purity of their respective doctrines. Both assumed pedagogical and tutelary responsibilities never before exercised by men outside of religious orders.

By 1918, Mussolini had abandoned the term *socialism* as incapable of identifying his social and political convictions. He insisted that so many revisions had beset classical Marxism that the term no longer had cognitive significance. Lenin, on the other hand, insisted on his Marxist orthodoxy. He had permitted Marxism to "evolve" in order to make it viable to a new epoch, the final stage of capitalism. This "new stage" saw the inversion of several critical Marxism theses. Marx and Engels had both foreseen the socialist revolution in the advanced capitalist countries where objective conditions had produced the requisite economic base and attendant consciousness that were the conditions necessary for the establishment of a socialist democracy. Engels had systematically maintained that a restricted productive base could only produce the class cleavages against which Communism was unalterably opposed.

The separation of society into an exploiting and an exploited class, a ruling and an oppressed class, [is] the necessary consequence of the deficient and restricted development of production. . . . So long as the total social labor only yields a produce which but slightly exceeds that barely necessary for the existence of all; so long . . . is society divided into classes.[71]

The division of society is based "upon the insufficiency of production," which can be overcome only in the advanced capitalist nations. Socialism, therefore, can arise only on the productive base inherited from mature capitalism. Lenin, having committed himself to the mobilization of the elemental revolutionary potential in the backward countries, argued that revolution might first erupt in societies possessed of deficient and restricted industrial productivity, in essentially agrarian nations. It was equally clear, however, that Lenin conceived such revolutions as preliminary to the world-wide revolution of the proletariat, a revolution that would restore to the socialist movements the economic base necessary for the erection of a classless society.

Mussolini had, on the other hand, abandoned classical Marxism and had committed himself to a form of national socialism. He recognized that his revolution would inherit a backward economy. His economic and political program was therefore predicated on this recognition. The imperative governing the tactical and strategic program of the first Fascist organization was increased national production. Italy was a "proletarian nation." Its critical problem was not overproduction and maldistribution, the central concepts of classical Marxism, but underproduction and a lack of political and economic discipline. Mussolini contended that increased national production was a function of national discipline and charged the Fascist cohorts with the responsibility of infusing that sense of national purpose in the restive majority and imposing upon them the tutelary control that their conditions required.

Lenin, on the other hand, in his *State and Revolution,* written on the eve of the Bolshevik revolution, argued as though Russia had already attained maturity as a capitalist nation. It was only after the first six months of Bolshevik control that he admitted that the obligation which faced his minoritarian government was, in fact, to increase national production. Thereafter, his imperatives increasingly turned on the issue of expanding production. Russia was not beset with the problems Marx and Engels had analyzed. It was not a country afflicted with the "absurdity of overproduction." Russia's economy was basically agrarian and it was underproductionist. Russia was an underdeveloped nation. In April, 1918, at approximately the same time Mussolini was developing his productionist conceptions in Italy, Lenin announced that it would be necessary to impose upon revolutionary Russia "the organization of the strictest . . . nationwide accounting and control of production" and "the raising [of] the productivity of labor on a national scale."[72] It was obvious to Lenin that "the use of compulsion," an "iron hand," and "iron rule" were necessary if such imperatives were to be fulfilled.[73]

It was only after the death of Lenin, in 1924, that Bolshevism underwent the transformation from an international to a national socialism. Lenin had anticipated a world-wide proletarian uprising that would provide nascent socialism with the economic base necessary for a socialist society. He waited in vain. Similarly, in 1924, after the death of Lenin, Stalin could still write that "the principal task of socialism—the organization of socialist production—has still to be fulfilled. Can this task be fulfilled, can the final victory of socialism be achieved in one country, without the joint efforts of the proletarians in several advanced countries? No, it cannot."[74]

Only months later did Stalin reverse himself and organize Russia behind a vast program of rapid and exacting national industrialization. So immense a program required the marshalling of all resources behind a highly centralized developmental program. Bolshevism, like Fascism, became a national developmental dictatorship. That development was directed by a small minority of men who possessed a monopoly over all communication and control media. A program of accelerated industrialization was undertaken which required dedication, discipline, and sacrifice. And it was left to the revolutionary and unitary party to impose them upon an entire society. It was this development which permitted Leon Trotsky to maintain that Stalinism and Fascism were "symmetrical phenomena."[75]

The principal product of the Stalin period was a contrived but viable national socialism or, if one prefers, a national Bolshevism. Its programmatic goals were indistinguishable from those of revolutionary developmental nationalism. All classes and categories in the Soviet Union, characterized as they were by differential income and status, were nonetheless exhorted to identify with the Soviet "fatherland." Thus, during World War II, Russians of whatever class were called upon to defend their homeland in a "Great Patriotic War." The nation became the charismatic object of loyalty. After 1955, the internationalism of world communism further disintegrated under the centrifugal forces of what is today loosely referred to as "national communisms."[76] Soviet internationalism remains but a vestigial doctrinal element in Marxism-Leninism. The "socialist world system" is conceived not as an international association of the proletarian class, but a "fraternity of proletarian nations" polycentrically organized in a loose consortium of sovereign states, those of lesser viability and economic potential gravitating around the larger and more commanding socialist states. At the moment what remains of classical Marxism's internationalism is the Soviet conviction that "patriotism is one of the best feelings of man," and that "some time in the future, all nations of the world will be members of a single communist family. Then, patriotism and internationalism will blend into a single great love for all humanity."[77]

Leninist and Fascist Internationalism

The trajectory traced by these latter developments follows those of paradigmatic Fascism with remarkable precision. As early as 1930, Fascist theoreticians had begun to speak of an *Internazionale fascista,* a pan-fascist union of kindred have-not, or proletarian, nations. By 1935, Fascists maintained that Fascism recognized that the ravages of war and depression in Europe could only be undone by international "antiplutocratic" reconstruction and argued, as a consequence, that Fascism was to be both "patriotic and international at the same time."[78] A pan-European federation of fascist nations was anticipated that would function through a "polyarchic directorate," providing Europe with the minimum political unity that Mussolini insisted, as early as 1933, was necessary for its viability.[79] By 1942, this conception of a European consortium of fascist nations united in what was called a "European regime of federal union" had become a commonplace in Fascist literature.[80] In 1943, one of the principal planks of the Fascist Republican Party was "the realization of an European community, with a federation of all nations," dedicated to "the abolition of the capitalist system; the struggle against the world plutocracies, and the development, for the benefit of European peoples and of the natives, of Africa's natural resources, with absolute respect for those peoples . . . who . . . have already achieved civil and national organization."[81] Just prior to his death Mussolini spoke of a world-wide "New Order," based on the "axis" of proletarian nations, in which patriotism would finally unite with internationalism.[82]

Nationalism, which classical Marxism had dismissed as an anachronism, has proven itself to be one of the most potent political forces in the socialist nations. Socialist nations have in the past, and continue in the present, to pursue national interests with as much, if not more, dedication than non-socialist nations. There is little, in fact, to distinguish the nationalism and internationalism of contemporary socialism from that of paradigmatic Fascism. The internationalism of both ideologies was, in fact, equally diaphanous. Nationalism alone was vital.

The Leninist and Fascist Conceptions of the State

Such parallelisms can be traced throughout the Leninist and Fascist systems. The political program, for example, of the Leninist or Fascist unitary party involved a developmental program that required the extensive use of coercion and elaborate institutions of control. For Mussolini, who had early divested himself of classical Marxism, the construction of a suitable apparatus to implement his policies was overt. Fascism required the existence of a strong and centralized state. The concept of the strong state, whose will was identified with the ultimate interests of every citizen of whatever class, became central to Fascist ideology. Leninism, on the other hand, still embroiled in the theoretical constraints it had inherited from classical Marxism, proceeded on the same course, but its rationale was delivered in vague, confused and contradictory arguments.

Lenin had initially made it clear that Marxism, as he understood it, conceived the state as nothing more than "an organ for class rule, an organ for the oppression of one class by another," and that "so long as the state exists there is no freedom."[83] The task of the revolutionary proletariat was to smash the bourgeois state, then reduce the proletarian state to its simplest, most rudimentary form, to make it not a state at all. And yet, by 1925, the Soviet state had assumed so many enterprisory, tutelary, and pedagogical functions that Stalin could no more countenance its "withering away," its reduction to a residual institution, than could Mussolini. In his report before the Sixteenth Party Congress of 1930 Stalin, quite seriously, maintained that

We stand for the withering away of the state. At the same time we stand for the strengthening of the dictatorship of the proletariat, which is the mightiest and strongest state power that has ever existed. The highest development of state power with the object of preparing the conditions for the withering away of state power—such is the Marxist formula. Is this "contradictory?" Yes, it is "contradictory." But this contradiction is bound up with life, and it fully reflects Marx's dialectics.[84]

At one time a *prima facie* doctrinal distinction could be drawn between Left and Right Wing revolutionary movements on the basis of their postures *vis-à-vis* the state. Fascism clearly and unequivocally advocated a state that stood above class and category interests and represented the "true and ultimate will of the entire people."[85] Fascists insisted that all classes and productive categories in the nation shared ultimate interests. As a consequence a unitary party in a totalitarian state could effect the harmonious national and popular will.

These contentions were mocked, at the time, by socialist theoreticians. The state, by Marxist definition, was the organ of class control. This conviction was exemplified in the Soviet Union by identifying the state, throughout the Stalin period, as the "dictatorship of the proletariat." At the Twenty-Second Party Congress in 1961, however, it was announced that Marxist-Leninist thought had attained a new level of theoretical maturity. Soviet Marxists announced a new political concept: "the all-people's state." Nikita Khrushchev announced that the Soviet Union had produced a new political phenomenon, hitherto unknown in history, a state that embodied the will, not of a class or classes, but of the entire people.[86] We were informed that "the Soviet state of the dictatorship of the proletariat has become a state of the whole people, expressing the will of all the people, while the Communist Party has changed from the Party of the working class to the Party of the whole people."[87]

Contemporary Marxists argue that "the substance of the state changed radically under the impact of the socialist revolution."[88] The state no longer represents class interests; it is no longer conceived as an organ of class struggle. It is the juridical expression of the collective popular will. While this is advertised as "a new stage in the materialization of the revolutionary theory of Marx, Engels, and Lenin," it is candidly admitted that "we may not find any direct reference to a state of the whole people in anything Lenin wrote or said"[89] (nor, one might add, in anything either Marx or Engels ever wrote or said). We are assured, nonetheless, that this conception of the state is unimpeachably Marxist. As a matter of fact, the conception of "the all-peoples' state" is Khrushchev's contribution to the transformation of Marxism. It renders the rationale offered in support of Soviet totalitarianism all but indistinguishable from that offered by Fascists in support of their own.

Leninism as an Inconsistent Fascism

Lenin's contribution to this involution of classical Marxism was his concept of minoritarian revolution and the implicit voluntarism upon which it trafficked.[90] Stalin, in turn, transformed Marxism into a rationale for national socialism. Khrushchev provided the concept of the "state of the whole people."

All of this could hardly go unnoticed. When Lenin bruited his conception of introducing consciousness from "without," via an elite of professional revolutionaries, socialist theoreticians of the caliber of Rosa Luxemburg and Karl Kautsky were quick to indicate that he thereby threatened the entire fabric of classical Marxism and the values it supported. Leon Trotsky was equally quick to condemn the advocacy of socialism in one country, a commitment which further eroded classical Marxism. The Chinese Communists have been no less quick to take issue on the subject of the "state of the whole people."

The fact is that Soviet Leninism, through a process of gradual involution, has taken on more and more of the attributes of paradigmatic Fascism. It is not Fascism largely because its vindications, given the legacy of its inherited Marxism, fail to provide justifications for the most significant aspects of the regime. The revolutionary mass-movement regimes of our time (of which the Soviet Union is one), all seem to harbor a prevailing tendency to take on more and more of the features of totalitarianism in the service of rapid national industrialization. In order to accomplish such modernization, which requires centralized control over resources both material and human, "nationalism," which operationally means a generalized readiness on the part of the participant population to sacrifice in the service of the community, becomes central to the system. Classical Marxism and its contemporary variants can but poorly legitimize the nationalism that is now recognized as inherent in mobilizing strategies. Moreover, such strategies require the instrumentalities provided by a central and authoritative administrative and enterprisory agency: the state. All revolutionary mass-movement regimes now disport a powerful state apparatus. Classical Marxism and Leninism (until its most recent "progressive development") could provide no legitimizing warrant for the continued existence of the state, much less its phenomenal growth and increasing tutelary and directive functions. Finally, in all revolutionary mass-movements, voluntaristic elites, characteristically composed of declassed intellectuals, have exercised a measure of dominance and organizational significance impossible to vindicate within the context of classical Marxism. Only Leninism, as a variant of the Marxism of Marx and Engels, attempted to legitimate elite roles and the voluntarism they presuppose—and then only at the expense of some of the basic precepts of Marxism. Only totalitarianism, the identification of the individual with his collectivity, finds its unambiguous rationale in the classic Marxism of the nineteenth century. Even in this instance the totalitarianism of classical Marxism compared to that of Leninism was, in a significant sense, benign. Marx conceived "communist consciousness," the seamless identification of the individual with his society, to be a determinate product of a special stage of capitalist economic development, the spontaneous and uncoerced "efflux" of the material life conditions of the "vast majority of men." For Leninism, that consciousness is the product of the pedagogical, tutelary, and sometimes terroristic control of the elite party.

The fact is that Soviet society, like many of the societies being constructed under the auspices of revolutionary mass-movement regimes, has taken on features which are manifestly fascistic. In 1957, approximately a decade after the death of Mussolini, Ugo Spirito, the principal advocate of the radical corporativism of the Fascist Congress of Ferrara of 1932, and Gentile's foremost philosophic heir, published his reflections on the Soviet Union. His essay revealed the critical and essential continuity he saw between paradigmatic Fascism and the "state of the whole people" as it has manifested itself in a society that had once committed itself to the "withering away of the state."

Spirito saw in the Soviet Union a transcendence of the dual world of the bourgeoisie, a transcendence of the "liberal" social order, the "order" riven into public and private domains that is the characteristic product of the bourgeoisie. Soviet society, Spirito contended, has transcended the bourgeois distinction between public and private; in the Soviet Union "the particular and the universal are intrinsically bound up in a single expression of life. . . . Russian communism is rooted in the reality of a people that conceives the values of the collectivity as constituent elements of its very life. Communion and faith are its principal characteristics . . ." and myth its sustaining strength.[91] This is manifestly the language of his communication before the Fascist Congress of Ferrara. Soviet society has fulfilled, in part, the Fascist dream of his young manhood.

Totalitarianism and Revolutionary Mass Movements

Contemporary national totalitarianism, its statism, voluntarism, and elitism, finds its most consistent rationale in the arguments of paradigmatic Fascism. More and more frequently, and more and more explicitly, Fascism's arguments, couched in the idiom of "socialism" and "democracy," find a place in the ideological and doctrinal literature of contemporary radical mass-movements. What this suggests is the poverty of available "theories of Fascism," particularly those of Marxist provenience.

First and foremost, there is an ideology of totalitarianism, a collection of reasoned vindications in support of a type of society minimally characterized by a mass-movement of solidarity animated by a relatively specific *Weltanschauung*, rule by a single party hierarchically organized under the charismatic or pseudocharismatic rule of a leader in an institutional system that provides for state monopoly of communication, coercion, and economic control. The ideology is the product of declassed intellectuals. Such an ideology, in whatever guise it originally appears (for example, Bolshevism's original protestations of perfervid internationalism), ultimately reveals itself as an avowed nationalism committed to explicit national purpose. Its clear intention is to win a place for the national community in the arena of international competition. One of the critical doctrinal elements of its organizing and charter mythology is the harkening back to real or imagined ancient glories—the achievements of ancient Rome, the superiority of Russian culture and the "priority" of Russian inventiveness, the "timeless" national traditions of Chinese culture, the ideal Akan society, the "communal" fraternity of the Baluba, or Germanic creative genius. There is a commitment to the total mobilization of a society's human and material resources to the restoration or achievement of the nation's place in the modern world. The most consistent and mature ideological rationale for the mobilizing strategies of such national totalitarianism was paradigmatic Fascism. As an ideology, it cannot be effectively reduced to a rationalization of the interests of any specific class or strata of contemporary society. Whatever its recruitment base, and whatever class or strata interests the historic Fascist regime did in fact partially satisfy, its arguments are paradigmatic of totalitarian vindications.

The "fascisms" of which contemporary academicians speak represent mass movements of solidarity that matured in relatively advanced economies under the goad of severe and protracted crisis. The theme of "class collaboration," which at one time was conceived as a specific species trait of fascism, was prominent because such relatively advanced economies had articulated a variety of class and strata groupings with which the movement had to contend. Totalitarian movements that develop in primitive economic circumstances, however, can afford the initial luxury of a putative class appeal. Mao Tse-Tung's early appraisals of China's revolutionary potential, for example, turned on his assessment of the available demographic resources his movement might exploit. To the total neglect of Marxist insights into the economic and social role of classes, he argued that even if the "big-property class" and the "middle-property class" combined to resist the revolution of national revival, there remained a recruitment base of 395 million peasants and peripheral elements that could be called to the service of the movement. Under these circumstances there was little initial disposition to make appeal to all classes and categories. Nonetheless Mao's ultimate appeal, which has become increasingly emphatic in the years of Sino-Soviet rivalry, is to the *people* of China rather than to any constituent class or population strata. The contemporary appeal is to a "national bloc" that includes "workers, peasants, soldiers, intellectuals, businessmen and other patriots . . . ," and it is now conceived that the Communist Party of China "shares the destiny and life-breath of the Chinese *people*."[92] Revolutionary mass movements in our own time have, in fact, a prevailing tendency to make their appeals to the people—the category to which nationalism must make final recourse.

Totalitarian movements, like Fascism and National Socialism, which develop in environments where there are well-articulated classes, must make such an appeal at the very commencement of their enterprise if they seriously aspire to mass membership. Given their clear intentions they cannot advance themselves as class movements. For this reason G. D. H. Cole is correct in characterizing them as "not fundamentally class movements," a fact that "orthodox" Marxist analysts simply cannot appreciate. At their very commencement such movements, in fact, appeal to what they conceive to be the more fundamental strata of consciousness, the prepotent ethnocentric sentiments that subtend calculated interests—those sentiments which characterize the human being as a herd animal.[93] Because such sentiments are not rational products, are not the result of calculation, appeal to them is most effectively made through emotion, suggestive contagion, and mimetism. These are the tactics which gave the prewar fascisms their "irrational" features. More significantly, from the point of view of analysis, the conviction that the "masses" were motivated by prelogical sentiments gave rise, among fascists, to a recurrent set of correlative attitudes. On the one hand the influences to which the masses are exposed must be carefully controlled; the masses harbor a variety of sentiments, some of which, under the influence of dissident political stimuli, can be turned to purposes that could only threaten what the mass-movement regime conceived to be the "national interests." As a consequence of such considerations, the totalitarianism that develops in a relatively industrialized society tends to advocate and adopt extensive censorship controls—to be disdainful of the masses, pessimistic, in fact, with respect to its subjects' capacity for constancy and virtue. Mussolini's judgments concerning the endemic limitations of the masses are too well known to bear repeating—Hitler's no less notorious.

Class-based movements, on the other hand, originally suffused with the conviction that society is composed of groups of men, each cognizant of its own special and specific interests, tend to be optimistic at least concerning the tractability of human nature. Class-based movements, whatever their practice, rarely express with candor, their reservations concerning the quality of mass intelligence, although it has become increasingly commonplace for revolutionary class-based mass movements to search out "virgin intellects," i.e., peasants rather than relatively sophisticated urban workers, into which to instill their radical ideologies—clear evidence of their reservations concerning the sapience of the masses. Moreover, the strict censorship that characteristically prevails in such circumstances, and the emphasis upon the pedagogical role of the single party, are *prima-facie* evidence that, as the class-based movements take on more and more of the features of national totalitarianism, fascism's attitudes, if not its rationale, come to govern manifest practice.

Other than the totalitarianism that develops in relatively industrialized environments and the class-based revolutionary mass movements that develop in the underdeveloped nations, there is a third kind of revolutionary mass movements that, although crystallizing in underdeveloped areas, has not been class-based even during the initial insurrectionary stages. Such movements, their principal representatives now identified as "African socialisms," arise displaying literally all the species traits of paradigmatic Fascism. They originate as movements of national solidarity; their appeal is to the "people," to class collaboration (with an explicit rejection of the "class struggle") in the service of national purpose under the organized cadre of the unitary single party and the leadership of the charismatic or pseudocharismatic leader. In Ghana this process devolved into a caricature of fascist rule with the *Osagyefo* (the Savior) Nkrumah identified as the Messiah of our time and his party as representing the ultimate will of the people of Ghana.

Fascism, Totalitarianism, and the "Third World"

The circumstances which conduce to such developments can be suggested in broad outline. National insurgency and anticolonialist movements in Africa and Asia have enjoyed special recruitment advantages. Such "national liberation" movements have had a specific enemy, generally identified with racial traits of high social visibility, a circumstance which has created a reactive sense of group identity on the part of colonial subjects. Almost all classes and strata in the colonial dependencies have suffered economically, or by the loss of personal dignity or collective status, at the hands of their European suzerains. There was, consequently, no strategic or tactical need to appeal to real or fancied class interests among the population of the dependencies to mobilize them to revolutionary purpose—reactive national solidarity was the predictable response to colonialism. A status-deprived people, composed of a variety of classes, social strata, and productive categories aspire to bridge the distance between themselves and their former superiors. Under such circumstances class appeals could only dissipate the elemental energies already reactively united as the consequence of historical, social, and political circumstances.

Under such conditions not only classical Marxism but Marxism-Leninism is largely irrelevant. Marx's original analysis was largely restricted to the economic circumstances that prevailed in the countries of western Europe.[94] He was preoccupied with the redistribution of "surplus value," with the modification of prevailing productive relations and the ownership of the means of production, with crises of overproduction (or, more accurately, underconsumption), with falling rates of profit in industries laboring under heavy capital investment, and with the problems of technological unemployment. None of these concerns are relevant to the revolutionary movements in the former colonial dependencies or in the developmental dictatorships of our time. Mussolini insisted that they were irrelevant for Italy, a largely agrarian country only beginning its substantive economic development. Against the distributionist biases of classical Marxism Mussolini advanced the avowedly productionist intentions of Fascism. Fascism's avowed aim was to increase the industrial productivity of the Italian peninsula in an effort to reduce the gap between it and the favored nations of Europe. Lenin, and more emphatically Stalin, were forced to recognize that the problems of socialist Russia were not problems of redistribution of surplus and the transfer of ownership, but problems of mobilizing collective energies in the service of national industrial development. The "class struggle," the destruction of strategic industrial elites, the initial massive loss of "bourgeois" talents, were all suffered as a payment for having misunderstood the historic task of the revolution. The radical modernizing movements of this half of the twentieth century are not likely to emulate that phase of the Leninist program. Thus the various forms of African socialism that have appeared on the African continent have made it abundantly clear that any form of traditional Marxism is inappropriate to African circumstances. Before the military coup that deposed Nkrumah, J. H. Mensah, Chairman of the Ghanaian National Economic Planning Commission, explained that it was impossible to apply "traditional Marxian theory" which "aimed at the reorganization of the ownership of existing property" to Ghana because "by and large, the means of production do not exist." The real problem to which "socialists" should address themselves "is not the rearrangement of the ownership of the means of production. The central concern must be with the building up of the nation's stock of productive assets."[95]

Leopold Senghor has propounded essentially the same thesis. Private capitalism has not been suppressed in Senegal nor has there been any nationalization.[96] The primary and almost exclusive concern of African socialism is national industrial development. The mobilization of the national community in the service of such development receives recurrent and varied expression in the statements of the theoreticians and practitioners of African socialism. Neither class-based appeals nor adherence to Marxist economic and political theory is permitted to obstruct the nationalist developmental programs of African socialism, for ". . . development requires," according to Mamadou Dia (formerly Prime Minister of Senegal), "a complete and conscious association of the entire people. It is, before anything else, a collective will for development. . . ."[97]

Since appeal is made to the "people" as distinct from any constituent class, stratum or productive category, that appeal, as has been already suggested, must be primitive, general, and more emotional than cognitive. We find, therefor, Senghor talking of the political "myths" which animate the masses in the services of national purpose and Quaison-Sackey of Ghana addressing himself to the "faith" of the "people" by virtue of which they are "propelled to action. . . ."[98]

It is obvious that class, as such, has ceased to be a serious analytic, theoretic, or organizational concern for the ideologists of African socialism. The revolutionary protagonists in the African socialist "class struggle" are "proletarian" *nations* whose respective citizenries, animated by "myths" and "faith," acknowledge no class distinctions and merge into an all-encompassing category, the *people*. Thus Senghor explicitly maintains that his attempt "to define an 'African road to Socialism'" involves "national values and [starts] from national realities."[99] African socialism seeks to create a nation, a people in which "each individual will identify himself with the collective whole and vice versa."[100] Sékou Touré, the most "Marxist" of the African socialists, nowhere affirms that the Guinean proletariat is the prime mover of national revolution and national reconstruction, but rather consistently alludes to the historic and national role of the people of Guinea. The entire people is conceived as the prime mover of historical development; it is both object and agent of historical development. Senghor thus specifically maintains that it is necessary to "subordinate the proletarian revolution to the national revolution," and Nkrumah enjoined the "entire people" of Ghana, including "whatever . . . occupation or status . . . farmers, fishermen, masons, lawyers, doctors, and laborers, businessmen, engineers, architects, traders, teachers and students," to devote themselves to the production of a "wider and fuller life for our nation."[101] The axis of conflict has clearly been transposed from the class to the national level. What once was conceived as a defining characteristic of Fascism is now characteristic of a variety of related doctrines called African socialism. In 1927, Fascist syndicalists identified the "principal defining trait of Fascism" as its "nationalist character" in order to distinguish it from the various expressions of internationalist socialism. Fascist theoreticians maintained,

There exists among the various classes . . . a compelling necessity for solidarity that transcends the contrasts of category, the solidarity of a proletarian *nation* that must struggle for its existence against wealthy and economically powerful and favored nations.[102]

The distinction Fascists drew between themselves and socialists of whatever sort turned chiefly on their substitution of the formula "inter-class solidarity and national struggle" for the Marxist formula "international solidarity and class struggle," for chief among the elements of Fascist social theory was the conviction that "the struggle between nations is more serious and critical than the class struggle . . . ,"[103] the echo of which is now heard in the ideological pronouncements of Senghor and Nkrumah.

Whatever socialism the African socialists are advocating, it is abundantly clear that the analytic, theoretic, and charismatic entity upon which they focus their attention is the *nation* and its *people* rather than a *class* or *classes,* however defined. Both Senegal and Ghana, for example, possess reasonably well-articulated socio-economic classes that either have special entrepreneurial functions in the economy or enjoy special status or income, but both reject the Marxist conception of class struggle and emphatically advocate class collaboration in the service of national development.

The socialism of African socialism is national and nationalist rather than international and internationalist. Its recruitment base is, and its appeal is directed toward, the people rather than any specific class or classes. Since its appeal is to the collective people rather than any interest group, its language tends to be exhortative, and its admonitions are directed toward the "will," the "sacrifice," the "dedication" and the forbearance of the people rather than to their immediate material interests. Thus at the Dakar Colloquium on African Socialism, Seydou Kouyate, Mali Minister of Development, expressed himself as follows:

We can say that the socialist path we have adopted is based on two fundamental notions: (1) a socialism set up by a movement led by elements not essentially proletarian; and (2) a socialism recognizing spirituality as an integral part of man. . . . [We] believe that the political organization of the people, considered as the driving force of the people, can lead the country in setting up socialism. . . .[104]

The "socialism" to which Kouyate refers is indistinguishable from economic development and its necessary condition is the political mobilization of the entire people. That mobilization requires a collective *will* which finds concrete expression in the *state*. Thus, Senghor maintains that

"if the nation is a conscious determination to reconstruct, the state is its major means. . . . It fulfills the nation's will and ensures its permanence. . . . [The] state is the expression of the nation; it is primarily a means to achieve the nation."[105]

Since the state is so conceived the theoreticians of African Socialism have been ill-disposed toward any Marxian suggestion of the "withering away" of the state.[106] All advocates of African socialism have insisted upon the need of a strong and centralized state authority.[107] The state is conceived as the most efficient agency for effecting the nation's will, a will that can only become conscious via an explicit and exclusive political ideology. Thus Amidou Kane, Commissioner-General of the Senegal Development Plan, has indicated that "the socialist revolution is above all structural change animated by ideology. . . ."[108] The classic Marxist conception of a specific economic base supporting an ideological superstructure is inverted and ideology is infused with causal and explanatory properties completely alien to any form of Marxian socialism. Social consciousness and organized will are conceived as creating a specific economic base. Senghor has argued,

The problem is to awaken "dormant energies." . . . In a word, we must awaken the national conscience. . . . Understanding this, the Senegalese Government decided to awaken the consciousness of the masses. . . . But the Government cannot and must not do it all. It must be guided and helped by the party. . . . Our party must be the consciousness of the masses, who lack education and culture, still remains confused, lost in the fog of animal needs. It does not rise to the level of "political consciousness, a superior form of consciousness." This can only reach the masses from the outside, from the intellectuals.[109]

This is the African socialist analogue of the elitism that was central to Mussolini's thought as early as his first formulations of "revolutionary socialist" theory. Lenin developed essentially the same conception of the relationship between the masses and the elite. But Senghor's appeal to political myths, to "will" and to "faith," characterize his conceptions as fascist rather than Leninist.

"[The] nation," Senghor insists, "must inspire all its members, all individuals, with faith in nationhood. . . ." To effect his purpose the state "shapes the individuals into the mold of the archetype. . . . For only this action can make of our various populations a People, that is to say, a Community, where each individual will identify himself with the collective whole and vice versa."[110] This is clearly a fascist responsibility, the pedagogical and tutelary task of a totalitarian and Gentilean ethical state.

The parallels could be pursued on the doctrinal level to include a survey of Senghor's "anti-racist racism," his myth of "Negritude," as the African analogue of Fascism's dynamic race concept. Pan-Africanism has its equally revealing analogue in the conception of pan-fascism that became increasingly prominent in Fascist thought throughout the years before the Second World War. The fact is that the prevailing tendencies which characterize African socialism are totalitarian and the specifics of its ideology reveal it to be, in a significant sense, a variant of paradigmatic Fascism.[111]

African socialism is neither fully totalitarian nor fully fascist. Some of the principal identifying structural and organizational features of totalitarian and fascist society are technologically conditioned. Effective totalitarian control over communications, the security and defense establishments, and the economy, for example, require as a necessary condition an elaborate infrastructure which simply does not obtain in Africa south of the Sahara and north of the Limpopo. Furthermore, the militarism, the expansionism, and the aggressiveness which were insistent features of fascism in the relatively advanced countries of Europe are impossible to mount, for the time being, in underdeveloped Africa. This is to suggest that just such features can be expected to manifest themselves with the development of an appropriate industrial base. If the postures assumed by Nkrumah's Ghana suggest anything they suggest that such an eventuality is not at all improbable. Moreover, given an adequate industrial and military capability, black Africa's effort to resolve the problem of a white South Africa might very well take on the character of a military adventure. To all this one must add the potential violence which hovers over Africa's non-Negro minorities given the Africanist postures of some of its indigenous nationalist movements. That these minorities enjoy favored positions in the economy merely increases their potential danger and the real possibility of a baleful African socialist racism.

Totalitarian Revolutionary Mass Movement Regimes

Totalitarianism is a form of authoritarianism developed in an age of nationalism and rapid industrial development. It is a response to some critical and pervasive problems of the twentieth century. Revolutionary mass movements from a variety of historic and cultural traditions and from areas at diverse levels of industrial sophistication advance ideologies which display a marked family resemblance. They share one or another of several features in common and represent different species of the same political genus. They all embrace some form of the leadership principle, making one man responsible for functions ordinarily deployed over a variety of agencies in parliamentary regimes; they are all in some substantial sense elitist, with the strategic and functional cadre organized in a single party that permits no organized opposition. The single party becomes the focal institution for the reorganization of society. Effective control of the mass media, the means of security and coercion, and the direction of the economy pass into the hands of a political elite. Entire societies are politicized. The arguments employed by the mass movement to recruit, and to vindicate policy, take on the form of a relatively specific revolutionary ideology which subsequently becomes the charter myth of the mass movement regime. The operation of such a society has as its predictable by-product a society with a high conformity index, ritual acquiescence, and institutionalized anxiety.[112]

What have been described are totalitarian revolutionary mass movement regimes under single-party auspices. There is, of course, a class of revolutionary mass-movement regimes under single-party auspices that do not have totalitarian aspirations. Such regimes, like that of Kemal Atatürk, and China under Sun Yat-sen, may satisfy all the requirements of revolutionary mass-movement regimes and yet fail to countenance, for example, bureaucratic control of the economy. There is a tendency, of course, to move in this direction in a revolutionary one-party environment, but there are an indeterminate set of counterinfluences that make unrestricted generalizations about the future policies of revolutionary mass-movement regimes hazardous. In the case of Fascism in Italy the totalitarian aspirations of the movement were already implicit in its ideological commitment and knowledge of those commitments would have suggested to analysts at the time that the regime would move in the direction of total control of the economy. Since, however, a finite, if indeterminate, set of factors exercise an influence on the maturation of such a tendency, such a prediction could have been made with only a minimal degree of confidence. The Franco regime in contemporary Spain, by way of illustration, is a case in which totalitarian tendencies have become extinct. The revolutionary mass movement led by José Antonio had made clear totalitarian commitments,[113] but the execution of José Antonio and the accession of Franco to political control reduced the Falangist movement to a supportive adjunct to a basically conservative political system.[114]

Among the totalitarian revolutionary mass movements their respective development seems to be governed by the circumstances surrounding their initial organization and the conditions under which they assume political power. Thus by 1921 paradigmatic Fascism had articulated what were to be its totalitarian aspirations. Nonetheless, developing as it did within a situation in which the disposition of forces had polarized allegiances and exacerbated special interest groups, the movement found itself allied, in its struggle against orthodox socialism, with essentially conservative forces. Fascism, originally opposed to orthodox socialism because of socialism's anti-interventionist and internationalist postures, suddenly found itself the paladin of a reactive coalition of rabidly antisocialist elements. By 1921, Mussolini found himself in the unenviable position of having to choose between cutting himself free from conservative support in order to effect Fascism's radical purpose, and thereby politically isolating the nascent movement (since it was by that time impossible to make common cause with the orthodox socialists, although Mussolini did make gestures in that direction[115]), or tempering the radical demands of the totalitarian movement.

He chose to temper Fascism's demands—at least until it found itself possessed of increased political leverage. This constitutes the evidence on which Marxist, or quasi-Marxist, theorists support their interpretation of Fascism as the "armed defense of the bourgeoisie," and "a reactionary mass movement [barring] the road to revolution."[116] That large sections among the industrial bourgeoisie and the landed classes interpreted Fascism similarly is clear. But such an analysis is grossly inadequate and such an interpretation mistaken. The more sophisticated Marxists rejected it even before it was officially accepted as the "definition" of Fascism by the Comintern. Clara Zetkin, Antonio Gramsci, and Angelo Tasca all rejected such an analysis as, in one way or another, simplistic. Clara Zetkin insisted that

The mistakes of the Communist Party . . . lie above all in considering Fascism to be only a military-terrorist movement, and not as a mass movement with deep social roots. It must be expressly emphasized that before Fascism had won militarily, it had already achieved the victory politically and ideologically. . . .[117]

Similarly Gramsci, in 1926, maintained that Fascism was not solely "a body guard of the bourgeoisie"—it was also a "social movement."[118] Gramsci recognized that the characterization of Fascism as simply "armed reaction" was grossly misleading. He recognized that the recruitment resources of Fascism lay essentially in the urban petty bourgeoisie and the new agrarian bourgeoisie, but he also argued that a variety of circumstances had provided Fascism with an "ideological unity" that permitted the movement to oppose the traditional political leaders with an ideological system essentially antiliberal and potentially totalitarian.[119] Even Angelo Tasca understood Fascism as a movement that, for its own political ends, imposed strategic and functional political controls on every class represented in Italian social and economic life.[120]

Non-Marxist commentators have generally been even more astute. In 1922, Arturo Labriola tendered a brief analysis of Fascism that is remarkable for its insights. He saw the development of Fascism as having, by that time, traversed three stages: (1) a spontaneous movement defending the nation's involvement in, and sacrifice during, World War I; (2) as subsequently having attracted to itself conservative elements because of its opposition to orthodox socialism; and (3) as a political mass movement composed essentially of agrarian and urban petty-bourgeois elements of essentially socialistoid (if not socialistic) disposition. Furthermore, he indicated that Fascism had attracted a significant section of the proletariat (a phenomenon to which many Marxist commentators allude[121]). Labriola saw in Fascism a revolutionary mass movement, supported largely by petty-bourgeois elements, that aspired to a new form of national socialism. Its opposition to orthodox socialists and communists had attracted to its standards the representatives and the support of the vested interests threatened by organized class-based revolution. It was this association with threatened class interests—a reaction to the class politics of orthodox socialism—that gave Fascism the appearance of an "armed militia in the service of the old order," when, in fact, its intentions were clearly revolutionary.[122]

Marxists have long recognized that the doctrinal and ideological commitments of Fascism were, in a significant sense, revolutionary. However, in order to assimilate Fascism into their conceptual schemata they have chosen to dismiss the ideology of Fascism as irrelevant. Fascism's "essence" was its defense of capitalism. Its ideology was calculated to gull the citizenry or foreign opinion. Such an interpretation has little theoretic yield and is difficult to defend. The fact is that Fascism gradually extended, in accordance with its doctrinal commitments, its control over the entirety of Italian social and economic life. The landed and propertied classes that had given active or passive support (and that support was far from universal—the bulk of the bourgeoisie opposed Fascism[123]) had completely misassessed the dynamics of the movement. In Carsten's judgment, "Hardly anyone recognized that the Fascists represented an entirely new political and revolutionary force which could not be 'tamed' or brought under control, but would continue to develop its own dynamism, and would finally sweep away the old order."[124]

The contemporary interpretation of Fascism has, as a consequence, focused critical attention on the ideological rationale of the revolutionary mass movement as an indicator of its intentions. Eugen Weber has suggested that the "essence" of such movements is to be found in the "doctrines when they have not yet 'arrived'. . . ."[125] The struggle to attain and maintain power requires all the compromise and hedging that results when revolution must adapt itself to the exigencies of traditional political tactics and strategy. But the ideology remains as evidence of an emphatic disposition— a totalitarian disposition that was already, in the case of Fascism, evident in its earliest formulations.

In the course of its history, Fascism revealed itself as a revolutionary mass movement composed of a variety of social classes and population strata that propelled a revolutionary counter-elite into the position of power in which the entire machinery of the state was, in the words of G. D. H. Cole,

applied to the issuing of positive orders, in the name of the awakened Nation, to the capitalists themselves as well as to the defeated workers and to the middle classes. . . . In the ensuing struggle, the victory goes neither to the great capitalists nor to the small. It does not go to any *class;* for Fascism, though it wages war upon the working class and uses other classes as its instruments, is not fundamentally a class-movement. . . . Far . . . from controlling Fascism, the great capitalists come to be controlled by it, and are compelled to subordinate their money-making impulses to the requirements of the Fascist State as an organizer of national aggression.[126]

This analysis is essentially that of Iring Fetscher. Fascism was a revolutionary movement led by a declassed minority counter-elite which, while it exploited whatever support it could attract from interest groups deployed in its political environment, did not represent the specific interests of any. Fascism was as much of a threat to the specific immediate interests of the industrial bourgeoisie as it was to those of the working class movements. The principal specific goal of Fascism, explicit in its formulations as early as 1921, was "the destruction of political and social pluralism and the establishment of unrestricted rule of a new 'elite' . . . ,"[127] in the service of what it understood to be national renaissance.

Fascism was a minority movement of national insurgency, a national totalitarianism that conceived itself creating a social and political order of solidarity in which all classes, strata, and categories would unite under the leadership of the single party to restore the grandeur of Italy. The circumstances in which the movement matured influenced its political tactics and historic expression. In a partially industrialized environment, the movement found it necessary to contend with a specific constellation of forces that gave Fascism its local and contingent character. One of its first concerns, as Franz Borkenau has suggested, was the rapid expansion of the industrial potential of the nation—a prime requisite for competition in the modern world. In order to expand that potential, social peace was necessary as well as a rapid accumulation of investment capital.[128] Such concerns explain, at least in part, the tactics and strategy with respect to labor relations. In order to create an industrial base for modern society, systems as varied as Soviet communism and African socialism have similarly suppressed labor's traditional right to strike, have disciplined organized labor, and have favored the accumulation of capital, at least initially, in the hands of a special entrepreneurial class. The period of the New Economic Program in the Soviet Union represented such a phase; the contemporary treatment of labor as agents of the state, and the creation of attractive investment opportunities for foreign capitalists in the African socialist states evidence analogous tendencies.

Fascism, however, arose in a partially industrialized environment in which well-entrenched and vital vested interests obtained (expressly represented in an established and traditional aristocracy, a military establishment, and a historic church) that were independent foci of social, economic, and political force. Fascism was compelled, because of its special history as a heretical socialist movement, to ally itself with available, but essentially conservative, forces. The movement itself was not conservative. It was revolutionary. Its clear intention was to destroy all the social, economic, and political artifacts of classical liberalism. To effect this purpose, once orthodox socialism and communism were no longer contenders for power or effective opponents, Fascism undertook the long and protracted struggle against the aristocracy, the church, and the bourgeois representatives of heavy industry.

Totalitarian movements which develop in substantially different environments develop distinct and sometimes unique features. Bolshevism's struggles with its opponents were more direct and consequently more violent. The aristocracy and the church in Russia were thoroughly discredited by the debacle of World War I. Soviet Russia could, after 1924, embark with less restraint on a totalitarian program of compelling scope and intensity.

African socialism, in turn, has evident totalitarian and solidarist aspirations. The singular conditions surrounding the anticolonialist struggle have provided it with at least a temporary national consensus on which to attempt the erection of some form of national socialism. The ideological postures and evident intent are national and totalitarian, and the rationale singularly fascist. The manifest lack of aggressiveness is probably a function of gross underdevelopment. The inability of African socialism to effect totalitarian controls within the confines of its single party state can be similarly interpreted. Totalitarian political practice is the consequence of totalitarian intention conjoined with an appropriate infrastructure capable of supporting communication and weapons monopoly, as well as an industrial base that makes planning and bureaucratic control a real possibility. Finally, totalitarian control requires a population sufficiently literate to make political propaganda effective.

Totalitarian Ideologies

Totalitarian political movements express their intentions in a set of related propositions having both emotive and cognitive force: an ideology. Paradigmatic Fascism, the Fascism that has been the subject of this volume, provides its most consistent expression. All other totalitarian movements have either adopted all or significant component parts of Fascist ideology or are driven, by the logic of social and political circumstance, recruitment, mobilization, and control, to create its analogue.

Mussolini's Fascism was paradigmatic of national totalitarian revolutionary mass movements insofar as Fascist ideology is the only consistent rationale for a society in which the "people" are identified without remainder with the "state"—in which a minority single-party maintains (or aspires to attain) absolute control. Leninism is an inconsistent and incongruent rationale for the society Leninists have created. National Socialism ultimately revealed itself as dedicated not to the nation as the charismatic object of loyalty, but to a vaguely defined racial community. African socialism has proved itself more consistent—and its ideology most closely approximates that of Fascism.

Eugen Weber has recently suggested that the rationale for fascisms that develop in environments that are essentially agrarian, underdeveloped, and underindustrialized, whose recruitment base is essentially peasant, and that are led by declassed intellectuals, take on features of Africa's "cargo cults." The organizing and functional myths employed are myths of communalist embrace, functional analogues of Fascist myths.[129] Romanians, for example, in a nation essentially agrarian, conceived themselves colonials, ruled over by an exiguous clique of foreign capitalists. In 1938, the *Romanian Encyclopedia* contended, "All manufactured articles sold in the principalities came from Austria and Prussia. . . . Our goods were taken at very low prices, as from any other colony. . . ." Foreign capital and foreign control created circumstances in which Romania remained forever in danger

of being permanently a colony, open or disguised, of the foreigners. [This] not only keeps the whole national life in a situation of poverty, exploitation and slavery, but brings also gradual political serfdom, stifling any attempt to conquer one's rightful place in the world.[130]

These were the circumstances Romanian fascists exploited, and their language was all but identical to the language of the Corridonian nationalists of pre-Fascist Italy and anticolonialist Africa. Labriola and his syndicalists, furthermore, had spoken of Italy as a colony of "plutocratic Europe," Edmondo Rossoni, leader of the Fascist syndicates, insisted that Italians were the "Negroes" of European capitalism.[131] Senghor and Nkrumah have assumed the same postures. Fascists regularly and systematically employed the language of moral outrage against the "interventionism" and "imperialism" of the "plutocratic and capitalist powers," language that has its obvious echo in the declamations of the contemporary national socialisms of the underdeveloped countries.[132]

In environments where a viable class-based mass movement does not exist, fascist and proto-fascist movements can identify themselves without equivocation as "socialist"—always with the proviso that their socialism is understood to be nationalist, elitist, authoritarian, and productionist—that is to say fascist.

What have been traditionally identified in the literature as "fascist" regimes can best be characterized as totalitarian, revolutionary mass movements that have come to power in relatively or partially advanced industrial environments; environments in which there already exist entrenched and vital propertied classes as well as peripheral elements threatened with status deprivation. Fascist movements thus come to power in circumstances in which some accommodation with established interest groups must, at least initially, be effected if the revolution is not to drown in blood and/or the productionist aspirations of the movement are not to be faulted. Thus, those revolutionary mass-movement regimes that have been identified as "fascist" in the literature of political analysis are radically disposed mass movements supported by elements of the traditional and conservative propertied elites. Historically, such support has been the conservative reaction to the existence of an endogenous and imposing class-based mass movement which threatens not only the propertied elites with expropriation and/or downward status mobility but national solidarity as well. The existence of such opponents, however, is neither necessary nor sufficient for the appearance or the political success of fascist movements recognized as fascist even within the compass of tradi- tional interpretations. The success of Peronism in Argentina and that of Codreanu in Romania did not require the contemporaneous existence of a strong class-based opposition movement. The exist- ence of such opposition does, of course, facilitate the recruitment of membership for fascist mass movements in circumstances where well-articulated classes and productive categories exist. The price the fascist movements pay for such recruitment is a damping and a possible faulting of revolutionary purpose. Fascist movements in Europe have historically acceded to power only with the support of manifestly non-fascist allies. In the case of paradigmatic Fas- cism, the struggle between conservative and revolutionary elements behind the facade of the monolithic state continued through the Fascist Ventennial and into the war years, at which time there was massive betrayal of the Regime by conservative elements at critical loci in the state, the economy, and the military high commands. Only with the catastrophe of military defeat did the Fascist move- ment succeed in separating itself from the conservative elements that had assisted it to power. Separated from the burden of such "allies," Fascism clearly revealed itself as a radical revolutionary movement. The circumstances surrounding National Socialism in Germany were similar in significant respects. National Socialism came to power with the connivance of the propertied and strategic elites of the old order. Some commentators misconstrued this to mean that National Socialism was a movement dedicated to the protection of vested interest.[133] The conservative forces which had allied themselves with National Socialism, however, rapidly capitulated before its evident power. National Socialism, like paradigmatic Fascism, was intrinsically neither procapitalist nor antilabor.[134] It aspired to a society in which class, category, and confession would merge in one total charismatic community.

Fascisms of this kind develop in industrial communities in which classes are reasonably well articulated and vital and in which a traditional aristocracy exists that is threatened by displacement or downward mobility. These forces lend support to fascist movements and either contain it, as is the case in Spain, render it quiescent, as was the case for a considerable length of time in Fascist Italy, or submit to it, as was the case in National Socialist Germany.

Much of the substance of Barrington Moore's analysis of fascism turns on the presence of traditional aristocratic and landed elements in fascist regimes.[135] But fascist regimes, as they have been traditionally identified, have always represented the union of the *fascist movement* with *nonfascist allies*.[136] Whether the fascist movement succeeds in dominating its original allies in a contest that is conducted after the conquest of the state by fascists is determined by circumstances obtaining in each specific environment. In all environments the movement has radical and totalitarian pretensions. Circumstances may compel the movement to surrender its revolutionary program or significantly qualify it. The movement, nonetheless, has totalitarian and revolutionary aspirations, and with a change in the disposition of forces such aspirations govern the renewed dynamic of the movement. In circumstances where conservative allies are nonexistent, unavailable, or unnecessary, the national developmental and totalitarian goals of the movement are identified as "socialist." That such "socialism" has precious little to do with the internationalist, distributionist, libertarian, democratic, and class-orientated socialism of the nineteenth century is painfully obvious. In a significant sense it can be said that contemporary radical revolutionary mass movements possessed of nationalist and developmental intentions, and animated by totalitarian aspirations, are variants of paradigmatic Fascism.

Contemporary Fascisms

Such fascist and quasi-fascist movements occupy one end of the continuum occupied by contemporary revolutionary mass movements. They constitute an extreme type: their purpose is the rapid attainment of status for status-deprived national communities. To this end all energies are mobilized and directed, under single-party auspices, in a communalist regime of totalitarian character.

The circumstances surrounding rapid industrialization in the contemporary world seem to favor centralized resource mobilization, allocation, and management. Development today requires broader programs, more central control, and more intensive capital outlays than at any previous time in the history of national modernization. Moreover, it tends to require massive change in the traditional structure of society—a structure that, in general, obstructs rapid technological change.[137] Rapid development seems to require revolutionary ideologies calculated to undermine traditional loyalties and traditional covenants: ideologies that favor revolutionary change in the prevailing patterns of rights and obligations and that favor the political centralization of the processes of deliberation, decision, and management. Such ideologies, to effect their historic mandate, can be expected to seek to reduce anxiety during periods of high moral tension and protracted sacrifice by increasing collective self-confidence through the use of ritual, exhortation, and collective self-aggrandizement. What such efforts require for minimal efficiency is information management and the systematic suppression of dissidence. Such ideologies are required, furthermore, to provide the basis for shared feelings, to limn goals commonly understood, and to convey a sense of identity and solidarity that is the ground of effortless discipline and habitual conformity. Such ideologies can be expected, as a consequence, to make fewer and fewer references to internal class enemies in an effort to displace the hostilities that discipline and sacrifice tend to generate to real or imagined out-group opponents. They will tend to explicitly reject all forms of political liberalism and the individualism and pluralism that are the natural product of liberalism, and will tend to place an increasing emphasis upon the organic and natural character of the national society.[138] In effect, such ideologies will tend to take on more and more of the defining characteristics of paradigmatic Fascism—the first fully articulated ideology for a national socialist totalitarianism produced in the twentieth century.

Appendix A:
The Manifesto of
Fascist Racism

A GROUP of Fascist academicians from Italian universities, under the aegis of the Minister of Popular Culture, have formulated in the following terms the position assumed by Fascism with respect to the racial problem.

1. Human races exist. The existence of human races is not an academic abstraction, but corresponds to a concrete, material reality perceptible by the human senses. This reality is the reality represented in the heritability of physical and psychological similarities among millions of men, traits that were inherited and that continue to be inherited. To say that human races exist is not to say *a priori* that there exist superior or inferior races, but only to say that there exist different human races.

2. There exist geographic and local races. Not only do there exist systematic major groups that one commonly calls races and that are characterized by certain traits, but it is necessary also to admit that there exist systematic minor groups (for example, Nordics, Mediterraneans, and Dinarics), characterized by a reasonably large number of common traits. These groups constitute, from the biological point of view, true races, the existence of which is an evident reality.

3. The concept of race is a concept essentially biological. The concept of race is therefore based upon considerations other than those of people or of nations, founded essentially on historical, linguistic, or religious considerations. However, at the base of the differences between peoples and nations there are differences of race. If the Italians differ from the French, the Germans differ from the Turks, and so forth, it is not only because these people have diverse languages and diverse histories. They have been composed of different proportions of different races that since antiquity have constituted their diverse populations, whether it be the case that one race has absolute dominion over others, or whether all the races are fused harmoniously, or, finally, whether there exist even unto our own times unassimilated groups of the diverse races.

4. The population of Italy is Aryan in origin and its civilization is Aryan. This population and civilization which we call Aryan occupied for many millennia the Italian peninsula. Little is left of the civilizations of the pre-Ayran populations. The origins of contemporary Italy are rooted essentially in the same races which constituted and constitute the living biological elements of Europe.

5. The suggestion that Italy has been inundated by large groups of people in historic times is erroneous. After the invasions of the Longobards there have not been large population movements in the Italian peninsula capable of influencing the racial physiognomy of the nation. Therefore, while all the nations of Europe have suffered racial intrusions even within modern times, in Italy, fundamentally, the racial composition of today is that which it was a thousand years ago. The forty-four million Italians of today derive, in the absolute majority, from families that have lived in Italy for a millennium.

6. There exists therefore a pure "Italian race." This pronouncement is not based upon a confusion of a biological concept of race with the historical-linguistic conception of a people or of a nation, but upon the continuity of blood that unites the Italians of today to the millennial populations of historic Italy. This unity of blood is the supreme justification for the nobility of the Italian nation.

7. It is time that the Italians proclaimed themselves frankly racist. All the work that until our own time the Fascist regime in Italy has concluded has been based upon racism. Frequently it has

been a topic of the discourses of the Duce, whose references to the concept of race are frequent. The question of racism in Italy should be treated from the purely biological point of view independent of philosophical or religious considerations. The conception of racism in Italy must be unqualifiedly Italian and of Aryan-Nordic orientation. This is not to say that one wishes to introduce into Italy the theories of racism prevalent in Germany in order to affirm that the Italians and the Scandinavians are the same thing. But rather it wishes to provide for the Italians a physical and psychological normative model of the human race whose characteristics are unqualifiedly European and that separates itself completely from the races which are extra-European, and to instill in Italians an ideal of superior consciousness of themselves and of their major responsibilities.

8. It is necessary to make a sharp distinction between the Mediterraneans of Europe and the Eastern Mediterraneans and Africans. Those theories that contend that the Mediterranean race has had an African origin, and that conceive of a common racial unity for all the Mediterranean populations, whether they be Semitic or Hamitic, introduces relations and ideological sympathies which are absolutely inadmissible.

9. The Jews do not belong to the Aryan race. Of the Semites who, in the course of centuries, have sequestered themselves upon the sacred soil of our country, little in general has remained. Even the Arab occupation of Sicily has left little outside the record of certain names; the extremely rapid process of assimilation in Italy has absorbed the remainder. The Jews represent, on the other hand, the only population which has not been assimilated in Italy because it is composed of racial elements substantially diverse from those that gave rise to the Italians.

10. The physical and psychological characteristics of Italians, which are essentially European, should not be altered in any manner. Marriage is admissible only within the confines of the European races, among which one must not speak of real miscegenation, given that all these races belong to a common body and differentiate themselves only in minimal characteristics while they share a multitude of others. The essentially European characteristics of Italians are

modified in the miscegenation with any extra-European race, originators of a civilization other than that millennarian civilization of the European Aryans.

15 July, 1938.

[For the Italian text, vide Antonio Banzi, *Razzismo fascista* (Palermo, 1939), pp. 226–31; and Aldo Capasso, *Idee chiare sul razzismo* (Rome, 1942), pp. 5f.]

Appendix B:
The Program
Manifesto of
the Fascist
Republican Party

Verona, 14 November 1943

Constitutional and Internal

1. A Constituent Assembly shall be convened, possessed of sovereign power, and of popular origin, which shall declare the fall of the Monarchy, shall solemnly condemn the last King as a traitor and deserter, and shall proclaim the Social Republic and appoint its Head.

2. The Assembly shall be composed of representatives of all the syndical associations and administrative organizations, including representatives of the invaded provinces (by means of delegations from those who have escaped and reached free territory), of combatants and prisoners-of-war, Italians abroad, the magistracy, the Universities, and other bodies whose participation helps to make this Assembly a synthesis of all the valuable elements in the nation.

3. The Republican Constitution will ensure to citizens, soldiers, and workers the right of control over and responsible criticism of the public administration. Every five years citizens will be summoned

to express their opinion on the appointment of the Head of the Republic. No citizen arrested *in flagrante,* or detained for preventive measures, can be detained over seven days without an order from the judicial authority. Except in cases *in flagrante,* an order from the judicial authority is necessary for domiciliary search. In the exercise of its functions the magistracy will act in full independence.

4. Italy's negative electoral experience, and the partially negative experience of a method of appointment too rigidly hierarchic, suggests that a mixed system would give better results, e.g., the election by the people of representatives to the Chamber, combined with the appointment of Ministers by the Head of the Republic and of the Government, who will also ratify elections made within the Party, and appoint a National Directorate.

5. The organization which must complete the people's education on political problems is indivisible. The Party, an order of fighters and believers, must prove itself an organization of absolute political purity, worthy of being the guardian of the revolutionary idea. The Party membership card will not be asked for in connection with any post or employment.

6. The Republic's religion is the Catholic-Apostolic-Roman. Any other cult which does not conflict with the laws will be respected.

7. Members of the Jewish race are foreigners. For the duration of this war they belong to enemy nationality.

8. The main objective of the Republic's foreign policy must be the motherland's unity, independence, and territorial integrity within the sea and Alpine boundaries assigned by nature, by the sacrifice of blood, and by history—frontiers which are now threatened by the enemy through invasion and through promises made to the Governments which have taken refuge in London. Another essential objective will be the maintenance of the living space indispensable to a people of 45,000,000 souls who have insufficient room to live. This policy must also be directed towards the realization of a European community, with a federation of all nations which accept the following principles: (a) the elimination of age-old British intrigue from our continent; (b) the abolition of the capitalist system; (c) the struggle against the world plutocracies; (d) the development, for the benefit of European peoples and of the natives,

of Africa's natural resources, with absolute respect for those peoples, especially Moslems, who, as in Egypt, have already achieved civil and national organization.

Social 9. The basis of the Social Republic and its primary objective is manual, technical, and intellectual labor in every form.

10. Private property, the fruit of individual work and savings, the integration of human personality, will be guaranteed by the State. It must not, however, be allowed to undermine the physical and moral personality of others through exploiting their labor.

11. In the national economy, everything that, in scope or function, goes beyond private interests and affects those of the community comes within the State's sphere of action. Public services and, in general, war manufacture must be administered by the State through semi-State bodies.

12. In every industrial, private, semi-State, and State firm, technicians' and workers' representatives shall cooperate closely, through their intimate knowledge of the administration, in the fair apportioning of wages and in the distribution of profits between the reserve funds, interest on share capital, and the participation of the workers themselves in these profits. In certain firms this can be managed by an extension of the prerogatives of the present factory commissions, in others by the replacement of the executive board by administrative councils consisting of technicians, workers, and a State representative, and in others by semi-syndical cooperative means.

13. In agriculture, the proprietor's private initiative reaches its limit at the point where such initiative fails to be effective. Expropriation of undeveloped land and badly-managed enterprises may lead to the allotment of the land among the farm-workers, transforming them into direct farmers, or to conversion into semi-syndical cooperative or semi-State enterprises, according to the various exigencies of agricultural economy. This is already established by the existing laws, the application of which is being infused with the necessary impulse by the Party and syndical organizations.

14. Direct producers, artisans, professional people, and artists are fully authorized to carry on their individual productive activities for family or group purposes, provided they fulfill the obligation of handing over to the pools the quantity of goods fixed by law at the prices established by the controls.

15. The house will no longer be merely a right of property, but a right to property. The Party includes in its programme the establishment of a national organization to provide working-class houses, which, by absorbing the present housing organization and enlarging its scope, will ensure that the house shall become the property of the worker's family in every category, by means of direct building of new dwellings, or by the gradual acquisition of existing ones. The intention is to affirm the general principal that, once the rent paid covers the capital and interest involved, that payment establishes a title of purchase. As its first task the organization will solve the problems arising from war destruction by the requisition and allocation of empty buildings and by temporary construction.

16. The worker is automatically inscribed as a member of his category syndicate, without impediment to his transfer to another syndicate when he so demands. The syndicates will converge in one Confederation, including all workers, technicians, and professional men, with the exclusion of owners who are not directors or technicians. It will be called "The General Labor, Technical, and Arts Confederation." Employees of State industrial concerns and public services will belong to category syndicates, like any other workers. All the impressive social measures established by the Fascist Regime during two decades remain in their entirety, as well as the Labor Charter which, in its spirit, is the starting point of further developments.

17. The Party regards adequate wages for workers as an inviolable principle, to be achieved through the adoption of minimum national scales and through prompt revision of local scales. This will affect particularly the lower and middle-class employees, both State and private. In order that this measure may be fully effective, part of the wages will be paid in foodstuffs at official prices through canteens provided by firms. Only in this way can prices and currency be stabilized and market equilibrium restored. Black mar-

ket speculators, like traitors and defeatists, must come within the sphere of the Special Tribunals and be liable to the death sentence.

18. With this preamble to the Assembly, the Party demonstrates that it is not only "going out to meet the people," but that it remains among them.

Notes

The following abbreviations are employed in the notes:

CF   G. Gentile, *Che cosa è il fascismo?* (Florence, 1925).

EPM   K. Marx, *Economic and Philosophic Manuscripts of 1844* (Moscow, n.d.).

FD   G. Gentile, *Fondamenti della filosofia del diritto* (Florence, 1955).

GG   *Giovanni Gentile: la vita e il pensiero* (Florence, 1948–61), 9 vols.

GS   G. Gentile, *Genesi e struttura della società* (Florence, 1946).

IF   G. Gentile, *Introduzione alla filosofia* (Rome, 1933).

OD   G. Gentile, *Origini e dottrina del fascismo* (Rome, 1929).

Opera   B. Mussolini, *Opera omnia* (Florence, 1951–61), 36 vols.

PF   G. Gentile, *Preliminari allo studio del fanciullo* (Florence, 1958).

RE   G. Gentile, *Riforma dell'educazione* (Florence, 1955).

CHAPTER ONE

1. Cf. P. A. Sorokin, *Social and Cultural Dynamics* (New York, 1962), *passim,* but especially III, 486f.; *vide* also P. A. Sorokin, *The Crisis of our Age* (New York, 1941).

2. D. Bell, *The End of Ideology* (New York, 1962), p. 333; P. Corbett, *Ideologies* (New York, 1965), pp. 12f.; H. D. Aiken, "Mortality and Ideology," in *Ethics and Society,* ed. R. T. De George (Garden City, N.Y., 1966), p. 161; C. B. Macpherson, "Revolution and Ideology in the Late Twentieth Century," in *Revolution,* ed. C. J. Friedrich (New York, 1966), p. 140. The discussion which follows is, in essence, compatible with the analysis of ideologies into three constituent components: *credenda, miranda,* and *political formula,* as offered by Harold Lasswell in H. D. Lasswell, N. Leites, *et. al., Language of Politics* (Cambridge, Mass., 1965), pp. 9–12.

3. C. Johnson, *Revolution and the Social System* (Stanford, 1964).

4. This syndrome of traits is an abbreviation of that advanced by C. J. Friedrich and Z. K. Brzezinski, *Totalitarian Dictatorship and Autocracy* (New York, 1962), pp. 9f. It is abbreviated in the effort to reduce the amount of prejudgment otherwise necessitated by the cited account. Cf. also C. J. Friedrich, "The Unique Character of Totalitarian Society," in *Totalitarianism*, ed. C. J. Friedrich (New York, 1964), pp. 52f., and R. Aron, *Democratie et totalitarisme* (Saint-Amand, 1965), pp. 287f.

5. Cf. F. Engels, "Grundsaetze des Kommunismus," in *Marx-Engels Werke* (Berlin, 1959), IV, 372; H. Kelsen, "Vom Wesen und Wert der Demokratie," in *Archiv fuer Sozialwissenschaft und Sozialpolitik*, XLVII (1920), 82, 56.

6. B. Russell, *Roads to Freedom* (New York, 1966), p. 21.

7. V. I. Lenin, "The State and Revolution," in *Collected Works* (Moscow, 1964), XXV, 456.

8. A. Meyer, *Leninism* (New York, 1962), p. 58.

9. In 1905 Lenin maintained that the democratic "elective principle" could govern Party organization only under "*free* political conditions," which suggested that in a political democracy a Leninist party would abandon the characteristics of hierarchical "democratic centralism" required in an autocratic political environment. Cf. Lenin, "General Plain of the Third Congress Decisions," in *Collected Works*, VIII, 186. Cf. Meyer, *op. cit.*, chap. 5.

10. Cf. R. Luxemburg, *The Russian Revolution and Leninism and Marxism* (Ann Arbor, 1962).

11. F. V. Konstantinov, *Grundlagen der marxistischen Philosophie* (Berlin, 1964), pp. 567ff.

12. Lenin, "The State and Revolution," p. 387; N. S. Khrushchev, *Report on the Program of the Communist Party of the Soviet Union* (New York, 1961), p. 107.

13. Lenin, *op. cit.*, p. 468.

14. Khrushchev, *op. cit.*, pp. 108, 109.

15. *The Polemic on the General Line of the International Communist Movement* (Peking, 1965), p. 445.

16. Cf. A. F. Schischkin, *Grundlagen der marxistischen Ethik* (Berlin, 1964), pp. 532f.; *Die Grundlagen der kommunistischen Erziehung* (Soviet Academy for Pedagogical Science. Berlin, 1964), p. 147.

17. G. L. Mosse, "Introduction: The Genesis of Fascism," in *Journal of Contemporary History*, I, 1 (1966), 14; H. Seton-Watson, "Fascism, Right and Left," *ibid.*, p. 183.

18. S. W. Halperin, *Mussolini and Italian Fascism* (New York,

1964), p. 71; J. Comas, "Racial Myths," in *Race and Science* (New York, 1961), p. 34.

19. E. Nolte, *The Three Faces of Fascism* (New York, 1966), p. 240.

20. E. Weber, *Varieties of Fascism* (New York, 1964), p. 9. Even as competent a scholar as Barrington Moore, Jr. makes this error. Vide B. Moore, *Social Origins of Dictatorship and Democracy* (Boston, 1966).

21. H. S. Harris, *The Social Philosophy of Giovanni Gentile* (Urbana, 1960).

22. M. Rosental and P. Iudin, *Diccionario filosofico abreviado* (Montevideo, 1959), p. 182. This definition is repeated without qualification in the most recent analysis to come from Leninist sources. Vide M. Bohr and A. Kosing, *Kleines Woerterbuch der marxistisch-leninistischen Philosophie* (Berlin, 1966), p. 56.

23. L. Trotsky, *Fascism: What It Is; How to Fight It* (New York, 1944), p. 11. Cf. R. Palme Dutt, *Fascism and Social Revolution* (New York, 1934), p. 80.

24. Friedrich and Brzezinski, *op. cit.*, chap. ii; A. Aquarone, *L'organizzazione dello stato totalitario* (Turin, 1965), chap. v.

25. Cf. E. Weber, "The Men of the Archangel," in *Journal of Contemporary History*, I, 1 (1966), 101–26; S. M. Lipset, *Political Man* (New York, 1963), chap. v; W. G. Runciman, *Social Science and Political Theory* (New York, 1965), pp. 150f.

26. R. De Felice, *Mussolini il rivoluzionario, 1883–1920* (Turin, 1965), chap. ix; G. Pini, D. Susmel, *Mussolini: l'uomo e l'opera* (Florence, 1953), I, chap. viii.

27. R. De Felice, *Storia degli ebrei italiani sotto il fascismo* (Turin, 1962), p. 286.

28. Moore, *op. cit.*, p. 447.

29. "One must bear in mind: human life is sacred. Why? Man is spirit, and as such he possesses absolute value. Things are means, men are ends." *CF*, p. 35.

30. A. Hitler, *Mein Kampf* (Cambridge, Mass., 1943), pp. 291–300.

31. Cf. Runciman, *op. cit.*, chap. viii; I. Berlin, "Does Political Theory Still Exist?" in *Philosophy, Politics and Society*, Second Series, ed. P. Laslett and W. G. Runciman (Oxford, 1964), pp. 1–33.

32. Cf. T. Pirker, *Komintern und Faschismus: Dokumente zur Geschichte und Theorie des Fascismus* (Stuttgart, 1966); J. M. Cammett, "Communist Theories of Fascism, 1920–1935," in *Science and Society*, XXXI (Spring, 1967), 149–63; I. Fetscher, "Zur Kritik des

sowjetmarxistischen Faschismusbegriffs," in *Karl Marx und der Marxismus* (Munich, 1967), pp. 219-37.

33. Dutt, *op. cit.*, pp. 177, 178, 181.

34. Editorial, *Washington Post*, February 15, 1944.

35. D. Katz and H. Cantril, "An Analysis of Attitudes Toward Fascism and Communism," in *Journal of Abnormal and Social Psychology*, XXXV (1940), 362.

36. R. Stagner, "Fascist Attitudes: An Exploratory Study," in *Journal of Social Psychology*, VII (1936), 310, 318; A. L. Edwards, "Unlabeled Fascist Attitudes," in *Journal of Abnormal and Social Psychology*, XXXVI (1941), 575.

37. Dutt, *op. cit.*, p. 190 n.

38. J. F. Brown, *Psychology and the Social Order* (New York, 1936), pp. 387, 388.

39. T. W. Adorno, E. Frenkel-Brunswik, D. J. Levinson and R. N. Sanford, *The Authoritarian Personality* (New York, 1950), p. 1.

40. R. Brown, *Social Psychology* (New York, 1965), p. 478; cf. p. 485.

41. There have been, at best, only oblique validation tests attempted of instruments like the California "Fascist Scale." T. S. Cohn and H. Carsch administered the F Scale to workers in a German cosmetics factory (T. S. Cohn and H. Carsch, "Administration of the F Scale to a Sample of Germans," in *Journal of Abnormal and Social Psychology*, XLIX [1954]). They found the mean score of responses made by their sample to be the highest recorded until that time. Since there was no indication how many, if any, of the German workers had been or were National Socialists, the results could hardly be construed as providing a significant test validation even for National Socialist much less fascist attitudes. Such validation procedures, as long as they employ sample populations composed of National Socialists, cannot validate the claim that the scale measures "Fascist" attitudes unless the auxiliary assumption is made that the same attitudes subtend both National Socialism and Fascism—an assumption for which there is little, if any, evidence.

Another attempt at validation of the F Scale was that conducted by Thelma Coulter who administered the scale to members of Sir Oswald Mosley's British Union Movement—a group described as "avowedly fascist" (cf. H. Eysenck, *The Psychology of Politics* [London, 1954]). The mean score of the "fascists" was among the highest recorded. Brown construes such findings as "strong confirmation of the claim that the F Scale measures fascistic trends." (Brown, *Social Psychology*,

p. 528). There are, however, a number of reservations that can be legitimately raised against such an assessment.

First of all, the British Union Movement has attracted, for all intents and purposes, only National Socialist sympathizers since its incubation period before World War II. A content analysis of its doctrinal and propaganda literature prior to the War would clearly indicate a predominance of National Socialist themes. Since the end of the war, the Mosley group has exploited racial tensions in Britain. In effect the sample would represent, if it represents anything at all, National Socialist persuasions as they are understood by Englishmen.

More than that, few, if any, of the national leadership and the general membership of Mosley's small group, either prior to or after World War II, could read Italian. Whatever conception of fascism they entertained was by and large the by-product of available English language material. Since the prevailing stereotype fostered by that material characterized fascism as arch-conservative, antiradical, and anti-Semitic, the membership of British Union was largely, if not exclusively, self-selected on the basis of positive response to the English language stereotype. Testing members of British Union in order to validate a test vehicle like the F Scale exploits some of the same elements as instances of self-fulfilling prophecy. Intellectuals in England "interpreted" Fascism to mean exacerbated middle-class conservatism. As a consequence a few particularly exacerbated middle-class conservatives (of whatever class provenience) identified themselves as fascists. They were then subjected to the F Scale and found to be exacerbated middle-class conservatives. Cf. also H. H. Hyman and P. B. Sheatsley, "The Authoritarian Personality—A Methodological Critique," in *Studies in the Scope and Method of "The Authoritarian Personality,"* ed. R. Christie and M. Jahoda (Glencoe, 1954), pp. 50–122.

42. G. D. H. Cole, *The Meaning of Marxism* (Ann Arbor, 1964), 149f., 147.

43. Cf. H. S. Hughes, *Consciousness and Society* (New York, 1958), p. 272; R. Michels, *First Lectures in Political Sociology* (New York, 1965), pp. 113–15, 119, 126, 128, 131, 137, 153; C. Gini, "The Scientific Basis of Fascism," in *Political Science Quarterly*, XLII (March, 1927).

44. Cf. R. Melis, ed. *Sindacalisti Italiani,* (Rome, 1964), p. 144.

45. G. Bottai, *Vent'anni e un qiorno* (Cernusco sul Naviglio, 1949).

46. De Felice, *Mussolini,* p. 86; G. Roux, *Vita di Mussolini* (Rome, 1961), p. 33.

CHAPTER TWO

1. N. Colajanni, *Latini e Anglo-sassoni* (Rome, 1906), pp. 370f.

2. R. Michels, *Elemente zur Entstehungsgeschichte des Imperialismus in Italien* (Berlin, 1912), p. 58.

3. Cf. L. M. Hartmann, *Hundert Jahre italienischer Geschichte 1815–1915* (Munich, 1916), p. 190.

4. G. Giolitti, *Denkwuerdigkeiten meines Lebens* (Stuttgart, 1923), p. 85.

5. V. Pareto, *The Mind and Society* (New York, 1935), II, para. 855.

6. Cf. J. Meisel, *The Myth of the Ruling Class: Gaetano Mosca and the "Elite"* (Ann Arbor, 1958), pp. 169–83; and A. Livingston's Introduction to G. Mosca, *The Ruling Class* (New York, 1939), pp. xxxvi–xxxix.

7. V. Pareto, *Corso di economia politica* (Turin, 1949), II, para. 624, 659–62.

8. Both Mosca and Gumplowicz give 1881 as the date of publication of *Der Rassenkampf* (Mosca, *The Ruling Class*, p. 331; Gumplowicz, *Die sociologische Staatsidee* (Innsbruck, 1902), p. iii. The only edition I have been able to locate is published with the date 1883 (Innsbruck). In his preface to *The Outlines of Sociology* (Philadelphia, 1899) Gumplowicz gives 1883 as the date of publication for *Der Rassenkampf*. While this does not effect the question of priority, since *Rechtsstaat und Socialismus* was published in 1881, there does appear to be some confusion. All references to *Der Rassenkampf* in this text will be to the 1883 edition.

9. Cf. J. Burnham, *The Machiavellians* (Chicago, 1943).

10. Cf. G. Lundberg, *Can Science Save Us?* (New York, 1961) for a typical expression of contemporary sociological positivism. Cf. P. Sorokin, *Contemporary Sociological Theories* (New York, 1928), pp. 40f.

11. Mosca, *Teorica dei governi e governo parlamentare* (Turin, 1925), p. 16.

12. Mosca, *Ruling Class*, p. 50.

13. The *Sistemi* is employed for exposition because it appeared during the period with which we are concerned. The *Trattato* was published only in 1916, after Mussolini had formulated his basic social and political concepts.

14. Pareto, *I sistemi socialisti* (Turin, 1954), p. 19.

15. Pareto, *Corso*, II, paras. 667,993.

16. This conclusion is already implied in the *Corso,* II, para. 624.

17. Pareto, *Sistemi,* pp. 24–31.

18. L. Gumplowicz, *Rechtsstaat und Socialismus* (Innsbruck, 1881), p. 503.

19. Gumplowicz, *Rassenkampf,* pp. 193, 206, 218.

20. Gumplowicz, *Outlines of Sociology,* pp. 117f., 121.

21. Gumplowicz, *Rassenkampf,* p. 207. Cf. *Outlines,* p. 207; *Die sociologische Staatsidee* (Innsbruck, 1902), pp. 3f.

22. *Ibid.,* p. 219.

23. *Ibid.,* p. 234.

24. Pareto, *Corso,* II, para. 624.

25. *Ibid.,* para. 661f.

26. Gumplowicz, *Rassenkampf,* pp. 231–240.

27. Cf. G. Salomon's Preface to L. Gumplowicz, *Geschichte der Staatstheorien* (Innsbruck, 1926), p. vii; and H. Becker and H. E. Barnes, *Social Thought from Lore to Science* (New York, 1961), III, 1005.

28. Cf. the comments of M. Delle Piane, *Gaetano Mosca, classe politica e liberalismo* (Naples, 1952), p. 55, n. 10.

29. Mosca, *Ruling Class,* p. 163.

30. *Ibid.*

31. *Ibid.,* pp. 71f.

32. Cf. *Ibid.,* pp. 72, 115.

33. *Ibid.,* pp. 65–67, 158f.

34. *Ibid.,* p. 116.

35. Pareto, *Sistemi,* p. 80.

36. *Ibid.,* p. 45.

37. Cf. *Ibid.,* p. 28f.

38. Pareto, *The Mind and Society,* II, para. 868, III, para. 1397.

39. Pareto, *Sistemi,* p. 41.

40. *Ibid.,* p. 85.

41. Gumplowicz, *Rechtsstaat und Socialismus,* pp. 86, 100; Pareto, *Sistemi,* pp. 27, 530f.; Mosca, *Ruling Class,* p. 190.

42. Gumplowicz, *Outlines of Sociology,* p. 121, 126.

43. Gumplowicz, *Rechtsstaat und Socialismus,* p. 133, anm. a.

44. Pareto, *Sistemi,* p. 25; Mosca, *Ruling Class,* p. 51, cf. 154f., 184, 187. Gumplowicz advances these notions throughout his works, but his account in *Sozialphilosophe im Umriss* (Innsbruck, 1910), pp. 123–127 is particularly explicit. Cf. Gumplowicz, *Rechtsstaat und Socialismus,* p. 500.

45. Mosca, *Ruling Class,* pp. 51, 53.

46. Gumplowicz, *Outlines of Sociology,* pp. 143, 146.

47. Gumplowicz, *Rechtsstaat und Socialismus,* pp. 503–5; Pareto, *Sistemi,* pp. 24–36; Mosca, *Ruling Class,* pp. 65–69.

48. Cf. Gumplowicz, *Rassenkampf,* p. 228; *Outlines of Sociology,* p. 112. Reference is made here only to such elements in the works of Gumplowicz; their appearance in the works of Mosca and Pareto is too well known to warrant specific citations.

49. Mosca provides a particularly clear expression of these theses in *Ruling Class,* pp. 175f.

50. D. T. Campbell, R. A. LeVine, "A proposal for cooperative cross-cultural research on ethnocentrism," in *Journal of Conflict Resolution,* V (March, 1961), 83.

51. Cf. J. Gould, W. L. Kolb, *A Dictionary of the Social Sciences* (New York, 1964), p. 245.

52. W. G. Sumner, *Folkways* (New York, 1960), pp. 541, n. 75; 543, n. 69; 547, ns. 3 and 5; 574.

53. Gumplowicz, *Rechtsstaat und Socialismus,* pp. 70–73.

54. Gumplowicz, *Rassenkampf,* pp. 236–39, *Outlines of Sociology,* p. 123; *Rechtsstaat und Socialismus,* p. 74.

55. Gumplowicz, *Rassenkampf,* p. 248; *Outlines of Sociology,* pp. 139, 141–43.

56. Gumplowicz, *Outlines of Sociology,* pp. 157–77. By 1902 these ideas are fully articulated in *Die sociologische Staatsidee,* pp. 205–14.

57. Gumplowicz, *Die sociologische Staatsidee,* pp. 94f., n. 1, 209.

58. Cf. Delle Piane, *op. cit.,* Meisel, *op. cit., passim.*

59. R. Michels, *Political Parties* (New York, 1959), p. 379.

60. *Ibid.,* pp. 390f.

61. K. Marx, F. Engels, "The Communist Manifesto," *Selected Works in Two Volumes* (Moscow, 1955), I, 36, 44.

62. All commentators on Sorel refer to this shortcoming and he, himself, was conscious of it. Cf. G. Sorel, *Reflections on Violence* (New York, 1950), pp. 31–34.

63. H. Barth, *Masse und Mythos: Die Theorie der Gewalt: Georges Sorel* (Hamburg, 1959), pp. 10f., 18f.; E. von Beckerath, *Wesen und Werden des faschistischen Staates* (Berlin, 1927), p. 26; J. Variot, *Propos de Georges Sorel* (Paris, 1935), pp. 31, 261; cf. however P. Andreu, *Sorel, il nostro maestro* (Rome, 1966), p. 256.

64. Cf. J. Meisel, *The Genesis of Georges Sorel* (Ann Arbor, 1951), p. 41, n. 91; Sorel, *op. cit.,* p. 73, n. 11.

65. Sorel, *op. cit.,* pp. 142f.

66. Sorel, "The Decomposition of Marxism," in I. Horowitz, *Radi-*

calism and the Revolt against Reason: The Social Theories of Georges Sorel (New York, 1961), pp. 226–28, 245–47; "Apology for Violence," in *Reflections,* p. 301.

67. Sorel, *Reflections,* pp. 87, 133, 269.

68. Cf. V. Racca's introduction to G. Sorel, *Saggi di critica del Marxismo* (Milan, 1903), p. xli.

69. Sorel, *Saggi,* p. 163f.

70. Sorel, *Reflections,* pp. 189, 194. Cf. Sorel, *Saggi,* pp. 38–40; Horowitz, *op. cit.,* pp. 60f.

71. Sorel, *Reflections,* p. 189.

72. Cf. Sorel, "Unity and Multiplicity," in *Reflections,* pp. 279–300, also p. 247.

73. Sorel, *Reflections,* p. 106.

74. Sorel quoting Nietzsche, *Reflections,* p. 257.

75. Marx, Engels, *op. cit.,* p. 48.

76. A. O. Olivetti, *Questioni contemporanee* (Naples, 1913), pp. 24, 104. This is an unaltered reprint of 1906.

77. *Ibid.,* p. 154.

78. Sorel, *Saggi,* p. 39; *Reflections,* p. 194.

79. Pareto, *Sistemi,* p. 27; *Mind and Society,* IV, paras, 2182, 2184f., 2189f.

80. Cf. Meisel, *Genesis,* pp. 89f., 292.

81. Cf. Gumplowicz, *Rechtsstaat und Socialismus,* p. 26.

82. Gumplowicz, *Outlines,* pp. 178, 136, 133.

83. Cf. Engels, "The Origin of the Family, Private Property and the State," in Marx, Engels, *op. cit.,* II, 317–321; S. W. Moore, *The Critique of Capitalist Democracy* (New York, 1957), chap. i; J. Barion, *Hegel und die marxistische Staatslehre* (Bonn, 1963), pp. 132–41.

84. F. Engels, *Anti-Duehring* (Moscow, 1962), pp. 219–54.

85. Sorel, "La necessità e il fatalismo nel Marxismo," in *Saggi,* pp. 59–94.

86. Sorel, *Saggi,* p. 270.

87. Sorel, *Reflections,* p. 142. Sorel is specifically referring to "the errors of Marx" which are "numerous and sometimes enormous."

88. Horowitz, *op. cit.,* p. 127.

89. G. Sorel, "Avenir socialiste des syndicats," in *Matériaux d'une théorie du prolétariat* (Paris, 1929), p. 127.

90. R. Humphrey, *Georges Sorel: Prophet Without Honor* (Cambridge, Mass., 1951), p. 69.

91. Sorel, *Reflections,* pp. 55f.

92. *Ibid.,* p. 57.

93. The literature on the relationship between Sorel, Bergson, James, and Nietzsche is abundant; cf. Humphrey, *op. cit.*, chap. ii; Horowitz, *op. cit.*, pp. 39–56; G. La Ferla, *Ritratto di Georges Sorel* (Milan, 1933), pp. 58f.; Barth, *op. cit.*, pp. 72f.

94. Sorel, *De l'utilité du pragmatisme* (Paris, 1928), pp. 46f.

95. Sorel, *Saggi*, p. 14.

96. *Ibid.*, p. 48.

97. Sorel, *Reflections*, p. 140.

98. *Ibid.*, pp. 136f.

99. *Ibid.*, p. 144.

100. Sorel, "Multiplicity and Unity," in *ibid.*, p. 300.

101. *Ibid.*, p. 52.

102. *Ibid.*, p. 142.

103. *Ibid.*, p. 140.

104. Pareto, "Georges Sorel," in *La Ronda* (1922), p. 542.

105. Sorel, *Saggi*, p. 14.

106. Sorel, *Reflections*, p. 56.

107. *Ibid.*, p. 68.

108. Cf. Horowitz, *op. cit.*, pp. 36–39.

109. G. Le Bon, *The Crowd: A Study of the Popular Mind* (London, 1952), p. 41. Le Bon speaks of "crowds" rather than "social elements," and yet "crowds," for Le Bon, denotes social groups variously composed and structured. He speaks of sects, parties, casts, classes, and nations as "crowds." For the sake of exposition, these social groups of various kinds will be referred to as "social elements." Cf. Book III, chap. 1.

110. *Ibid.*, p. 70, cf. p. 116.

111. *Ibid.*, p. 21.

112. *Ibid.*, pp. 80f.

113. Sorel, *Saggi*, pp. 97f.; *Reflections*, p. 240.

114. Sorel, *Reflections*, p. 145.

115. *Ibid.*, p. 167.

116. Sorel, "Multiplicity and Unity," in *ibid.*, p. 298.

117. *Ibid.*, p. 300.

118. E. Shil, introduction to *ibid.*, p. 17.

119. *Ibid.*, p. 158.

120. *Ibid.*

121. *Ibid.*, p. 53.

122. Sorel, "Apology for Violence," *ibid.*, p. 302.

123. Sorel, *Saggi*, pp. 99f.

124. Shil, in Sorel, *Reflections*, p. 18.

125. *Ibid.*, p. 277.

126. As cited in Meisel, *Genesis*, p. 219.

127. Cf. E. Corradini, *Discorsi politici* (Florence, 1923), pp. 85–87, 128–30, 132–34; *Il volere d'Italia* (Naples, 1911), pp. 116–20, 199–201; *L'ora di Tripoli* (Milan, 1911), pp. 227–41.

128. Cf. Meisel, *Genesis*, pp. 218f.

129. Corradini, *Discorsi politici*, pp. 36f.; *L'unità e la potenza delle nazioni* (Florence, 1922), p. 61, 89–91; *Il nazionalismo Italiano* (Milan, 1914), p. 5.

130. Corradini, *L'ombra della vita*, p. 287.

131. *Ibid.*, p. 286. *Il nazionalismo italiano*, p. 11

132. Corradini, *L'unità e la potenza delle nazioni*, pp. 208f.

133. *Ibid.*, pp. 61f., 221f.

134. *Ibid.*, pp. 256–59.

135. Corradini, *Il nazionalismo italiano*, p. 234.

136. Corradini, *Discorsi politici*, pp. 173f.

137. Corradini, *La vita nazionale*, pp. 37ff.

138. Corradini, *Il volere d'Italia*, pp. 174f.

139. Corradini, *Discorsi politici*, p. 58.

140. *Ibid.*, p. 60.

141. Corradini, *L'unità e la potenza delle nazioni*, pp. 117–23.

142. For a compact exposition of Corradini's views, cf. J. Mannhardt, *Der Faschismus* (Munich, 1925), pp. 113–34.

143. *Contro il parlamentarismo* was written in 1895 and republished in *L'intelligenza della folla* (Turin, 1922) in successive editions. All references to Sighele's work will refer to the above edition.

144. Barnes and Becker, *op. cit.*, III, 1008f., cite the publication of Sighele's *La folla delinquente* as 1903. It was actually published in 1891. Cf. A. Stratico, *La psicologia collettiva* (Milan, n.d., but probably 1905), p. 26.

145. Cf. H. Spencer, *The Study of Sociology* (Ann Arbor, 1961), pp. 44f.

146. Stratico, *op. cit.*, pp. 26f.

147. Gumplowicz, *Die sociologische Staatsidee*, p. 211. Cf. Le Bon, *op. cit.*, 27.

148. Sighele, *L'intelligenza della folla*, pp. 97f.

149. *Ibid.*, pp. 111–19.

150. Le Bon, *op. cit.*, p. 187. Compare Sighele, *op. cit.*, p. 99.

151. Sighele, *op. cit.*, p. 125.

152. *Ibid.*, p. 128.

153. *Ibid.*, p. 132.

154. Pareto, *Sistemi*, 58, 83, 521, 523.

155. Gumplowicz, *Die sociologische Staatsidee*, pp. 205–24. By the time Gumplowicz wrote the *Sozialphilosophie im Umriss* in 1910, Sighele's ideas had become constituent elements of his account.

156. Pareto, *Corso*, II, para. 1036.

157. E. Corradini, *Pagine degli anni sacri* (Milan, 1920), pp. 134–137.

158. Corradini, *Discorsi politici,* p. 38; cf. *Il volere d'Italia,* pp. 161–65.

159. Corradini, *Discorsi politici,* pp. 56–58.

160. *Ibid.,* pp. 54–61.

161. *Ibid.,* p. 59.

162. Corradini, *Il volere d'Italia,* pp. 177f.

163. Corradini, *Discorsi politici,* p. 116.

164. "The Manifesto of Futurism," in J. Joll, *Three Intellectuals in Politics: Blum, Rathenau, Marinetti* (New York, 1960), pp. 181f. Minor changes have been made in translation, vide "Manifesto del Futurismo," in F. T. Marinetti, *Futurismo e fascismo* (Foligno, 1924), p. 21.

165. "Primo manifesto politico futurista, 1909," in Marinetti, *op. cit.,* p. 22 and Corradini, *Discorsi politici,* p. 196.

166. Marinetti, *op. cit.,* pp. 58f.

167. *Ibid.,* pp. 46f.

168. *Ibid.,* pp. 61, 66f., 207–10.

169. Cf. R. T. Clough, *Futurism: The Story of a Modern Art Movement* (New York, 1961), p. 30.

170. Michels, *op. cit.,* p. viii.

171. *Ibid.,* pp. 24f., 25, ns. 5 and 6.

172. Cf. Michels, *First Lectures in Political Sociology,* p. 63. Michels cites Mosca's *Elementi* and Pareto's *Sistemi* in this general connection; cf. *Political Parties,* p. 16, n. 7. Cf. also p. 379.

173. Michels, *Political Parties,* p. 86.

174. *Ibid.,* pp. 346f.

175. *Ibid.,* p. 353.

176. *Ibid.,* p. 390.

177. *Ibid.,* p. 393.

178. Michels, *First Lectures in Political Sociology,* p. 160.

179. R. Albrecht-Carrie, *Italy from Napoleon to Mussolini* (New York, 1960), p. 147.

180. P. Alatri, *Le origini del fascismo* (Rome, 1963).

181. B. Croce in *La Stampa,* May 15, 1924.

182. R. MacGregor-Hastie, *The Day of the Lion: The Rise and Fall of Fascist Italy (1922–1945)* (New York, 1963), p. 29.

183. G. Megaro, *Mussolini in the Making* (London, 1938), p. 327.

184. Considering the difficulties which attend the appraisal of a contemporary and highly controversial figure, one is compelled, at least grudgingly, to grant that perhaps such exclusive and definitive judgments require some, if not extensive, qualification. There are so many possible sources of error even when research is objective and well-intentioned. MacGregor-Hastie, for example, quotes from a police report of 1876 devoted to Alessandro Mussolini, Mussolini's father, to the effect that Alessandro had blue eyes. The quote is perfectly accurate. In fact, in 1882, when Alessandro Mussolini was twenty-eight, a police report dated July 24 listed his eyes as blue (*cerulei*). But in 1902, when Alessandro Mussolini was forty-eight and being interrogated in connection with electoral disturbances, the police description informs us that his eyes were brown (*castagne*). As a matter of fact, there were authors who even insisted that *Benito* Mussolini's eyes were *blue*. Now, if there can be dispute concerning such elementary empirical facts, one wonders what degree of caution should govern unrestricted generalizations concerning states of mind, moral dispositions, and psychological character traits.

These considerations are particularly urgent when scholarship devotes its attention to a figure as generally deplored as Mussolini. There is a conscious or unconscious tendency to create as damning a characterization as possible. This would be the most generous interpretation of the curious manner with which the facts of Mussolini's private life are treated by MacGregor-Hastie. He tells us that at Tolmezzo in 1907 "Mussolini is supposed to have contracted syphilis, which remained uncured for the rest of his life." Furthermore, a "law student" who knew Mussolini during this period "died under mysterious circumstances in 1928, a reported 'suicide,' which may have been Mussolini's way of suppressing evidence and eliminating witnesses."

This entire sequence, beginning with the "supposed" syphilitic infection, leading to the suggestion that Mussolini "may" have had people who might have defamed his character assassinated, is instructive. The evidence for the supposed infection comes from a book by Paolo Monelli published originally in 1950. In 1953 Giorgio Pini and Duilio Susmel published their first volume of a four volume biography of Mussolini, *Mussolini: l'uomo e l'opera*. In it they reviewed the available evidence concerning Mussolini's illness of 1907. Arnaldo Pozzi indicated that the medical records kept on Mussolini and the subsequent minute autopsy to which his body was subjected failed to reveal the least evidence of any syphilitic infection. Mussolini's disorder was diagnosed in September, 1907, by a specialist in Bologna, as "acute gonorrhea."

MacGregor-Hastie makes references to the work of Pini and Susmel in his notes and bibliography and yet chooses to neglect the results of their inquiry in his text. That the evidence provided by Pini and Susmel is compelling is indicated by the fact that Renzo De Felice, in his *Mussolini il rivoluzionario,* certainly no apologetic for Mussolini, simply accepts it without comment. For some curious reason MacGregor-Hastie chooses to entertain Monelli's supposition. Without that supposition his suggestion that Mussolini had possible witnesses assassinated would hardly apply in the chosen context.

Similar shortcomings recur in a variety of places in MacGregor-Hastie's book. He tells us, for example, that Mussolini had "a violent love affair with a schoolteacher, Ida Delser" (*sic*) in Trent during the summer of 1909, "by whom he had a son later in the year. The child was always sickly, and both he and his mother died eventually in lunatic asylums from—it was said—the general paralysis of the insane which developed out of the syphilis Mussolini passed on."

Even without knowing any of the historic facts the account is strange. If Mussolini was disposed to assassinate witnesses who might defame him, why would he permit a former paramour whom he had infected with syphilis to languish until her natural death in 1935? Or for that matter permit his illegitimate son, Benito Albano, whom he had recognized before the law, to continue to live until 1942 as a monument to his venereal disease? If Mussolini was disposed to dispatch witnesses it would seem that these would be prime candidates.

The fact of the matter is that MacGregor-Hastie's account is terribly confused. Mussolini's particularly unhappy affair with Ida Irene *Dalser* took place in Milan (although Mussolini had apparently met her in Trent), and it was on November 11, 1915 (not 1909) that the child was born. This puts the story in an entirely different context. Mussolini had, by that time, already established the relationship with Rachele Guidi, who was to become Rachele Mussolini in a civil ceremony in 1915 and who had already borne him two children: Edda in 1910, and Vittorio in September, 1915. Neither Rachele, Edda, nor Vittorio Mussolini contracted syphilis. The disease, apparently, must have been selective.

If such accounts, dealing with facts and the reporting and interpretation of facts, leave much to be desired, it would seem obvious that any judgment about the influence of philosophers on Mussolini's thought would have to be very carefully scrutinized indeed. Even as careful a scholar as Megaro, whose sweeping judgment we have already cited, by misreading a section of Mussolini's *Vita di Arnaldo* credits Mr. Richard Washburn Child with the authorship of the volume published over Mussolini's name, *My Autobiography*. Megaro charges Mussolini with perpetrating a "shameless literary fraud."

If Megaro were right, not only could Mussolini be charged with "literary fraud" but Mr. Child, the American Ambassador to Italy from 1921 to 1924, would have been not only a coconspirator but a rank liar as well. In the introduction to the book in question, Mr. Child says that he received the manuscripts from Mussolini. The explanation is not difficult. Megaro misinterpreted a section in Mussolini's *Vita di Arnaldo*. Mussolini indicates there that he asked Arnaldo (not Mr. Child) to write the text, based upon materials which he, Mussolini, would provide. We know now that Mussolini decided not to undertake the obligation of writing such a biography because of the press of governmental duties. And yet he was interested in obtaining favorable copy in the English speaking countries. As a solution he provided Arnaldo with documents and a biography he himself had written when he was twenty-eight, and asked him to prepare a draft manuscript which he, Mussolini, would then read and alter and/or approve. Arnaldo Mussolini's editorial work was done under the constant supervision of Mussolini. So it would seem that (1) it was not as "shameless" a "literary fraud" as Megaro suggests, and (2) that Mr. Child was not the author in any sense of the word, and (3) the entire confusion arose out of Megaro's mistranslation of a passage out of Italian.

There are a multitude of such instances in the literature devoted to Mussolini. These illustrations have been provided merely to indicate that broad and unqualified judgments concerning Mussolini's thought must be well-supported before they can be accepted.

CHAPTER THREE

1. For an account of Alessandro Mussolini, cf. 1. De Begnac, *Vita di Benito Mussolini* (Milan, 1930), I, chap. iv.

2. As cited in De Felice, *Mussolini il rivoluzionario*, p. 7.

3. "Mio padre," in *Opera*, III, 276.

4. De Felice, *Mussolini*, p. 13; cf. S. Bedeschi, R. Alessi, *Anni giovanili di Mussolini* (Milan, 1939), p. 21.

5. "Il romanzo Russo," in *Opera*, I, 3f.

6. Megaro, *op. cit.*, p. 318.

7. The novel was translated into English, years later, and appeared as B. Mussolini, *The Cardinal's Mistress*, trans. H. Motherwell (New York, 1928).

8. Letter to Torquato Nanni, December, 1909, in *Opera*, II, 269.

9. B. Mussolini, *Scritti e discorsi* (Milan, 1933–40) vols. 1–13.

10. Cf. "Premessa," in *Opera*, I, viif.

11. For a discussion of the development of both Marx's and Lenin's thought, cf. A. J. Gregor, *A Survey of Marxism* (New York, 1965).

12. Cf. A. Meyer, *Leninism* (New York, 1957), pp. 195–97. I. Lapenna, *State and Law: Soviet and Yugoslav Theory* (New Haven, 1964) provides a convenient discussion of developments in the Leninist theory of the state.

13. Bedeschi and Alessi, *op. cit.*, p. 26; M. Sarfatti, *Dux* (Milan, 1929), p. 51; P. Alatri, *op. cit.*, p. 256.

14. *Opera*, I, 92, II, 31, 123, 366, III, 47, 67, 197, 314, 365, 366, 367, IV, 153, V, 96, 327, VI, 9, 78.

15. *Opera*, II, 30f., III, 5, 86, 366, V, 94.

16. *Opera*, III, 315, IV, 154.

17. *Opera*, V, 96, 110, 204, 327, VI, 431, 9.

18. *Opera*, I, 143, V, 206, VI, 7378.

19. R. Michels, *Sozialismus in Italien: Intellektuelle Strömungen* (Munich, 1925), p. 365.

20. A. Labriola, *Essays on the Materialist Conception of History* (Chicago, 1904), *Socialism and Philosophy* (Chicago, 1934) originally published as *Discorrendo di socialismo e di filosofia: lettere a G. Sorel* (Rome, 1898).

21. E. Susmel, *Mussolini e il suo tempo* (Cernusco sul Naviglio, 1950), p. 34.

22. Megaro, *op. cit.*, p. 11; De Felice, *Mussolini*, pp. 23f.

23. "L'uomo e la divinità," in *Opera*, XXXIII, 6f. This thesis appears again in "Edmondo De Amicis," *Opera*, I, 106.

24. F. Engels, *Anti-Duehring* (Moscow, 1962).

25. "L'uomo e la divinità," in *Opera*, XXXIII, 22f. In 1908 this thesis is framed in the following fashion: ". . . Marx construed material interest the prime mover of human actions and considered all the

ideological superstructure of society (art, religion, morals) as a reflex and the consequence of economic conditions, more precisely, the mode of material production." "Karl Marx," in *Opera*, I, 103.

26. "La filosofia della forza," in *Opera*, I, 175.

27. "Uomini e idee: 'L'individuel et le social,'" in *Opera*, I, 73f.

28. Marx, "Contribution to the Critique of Hegel's Philosophy of Right," in *Early Writings*, trans. T. B. Bottomore (New York, 1964), p. 43; and "Theses on Feuerbach," in Marx and Engels, *The German Ideology* (New York, 1947), p. 198.

29. *EPM*, pp. 104f.

30. Marx, *Grundrisse der Kritik der Politischen Oekonomie (Rohentwurf)* (Berlin, 1953), p. 6.

31. "Centenario Darwiniano," in *Opera*, II, 9.

32. "Fra libri e riviste," in *Opera*, II, 248f.

33. "Uomini e idee: 'Individuel et le social,'" in *Opera*, I, 74.

34. "Socialismo e movimento sociale nel secolo XIX," in *Opera*, I, 43. Compare Engels, "The Origin of the Family, Private Property and the State," in Marx, Engels, *Selected Works*, II, 317f.

35. "Socialismo e socialisti," in *Opera*, I, 142.

36. "Karl Marx," in *Opera*, I, 103. Cf. "Socialismo e movimento sociale nel secolo XIX," in *Opera*, I, 44.

37. "L'uomo e la divinità," in *Opera*, XXXIII, 18, cf. pp. 22f.

38. Pp. 130–32.

39. "Pagine rivoluzionarie: 'Le parole d'un rivoltoso,'" in *Opera*, I, 51.

40. Mussolini's "human morality" was based on the "principle of universal fraternity. . . ." "L'uomo e la divinità," in *Opera*, XXXIII, 23; "Socialism," he maintained, "does not recognize nationality. . . ." *Opera*, I, 24. He maintained that "the religious ideal signifies coercion, slavery, and renunciation. . . ." He advised that one "should abandon the Church and labor for the triumph of human reason and the destruction of dogma. Only with the death of the gods can the lives of all mankind become fecund." *Ibid.*, pp. 27, 36. He maintained that "science had already destroyed God. . . ." "Sport dei coronati," in *Opera*, I, 32. He sought to "free men's minds from the absurdity of religion," and advocated the substitution of the "pagan conception of life" for the Christian. "Gli orrori del chiostro," in *Opera*, I, 38. "We are decisively anti-Christian and consider Christianity as the immortal stigma of opprobrium. . . ." "La libertà nera," in *Opera*, I, 111. He identified the goal of the movement as "collectivization of property." "Del socialismo svizzero nella Svizzera," in *Opera*, I, 23.

41. "Ne l'attesa," in *Opera*, I, 41.

42. F. Engels, "Preface of 1890 to the Communist Manifesto," in Marx and Engels, *Selected Works*, I, 31.

43. Cf. Gregor, *op. cit.*, pp. 178f.

44. "Pagine rivoluzionarie: 'Le parole d'un rivoltoso,'" in *Opera*, I, 51.

45. "Intorno all notte del 4 agosto," in *Opera*, I, 61.

46. "Uomini e idee: 'L'individuel et le social,'" in *Opera*, I, 73.

47. H. Stuart Hughes, *Consciousness and Society* (New York, 1958), p. 271; Megaro, *op. cit.*, pp. 112f.

48. As cited in De Felice, *Mussolini*, p. 38.

49. "La mia vita dal 29 luglio 1883 al 23 novembre 1911," in *Opera*, XXXIII, 257; *My Autobiography*, p. 27; Pini and Susmel, *op. cit.*, I, 72f., 82f.

50. "Intermezzo polemico," in *Opera*, I, 128, 129.

51. "La teppa," in *Opera*, I, 92; "Karl Marx," in *Opera*, I, 103f. Compare Pareto, *Sistemi*, pp. 26f.

52. ""Opinioni e documenti: La crisi risolutiva," in *Opera*, I, 70.

53. "La teoria sindacalista," in *Opera*, II, 128.

54. A Oriani, *La rivolta ideale* (Bologna, 1943), pp. 29f., 36.

55. Marx, "Hegel's Philosophy of Right," p. 59. Cf. S. Moore, *Three Tactics: The Background in Marx* (New York: 1963), pp. 14–16. Vide Mussolini's comments, "Il Programma del Partito Socialista," in *Opera*, V, 327.

56. Cf. B. D. Wolfe, *Marxism: 100 Years in the Life of a Doctrine* (New York, 1965), chap. 9.

57. Engels, "The Origin of the Family," 320f.

58. *Ibid.*, p. 325.

59. Michels, *Sozialismus in Italien*, pp. 368f.

60. For characteristic expressions of these views, cf. A. O. Olivetti, *Problemi del socialismo contemporaneo* (Lugano, 1906), published in a later edition as *Questioni contemporanee* (Naples, 1913); G. Prezzolini, *La teoria sindacalista* (Naples, 1909); E. Leone, *Il sindacalismo* (Palermo, 1905).

61. Engels, "On Authority," in Marx and Engels, *op. cit.*, I, 635f.

62. A. O. Olivetti, "I sindacalisti e la elite," in *Sindacalisti Italiani*, ed. R. Melis (Rome, 1964), pp. 191–93.

63. S. Panunzio, "La persistenza del diritto," in Melis, *op. cit.*, p. 226.

64. Stuart Hughes, *op. cit.*, p. 272.

65. "Fra libri e riviste," in *Opera*, II, 248f. R. Michels, *L'uomo economico e la cooperazione* (Turin, 1909).

66. Panunzio, *op cit.*, p. 231, and n. 1.

67. Mussolini, *My Autobiography*, pp. 25, 36.

68. "Atei," in *Opera*, I, 49.

69. Pini and Susmel, *op. cit.*, I, 72; De Felice, *Mussolini*, p. 40, n. 4.

70. "Lo sciopero generale e la violenza," in *Opera*, II, 163–68.

71. Megaro, *op. cit.*, p. 233.

72. "La necessità della politica socialista in Italia," in *Opera*, I, 17.

73. "La democrazia di domani," in *Opera*, VI, 121.

74. As cited in De Begnac, *Palazzo Venezia*, p. 118.

75. "Il valore storico del socialismo." in Opera, VI, 80, 81; compare "Le ragioni del cosidetto 'Pacifismo,'" in *Opera*, V, 134.

76. "L'impresa disperata," in *Opera*, VI, 51; compare "Lo sviluppo del partito," in *Opera*, V, 122.

77. "Lo sviluppo del partito," in *Opera*, V, 122f.; "Da Guicciardini," in *Opera*, IV, 171–74; "Socialismo e sindacalismo," *Opera*, IV, 207f.

78. "Il Congresso di Modena," in *Opera*, IV, 237, 'Da Guicciardini," in *Opera*, IV, 174.

79. "Da Guicciardini," in *Opera*, IV, 173.

80. Cf. Mussolini's subscription to the judgments of Bourchet in "Dopo lo sciopero generale," in *Opera*, V, 256f.

81. "Il programma del Partito Socialista," in *Opera*, V, 325.

82. "Pio Battistini," in *Opera*, III, 172.

83. "Vecchiaia," in *Opera*, III, 131.

84. "La teoria sindacalista," in *Opera*, II, 124.

85. "Socialismo e socialisti," in *Opera*, I, 137, 138. *Mussolini* indicated the distinction between a theory of motivation and a technique utilizing the theoretical insights thus obtained. Mussolini indicated that the Sorelian myth was itself a theoretical product. "Il valore storico del socialismo," in *Opera*, VI, 77.

86. "L'impresa disperata," in *Opera*, VI, 48.

87. "Per il socialismo romagnolo," in *Opera*, IV, 147.

88. "La crisi dell'inazione," in *Opera*, IV, 124.

89. E. Ludwig, *Colloqui con Mussolini* (Verona, 1950), pp. 119f.

90. As cited in Begnac, *Palazzo Venezia*, p. 652.

91. *Ibid.*, p. 186.

92. "We do not have formulae." "La necessità della politica socialista in Italia," in *Opera*, I, 17.

93. "Socialism e movimento sociale nel secolo XIX," in *Opera*, I, 43.

94. "Uomini e idee: 'l'individuel et le social,'" in *Opera*, I, 73.

95. "Karl Marx," in *Opera*, I, 103.

96. Cf. for example, "Socialismo e socialisti," in *Opera*, I, 142, "Edmondo De Amicis, *ibid.*, 105, "Karl Marx," *ibid.*, 103, "Opinioni e documenti: la crisi risolutiva," *ibid.*, 69–70, "Socialismo e movimento sociale nel secolo XIX," *ibid.*, 43f.

97. "Socialismo e socialisti," in *Opera*, I, 143.

98. "Evoluzione sociale e lotta di classe," in *Opera*, II, 30.

99. Cited in De Begnac, *Palazzo Venezia*, p. 118. Mussolini's references to Taine, Desmoulins, and Michelet indicate this period as the probable reference.

100. "'La Voce,'" in *Opera*, II, 53.

101. "La teoria sindacalista," in *Opera*, II, 125.

102. "Studi socialisti: tentativi di revisionismo," in *Opera*, V, 205f.; cf. "Come perirono gli dei di Roma," in *Opera*, V, 280.

103. "Lo sviluppo del partito," in *Opera*, V, 123.

104. E. Leone, "Il Sindacalismo," in Melis, *op. cit.*, p. 122.

105. "Prefazione a 'Il socialismo rivoluzionario," in *Opera*, V, 175.

106. "Il Congresso di Brest," in *Opera*, V, 94; "Il valore attuale del socialismo," in *Opera*, VI, 182.

107. K. Marx, *The Poverty of Philosophy* (Moscow, n.d.), p. 196; "Evoluzione sociale e lotta di classe," in *Opera*, II, 31.

108. "Intermezzo polemico: attute de preludio," in *Opera*, VI, 273.

109. "'La Voce,'" in *Opera*, II, 55.

110. "La teoria sindacalista," in *Opera*, II, 127.

111. "'La Voce,'" in *Opera*, II, 53.

112. R. B. Perry, *The Thought and Character of William James* (Cambridge, Mass., 1948), pp. 313–16. Cf. Mussolini's references to *Leonardo* in "'La Voce,'" in *Opera*, II, 53, and G. Papini, *Pragmatismo* (Florence, 1943), p. 7.

113. Letter to T. Nanni, July 2, 1913, in *Opera*, V, 358.

114. W. James, *Pragmatism* (New York, 1955), pp. 47, 61, 107, 167.

115. S. Panunzio, "La persistenza del diritto," in Melis, *op. cit.*, p. 223; Prezzolini, *La teoria sindacalista*, pp. 247f.

116. As cited in De Begnac, *Palazzo Venezia*, p. 118. Perry cites this reference as stemming from an interview in 1926. Perry, *op. cit.*, p. 317.

117. James, *op. cit.*, p. 47.

118. Papini, *op. cit.*, pp. 98, 102.

119. "Note e letture," in *Opera*, IV, 46. This constitutes the "pragmatism" of syndicalism; cf. "Cronaca cittadina: Conferenza Tancredi," in *Opera*, IV, 79.

120. "Lo sciopero generale e la violenza," in *Opera*, II, 163.

121. Papini, *op. cit.*, pp. 183f.

122. *Ibid.*, p. 120.

123. "L'uomo e la divinità," in *Opera*, XXXIII, 17.

124. "Al lavoro," in *Opera*, III, 5f., "Il valore storico del socialismo," in *Opera*, VI, 82.

125. "Il valere storico del socialismo," in *Opera*, VI, 81.

126. "La teoria sindacalista," in *Opera*, II, 125, cf. "Al lavoro," in Opera, III, 7, "Lo sciopero generale e la violenza," in *Opera*, II, 163–68, "Dichiarazione, in *Opera*, II, 5, "La Commune di Parigi," in *Opera*, II, 41.

127. "I 'sinistri' alla riscossa," in *Opera*, V, 91.

128. "Only with collectivism is individualism conceivable and realizable," "Il socialismo oggi e domani," in *Opera*, VI, 41, "La filosofia della forza," in *Opera*, I, 175f.

129. "Shermaglie," in *Opera*, I, 136.

130. "Nella morta stagione," in *Opera*, II, 256; "I 'sinistri' alla riscossa," in *Opera*, V, 91; "'I Canti di Faunus,' di Antonio Beltamelli," in *Opera*, I, 196.

131. "Replica a Graziadei," in *Opera*, VI, 249f.

132. "'L'A. B. C. sindacale,'" in *Opera*, III, 40.

133. "Cio che v'ha di vivo e di morto nel Marxismo," in *Opera*, III, 367.

134. "Al lavoro, in *Opera*, III, 5. In "Al largo" (in *Opera*, VI, 5), Mussolini refers to the empirical propositions entertained by Marxists as true. The propositions that misery is increasing and concentration of capital continues under capitalism are conceived to be true. One could grant their truth and still not be an orthodox Marxist, as Mussolini makes evident. What distinguishes an orthodox Marxist is his interpretation of such propositions within the context of an entire theoretical system. Mussolini refused to interpret them "positivistically." He insisted on a "progmatic," or "idealistic," interpretation that would permit will and conscious purpose to function as determinants in any assessment of political eventualities.

135. "Il valore storico del socialismo," in *Opera*, VI, 75.

136. "Profeti e profezie," in *Opera*, III, 313.

137. *Ibid.*, 314.

138. "Intermezzo polemico: lotta politica e lotta di classe," in *Opera*, VI, 279.

139. "Il 'delirium tremens' nazionalista," in *Opera*, VI, 343.

140. "In tema di 'neutralità' Italiana," in *Opera*, VI, 318.

141. "Una caduta," in *Opera*, I, 10; "Lo scipero dei cantonieri: Zivio!" in *Opera*, II, 196, n.

142. Cf. "Il contradditorio di Voltre," in *Opera*, III, 137.

143. "Attorno a una formula," in *Opera*, V, 232.

144. "Dalla neutralità assoluta alla neutralità attiva ed operante," in *Opera*, VI, 402.

145. Colajanni, *op. cit.*, p. 433.

146. "L'impresa disperata," in *Opera*, VI, 48.

147. G. Barni, "Tripoli e il sindacalismo," in *Pagine libere*, V (December 1–15, 1911).

148. "Note di guerra," in *Opera*, VI, 321–23.

149. "La situazione internationale," in *Opera*, VI, 363.

150. Olivetti, "La guerra di Tripoli," in Melis, *op cit.*, p. 201.

151. "Note di guerra," in *Opera*, VI, 321.

152. "L'attuale momento politico e partiti politici in Italia," in *Opera*, III, 288.

153. "Il contradditorio di Voltre," in *Opera*, III, 137.

154. "Nazionalismo," in *Opera*, III, 281.

155. "La concentrazione della ricchezza e il 'profeta fallito,' " in *Opera*, III, 308.

156. "Dalla neutralità assoluta alla neutralità attive e operante," in *Opera*, VI, 400f.

157. "La polemica Mussolini-Tancredi: fra la paglia e il bronzo," in *Opera*, VI, 391.

158. "Le dimissioni da direttore dell' 'Avanti!' " in *Opera*, VI, 404–408; cf. Nolte, *op. cit.*, pp. 170f.

159. "La situazione internazionale e l'atteggiamento del partito," in *Opera*, VI, 427–28.

160. "Mussolini riconferma la sua avversione alla neutralità," in *Opera*, VI, 431.

161. Michels, *Political Parties*, p. 393.

162. Mussolini, *My Autobiography*, p. 46.

CHAPTER FOUR

1. R. M. MacIver, *The Web of Government* (New York, 1965), p. 183.

2. "Dottrina del fascimo," in *Opera*, XXXIV, 122.

3. "Per l'espulsione dal Partito," in *Opera*, VI, 40.

4. "'Se credono di avermi imbavagliato sbagliano,'" in *Opera*, VII, 46.

5. "La necessità dell'intervento," in *Opera*, VII, 67.

6. "Fronda," in *Opera*, VII, 127.

7. "Il dovere dell'Italia," in *Opera*, VII, 98.

8. "La necessità dell'intervento," in *Opera*, VII, 66; "Per la libertà dei popoli, per l'avvenire dell'Itallia," *Ibid.*, 78.

9. "Popolo e borghesia," in *Opera*, VIII, 71f.

10. "Il dovere dell'Italia," in *Opera*, VII, 101; cf. "L'inevitabile cimento," *ibid.*, p. 189.

11. "Un appello ai lavoratori d'Italia dei Fasci d'Azione Rivoluzionaria," in *Opera*, VII, 117.

12. "La situazione internazionale," in *Opera*, VII, 148.

13. "Dopo l'adunata," in *Opera*, VII, 152f.

14. "E guerra sia!" in *Opera*, VII, 419.

15. "Il sangue è sangue!" in *Opera*, VIII, 32; cf. "'Usque ad finem,'" *ibid.*, p. 84.

16. "Per la libertà dei popoli, per l'avvenire dell'Italia," in *Opera*, VII, 77.

17. "Se fosse vivo," in *Opera*, VIII, 105; "Intermezzo," in *Opera*, IX, 293.

18. "Divagazioni pel Centenario," in *Opera*, XI, 46f.

19. "Guerra di popoli," in *Opera*, VII, 73, 72; cf. "Ombre e penombre," in *Opera*, VII, 341–43.

20. "Il sangue è sangue!" in *Opera*, VIII, 31f.

21. Cf. "'L'armee nouvelle,'" in *Opera*, XI, 118–27.

22. "Per la libertà dei popoli, per l'avvenire dell'Italia," in *Opera*, VII, 79.

23. "Gli Herveisti del Galles," in *Opera*, VIII, 90f.

24. "L'attimo che fugge," in *Opera*, IX, 150f.

25. "Malessere," in *Opera*, X, 143.

26. "Abbasso il Parlamento!," in *Opera*, VII, 366.

27. "L'adunata," in *Opera*, VII, 139f.

28. "I morti che vivono," in *Opera*, VII, 120.

29. "L'attimo che fugge," in *Opera*, IX, 150.

30. "Trincerocrazia," in *Opera*, XI, 140–42.

31. "Divagazione," in *Opera*, XI, 270f.

32. "Divagazioni pel Centenario," in *Opera*, XI, 47.

33. "Il fucile e la vanga," in *Opera*, XI, 35.

34. "'Tu quoque,' Jouhaux?" in *Opera*, XI, 357f.

35. "Il sindacalismo nazionale: per rinascere!" in *Opera*, XII, 11–14.

36. "Nel mondo sindacale Italiano: rettifiche di tiro," in *Opera*, XII, 250.

37. "La politica nazionale: primo squillo," in *Opera*, XII, 223.

38. "Conquiste e programmi," in *Opera*, XII, 245.

39. Cf. R. Farinacci, *Storia della rivoluzione fascista* (Cremona, 1937), I, 121f.; Pini and Susmel, *op. cit.*, I, 387f.

40. "Discorso di Dalmine," in *Opera*, XII, 314.

41. "Atto di nascita del fascismo," in *Opera*, XII, 325.

42. V. Pareto, *Transformazione della democrazia* (Rocca San Casciano, 1964), p. 33.

43. "Atto di nascita del fascismo," in *Opera*, XII, 326f.

44. *Ibid.*, p. 325.

45. *Ibid.*, p. 323. He had used the expression "proletarian nation" to identify Italy on an earlier occasion; cf. "Un altro passo," in *Opera*, XII, 229. Mussolini's specific objection to the League of Nations was that it was used by the "plutocratic nations" to maintain their positions of privilege; cf. "Il fascismo e i problemi della politica estera Italiana," in *Opera*, XVI, 158; "Le linee programmatiche del Partito Fascista," in *Opera*, XVII, 177f.

46. "Discorso di Trieste," *Opera*, X, 216; "La Babele e il resto," in *Opera*, XVIII, 235f. The same conviction is reaffirmed in 1924; cf. "'Occorre luce di peniero, di cultura, d'idealità,'" in *Opera*, XXI, 160f.

47. "Forze e programmi," in *Opera*, XVII, 282.

48. "Nel solco delle grandi filosofie: relativismo e fascismo," in *Opera*, XVII, 269.

49. "Fascismo e sindacalismo," in *Opera*, XVIII, 226; "Programma," in *Opera*, XVII, 321; "Al popolo di Ferrara," in *Opera*, XVI, 248.

50. "Le linee programmatiche del Partito Fascista," in *Opera*, XVII, 174f.

51. "'Rimango il capo del fascismo,'" in *Opera*, XIX, 63; "Il programma fascista," in *Opera*, XVII, 221.

52. "Discorso di Piazza Belgioioso," in *Opera*, XIV, 124.

53. "Il discorso di Napoli," in *Opera*, XVIII, 457.

54. "Breve preludio," in *Opera*, XVIII, 19.

55. "L'azione e la dottrina fascista dinnanzi alle necessità storiche della nazione," in *Opera*, XVIII, 419.

56. Cf. the entire discussion in "Stato, antistato e fascismo," in *Opera*, XVIII, 258–63.

57. "Il diritto della vittoria," in *Opera*, XIV, 53.
58. "Il programma fascista," in *Opera*, XVII, 220.
59. De Begnac, *Palazzo Venezia*, p. 133.
60. "La filosofia della forza," in *Opera*, I, 175.
61. *Ibid.*
62. "Il socialismo oggi e domani," in *Opera*, VI, 41.
63. "Per Ferdinando Lassalle," in *Opera*, I, 65f.
64. "Vecchie usanze," in *Opera*, XIV, 194.
65. "Tra il vecchio e il nuovo: 'Navigare necesse,' " in *Opera*, XIV, 231f.
66. "Divagazione: l'ora e gli orologi," in *Opera*, XIV, 397.
67. "La marcia del fascismo," in *Opera*, XV, 299.
68. "Le linee programmatiche del Partito Fascista," in *Opera*, XVII, 174.
69. De Begnac, *Palazzo Venezia*, p. 133; cf. pp. 178f., 212f.
70. "Il programma fascista," in *Opera*, XVII, 221, 219.
71. "Discorso inaugurale al second Congresso dei Fasci," in *Opera*, XIV, 468.
72. "Il fascismo nel 1921," in *Opera*, XVII, 101f.
73. "Il primo discorso alla Camera dei Deputati," in *Opera*, XVI, 445.
74. "Programma e statuti del Partito Nazionale Fascista," in *Opera*, XVII, 335.
75. "Forze e programmi," in *Opera*, XVII, 282.
76. "Da che parte va il mondo?" in *Opera*, XVIII, 71.
77. "L'azione e la dottrina fascista dinnanzi alle necessità storiche della nazione," in *Opera*, XVIII, 414.
78. "Il programma fascista," in *Opera*, XVII, 220.
79. "I nostri postulati: per la storia di una settimana," in *Opera*, X, 87.
80. "L'azione e la dottrina fascista dinnanzi alle necessità storiche della nazione," in *Opera*, XVIII, 415.
81. "Adagio," in *Opera*, XVIII, 410.
82. "Fiera di 'Demos,' " in *Opera*, XVIII, 360.
83. "Nel solco delle grandi filosofie: relativismo e fascismo," in *Opera*, XVII, 268.
84. "Discorso di Monza," in *Opera*, XVI, 128; "Discorso di Piazza Belgioioso," *Ibid.*, p. 124; cf. "Illusioni e mistificazioni: il paradiso Leninista," *Ibid.*, p. 117.
85. Pareto, *Corso*, II, para. 1036.

86. Cf. "Ai fascisti della Lombardia," in *Opera*, XVI, 174; "Dopo due anni," *Ibid.*, p. 212; "Discorso di Piazza Belgioioso," *Ibid.*, p. 300; "Prefazione al programma," in *Opera*, XVII, 352.

87. "Atto di nascita del fascismo," in *Opera*, XII, 325.

88. "Nel mondo sindacale Italiano: rettifiche di tiro," in *Opera*, XII, 250.

89. "Sindacalismo," in *Opera*, XVIII, 386.

90. "Discorso di Piazza Belgioioso," in *Opera*, XVI, 300; cf. "Salandra," *Ibid.*, 320; "Discorso di Verona," *Ibid.*, 335, "Scoperte," in *Opera*, XVII, 186.

91. "Discorso di Piazza Belgioioso." in *Opera*, XVI, 301; "Discorso di Piazza Borromeo," *Ibid.*, p. 347; "Il discorso di Napoli," in *Opera*, XVIII, 459.

92. "Il Libro Bianco," in *Opera*, XVII, 278f.

93. "Dove impera Lenin," in *Opera*, XVII, 78; cf. "Sindacalismo Francese: una dichiarazione-programma," in *Opera*, XIV, 247.

94. "L'azione e la dottrina fascista dinnanzi alle necessità storiche della nazione," in *Opera*, XVIII, 419.

95. This is the conception of Jean Jaures, but it was a view of the ideal structure of the nation to which Mussolini subscribed and that remained constant throughout his political life. A similar conception of the organization of social forces was evident during his socialist period as well. " 'L'armee nouvelle,' " in *Opera*, VIII, 121.

96. H. Finer, *Mussolini's Italy* (New York, 1965), p. 146.

97. As cited in Meisel, *Genesis*, p. 230, and G. Pini, *The Official Life of Benito Mussolini* (London, 1939), p. 104.

98. P. Gorgolini, *Il fascismo nella vita Italiana* (Turin, 1923), p. 3. Originally published in 1921, but all references will be to the second edition.

99. *Ibid.*, p. 43.

100. *Ibid.*, pp. 33, 35, 131.

101. *Ibid.*, pp. 42–4.

102. *Ibid.*, pp. 48, 73f.

103. This is De Marsanich's contention and appears to be substantially correct. Cf. A. De Marsanich, *Lo stato nel ventennio fascista* (Rome, n.d.), p. 7.

104. As cited in Pini and Susmel, *op. cit.*, II, 259.

105. "Il primo discorso presidenziale alla Camera dei Deputati," in *Opera*, XIX, 15–24 and "Replica ai Deputati," *Ibid.*, pp. 25–28.

106. K. Marx, *Das Kapital, Werke* (Berlin, 1962), XXIII, 346. This is translated as "man is . . . a social animal" in *Capital* (Moscow, 1954), I, 326.

107. K. Marx, *Grundrisse der Kritik der politischen Oekonomie* (Berlin, 1953), p. 6.

108. Gumplowicz, *Outlines* p. 39.

109. Gumplowicz, *Die sociologische Staatsidee*, p. 211.

110. A. O. Olivetti, *Il sindacalismo come filosofia e come politica* (Milan, 1924), p. 28. Cf. G. Pighetti, *Sindacalismo fascista* (Milan, 1924), pp. 88, 143.

111. Olivetti, *Il sindacalismo come filosofia e come politica*, pp. 28, 30f., 92. Cf. I. Kant, *Anthropologie in pragmatischer Hinsicht* (Berlin, 1869), pp. 260–62.

112. B. Giuliano, *L'esperienza politica dell'Italia* (Florence, 1924), pp. 198–204.

113. *Ibid.*, p. 200.

114. S. Panunzio, *Lo stato fascista* (Bologna, 1925), p. 51. Cf. S. Panunzio, *Che cos'è il fascismo?* (Milan, 1924), p. 77.

115. S. Panunzio, "Principio e diritto di nazionalità," in *Popolo, nazione, stato* (Florence, 1933), p. 80. This essay was written in 1917. Cf. Panunzio's objections to the "atomistic and contractual" conception of society and the state: Panunzio, *Stato nazionale e sindacati* (Milan, 1924), p. 93.

116. Panunzio, *Che cos'è il fascismo?* p. 79; *Lo stato fascista*, pp. 21–30. Cf. M. Rocca, *Il primo fascismo* (Rome, 1964), p. 53.

117. "L'instaurazione dello stato fascista," in *Opera*, XIX, 82.

118. Pighetti, *op. cit.*, p. 18. The passage refers to the first formulation of the doctrinal commitments of fascist syndicalism made on the 24th of January, 1922, by Michele Bianchi.

119. *Ibid.*, p. 222; Panunzio, *Stato nazionale*, p. 38.

120. Panunzio conceived *jurisdictio* and *imperium* as one thing, not two. Cf. Panunzio, *Lo stato fascista*, pp. 92, 134; cf. "la riforma elettorale," in *Opera*, XIX, 316.

121. Panunzio, *Che cos'è il fascismo?* p. 16.

122. Cf. R. Farinacci, *Storia della rivoluzione fascista*, III, 230–262, particularly p. 256.

123. *Ibid.*, pp. 265, 238.

124. *Ibid.*, p. 265.

125. Panunzio, *Lo stato fascista*, p. 169; Pighetti, *op. cit.*, pp. 149, 155f.

126. "Forza e consenso," in *Opera*, XIX, 195; "La riforma elettorale," *Ibid.*, p. 310.

127. Panunzio, *Lo stato fascista*, pp. 145f.

128. E. Susmel, *Mussolini e il suo tempo* (Cernusco sul Naviglio, 1950), p. 179; cf. C. Quaglio, *Orientamenti della rivoluzione fascista* (Lucca, 1937), p. 69.

129. Rocca, *op. cit.*, pp. 191, 31f. Compare "Replica ai Senatori," in *Opera*, XIX, 47.

130. There are any number of competent accounts of the historic events that transpired during this period. I have found the accounts of H. Finer, *Mussolini's Italy* (New York, 1965) and H. W. Schneider, *Making the Fascist State* (New York, 1928) most serviceable.

131. "Sull'indirizzo di risposta al discorso della Corona," in *Opera*, XX, 317, cf. pp. 320, 324.

132. Cf. A. Rocco, *La trasformazione dello stato* (Rome, 1927), pp. 8f.

133. G. Bottai, *Experienza corporativa (1929–1935)* (Florence, n.d.), p. 22. Cf. S. Panunzio, *Il sentimento dello stato* (Rome, 1929), part II.

134. Cf. G. Bottai, *La Carta del Lavoro* (Rome, 1928), pp. 6f.; E. M. Olivetti, *Sindacalismo nazionale* (Milan, 1927), pp. 157–61; A. Turati, "The Labour Charter," in International Center of Fascist Studies, *A Survey of Fascism* (London, 1928), pp. 136–40. Contemporary neo-Fascists such as De Marsanich, *op. cit.*, pp. 9f., assign the same doctrinal significance to the *Carta*.

135. Part II of the *Dottrina*, that portion actually written by Mussolini, became the preamble to the Statutes of the Partito Nazionale Fascista in 1938.

136. S. Panunzio, *Il diritto sindacale e corporativo* (Perugia, 1930), pp. 38f., 46f. Vincenzo Zangara speaks of the *Carta* as "affirming general principles. . . ." V. Zangara, *Rivoluzione sindacale: lo stato corporativo* (Rome, 1927), p. 149.

137. "Il 'Fascismo,'" in *Opera*, XIII, 220.

138. "Dopo i fatti del 15 Aprile 1919," in *Opera*, XIII, 63; "Per un'azione politica," *Ibid.*, p. 209, "Il 'Fascismo,'" *Ibid.*, pp. 218f., "I diritti della vittoria," in *Opera*, XIV, 51.

139. "La prima adunata fascista," in *Opera*, XIV, 44.

140. "Per l'intesa e per l'azione fra gli interventisi di sinistra," in *Opera*, XIII, 252; "Chi possiede, paghi!" *Ibid.*, p. 224.

141. "Per i Fasci di Combattimento," in *Opera*, XIII, 113; "I postulati fondamentali del blocco fascista," in *Opera*, XIV, 111.

142. "Per un'azione politica," in *Opera*, XIII, 208; "Prima vittoria," *ibid.*, pp. 221f., "Sbrigatevi, signori!" *ibid.*, p. 265.

143. "Per l'intesa e per l'azione fra gli interventisti di sinistra," in *Opera*, XIII, 254.

144. Cf. A. Canepa, *Sistema di dottrina del fascismo* (Rome, 1937), I, 10ff.

145. In 1926, Puchetti insisted that fascism and its doctrine could be explicated on the basis of "strictly sociological considerations." A Puchetti, *Il fascismo scientifico* (Turin, 1926), p. 4.

146. "Dottrina del Fascismo," in *Opera*, XXXIV, 117.

147. For a contemporary review of the "organicistic" tradition, with some reference to its function in fascism, cf. M. Marotta, *Organicismo e neo-organicismo* (Milan, 1959).

148. These conceptions are developed, in essentially the same language, in Corso, *Lo stato fascista*, pp. 69–72. Cf. also Panunzio, *Popolo, nazione, stato*, pp. 13–28.

149. *Ibid.*, p. 70.

150. S. Raguso, *Elementi di scienza politica corporativa* (Florence, 1935), p. 28.

151. C. Gini, *Il neo-organicismo* (Catania, 1927), pp. 27, 42f.

152. C. Gini, "The Scientific Basis of Fascism," in *Political Science Quarterly*, XLII (March 1927), 102f.

153. A. Rocco, "The Political Doctrine of Fascism," in *Communism, Fascism and Democracy*, ed. C. Cohen (New York, 1964), pp. 341, 342f., 344.

154. In 1927, Rocco restated the fascist doctrine of society, the state, and the relationship with the individual in essentially the same manner. Cf. Rocco, *La trasformazione dello stato*, pp. 16f.

155. G. Bortolotto, *Faschismus und Nation* (Hamburg, 1932), pp. 32f.

156. Rocco, "The Political Doctrine of Fascism," p. 342.

157. Gini, *Il neo-organicismo*, p. 8.

158. Olivetti, *Il sindacalismo come filosofia e come politica*, pp. 11, 15, 21, 39, 40f. Cf. Corso, *op. cit.*, chap. 2.

159. A. Labriola, *Socialismo contemporaneo* (Naples, 1924), p. 303.

160. A. Labriola, "La patria come sentimento," in Melis, *op. cit.*, pp. 77f.

161. This harks back to Mazzini; cf. G. Mazzini, "Dell'unità italiana," in *Scritti editi e inediti* (Rome, 1906), II, 125. Cf. P. S. Mancini, *Prolusione al corso di diritto costituzionale* (Rome, 1931), as cited in C. Costamagna, *Dottrina del fascismo* (Turin, 1940), p. 187. Cf. Panunzio, *Popolo, nazione, stato*, pp. 14f.; C. Costamagna, *Elementi di* *diritto costituzionale corporativo fascista* (Florence, 1929), pp. 23–25.

162. Michels, "Patriotism," *First Lectures in Political Sociology,* p. 157. Cf. also his *Der Patriotismus. Prolegomena zu seiner soziologischen Analyse* (Munich, 1929).

163. Mussolini, in a letter to A. O. Olivetti, dated November 22, 1927, in *Opera,* XXIII, 301.

164. E. M. Olivetti, *Sindacalismo nazionale,* p. 95.

165. Costamagna, *Dottrina del fascismo,* p. 80.

166. *Ibid.,* p. 149; cf. Quaglio, *op. cit.,* p. 161; G. Bortolotto, *Massen und Fuehrer in der faschistischen Lehre* (Hamburg, 1934), p. 25.

167. Costamagna, *Elementi,* p. 19.

168. Raguso, *op. cit.,* p. 28.

169. Cf. S. Panunzio, *Il diritto sindacale e corporativo.*

170. Costamagna, *Dottrina del fascismo,* pp. 145f.

171. "Per la Medaglia dei Benemeriti del Commune di Milano," in *Opera,* XXI, 425.

172. "The Charter of Labor," in W. G. Welk, *Fascist Economic Policy* (Cambridge, 1938), p. 287. (Retranslated from the Italian.)

173. Partito Nazionale Fascista, *L'ordinamento dello stato fascista* (Rome, 1936), p. 27.

174. "Dottrina del fascismo," in *Opera,* XXXIV, 129.

175. This was a constant and recurring theme in statements of Fascist doctrine. G. Bortolotto, *Massen und Fuehrer in der faschistischen Lehre,* p. 13; P. Gorgolini, *Il fascismo spiegato al popolo* (Turin, 1935), pp. 69f.

176. Cf. Costamagna, *Dottrina del fascismo,* pp. 111f.

177. Canepa, *op. cit.,* 111, 78f.

178. V. Pareto, *The Mind and Society,* III, para. 1868.

179. Mussolini, in his Introduction to R. Korherr, *Regresso delle nascite, morte dei popoli* (Rome, 1928), p. 22, "Il numero come forza," in *Opera,* XXIII, 215.

180. Cf. Pareto's discussion of myths and sentiments in Pareto, *La trasformazione delle democrazia,* pp. 43–8.

181. Costamagna, *Dottrina del fascismo,* pp. 111, 129; C. Pellizzi, *Fascismo-aristocrazia* (Milan, 1924), p. 192; cf. Canepa, *op. cit.,* III, 79, n. 14.

182. O. di Giamberardino, *L'individuo nell'etica fascista* (Florence, 1940), p. 5.

183. The most notorious, though certainly not the only, author in this tradition was Julius Evola. In 1928, he insisted that Fascism must "oppose profane, democratic, and material science, always relative and conditional, the slave of phenomena and of incomprehensible laws, mute with respect to the profound reality of man. . . ." He insisted that "true" Fascism restore ". . . sacred, interior, and secret science . . . the science that leads to the occult forces that rule our organism. . . ." His appeal was to occult tradition. J. Evola, *Imperialismo pagano: il fascismo dinnanzi al pericolo Euro-Cristiano* (Rome, 1928), p. 12. Cf. J. Evola, *Rivolta contro il mondo moderno* (Milan, 1934). Generally, Fascist "mysticism" meant no more than some form of ethical idealism. Cf. E. Martinoli, *Funzione della mistica nella rivoluzione fascista* (Udine, 1940).

184. "Preludio al Machiavelli," in *Opera,* XX, 251–54.

185. Such convictions turn on a set of theoretical and descriptive generalizations expressed by Rocco in the following manner: "By a fundamental law of social life, which Maine calls the law of 'imitation,' the mass of men tend to follow the will of some dominating element, some so-called 'guiding spirits.' " A. Rocco, "The Transformation of the State," in *What is Fascism and Why?* ed. T. Sillani (New York, 1931), p. 22. Cf. A. Marpicati, *Il Partito Fascista* (Milan, 1938), p. 69; Partito Nazionale Fascista *La cultura fascista* (Rome, 1936), pp. 9–17.

186. Costamagna, *Dottrina del fascismo,* pp. 99–116.

187. Michels, *First Lectures in Political Sociology,* p. 126.

188. Partito Nazionale Fascista, *Il Partito Nazionale Fascista* (Rome, 1936), p. 50.

189. "Dottrina del fascismo," in *Opera,* XXXIV, 128.

190. There are a number of substantial accounts of the institutional structure of the Fascist Corporative State. Those that I have found most useful include: Welk, *op. cit.;* G. L. Field, *The Syndical and Corporative Institutions of Italian Fascism* (New York, 1938). Accounts in English of the early structure of the Corporative State can be found in A. Pennachio, *The Corporative State* (New York, 1927); C. Haider, *Capital and Labor under Fascism* (New York, 1930); F. Pitigliani, *The Italian Corporative State* (London, 1933); H. Goad, *The Making of the Corporate State* (London, 1934). A critical account can be found in C. Schmidt, *The Corporate State in Action: Italy under Fascism* (New York, 1939). Among the best accounts written by Fascists themselves are N. Jaeger, *Principii di diritto corporativo* (Padua, 1939); A. Serpieri, *Principii di economia politica corporativa* (Florence, 1944). The most comprehensive postwar Italian exposition is to be found in A. Aquarone, *L'organizzazione dello stato totalitario.* A collection of Fascist legislation governing the organization of the Corporative State can be found in *Codice corporativo e del lavoro* (Milan, 1940), 2 vols.

191. ". . . Fascism never raises the question of methods, using in its political praxis now liberal ways, now democratic means and at times even socialistic devices. This indifference to method often exposes Fascism to the charge of incoherence on the part of superficial observers, who do not see that what counts with us is the end and that therefore even when we employ the same means we act with a radically different spiritual attitude and strive for entirely different results. The Fascist concept then of the nation, of the scope of the state, and of the relations obtaining between society and its individual components, rejects entirely the doctrine which I said proceeded from the theories of natural law developed in the course of the sixteenth, seventeenth and eighteenth centuries and which for the basis of the liberal, democratic and socialistic ideology." Rocco, "The Political Doctrine of Fascism," p. 341.

CHAPTER FIVE

1. Vide H. Kohn, *Political Ideologies of the Twentieth Century* (New York, 1966), p. 149. Cf. H. Marcuse, *Reason and Revolution* (New York, 1954), p. 404.

2. Papini, *Pragmatismo,* p. 35. It is in this sense that Mussolini spoke of "action" having "buried" philosophy. "Il programma di Mussolini," in *Opera,* XVIII, 465.

3. Prezzolini, *La teoria sindacalista,* pp. 240–53.

4. Papini, pp. 19f., 95, 98, 110, 151, 199.

5. *Ibid.,* p. 115.

6. Schneider, *op. cit.,* p. 7; cf. Papini, p. 9.

7. Spirito wrote a searching criticism of pragmatism before the March on Rome. U. Spirito, *Il pragmatismo nella filosofia contemporanea* (Florence, 1921).

8. U. Spirito, *Inizio di una nuova epoca* (Florence, 1961), p. 229.

9. "Relativismo e fascismo," in *Opera,* XVII, 267–69. Mussolini apparently soon became embarrassed by the rank relativism he seemed to espouse in this brief essay and prohibited its republication in the so-called "definitive" edition of his works undertaken during the Fascist period. Cf. E. Susmel, *Venticinque scritti e un discorso di Benito Mussolini da lui proibiti* (Milan, 1950), pp. 189, 195.

10. "Not only does the dualism between matter and spirit not exist for us, we have overcome this antithesis in the synthesis of the spirit. The spirit alone exists, nothing more; neither you nor this hall, neither the things and objects that pass in the fantastic cinematography of the universe. They exist in so much as I think them and only in my thought, not independent of my thought. It is the spirit [*l'anima*], gentlemen, that has returned." "Per la vera pacificazione," in *Opera,* XVII, 298.

11. Spirito, *Inizio di una nuova epoca,* pp. 229–33. Because the relationship between Gentilean idealism and pragmatism had been so close it was necessary, years later, to emphasize the differences. Cf. F. Modica-Cannizzo, "Antiprammatismo e antiattivismo di Giovanni Gentile," *GG,* II, 121–27.

12. Cf. G. Gentile, *La filosofia Italiana contemporanea* (Florence, 1941), pp. 48–51; *OD,* pp. 38f.; 58, *CF,* 47, 98; F. Chilanti, "Il popolo e l'intelligenza," *Gerarchia,* XIX (September, 1940), 481–83; O. Valle, "Dell'intelligenza fascista," *Gerarchia,* XIX (October, 1939), 702–3.

13. Cf. the similar definition suggested by Lasswell and Larner. H. Lasswell and D. Lerner, *World Revolutionary Elites: Studies in Coercive Ideological Movements* (London, 1966), p. 17.

14. "Socialismo e socialisti," in *Opera,* I, 142; cf. p. 139.

15. "Dottrina del Fascismo," in *Opera,* XXXIV, 117.

16. "Al congresso delle scienze prima del quarto attentato," in *Opera,* XXII, 251.

17. Cf. "All 'Assemblea delle Corporazione," in *Opera,* XXVI, 379, and "Discorso del XIII Gennaio per lo Stato Corporativo," *Ibid.,* pp. 86–96.

18. "Dottrina del fascismo," in *Opera,* XXXIV, 122.

19. "Da che parte va il mondo," in *Opera,* XVIII, 70f.

20. This is true of his political thought in general, but an explicit statement to this effect is found as early as "Il 'PUS' a congresso," in *Opera,* XVI, 116, 117.

21. "Dottrina del fascismo," in *Opera,* XXXIV, 117.

22. Canepa, *op. cit.,* III, 57, n. 5. cf. G. S. Spinetti, *Fascismo e libertà* (Padua, 1941), chaps. i, ii.

23. Canepa, III, 65.

24. Panunzio, *Lo stato fascista,* pp. 15f.

25. Volpicelli, *Motivi su Mussolini,* p. 18.

26. L. Volpicelli, "La realtà storica del Fascismo," in *Educazione Fascista,* VIII (1929), 580.

27. "Fascist doctrine is not a philosophy in the common sense of the word. . . . Fascism is opposed to abstract and intellectualistic philosophies. . . . The Fascist, because of the patrimony of certain Marxist

and Sorelian insights (since many Fascists and the Duce himself received their first intellectual education in the school of Marx and Sorel) as well as the influence of contemporary Italian idealist doctrines in which Fascist mentality matured, conceives philosophy as philosophy of practice." *OD*, pp. 37, 58.

28. "La filosofia della forza," in *Opera*, I, 174; cf. "La teoria sindacalista," in *Opera*, II, 128, and "Alla nuova sede dei mutilati," in *Opera*, XIX, 168f.

29. Mussolini, as cited in G. A. Chiurco, *Storia della rivoluzione fascista* (Florence, 1929), I, 201.

30. "Navigare necesse," in *Opera*, XIV, 231.

31. "Aspetti del dramma," in *Opera*, X, 8.

32. ". . . one must not imagine that Fascism has been without theory. This would be a very grave error." "Fascismo e nazionalismo," in *Opera*, XIX, 162.

33. "Al congresso dei filosofi," in *Opera*, XXIV, 109.

34. Mussolini, letter to Bianchi, August 26, 1921, in *Opera*, XVII, 415.

35. M. Marchello, *La morale eroica del fascismo* (Turin, 1934), p. 14; G. Gentile, "La formazione politica della coscienza nazionale," in *Educazione Fascista*, VIII (1930), 675.

36. Canepa, *op. cit.*, I, 15, n. 1.

37. *Ibid.*, n. 2. Cf. also, A. Carlini, *Filosofia e religione nel pensiero di Mussolini* (Rome, 1934), p. 11.

38. Cf. *Opera*, XXXIV, vi.; Pini and Susmel, *op. cit.*, III, 255; N. Tripodi, *Vita e ideali di Giovanni Gentile* (Rome, 1954), p. 16; Harris, *op. cit.*, pp. 188f.

39. Cf. Canepa, *op. cit.*, III, 17; Martinoli, *op. cit.*, p. 13.

40. Some of the most important Fascist theoreticians, including Panunzio, Costamagna, Canepa, and Tripodi, attempted to disassociate the philosophy of Fascism from that of Gentile.

41. G. Gentile, "Discorso agli Italiani," in *GG*, IV, 67; cf. A. Carlini, "Studi Gentiliani," in *GG*, VIII, 115.

42. Cf. Gentile's letter to Mussolini on the occasion of Gentile's formal entry into the *Partito Nazionale Fascista;* Harris, *op. cit.*, pp. 167f.

43. De Begnac, *Palazzo Venezia*, p. 133.

44. A. Labriola, *Studio su Marx* (Naples, 1926), p. 42, n. 37. This volume was originally published in 1908 and the second edition was unaltered.

45. Pini and Susmel, *op. cit.*, I, 279.

46. Mannhardt, *op. cit.*, p. 114; Schneider, *op. cit.*, p. 102.

47. De Begnac, *Palazzo Venezia*, p. 130.

48. *Ibid.*, p. 158.

49. Mussolini, letter to M. Bianchi, August 26, 1921, in *Opera*, XVII, 414f.

50. B. Croce, *Storia d'Italia dal 1871 al 1915* (Bari, 1942), pp. 279f.; cf. Carlini, *Filosofia e religione nel pensiero di Mussolini*, p. 14; "Studi Gentiliana," in *GG*, VIII, 106.

51. "Il primo discorso alla Camera dei Deputati," in *Opera*, XVI, 440.

52. Cf. "Al congresso delle scienze prima del quarto attentato," in *Opera*, XXII, 251; Volpicelli, *op. cit.*, p. 22.

53. Cesare Rossi, an intimate of Mussolini at this time, maintained that Mussolini's knowledge of Gentile in 1922 was "very vague"; C. Rossi, *Trentatre vicende Mussoliniane* (Milan, 1958), p. 423. Rossi harbors a most emphatic (and understandable) anti-Mussolini bias which should be weighed in assessing his judgments.

54. Harris, *op. cit.*, pp. 160f.

55. Mussolini's speech of December 1, 1921, before the Chamber, in which he took up a commitment to epistemological idealism, contains a paraphrase of Gentile's first two chapters in the *Teoria generale*. Compare "Per la vera pacificazione," in *Opera*, XVII, 298, with Gentile, *Teoria generale dello spirito come atto puro* (Bari, 1924), chaps. i and ii. This edition is substantially unchanged from the edition of 1916.

56. De Begnac, *Palazzo Venezia*, p. 212.

57. Harris, *op. cit.*, p. 189, n. 72.

58. Cf. N. Tripodi, *Commento a Mussolini: Note sulla "Dottrina del fascismo"* (Rome, 1956), p. 10.

59. "L'uomo e la divinità," in *Opera*, XXXIII, 22.

60. *GS*, p. 44.

61. Gentile insisted that the conception of the state was the essential commitment of fascism, a judgment with which Mussolini concurred. Cf. *CF*, p. 103; *OD*, pp. 42f.; "Dottrina del fascismo," in *Opera*, XXXIV, 129; "All'Assemblea Quinquennale del Regime," in *Opera*, XXIV, 15.

62. Tripodi, *Commento a Mussolini*, p. 20.

63. *IF*, p. 181.

64. *RE*, p. 28.

65. Cf. *GS*, p. 14; *FD*, pp. 103f.; *IF*, p. 182; M. Aebischer, *Der Einzelne und der Staat nach Giovanni Gentile* (Freiburg, 1954), p. 56.

66. A. D. Lindsay, in his objections to Mill, maintains: "Real liberty is possible, not in a world where we have no relations with other people, but where our relations with them are the expression of reason. In so far, therefore, as the state substitutes ordered and reasonable interference for the arbitrary interference of individuals, it increases freedom." Introduction to J. S. Mill, *Utilitarianism, Liberty and Representative Government* (New York, 1950), p. xxv.

67. Cf. *RE*, pp. 20f.; *GS*, pp. 60, 65f., 109f., 115.

68. Cf. *PF*, p. 53.

69. *FD*, p. 105, cf. p. 108.

70. *GS*, p. 15.

71. *GS*, pp. 33, 38.

72. *GS*, p. 44.

73. *GS*, p. 15.

74. *GS*, p. 16.

75. Cf. Puchetti, *op. cit.*, p. 112.

76. *RE*, pp. 8–16.

77. Cf. *CF*, pp. 10f.

78. *RE*, p. 14.

79. *CF*, p. 34.

80. *FD*, p. 67.

81. *CF*, pp. 34, 47, 51; *GS*, p. 58.

82. *IF*, p. 180.

83. Cf. G. Pannese, *L'etica nel fascismo e la filosofia del diritto e della storia* (Rome, 1942), pp. 149f.; Costamagna, *Dottrina del fascismo*, pp. 337–65; Corso, *op. cit.*, pp. 44f.

84. *RE*, pp. 24f.

85. *OD*, pp. 49, 63. Cf. S. Longhi's Preface to A. Sermonti, *Diritto sindacale Italiano* (Rome, 1929), I, ix.

86. *FD*, p. 111.

87. Cf. V. Bellezza, *L'esistenzialismo positivo di Giovanni Gentile* (Florence, 1954), chap. x.

88. Cf. U. Spirito, *Capitalismo e corporativismo* (Florence, 1933), p. 29; Corso, *op. cit.*, p. 34.

89. *FD*, pp. 67, 81; cf. G. Maggiore, "Il problema del diritto nel pensiero di Giovanni Gentile," *GG*, I, 236.

90. *FD*, p. 80.

91. *GS*, p. 57.

92. *GS*, p. 58.

93. *CF*, pp. 90f.; *IF*, p. 183.

94. "The Fascist conception of the state differs profoundly from that of liberalism and democracy with regard to subjective political

rights and the liberty of citizens. In fact, the Fascist state does not recognize individual rights that prevail against the state; rather political rights and liberties are *concessions* that the state makes to citizens 'in order that they might conduct themselves under its authority in a manner conducive to social well-being.' " Pannese, *op. cit.*, p. 161.

95. Cf. particularly Panunzio, *Popolo, nazione, stato* and *L'ordinamento dello stato fascista*, pp. 19–26.

96. *CF*, p. 36; cf. p. 50.

97. *OD*, pp. 63f.; "La costituzionalizzazione del Gran Consiglio del Fascismo," in *Educazione fascista*, VI (February, 1928), 86f.

98. *CF*, pp. 109f.; *GS*, pp. 58f.; *FD*, pp. 117f.

99. Pannese, *op. cit.*, p. 158.

100. *GS*, pp. 32, 34, 39.

101. Cf. *DR*, p. 88.

102. *GS*, p. 48.

103. *OD*, p. 59.

104. *OD*, pp. 9f.; cf. Harris, *op. cit.*, p. 219.

105. *OD*, p. 59; *L'ordinamento dello stato fascista*, pp. 49–51.

106. "Dottrina del fascismo," in *Opera*, XXXIV, 117–20.

107. Cf. Harris, *op. cit.*; P. A. Zacchi, *Il nuovo idealismo Italiano di B. Croce e G. Gentile* (Rome, 1925); U. Spirito, *L'idealismo Italiano e i suoi critici* (Florence, 1930); N. Papafava, *L'idealismo assoluto* (Milan, n.d.); E. Chiocchetti, *La filosofia di Giovanni Gentile* (Milan, 1922).

108. Costamagna, *Dottrina del fascismo*, pp. 9, 31.

109. *OD*, pp. 22, 38.

110. *RE*, p. 11.

111. *GS*, p. 125.

112. *CF*, p. 51.

113. *GS*, pp. 59f.

114. *RE*, p. 34.

115. *IF*, pp. 177f., 179.

116. *RE*, p. 26.

117. *CF*, p. 193.

118. *GS*, p. 136.

119. Cf. "Il fascismo nella cultura," in *CF*, pp. 95–116, particularly p. 104.

120. *GS*, pp. 134–36.

121. Costamagna, *Dottrina del fascismo*, p. 13. G. Guizzardi argued that "Man is tired of justifying, explaining, reasoning. . . . Men have forgotten Reason. They desire Faith and invoke the Myth." G. Guizzardi,

"Dalla 'Ragione' alla 'Fede,'" in *Gerarchia*, XIX (April, 1940), 197, 198.

122. Costamagna, *Dottrina del fascismo*, p. 26.

123. Evola, *Imperialismo pagano*, p. 76.

124. Cf. J. Evola, *Gli uomini e le rovine* (Rome, 1953); "Gentile non è il nostro filosofo," in *Minoranza*, II (August–October, 1959), 22–7.

125. "Preludio a Machiavelli," in *Opera*, XX, 252, cf. pp. 251–4.

126. *Ibid.*, p. 253. Cf. also Mussolini's remarks in "Soliloquio in 'libertà' all'Isola Trimellone," in *Opera*, XXXII, 178.

127. "Pensieri Pontini e Sardi," in *Opera*, XXXIV, 286.

128. *CF*, p. 100.

129. "Il fascismo è una 'rivolta spirituale,'" in *Opera*, XX, 149.

130. Cf. Costamagna, *Dottrina del fascismo*, pp. 133f.

131. The only counterevidence for this assertion is Mussolini's admission that he "infected" socialism with "a little bit of Bergson." Since he did not indicate precisely what elements of Bergsonianism he advocated, it is difficult to make anything of this remark. On the other hand, as we have indicated, Mussolini did reject Sorel's intuitive mysticism. Cf. "Il primo discorso alla Camera dei Deputati," in *Opera*, XVI, 440. Nonetheless, the convenience of such a tactic led many Fascists to insist that "beyond truth and error there is the myth, the mystic force, since in order to act demonstration is not necessary; only belief is required." Such notions are consistent with Mussolini's theory of motivation, not necessarily with his conceptions of truth. F. Forni, "Fascismo e filosofia," in *Gerarchia*, XVIII (August, 1938), 579.

132. "If by mysticism one means the power to comprehend truth without the assistance of intelligence, I would be the first to declare myself opposed to any mysticism." As cited in De Begnac, *Palazzo Venezia*, p. 186. Thus, Spinetti described Fascist mysticism as essentially that moral discipline "intimate and reasonable," having no relationship to "transcendental or irrational" truth claims. Fascist mysticism could be "rationally explicated even if to some it remains as yet indemonstrable by reason and relegated to those things believed by faith, without discussion." G. S. Spinetti, "Nostra mistica," *Gerarchia*, XVIII (February, 1938), 79, 80, 81.

133. M. Palmieri, *The Philosophy of Fascism* (Chicago, 1936), pp. 70f. Calza maintained, in opposition, that "following Mussolini, the architect of a civilization, is a question of intelligence. . . . Following a man of genius is not, in fact, a political sentiment. . . ." G. Calza, "Intelligenza del fascismo," *Gerarchia*, XIX (May, 1939), 316.

134. Palmieri, *op. cit.*, p. 69. A. Zapponi spoke of the "mysticism" that manifested itself as the sense of "unity that merged the individual in the collectivity and the collectivity with the entire land and nation in that unwritten law that . . . is a law of human nature." This would function as Gentile's "sentiment," the initial impulse of spiritual life. But Zapponi goes on to speak of the manifestations of such sentiment as "irrational impulse," something that Gentile would consider outside the range of moral concerns. A. Zapponi, "P.N.F. Mistica fascista," *Gerarchia*, XIX (March, 1940), 157, 158.

135. Costamagna, *Dottrina del fascismo,* pp. 340, 341.

136. Pellegrini-Giampietro, *op. cit.*, pp. 68, 69, 73. Cf. in this regard, M. Rivoire, "Mistica fascista e mistica totalitaria," in *Gerarchia* XIX (March, 1940), 132; M. Jannelli, "Il dominio dello spirito nello stato fascista," in *Gerarchia*, XVIII (January, 1938), 3; A. Assanta, "Stato spirituale," in *Gerarchia*, XII (August, 1934), 666.

137. Martinoli, *op. cit.*, pp. 23–32; Carlini, *op. cit.*, p. 60.

138. Mussolini's Preface to Oriani, *op. cit.*, p. v; "Alfredo Oriani," in *Opera*, XX, 244–46.

139. Oriani, *op. cit.*, p. 243.

140. Di Giamberardino, *op. cit.*, pp. 60f., 62f., 65.

141. Carlini, *op. cit.*, p. 60.

142. Ludwig, *op. cit.*, pp. 129, 119.

143. Silus, "Civiltà, aristocrazia, intelligenza," in *Gerarchia*, XIX (March, 1939), 162f.; B. Damiani, "Democrazie authoritarie," in *Gerarchia*, XVIII (July, 1938), 485.

144. P. Ubaldi, "Per una realistica filosofia del fascismo," in *Gerarchia*, XVIII (September, 1938), 620, 621.

145. F. Paoloni, *Sistema rappresentativo del fascismo* (Rome, 1937), pp. 220f.

146. W. Cesarini Sforza, "La Camera dei Fasci e delle Corporazioni," in *La Camera dei Fasci e delle Corporazioni* (Florence, 1937), p. 250.

147. Ludwig, *op. cit.*, pp. 122, 123.

148. Cf. "Soliloquio in 'libertà' all'Isola Trimellone," in *Opera,* XXXII, 170.

149. *Ibid.*, p. 178.

150. Aquarone, *op. cit.*, has provided a brief but competent attempt at analysis. Cf. also D. L. Germino, *The Italian Fascist Party in Power. A Study in Totalitarian Rule* (Minneapolis, 1959).

151. G. Battaglini, "Stato fascista, stato di popolo," in *Gerarchia*, XII (May, 1934), 361; A. Fiaccadori, "L'autorità del fascismo," in *Gerarchia*, XII (October, 1934), 859. Cf. A. Navarra, "Governo e governati in regime fascista," in *La Camera dei Fasci e delle Corporazioni,* p. 166; Paoloni, *op. cit.,* p. 114.

152. S. Panunzio, "Contributo all'esame dei problemi alla istituzione della Camera dei Fasci e delle Corporazioni," in *La Camera dei Fasci e delle Corporazioni,* p. 228.

153. Di Giamberardino, *op. cit.,* pp. 303f. This is a paraphrase of Gentile (*OD,* p. 9), but the implications were obviously different.

154. Michels, *First Lectures in Political Sociology,* chap. vi.

155. Friedrich and Brzezinski, *op. cit.,* pp. 24f.

156. Bottai, *Vent'anni e un giorno,* p. 196.

157. "Pensieri Pontini e Sardi," in *Opera,* XXXIV, 278.

158. G. Gentile, "Ricostruire," in *GG,* IV, 86f.

159. *OD,* pp. 43f.

160. Tripodi, *Commento a Mussolini,* p. 19; cf. p. 14.

CHAPTER SIX

1. Cf. Susmel, *op. cit.,* chap. xxix; Roux, *op. cit.,* pp. 261f., 277; Bardech, *op. cit.,* chap. ii; J. Evola, *Il fascismo* (Rome, 1964), p. 95.

2. Nolte, *op. cit.,* p. 240.

3. Turin, 1962.

4. "Al Consiglio Nazionale del P.N.F.," in *Opera,* XXIX, 190.

5. Cf. "Il Partito e il razzismo Italiano," in *Difesa della razza* (hereafter referred to as *Difesa*), I (August 5, 1938), 2; E. Leoni, *Mistica del razzismo fascista* (Padua, 1941), pp. 19–27.

6. "Discorso di Bologna," in *Opera,* XVI, 239, 240, 243.

7. "La vittoria fatale," in *Opera,* XI, 81.

8. "Al popolo di Cagliari," in *Opera,* XIX, 267f.; "Il primo anniversario della Marcia su Roma," in *Opera,* XX, 64; "Per la Sagra dei Combattenti," in *Opera,* XIX, 288.

9. "La politica interna al Senato," in *Opera,* XXI, 201; "Il venticinquennio del Regno di Vittorio Emanuele III," in *Opera,* XXI, 343.

10. "Discorso di Genova," in *Opera,* XXII, 138.

11. R. Michels, *Lavoro e razza* (Milan, 1924), p. lx, cf. p. 1, n. 1.

12. Marinetti, *op. cit.,* pp. 25, 51, 60, 64, 67, 68, 79, 87, 90, 95, 101, 103, 109, 110, 111, 113, 114, 123, 136, 137, 174, 175, 176, 191, 198, 199, 200, 206, 208f., 210, 212, 218, 219, 228, 242.

13. *Ibid.,* p. 19.

14. *Ibid.,* p. 113.

15. *Ibid.,* 174, 175.

16. *Ibid.*, p. 199.

17. *Ibid.*, pp. 198–200.

18. "Discorso di Bologna," in *Opera*, XVI, 243; cf. "Al popolo di Piacenza," in *Opera*, XIX, 272.

19. Cf. Michels, *Lavoro e razza*, pp. 4, 97.

20. Pareto, *The Mind and Society* (New York, 1935), paras. 664, n. 3; 729; 779, n. 1; 782; 784; 2236, n. 1.

21. "Agli operai del Poligrafico," in *Opera*, XIX, 115.

22. Cf. A. Rocco, *Scritti e discorsi politici* (Rome, 1938), 1, 9, 71, 88; cf. De Felice, *op. cit.*, p. 33.

23. "Il discorso dell'ascensione," in *Opera*, XXII, 363, cf. pp. 361–63; "Il programma fascista," *Opera*, XVII, 219; vide also "Sintesi del regime," in *Opera*, XXVI, 190–91.

24. B. Spampanato, *Contromemoriale* (Rome, 1952), 11, 131.

25. Oriani, *op. cit.*, p. 112.

26. "Il numero come forza," in *Opera*, XXIII, 210.

27. Corradini, *L'ombra della vita*, pp. 170–73.

28. "I complici," in *Opera*, XIII, 169f. A year after this apparent identification of the Jews with Bolshevism, Mussolini explicitly affirmed that "Bolshevism, as it is thought, is not a Jewish phenomenon. . . ." "Ebrei, Bolscevismo e Sionismo Italiano," in *Opera*, XV, 269. Many Jews, by this time, were providing significant financial support to the first Fascist groups. Elias Jona, in fact, appears to have been one of the principal supporters of Mussolini's *Il Popolo d'Italia*. Cf. de Felice, *Storia*, p. 85; and De Begnac, *Vita di Benito Mussolini*, III, 603–9

29. I. Horowitz, *Radicalism and the Revolt against Reason: The Social Theories of Georges Sorel* (New York, 1961), pp. 39ff., n. 1; cf. J. Meisel, *The Genesis of Georges Sorel* (Ann Arbor, 1951), pp. 86, 176–80.

30. "It is ridiculous to think that one should close the Synagogues! The Jews were here in the times of prerepublican Rome. Perhaps they furnished the clothing after the rape of the Sabine women. There were fifty thousand of them in Rome at the time of Augustus and they requested permission to weep at the bier of Julius Caesar. They will remain unmolested. . . ." "Relazione alla Camera dei Deputati sugli Accordi del Laterano," in *Opera*, XXIV, 82; cf. Ludwig, *op. cit.*, p. 72.

31. M. Sarfatti, *Dux* (Milan, 1929).

32. De Felice, *Storia*, p. 277.

33. R. MacGregor-Hastie, *The Day of the Lion* (New York, 1963), p. 199.

34. Cf. Gentile, *Guerra e fede* (Naples, 1919), pp. 48–52; Harris, *op. cit.*, p. 133.

35. Marinetti, *op. cit.*, p. 199.

36. Gentile, *Guerra e fede*, pp. 156–61.

37. *Ibid.*, pp. 309–14; Harris, p. 139.

38. Cf. Pini and Susmel, *op. cit.*, I, 279; MacGregor-Hastie, *op. cit.*, p. 97.

39. Marinetti himself remained a Fascist and was honored by a state funeral when he died in 1944. Amicucci, *op. cit.*, pp. 195f.

40. Cf. E. Corradini, *La rinascita nazionale* (Florence, 1929), p. 147; Pighetti, *op. cit.*, p. 13; Panunzio, *Popolo nazione, stato*, pp. 14f.; cf. S. Raguso, *Elementi di scienza politica corporativa* (Florence, 1935), pp. 93f.; Bottai, *La Carta del Lavoro*, p. 137.

41. Cf. Olivetti, *Il sindacalismo come filosofia e come politica.*

42. Olivetti, *Sindacalismo nazionale*, pp. 172f.

43. Panunzio, *Stato nazionale e sindacati*, p. 35; Pighetti, *op. cit.*, p. 18.

44. Corso, *op. cit.*, pp. 34f.

45. Corradini, *Rinascita*, p. 144.

46. E. Santarelli, "Dal nazionalismo al razzismo," in *Difesa*, IV (January 5, 1941), 26f.

47. G. Acerbo, *I fondamenti della dottrina fascista della razza* (Rome, 1940), p. 25.

48. Cf N. Timofeeff-Ressowsky, "Genetica ed evoluzione," and "Sulla questione dell'isolamento territoriale entro popolazioni specifiche," in *Scientia Genetica*, I (1939); Gini, *Nascita*, p. 100, n. 31.

49. Acerbo, *op. cit.*, p. 26.

50. A Capasso, *Idee chiare sul razzismo* (Rome, 1942), p. 21; cf. Landra, "La razza italiana nella teoria dell'ologenesi," in *Difesa*, II (April 5, 1939), 10.

51. Capasso, *op. cit.*, p. 23; cf. Acerbo, *op. cit.*, p. 25; E. Canevari, "La politica di razza e il nuovo ordine europeo," in *Difesa*, IV (August 5, 1941), 9.

52. M. Canella, *Lineamenti di antropobiologia* (Florence, 1943), 8.

53. *Ibid.*, p. 4; M. Canella, *Razze umane estinte e viventi* (Florence, 1942), p. 8.

54. Capasso, p. 26; G. Landra, "L'influenza della città sulla forma della testa," in *Difesa*, IV, (December 20, 1940), 28–30; "Studi sull'aumento della statura in Scandinavia," in *Difesa*, IV (January 5, 1941); "Caratteri fisici della razza italiana," in *Difesa*, I (September 5, 1938), 12; Marro, *op cit.*, p. 13.

55. "Human societies, ethnic groups [*etnie*], nations, are concrete realities, essential expressions of the complex human psyche, developed as a consequence of the interaction of factors of diverse order, biological, geographic, climatic, historic, and social. In an ethnic group that is well individualized, historically and politically well integrated, even if racially relatively heterogeneous, a common civil life, common laws, common usages and customs, a common language, a common official religion, a common soil, a common state education, a common cultural climate, the same collective aspirations and ideals can, conjoined with the mixture of blood of the various races and regional subraces, produce a new mean racial type . . . . A nation, therefore, and this is the opinion of many anthropologists, can constitute the crucible of a new race in formation." Canella, *Lineamenti,* p. 8. Cf. Maggiore, *op. cit.,* pp. 204f.; Capasso, p. 18, 26.

56. Acerbo, p. 23.

57. Cf. Gini, *Nascita,* pp. 72ff.

58. A Solmi, "L'unità etnica della nazione italiana nella storia," in *Difesa,* I (August 5, 1938), 8–11; G. Landra, "Biondi e bruni nella razza italiana," in *Difesa,* I (September 20, 1938), 26–28.

59. Marro, *op. cit.,* p. 32; Canella, *Razze umane,* p. 18.

60. Canella, *Razze umane,* p. 17.

61. Maggiore, *op. cit.,* p. 41.

62. Capasso, *op. cit.,* p. 34.

63. *Ibid.,* pp. 28f.

64. *Ibid.,* pp. 31f.

65. Pareto, *Corso,* II, paras. 991, 992, and 992 n. 2.

67. N. Pende, "Il principio biotipologico unitario," in *Gerarchia,* XX, 1 (1940), 569–72.

68. ". . . All races give evidence of hybrid origin. Group sentiment, determined by physical, social, cultural, or administrative factors (race, caste, city, state, and so forth) and the hostility directed against adjacent groups serves to isolate, and in isolation to accomplish the gradual complete fusion of the mixed groups. This is the biological function of group sentiment. And it is understood that in such a fashion . . . the nation can be defined as a group of persons possessing a proper individuality, not only from the point of view of politics and culture, but also from the biological point of view. Political and social individuality inevitably brings with it a certain measure of isolation, which has the effect of producing characteristic biological features in the nation . . . . All human races are, as is often maintained today, of hybrid origin, in the sense that all derive from recent or remote genetic intermixture; there are in this sense no pure races but races which have become purified. . . .

"The populations of Nordic provenience which invaded the Roman Empire established themselves as suzerains over its territory and at first maintained themselves apart from the Latin population. In a successive period, when Latin civilization prevailed and was assimilated by the Germanic elements, the two races gradually merged and in time a new race was formed from which proceeded a new nation." C. Gini, *Nascita, evoluzione e morte delle nazione* (Rome, 1930), pp. 100, 86.

69. *Ibid.*, p. 89, n. 2.

70. Canella, *Principi*, p. viii.

71. Cf. A. Keith, *Nationality and Race from an Anthropologist's Point of View* (London, 1919), and *The Place of Prejudice in Modern Civilization* (New York, 1931).

72. (Turin, 1941), I, 300, 297.

73. Canella, *Razze umane*, p. 18.

74. *Ibid.*, p. 16. G. Landra, "Due anni di razzismo Italiano," in *Difesa,* III (July 5, 1940), 14. Cf. U. Redanò, "Dottrina Italiana della razza," in *Difesa,* III (November 20, 1939), 14f.; R. S. Salis, "Difesa legislativa della razza," in *Difesa,* III (April 5, 1940), 38; A. Modica, "Origine e classificazione della razza Italiana," in *Difesa,* IV (July 20, 1941), 21–4.

75. G. Landra, "Il convegno sul concetto di razza," in *Difesa,* III (February 20, 1940), 17f. Actually, Montandon employed a slightly modified vocabulary and referred to nations as "sub-ethnic" rather than "ethnic" communities that were developing or had developed into regional or parish races.

76. G. Montandon, "L'etnie putaine," in *Difesa,* III (November 5, 1939), 19.

77. Cf. A. Keith, *Evolution and Ethics* (New York, 1947), *A New Theory of Human Evolution* (New York, 1949).

78. Cf. A. J. Gregor, *Contemporary Radical Ideologies* (New York, 1968), chap. v.

79. S. Blaas, *Der Rassegedanke: seine biologische und philosophische Grundlegung* (Berlin, 1940), pp. 203, 240f.

80. Cf. De Felice, *Storia*, p. 295.

81. Canella, *Principi*, pp. 18–20.

82. P. Orano, *Gli Ebrei in Italia* (Rome, 1937); vide also P. Orano, ed., *Inchiesta sulla Razza* (Rome, 1940), pp. 5–48.

83. R. Michels, "Der Aufstieg des Faschismus," in *Neue Zuercher Zeitung*, December 29, 1922.

84. The number of Jews in Italy during the Fascist period is difficult to determine exactly. The most responsible sources give 40,000

as the best estimate. The Fascists generally gave 45–50,000. Dedicated anti-Semites like Preziosi gave estimates of 100,000.

85. "Il Trentino veduto da un socialista," in *Opera*, XXXIII, 153–61; cf. O. Reche, Introduction to *Woltmanns Werke* (Leipzig, 1936), I, 7; Rosenberg, *Der Mythus des 20. Jahrhunderts*, pp. 638f.; A Bullock, *Hitler: A Study in Tyranny* (New York, 1952), 72; Blaas, *op. cit.*, pp. 91, 97, 98, 104, 122, 137, 204, 235, 240, 252, 260.

86. "Da Guicciardini," in *Opera*, IV, 172.

87. Ludwig, *op. cit.*, p. 71.

88. Capasso, *op. cit.*, p. 27.

89. G. Maggiore, *Razza e fascismo* (Palermo, 1939), pp. 95ff.

90. Cf. Rosenberg, *Mythus*, p. 114.

91. Cf. J. Evola, *Il mito del sanque* (Milan, 1937), pp. 187, 190ff., 194f.; Leoni, *op. cit.*, p. 40; Costamagna, *op. cit.*, p. 200.

92. *Rosenberg*, p. 81.

93. This was Meisel's interpretation; vide Meisel, *The Myth of the Ruling Class*, p. 259. For Mosca's criticism's of biological racism, vide G. Mosca, "Cenni storici e critici sulle dottrine razziste," in *Rendiconti della R. Accademia Nazionale dei Lincei Classe di scienze morali, storici e filologiche* XI (1933), 455–70, *Storia delle dottrine politiche* (Bari, 1951), chap. xxxix.

94. G. Selvi, "Il mito di razza," in *Gerarchia*, XIV, 10 (1934), pp. 803f.

95. G. Bianchini, "Mistica e politica razziste," in *Gerarchia*, XIV, 7 (1934), 577.

96. J. Gomez de Teran, "Lo soluzione integrale della questione ebraica," in *Gerarchia*, XVI, 6 (1936), 408.

97. "Fallacia Ariana," in *Opera*, XXVI, 298.

98. "Razza e razzismo," in *Opera*, XXVI, 327–29.

99. G. Gentile, *Memorie Italiane* (Florence, 1936), p. 384.

100. Cf. Canepa, *op. cit.*, III, 225, n. 19; G. Magnoni, "I G.U.F. e la politica fascista della razza," in *Gerarchia*, XVIII, 9 (1938), 633; L. Franzi, *Fase attuale del razzismo tedesco* (Rome, 1939), pp. 56–9; Costamagna, Dottrina, pp. 185–210; Leoni, *op. cit.*, p. 27; Capasso, op. cit., pp. 35f. Cf. also A. Banzi, *Razzismo fascista* (Palermo, 1939), p. 13.

101. (Milan, 1937).

102. N. Pende, "Il principio biotipologico unitario," in *Gerarchia*, XIX, 11 (1940), 569; M. Canella, *Principi di psicologia razziale* (Florence, 1941), pp. 128f.; A. Modica, "Origine e classificazione della razza italiana," in *Difesa* IV (July 20, 1941), 21–4.

103. Franzi, *op cit.*, p. 15.
104. Cogni, *op. cit.*, p. 108.
105. *Ibid.*, p. 109.
106. *Ibid.*, p. 115.
107. Evola, *Il mito;* "Filosofia etica mistica del razzismo," in *Difesa*, IV (April 20, 1941), 27–9.
108. Cf. Capasso, *op. cit.*, p. 40, n. 7.
109. De Felice, *Storia*, p. 325; I. Kirkpatrick, *Mussolini: A Study in Power* (New York, 1964), p. 373.
110. Costamagna, *Dottrina*, p. 207.
111. *Ibid.*, p. 194.
112. Cf. Ludwig, *op. cit.*, pp. 70f.
113. Cf. Capasso, *op. cit.*, pp. 35ff.
114. Franzi, *op. cit.*, pp. 44f.
115. G. Landra, "Il concetto di razza," in *Difesa*, II (March 5, 1939), 12.
116. Capasso, *op. cit.*, p. 36.
117. Landra, "Il concetto," p. 12; Maggiore, *op. cit.*, p. 65.
118. Costamagna, *Dottrina*, pp. 193f.
119. Capasso, *op. cit.*, p. 11.
120. *Ibid.*, pp. 16f.
121. M. Canella, "Psicolgia differenziale delle razze umane," in *Rivista di Psicologia*, XXXVI (July–December, 1940), 312.
122. G. Marro, *Caratteri fisici e spirituali della razza italiana* (Rome, 1939).
123. A. Rosenberg, *Das Wesensgefuege des Nationalsozialismus* (Munich, 1934), p. 14; A. Baeumler, *Alfred Rosenberg und der Mythus des 20. Jahrhunderts* (Munich, 1943), pp. 13, 27f., 32f.
124. De Begnac, *op. cit.*, p. 642.
125. Ludwig, *op. cit.*, pp. 70f.
126. M. Missiroli, "Razza e cultura," in *Circoli* (July–August, 1939), pp. 981–89.
127. Cf. Gini, *Nascita*, p. 21.
128. Cf. G. Landra, "L'ologenesi del Rosa," in *Difesa*, II (March 20, 1939), 11–14; "La razza italiana nella teoria dell'ologenesi," *Ibid.*, II (April 5, 1939), 9–11; "Concetti del razzismo italiano," *Ibid.*, I (August 20, 1938), 9–11.
129. Cf. G. Marro, *op. cit.*
130. Cf. Capasso, *op. cit.*, pp. 35f
131. *Ibid.*, p. 41, n. 11. This is at variance with Maggiore, *op. cit.*, p. 33.

132. L. Cipriani, "Razzismo," in *Difesa*, I (August 5, 1938), 12–13; "Razzismo coloniale," in *Difesa*, I (August 20, 1938), 18–20; A. Petrucci, "Negri e bianchi in Africa," *ibid.*, pp. 34–6; L. Franzi, "Il metticiato insidia contro la salute e fisica del popoli," in *Difesa*, I (September 20, 1938), 29–31; A. Chiauzzi, "La scala metrica dell'intelligenza e l'inferiorità mentale dei negri," in *Difesa*, I (October 5, 1938), 32–33. A distinction should be made between the polemical writings of Fascist apologists and experimental scientists such as Mario Canella, who, while convinced that races where characterized by hereditary psychological differences, attempted to indicate the complexity of any judgment concerning hereditary racial differences. Given the circumstances under which it was written, his *Principi di psicologia razziale* is an interesting treatment of a vexed area of research. Many of his conclusions would, of course, have to be significantly qualified today (as Canella himself would no doubt admit). Cf. also the reservations of S. de Martino, *Lo spirito e la razza* (Rome, 1940), chap. xii.

133. N. Minovici, "Razza e nazione: Fascismo creatore," in *Difesa*, III (November 5, 1939), 52.

134. Cf. De Felice, *Storia*, pp. 280f. This should be qualified by the fact that Mussolini, as a young man, maintained that it was an "incontestable fact that intellectual potential stands in direct relation to brain weight and the number of cerebral convolutions." "L'uomo e la divinità," in *Opera*, XXXIII, 11. Should the logic of this be pursued, and racial differences in brain weight and cytoarchitecture taken seriously, the argument against racial misegenation might be essentially biological.

135. "Al Consiglio Nazionale del P.N.F.," in *Opera*, XXIX, 190–91.

136. "Secondo messaggio al popolo americano," in *Opera*, XXIV, 330.

137. "All the discussion about the term 'Aryan' is otiose, given the fact that the term has for some time been used to indicate all those individuals who belong to a variety of kindred anthropological types called respectively Nordic, Dinaric, Alpine, Dalonordic, Mediterranean, and Baltic." Landra, "Due anni di razzismo italiano," in *Difesa*, III (July 5, 1940), 14.

138. A. Donaggio, "Caratteri della Romanità," in *Difesa*, I (August 5, 1938), 22f.

139. Marro, *op. cit.*, p. 31.

140. *Ibid.*; E. Zavattari, "Ambiente naturale e caratteri biopsichici della razza italiana," in *Difesa*, I (August 5, 1938), 20.

141. Canella, *Lineamenti,* p. 239.

142. Zavattari, *op. cit.,* p. 21.

143. Capasso, *op. cit.,* p. 17.

144. *Ibid.,* p. 23.

145. *Ibid.,* p. 19.

146. G. Landra, "Die wissenschaftliche und politische Begruendung der Rassenfrage in Italien," *Nationalsozialistische Monatshefte,* CIX (April, 1939), 201, cf. 298.

147. Cf. Canella, *Razze umane,* pp. 18f.; cf. G. Montandon, "L'ethnie putaine," in *Difesa,* III (November 5, 1939), 18–20.

148. Marro, *op. cit.,* p. 30.

149. Capasso, *op. cit.,* p. 27.

150. Cf. G. Landra, "Due anni di razzismo italiano," in *Difesa,* III (July 5, 1940), 14.

151. Canella, *Razze umane,* p. 234; cf. G. Genna, "Gli ebrei come razza," in *Difesa,* I (September 5, 1938), 13–15.

152. L. Livi, *Gli Ebrei alla luce della statistica* (Florence, 1933); G. Montandon, "Da che cosa si riconosconogli Ebrei?" in *Difesa,* III (September 5–20, 1940), 6f.; "I caratteri del tipo giudaico," in *Difesa,* IV (June 20, 1941), 16–20.

153. Canella *Lineamenti,* p. 38.

154. *Ibid.,* p, 39.

155. Canella, *Razze umane,* p. 234.

156. Canella, *Lineamenti,* p. 236; *Principi,* pp. 206f., n. 1.

157. Cf. De Felice, *Storia,* p. 293.

158. Spampanato, *op. cit.,* II, 132.

159. Cf. Harris, *op. cit.,* p. 245.

160. De Felice, *Storia,* p. 443; Harris, *op. cit.,* p. 245, n. 3.

161. De Begnac, *op. cit.,* p. 643.

162. Cf. Susmel, *op. cit.,* chap. xxix; G. Pisanò, *Mussolini e gli Ebrei* (Milan, 1967).

163. De Felice, *Storia,* p. 148.

164. *Ibid.,* p. 286.

165. *Ibid.,* p. 293.

166. Cf. *Ibid.,* p. 659, document 30; cf. pp. 509f.

167. *Ibid.,* p. 511.

168. M. Missiroli, "Razza e cultura," in *Circoli* (July–August, 1939), 981–89.

169. "Memoriale di G. Preziosi a B. Mussolini," in De Felice, *Storia,* p. 670.

170. Cf. Preziosi in *Ibid.,* p. 670.

171. Amicucci *op. cit.*, pp. 19–27.

172. E. Cione, *Storia della Repubblica Sociale Italiana* (Caserta, 1948), p. 161.

173. Cf. B. Gentile, *Giovanni Gentile: dal discorso agli Italiani alla morte* (Florence, 1951), pp. 50ff.

174. Amicucci, *op. cit.*, p. 199; F. W. Deakin, *The Brutal Friendship: Mussolini, Hitler and the fall of Italian Fascism* (New York, 1962), p. 620; cf. *Opera*, XXXII, 76.

175. De Begnac, *op. cit.*, p. 643.

176. "Storia di un anno," in *Opera*, XXXIV, 305; "Alle Camicie Nere della Brigata Nera 'Aldo Resega,'" in *Opera*, XXXII, 115; "Brenno a Jalta," *ibid.*, p. 452; "Dell'ospitalità regale," *ibid.*, p. 264; "Roma o moret," *ibid.*, p. 371; "Trame del tradimento," *ibid.*, p. 269; cf. "Un nuovo Papa," *ibid.*, p. 264; "Consuntivo 1943," *ibid*, p. 284; "Brennero a Jalta," *ibid.*, p. 451; "Urbania," *ibid.*, p. 311.

CHAPTER SEVEN

1. Cf. "Pensieri Pontini e Sardi," in *Opera*, XXXIV, 278, 285.

2. *The Goebbels Diaries, 1942–1943*, ed. and trans. by L. P. Lochner (Garden City, N.Y., 1948), pp. 472, 469.

3. *Ibid.*, p. 468.

4. F. Martinelli, *Mussolini ai raggi X* (Milan, 1964), p. 448.

5. C. Silvestri, *Mussolini, Graziani e l'antifascismo* (Milan, 1949), p. 79.

6. Cf. Deakin, *The Brutal Friendship*, pp. 587–606.

7. "Il primo discorso dopo la liberazione," in *Opera*, XXXII, 4.

8. "1° riunione del Consiglio dei Ministri Repubblicano," in *Opera*, XXXII, 7.

9. Pini and Susmel, *op. cit.*, IV, 362f.

10. 5° riunione del Consiglio dei Ministri Repubblicano," in *Opera*, XXXII, 31–38.

11. *Idem.*

12. "6ª riunione del Consiglio dei Ministri Repubblicano," in *Opera*, XXXII, 41–56.

13. Tarchi to Mussolini, letter of February 11, 1944, as cited in Deakin, *op. cit.*, p. 668.

14. Deakin, *op. cit.*, pp. 670–73.

15. This represents the sentiments of commentators like G. Perticone, *La Repubblica di Salò* (Rome, 1947).

16. E. Amicucci, *I 600 giorni di Mussolini* (Rome, 1949), p. 152.

17. The communications of the Convention are contained in *Atti del Secondo Convegno di studi sindacali e corporativi, Ferrara 5–8 Maggio 1932* (Rome, 1932), vol. I: Relazioni; vol. II: Comunicazioni; vol. III: Discussioni.

18. U. Ojetti, *I taccuini, 1914–1943* (Florence, 1954), p. 394.

19. U. Spirito, *Capitalismo e corporativismo* (Florence, 1933), pp. xivf.

20. "I diritti della vittoria," in *Opera*, XIV, 53.

21. "Crepuscolo," in *Opera*, XIV, 69; cf. also "Fascismo e terra," in *Opera*, XVI, 170; "Discorso al Senato per lo Stato Corporativo," in *Opera*, XXVI, 147.

22. As cited in Deakin, *op. cit.*, p. 671.

23. "Sindacalismo Francese. Una dichiarazione-programma," in *Opera*, XIV, 247; "Dove impera Lenin," in *Opera*, XVII, 78.

24. "Discorso per lo Stato Corporativo," in *Opera*, XXVI, 87.

25. Cf. H. W. Schneider, *Making the Fascist State* (New York, 1928), p. 177.

26. A. Aquarone, *L'organizzazione dello stato totalitario* (Turin, 1965), p. 125.

27. *La Carta del Lavoro* (Edited by G. Bottai. Rome, 1928), p. 150. For the English text of the Charter, see F. Pitigliani, *The Italian Corporative State* (London, 1933), appendix A.

28. L. Merlino, "Il congresso dei sindacati fascisti," in *Gerarchia*, VIII (May 1928), 355.

29. Cf. "I problemi del lavoro," in *Il Lavoro fascista*, I (August 1, 1927), 15; and L. Rosenstock-Franck, *Les realisations pratiques et les doctrines du syndicalisme fasciste* (Paris, 1933); *L'Economie corporative fasciste en doctrine et en fait* (Paris, 1934); C. Haider, *Capial and Labor under Fascism* (New York, 1930).

30. "Le basi della nuova economia," in *Opera*, XXXII, 294. It is not certain that Mussolini himself wrote this article, but if he did not write it he certainly edited and approved it.

31. E. Corradini, "Dopo lo sciopero fascista," *Popolo d'Italia*, March 19, 1925.

32. U. Spirito, *Critica della democrazia* (Florence, 1963), p. 31.

33. G. Gentile, "Individuo e stato," in *Giornale critico della filosofia italiana*, III (1932), 313.

34. "Discorso al Senato per lo Stato Corporativo," in *Opera*, XXVI, 147.

35. Spirito, *Capitalismo e corporativismo*, pp. 55, 59.

36. *Ibid.*, p. 120.

37. *Ibid.*, pp. 14f.

38. U. Spirito, *Il Corporativismo Nazionalsocialista* (Florence, 1934), p. 6; cf. p. 13.

39. Cf. P. Drieu La Rochelle, *Socialisme fasciste* (Paris, 1934); *Socialismo, Fascismo, Europa* (Edited by J. Mabire. Rome, 1964); M. Manoilesco, *Le siècle du corporatisme: doctrine du corporatisme integral et pur* (Paris, 1938).

40. "Discorso agli operai di Milano," in *Opera*, XXVI, 356, 357.

41. *Giovanni Gentile*, ed. V. Vettori, (Florence, 1954), pp. 43f.

42. "Il piano regolatore della nuova economia Italiana," in *Opera*, XXVII, 241–48. Cf. H. A. Steiner, *Government in Fascist Italy* (New York, 1938), pp. 93–98.

43. "Il piano regolatore della nuova economia Italiana," in *Opera*, XXVII, 245, 246, 247.

44. "All Terza Assemblea Generale delle Corporazioni," in *Opera*, XXVIII, 175–81.

45. Steiner, *op. cit.*, pp. 97f.

46. "Rivoluzione sociale: primi sintomi," in *Opera*, XXXII, 267; cf. also "Ventennale sviluppo logico della dottrina fascista," in *Opera*, XXXII, 316.

47. "Storia di un anno," in *Opera*, XXXIV, 410.

48. "Il discorso al 'Lirico' di Milano," in *Opera*, XXXII, 126.

49. "Soliloquio in 'libertà' all'Isola Trimellone," in *Opera*, XXXII, 171.

50. "Elogio a Padova per la sua fede nella socializzazione," in *Opera*, XXXII, 154.

51. Amicucci, *op. cit.*, p. 143.

52. Archivio Centrale dello Stato, Roma, "Partito Nazionale Fascista, Situazione politica delle provincie, busta Genova," as cited in Aquarone, *op. cit.*, p. 197, n. 3.

53. Cf. F. Giolli, *Come fummo condotti alla catastrofe* (Rome, 1945), pp 71–9; E. Cione, *Storia della Repubblica Sociale Italiana* (Caserta, 1948), pp. 293f.

54. Amicucci, *op. cit.*, pp. 147f.

55. "Sindacalismo integrale," in *Gerarchia*, XV (August, 1935), 672.

56. "Precisazioni per il 'Borghese,'" in *Gerarchia*, XIX (February, 1939), 85.

57. S. Gatti, "Dalla concezione individualistica alla concezione fascista della proprieta privata," in *La concezione fascista della pro-*

prietà privata, ed. the Confederazione Fascista dei Laboratori dell'Agricoltura (Rome, n.d.), pp. 30f., 35; L. Barassi, "Il diritto di proprietà e la funzione sociale," *ibid.*, p. 191. The date 1939 attributed to this volume is based on internal evidence.

58. F. Carli, "La proprietà e il fascismo," *ibid.*, pp. 39, 55f.; C. Biggini, "Riforma dei codici e diritto di proprietà," *ibid.*, pp. 64f., 68-71; O. Censi, "La proprietà come rapporto di diritto pubblico," *ibid.*, pp. 141f.

59. Biggini, *ibid.*, p. 75; cf. Barassi, *ibid.*, p. 193.

60. S. Panunzio, "Prime osservazioni giuridiche sul concetto di proprietà nel regime fascista," *ibid.*, p. 115.

61. F. Ferrara, "La proprietà come 'dovere sociale,'" *ibid.*, p. 281.

62. G. Chiarelli, "Il fondamento pubblicistico della proprietà," *ibid.*, pp. 151, 153ff.; cf. pp. 148f.

63. P. Gasparr. "L'impresa come fenomeno sociale," *ibid.*, pp. 381-83; C. Arena, "La proprietà di impresa nell'ordine corporativo," *ibid.*, pp. 399-405.

64. Barassi, *ibid.*, pp. 187, 199.

65. A. Lanzillo, "La proprietà privata e la corporazione," *ibid.*, p. 337. Biggini maintained that "within each enterprise labor still remains distinct, disassociated and often opposed to capital. It is certain that a concrete and substantial corporative evolution in industry cannot but involve labor in the management, the responsibilities and the profits of enterprise itself." Biggini, *ibid.*, p. 78.

66. S. Panunzio, "L'impero Italiano del lavoro," in *Gerarchia*, XIX (September, 1940), 463.

67. "Alle Camicie nere della Brigata Nera 'Aldo Resega,'" in *Opera*, XXXII, 114.

68. "Ritornate!" in *Opera*, XXXII, 91.

69. "Soliloquio in 'libertà' all'Isola Trimellone," in *Opera*, XXXII, 178f.

70. C. Rossi, *Trentatre vicende mussoliniane* (Milan, 1958), p. 443.

71. Pavolini, as quoted in Amicucci, *op. cit.*, p. 143.

72. *Ibid.*, p. 144.

73. Silvestri, *op. cit.*, pp. 320f.

74. "Decreto sulla 'socializzazione' del C.L.N.A.I.," in Perticone, *La Repubblica di Salò*, p. 380.

75. Cf. N. Rotenstreich, *Basic Problems of Marx's Philosophy* (New York, 1965) (vide my review in *Journal of the History of Philosophy*, IV [October, 1966], 349f.); L. Dupré, *The Philosophical Foundations*

of Marxism (New York, 1966); A. J. Gregor, "Giovanni Gentile and the Philosophy of the Young Karl Marx," in *Journal of the History of Ideas,* XXIV (April 1963).

76. *ED,* p. 172, 173.

77. *Ibid.,* p. 175f.

78. *Ibid.,* p. 190; cf. pp. 238f.

79. *Ibid.,* pp. 245f.

80. *Ibid.,* p. 207; cf. K. Marx and F. Engels, *The German Ideology* (Moscow, 1964), p. 646, for the English text.

81. *FD,* p. 222.

82. Marx and Engels, *German Ideology,* pp. 37, 47, 49.

83. *Ibid.,* p. 80.

84. K. Marx, *The Poverty of Philosophy,* p. 196; cf. "Evoluzione sociale e lotta di classe," in *Opera,* II, 31.

85. *FD,* p. 303.

86. *Ibid.,* p. 264.

87. *Ibid.,* p. 298.

88. *GS,* p. 15.

89. U. Spirito, *La filosofia del comunismo* (Florence, 1948), pp. 12f.

90. *FD,* p. 148.

91. *Ibid.,* p. 215.

92. *PF,* p. 27.

93. Cf. M. Manfredini, "Gentile è vivo," in Vettori, *op. cit.,* pp. 179f.

94. *GS,* pp. 111f. I have utilized G. Gentile, *Genesis and Structure of Society,* trans. H. S. Harris (Urbana, 1961), pp. 171f.

95. *CF,* pp. 42f.

96. *OD,* p. 58.

97. G. Gentile, *Dopo la vittoria. Nuovi frammenti politici* (Rome, 1920), p. 178.

98. G. Gentile, "Individuo e stato," in *Giornale critico della filosofia Italiana,* III (1932), 314.

99. V. I. Lenin, "Karl Marx," in *Collected Works* (Moscow, 1964), XXI, 88.

100. Labriola, as quoted in Vettori, "Introduzione a Gentile," *op. cit.,* p. 44.

101. Cf. U. Spirito, *Critica della democrazia* (Florence, 1963), pp. 32–6.

102. G. Gentile, "Discorso agli Italiani," in B. Gentile, *Giovanni Gentile: Dal Discorso agli Italiani alla morte* (Florence, 1951), p. 69.

103. *Ibid.,* p. 72.

104. Vettori, "Introduzione a Gentile," *op. cit.,* pp. 54f.

105. Cf. D. Gaudenzi, "Dal sindacalismo eroico all'umanesimo del lavoro," in Vettori, *op cit.,* pp. 163–70.

106. Gentile, "Individuo e stato," *op. cit.,* p. 313.

107. *GS,* pp. 32, 34, 39.

108. *CF,* p. 56.

109. A. Carlini, *Studi Gentiliani* (Florence, 1958), p. 106.

110. *RE,* pp. 25, 14.

111. Spirito, *Capitalismo e corporativismo,* p. 33.

112. G. Pannese, *L'etica nel fascismo e la filosofia del diritto e della storia* (Rome, 1942), p. 158; cf. also O. Di Giamberardino, *L'individuo nell'etica fascista* (Florence, 1940), pp. 177f.

113. "Dottrina del fascismo," in *Opera,* XXXIV, 117, 118.

114. Di Giamberardino, *op. cit.,* p. 165.

115. Cf. Harris, *The Social Philosophy of Giovanni Gentile,* pp. 197–201.

116. "La proprietà privata nella concezione di Hegel," reprinted in Spirito, *La filosofia del comunismo,* pp. 135–50.

117. Cf. Spampanato, *Contromemoriale,* II, 33, 47. Cf. "13ª riunione del Consiglio dei Ministri Repubblicano," in *Opera,* XXXII, 125.

118. "Il discorso al 'Lirico' di Milano," in *Opera,* XXXII, 131; Circular of March 10, 1944, in *Opera,* XXXII, 236.

119. "Della vera libertà," in *Opera,* XXXII, 273.

120. "Le basi della nuova economia," in *Opera,* XXXII, 295.

121. "Leggenda di Muti," in *Opera,* XXXII, 396.

122. "Il sesso degli angeli," in *Opera,* XXXII, 121.

CHAPTER EIGHT

1. Cf. A. Thalheimer, "Ueber den Faschismus," in W. Abendroth, ed., *Faschismus und Kapitalismus* (Vienna, 1967), pp. 19–38; J. Cammett, "Communist Theories of Fascism," in *Science and Society,* XXXI (Spring, 1967), pp. 149–63.

2. H. Rogger seems to suggest something of this in an otherwise sound appraisal of Right Wing movements. Cf. H. Rogger, "Afterthoughts," in H. Rogger and E. Weber, eds., *The European Right* (Berkeley, 1966), p. 588.

3. R. Brown, *Social Psychology* (New York, 1965), pp. 478, 485; E. Shils, "Authoritarianism: 'Right' and 'Left,'" in R. Christie and

4444

4444

4444

4444

4444

4444

M. Jahoda, eds., *Studies in the Scope and Method of "The Authoritarian Personality"* (New York, 1954), pp. 26f.

4. *Shils*, pp. 27f.

5. H. J. Eysenck, *The Psychology of Politics* (London, 1954).

6. R. Christie, "Eysenck's Treatment of the Personality of Communists," in *Psychological Bulletin*, LII (1956), pp. 411–30.

7. M. Rokeach, *The Open and Closed Mind* (New York, 1960).

8. I. A. Taylor, "Similarities in the Structure of Extreme Social Attitudes," in *Psychological Monographs*, LXIV, 2 (1960), pp. 1–36.

9. H. McClosky and J. H. Schaar, "Psychological Dimensions of Anomy," in *American Sociological Review*, XXX (February, 1965), 14–40.

10. E. Halevy, *The Era of Tyrannies* (Garden City, N.Y., 1965), p. 267.

11. F. Borkenau, *World Communism* (Ann Arbor, 1962), p. 423.

12. *EPM*, pp. 104f.

13. M. Hess, "Die letzten Philosophen," in *Philosophische und sozialistische Schriften: 1837–1850* (Berlin, 1961), p. 381.

14. K. Marx, "Contribution to the Critique of Hegel's Philosophy of Right," in *Early Writings*, trans. and ed. T. B. Bottomore (New York, 1964), p. 43; "Theses on Feuerbach," in K. Marx and F. Engels, *The German Ideology* (New York, 1947), p. 198.

15. *EPM*, p. 145.

16. Cf. Marx's discussion in K. Marx and F. Engels, *The Holy Family* (Moscow, 1956), p. 142 and *The German Ideology*, particularly part I.

17. Marx, "Contribution," p. 52.

18. *Ibid.*, p. 59.

19. K. Marx, "Briefe aus den 'Deutsche-Franzoesischen Jahrbuechern," in *Werke* (Berlin, 1961), I, 338f.

20. K. Marx, *Grundrisse der Kritik der Politischen Oekonomie (Rohentwurf)* (Berlin, 1953), p. 6, emphasis supplied; cf. Rotenstreich, *Basic Problems of Marx's Philosophy*, chap. iv.

21. *EPM*, pp. 104f.

22. "Ueber die sozialistische Bewegung in Deutschland," *op. cit.*, p. 284.

23. *EPM*, p. 104.

24. Marx and Engels, *The Holy Family*, p. 56.

25. Marx, "On the Jewish Question," in *Early Writings*, p. 16.

26. K. Marx and F. Engels, "The Communist Manifesto," in *Selected Works* (Moscow, 1955), I, 54.

27. Marx, *Grundrisse*, p. 387.

28. Schaff, *op. cit.*, p. 60.

29. D. Bergner, "Dialektischer Materialismus, Psychologie und Ethik," in G. Heyden, ed., *Wissenschaft contra Spekulation* (Berlin, 1964), pp. 208f.

30. Cf. the "Collective Work," in *Die Grundlagen der kommunistischen Erziehung* (Berlin, 1964), p. 46; and F. V. Konstantinov, *Grundlagen der marxistischen Philosophie* (Berlin, 1964), p. 650.

31. K. Mácha, *Individuum und Gesellschaft* (Berlin, 1964), pp. 9, 14f., 297ff.

32. Schischkin, *op. cit.*, pp. 32, 238.

33. *Ibid.*, p. 264.

34. F. Engels, "Zwei Reden in Elberfeld: I," in K. Marx and F. Engels, *Werke* (Berlin, 1957), II, 539, 542.

35. S. I. Benn and R. S. Peters, *The Principles of Political Thought* (New York, 1964), pp. 259f.

36. G. Shakhnazarov, et al., *Man, Science and Society* (Moscow, 1965), p. 251.

37. Archangelski, *op. cit.*, p. 302.

38. Shakhnazarov, *op. cit.*, pp. 254, 255, 258.

39. Schischkin, *op. cit.*, p. 261.

40. This is particularly true of non-Soviet Marxists. Cf. J. Lewis, *Socialism and the Individual* (New York, 1961).

41. V. I. Lenin, *Philosophical Notebooks*, in Lenin, *Collected Works* (Moscow, 1960), XXXVIII, 361.

42. Cf. F. Burlatsky, *The State and Communism* (Moscow, n.d.), p. 85.

43. Mácha, *op. cit.*, p. 289.

44. R. T. Holt, *Radio Free Europe* (Minneapolis, 1964), p 26.

45. H. J. Berman, *Justice in the U.S.S.R.* (New York, 1963), p. 365.

46. Archangelski, *op. cit.*, pp. 303f. In its entirety, this reads: "Some men argue in the following fashion: Since the personal and the collective are not to be distinguished, one must in the first instance pursue his own interests and thereby serve the collective well-being. But this argument is fundamentally erroneous. In it petty-bourgeois aspirations find expression, and whoever takes this position defends outworn and moribund views which are incompatible with the essence of our socialist order."

47. U. Spirito, *La filosofia del communismo* (Florence, 1948), p. 13.

48. M. Ardemagni, "Deviazioni Russe verso il fascismo," in

Gerarchia, XIV (July, 1934), 571. For Mussolini's assessments of the same involution, cf. "Segnalazione," in *Opera*, XXVI, 84; "Atto quinto finora," in *Opera*, XXIX, 63.

49. L. Trotsky, *The Revolution Betrayed* (Garden City, N.Y., 1937), p. 278.

50. Marx, "Contribution," *op. cit.*, p. 52.

51. Marx, "Briefe aus den 'Deutsch-Franzoesischen Jahrbuechern,'" in *Werke*, I, 338f.

52. Engel's Preface to the English edition of 1888, "The Communist Manifesto," in K. Marx and F. Engels, *Selected Works*, I, 28; cf. p. 24.

53. Marx and Engels, "The Communist Manifesto," *Selected Works*, I, 34; F. Engels, *Anti-Duehring*, pp. 365, 367.

54. K. Marx and F. Engels, *The German Ideology* (Moscow, 1964), pp. 37f.

55. Cf. Engels, *Anti-Duehring*, pp. 130f., 145, 354; Marx and Engels, *The German Ideology*, pp. 48–51, 60f.; K. Marx, *Capital* (Moscow, 1954), I, 82 n.; Marx and Engels, "The Communist Manifesto," in *Selected Works*, I, 52.

56. Marx, *Capital*, I, 8–9, 763; F. Engels, *The Condition of the Working-Class in England in 1844* (London, 1950), p. 18.

57. Marx and Engels, "The Communist Manifesto," in *Selected Works*, I, 62.

58. Marx, Engels, *The Holy Family*, p. 52.

59. F. Engels, "Grundsaetze des Kommunismus," *Werke*, IV, 372.

60. Marx, Engels, *The Holy Family*, pp. 52f.; "The Communist Manifesto," in *Selected Works*, I, 45.

61. Engels, *The Condition of the Working-Class in England in 1844*, p. 295.

62. Marx and Engels, "The Communist Manifesto," in *Selected Works*, I, 44; cf. Engels, *Anti-Duehring*, p. 384.

63. F. Engels, Introduction to "Class Struggles in France 1848–1850," in *Selected Works*, I, 134.

64. Marx, Engels, "The Communist Manifesto," in *Selected Works*, I, 63.

65. Cf. Engels Introduction to K. Marx, "The Civil War in France," in *Selected Works*, I, 482f., 485; and Marx, *Ibid.*, pp. 520–21.

66. *Ibid.*, p. 521.

67. Engels to Marx, letter of November 18, 1868, in K. Marx, F. Engels, *Der Briefwechsel zwischen Friedrich Engels und Karl Marx* (Stuttgart, 1913), IV, 113; cf. letter of October 7, 1858, *ibid.*, II, 290.

68. Marx to Kugelmann, letter of March 28, 1870, in Marx and Engels, *Werke*, XXXII, 664.

69. V. I. Lenin, "A Talk with Defenders of Economism," in *Collected Works*, V, 316.

70. *Ibid.*, p. 318.

71. Engels, *Anti-Duehring*, p. 386.

72. Lenin, "The Immediate Tasks of the Soviet Government," in *Selected Works in Two Volumes* (Moscow, 1950–51), II, pt. 1, 455.

73. *Ibid.*, pp. 471, 477, 478.

74. J. Stalin, "Concerning Questions of Leninism," in *Works* (Moscow, 1952–55), VIII, 65.

75. Trotsky, *The Revolution Betrayed*, p. 278.

76. Cf. R. Lowenthal, *World Communism: The Disintegration of a Secular Faith* (New York, 1966), pp. 39–48.

77. Shakhnazarov, *op. cit.*, p. 247.

78. G. Maggiore, *Imperialismo e impero fascista* (Palermo, 1937), p. 145; cf. A. Gravelli, *Panfascismo* (Rome, 1935), *passim;* P. Gorgolini, *Il fascismo spiegato al popolo* (Turin, 1935), pp. 66–69.

79. Mussolini, "Discorso per lo stato corporativo," in *Opera*, XXVI, 91; cf. Mussolini's discussion with Emil Ludwig, *Colloqui con Mussolini*, p. 145.

80. C. Costamagna, "Grand spazio e etnarchia imperiale," in *Lo Stato*, XIII (January, 1942), 1–18; F. Lo Biancho, "L'azione euoropea," in *Lo Stato*, XIII (April, 1942), 119–123; "Il Convegno di Pisa per i problemi economici del'Ordine Nuovo," in *Lo Stato*, XIII (May, 1942), 162–65; A Tramonti, "Nazione o rivoluzione?" in *Lo Stato*, XIV (January, 1943), 24f.; C. Costamagna, "L'idea dell'Europea e la guerra," in *Lo Stato*, XIV (March, 1943), 65–78.

81. Cione, *Storia della Repubblica Sociale Italiana*, p. 175.

82. Mussolini, "Conversazione con Maddalena Mollier," in *Opera*, XXXII, 157–61.

83. Lenin, "The State and Revolution," in *Selected Works*, II, pt. 1, 204, 299.

84. Stalin, "Political Report of the Central Committee to the Sixteenth Congress," in *Works*, XII, 381.

85. *CF*, p. 36; cf. *ibid.*, p. 50, *OD*, p. 63, "La costituzionalizzazione del Gran Consiglio del Fascismo," in *Educazione fascista*, VI (February, 1928), 86f.

86. N. S. Khrushchev, *Report on the Program of the Communist Party of the Soviet Union* (New York, 1961), pp. 104, 107–9.

87. V. Podosetnik, *Marxist-Leninist Philosophy, the Theory of Revolutionary Practice* (Moscow, n.d.), p. 24.

88. Burlatsky, *op. cit.*, pp. 5f.

89. Ibid., p. 6.

90. Cf. M. M. Drachkovitch, "Introduction," in M. M. Drachkovitch, ed, *Marxism in the Modern World* (Stanford, 1965), pp. xif.; R. Aron, "The Impact of Marxism," *ibid.*, pp. 11, 31; B. D. Wolfe, "Leninism," *ibid.*, pp. 88f

91. U. Spirito, *Il comunismo* (Florence, 1965), pp. 199, 210.

92. Cf. D. Lowe, *The Function of "China" in Marx, Lenin and Mao* (Berkeley, 1966), pp. 121f.; "On the Question of the National Bourgeoisie and the Enlightened Gentry," Mao Tse-tung, *Selected Works* (New York, n.d.), V, 207; "On the People's Democratic Dictatorship," *Ibid.*, V. 415; Liu Shao-chi, *The Victory of Marxism-Leninism in China* (Peking, 1959), pp. 15, 37.

93. G. D. H. Cole, *The Meaning of Marxism* (Ann Arbor, 1964), pp. 146f.

94. Marx, letter to Vera Zasulich, March 8, 1881, in K. Marx and F. Engels, *Selected Correspondence* (Moscow, n.d.), p. 412.

95. J. H. Mensah, "The Relevance of Marxian Economics to Development Planning in Ghana," in *The Economic Bulletin of Ghana,* IX, 1, v, 4, 14.

96. Cf. B. Fitch and M. Oppenheimer, "Ghana: End of an Illusion," in *Monthly Review,* XVIII, 3 (1966), 111, n. 12.

97. "Dakar Colloquium: Search for a Definition," in *Africa Report,* VIII (May, 1963), 17.

98. Cf. L. Senghor, *On African Socialism* (London, 1964), p. 52; "What is Negritude?" in P. Sigmund, ed., *Ideologies of the Developing Nations* (New York, 1963), p. 250; "Eléments constitutifs d'une civilisation d'inspiration Négro-Africaine," in *Liberté 1: Négritude et Humanisme* (Paris, 1964), p. 284; A. Quaison-Sackey, *Africa Unbound* (London, 1963), p. 50.

99. Senghor, *On African Socialism,* p. 3.

100. *Ibid.,* p. 25.

101. Cf. G. Balandier, "Doctrines: From Negritude to Socialism," in *Jeune Afrique* (Tunis), December 3–9, 1962; K. Nkrumah, *I Speak of Freedom: A Statement of African Ideology* (New York, 1961), p. 169.

102. *Che cosa è il sindacalismo fascista?* (Rome, 1927), p. 7; cf. E. Nolte, *The Three Faces of Fascism,* p. 183.

103. Cf. H. Schneider, *Making the Fascist State* (New York, 1928), pp. 152f.

104. "Dakar Colloquium," *op. cit.*, p. 16.

105. Senghor, *On African Socialism*, pp. 12, 25.

106. R. S. Morgenthau, "African Socialism: Declaration of Ideological Independence," in *Africa Report*, VIII (May, 1963), 5f.

107. Cf. K. Nkrumah, *Africa Must Unite* (New York, 1964), p. 64; *Some Essential Features of Nkrumaism*, prepared by the Editors of *The Spark* (New York, 1965), pp. 42f.; Senghor, *On African Socialism*, p. 52.

108. C. A. Kane, "First Steps Toward a Planned Economy," in *Europe Outremer* (Paris), September, 1962.

109. Senghor, *On African Socialism*, p. 159.

110. *Ibid.*, pp. 3, 11f., 25.

111. This thesis is argued in more detail in A. J. Gregor, *Contemporary Radical Ideologies* (New York, 1968), chap. 7; and in "African Socialism, Socialism and Fascism: An Appraisal," in *Review of Politics*, XXIX (July, 1967), 324–53.

112. The literature on "totalitarianism" is abundant. The most significant works, in my opinion, include C. Friedrich, *Totalitarianism* (New York, 1964); C. Friedrich and Z. Brzezinski, *Totalitarian Dictatorship and Autocracy* (New York, 1961); R. C. Tucker, "Towards a Comparative Politics of Movement Regimes," in *American Political Science Review*, reprinted in *The Soviet Political Mind* (New York, 1963); A. Kassof, "The Administered Society: Totalitarianism Without Terror," in *World Politics*, XVI (July, 1964), 558–75. The characterization of totalitarianism here does not employ the disposition to "world conquest" as a serious defining attribute. World conquest may or may not have been a serious intention on Hitler's part, but it can hardly be conceived as the policy of the Soviet Union. The policies of the Soviet Union and Red China, for that matter, can be seen as the power politics of nationalism. The ascription of a lust for world conquest adds nothing to the analysis.

113. Jose Antonio Primo de Rivera, *Textos de doctrina politica* (Madrid, 1952), pp. 43–48, 53, 65–69, 85–93, 215, 281, 335f., 483–507, 559.

114. Cf. B. Nellessen, *La rivoluzione proibita: ascesa e tramonto della Falange* (Rome, 1965).

115. An exhaustive discussion of this period is available in R. De Felice, *Mussolini il fascista: la conquista del potere, 1921–1925* (Turin, 1966) particularly chaps. 1 and 2.

116. J. Degras, ed., *The Communist International, 1919–1943: Documents* (London, 1956), II, 459.

117. C. Zetkin, "Aus den Referat der Genossin Clara Zetkin ueber den Faschismus," in *Inprekorr* (June 27, 1923), reprinted in T. Pirker, *Komintern und Faschismus: Dokumente zur Geschichte und Theorie des Faschismus* (Stuttgart, 1966), p. 119.

118. Cf. R. De Felice, *Il fascismo e i partiti politici Italiani* (Rocca San Casciano, 1966), p. 12.

119. Cf. J. Cammett, *Antonio Gramsci and the Origins of Italian Communism* (Stanford, 1967), p. 179.

120. A. Tasca, *Nascita e avvento del fascismo* (Florence, 1950), pp. 543f.

121. A. Rosenberg, "Der Faschismus als Massenbewegung," in *Faschismus und Kapitalismus,* p. 111; G. Aquila, "il fascismo Italiano," in De Felice, *Il fascismo,* p. 428.

122. A. Labriola, "L'inchiesta del 'Resto del Carlino,'" *Ibid.,* pp. 512–15.

123. Cf. E. Nolte, *Die faschistischen Bewegungen* (Munich, 1966), pp. 65f.

124. F. Carsten, *The Rise of Fascism* (Berkeley, 1967), p. 66.

125. E. Weber, *Varieties of Fascism* (New York, 1964), p. 10.

126. Cole, *op. cit.,* pp. 146f.

127. Fetscher, *op. cit.,* p. 237; cf. pp. 226f.

128. F. Borkenau, "Zur Soziologie des Faschismus," in *Archiv fuer Sozialwissenschaft und Sozialpolitik,* 1933.

129. Cf. E. Weber, "The Men of the Archangel," in *Journal of Contemporary History,* I, 1 (1966), 101–26; "Romania," in Rogger, Weber, *op. cit.,* pp. 523f.

130. As quoted, *ibid.,* p. 504.

131. Cf. Schneider, *Making the Fascist State,* pp. 141f.

132. In this regard see the contemporary fascist discussion of revolution in the underdeveloped countries. There is a clear sympathy for anticolonialist aspirations. Bardèche, *Qu'est-ce que le fascisme?* chaps. ii, iii.

133. This is the central thesis in Dutt, *op. cit.,* and S. Roberts, *The House That Hitler Built* (London, 1937).

134. Cf. I. Fetscher, "Zur Kritik des sowjetmarxistischen Faschismus Begriffs," in *Karl Marx und der Marxismus* (Munich, 1967), pp. 218–37; A. Schweitzer, *Big Business in the Third Reich* (Bloomington, 1964); D. Schoebaum, *Hitler's Social Revolution: Class and Status in Nazi Germany, 1933–1939* (New York, 1966).

135. B. Moore, *Social Origins of Dictatorship and Democracy: Lord and Peasant in the Making of the Modern World* (Boston, 1966).

136. For an instructive discussion on these points see J. Kautsky, *Political Change in Underdeveloped Countries: Nationalism and Communism* (New York, 1962), pp. 101–6.

137. Cf. E. S. Mason, *Economic Planning in Underdeveloped Areas: Government and Business* (New York, 1958).

138. D. Apter, *The Politics of Modernization* (Chicago, 1965), pp. 328–30.

Selected
Bibliography

T H I S selected bibliography is provided to indicate materials basic to an adequate interpretation of Fascism as an ideology. The materials are classified under relatively specific subject headings. Although an effort has been made to exclude trivia, apologetic or polemic materials that succeed in making some contribution to the subject have been included. No effort has been made to indicate relevant journal articles. Such an undertaking would involve a bibliographical enterprise of unmanageable proportions. There are, however, a number of Fascist journals vital to the reconstruction of Fascist thought; the most important include *Critica fascista, Lo Stato, Gerarchia, Educazione fascista,* and *La difesa della razza.*

I. GENERAL HISTORICAL AND BIOGRAPHICAL MATERIAL

BEDESCHI, Sante and ALESSI, Rino. *Anni giovanili di Mussolini.* Milan: Mondadori, 1939.

BONOMI, Ivanoe. *Dal socialismo al fascismo.* Rome: Formiggini, 1924.

BOTTAI, Giuseppe. *Vent'anni e un giorno.* Cernusco sul Naviglio: Garzanti, 1949.

CIANO, Galeazzo. *The Ciano Diaries, 1939–1943,* ed. H. Gibson. Garden City, New York: Doubleday, 1946.

———. *Ciano's Hidden Diary, 1937–1938,* trans. A. Mayor. New York: Dutton, 1953.

DE BEGNAC, Yvon. *Palazzo Venezia: storia di un regime.* Rome: La Rocca, 1950.

———. *Trent'anni di Mussolini: 1883–1915.* Rome: Menaglia, 1934.

———. *Vita di Benito Mussolini.* 3 vols. Milan: Mondadori, 1936–40.

DE FELICE, Renzo. *Mussolini il fascista.* Turin: Einaudi, 1966.

———. *Mussolini il rivoluzionario.* Turin: Einaudi, 1965.

DOLFIN, Giovanni. *Con Mussolini nella tragedia.* Cernusco sul Naviglio: Garzanti, 1949.

FARINACCI, Roberto. *Storia della rivoluzione fascista.* 3 vols. Cremona: Cremona Nuova, 1937.

FINER, Herman. *Mussolini's Italy.* New York: Grosset and Dunlap, 1965.

GAETA, Franco, ed. *La stampa nazionalista.* Rocca San Casciano: Cappelli, 1965.

GERMINO, Dante. *The Italian Fascist Party in Power.* Minneapolis: Univ. of Minnesota Press, 1959.

LUDWIG, Emil. *Colloqui con Mussolini.* Verona: Mondadori, 1950.

MANNHARDT, Johann Wilhelm. *Der Faschismus.* Munich: Beck, 1925.

MARRONI, Cesare. *Mussolini se stesso.* Rome: I.C.N.F., 1941.

MELOGRANI, Piero, ed. *Corriere della sera (1919–1943).* Rocca San Casciano: Cappelli, 1966.

MISSIROLI, Mario. *Il fascismo e il colpo di stato dell'Ottobre 1922.* Rocca San Casciano: Cappelli, 1966.

NENNI, Pietro. *Vent'anni di fascismo.* Milan: Avanti!, 1964.

NOLTE, Ernst. *Die faschistischen Bewegungen.* Munich: Deutscher Taschenbuch Verlag, 1966.

———. *Three Faces of Fascism: Action Française, Italian Fascism, National Socialism,* trans. L. Vennewitz. New York: Holt, Rinehart and Winston, 1966.

PINI, Giorgio and Susmel, Duilio. *Mussolini: l'uomo e l'opera.* 4 vols. Florence: La Fenice, 1953–55.

ROCCA, Massimo. *Il primo fascismo.* Rome: Volpe, 1964.

ROSSI, Arturo [Angelo Tasca]. *The Rise of Italian Fascism,* trans. P. and D. Wait. London: Methuen, 1938.

ROSSI, Cesare. *Mussolini com'era.* Rome: Ruffolo, 1947.

———. *Trentatre vicende mussoliniane.* Milan: Ceschina, 1958.

ROUX, Georges. *La Italia fascista.* Barcelona: Subirana, 1933.

SALVATORELLI, Luigi and Mira, Giovanni. *Storia d'Italia nel periodo fascista.* Turin: Einaudi, 1964.

SALVEMINI, Gaetano. *Scritti sul fascismo.* Milan: Feltrinelli, 1966.

————. *Under the Axe of Fascism.* London: Gollanz, 1936.

SILVESTRI, Carlo. *Mussolini, Graziani e l'antifascismo.* Milan: Longanesi, 1950.

SPAMPANATO, Bruno. *Contromemoriale.* 3 vols. Rome: Illustrato, 1952.

SUSMEL, Edoardo. *Mussolini e il suo tempo.* Cernusco sul Naviglio: Garzanti, 1950.

TASCA, Angelo. *Nascita e avvento del fascismo.* Florence: La nuova Italia, 1950.

VINCIGUERRA, Mario. *Il fascismo visto da un solitario.* Florence: Le Monnier, 1963.

VOLPE, Gioacchino. *History of the Fascist Movement.* Rome: Novissima, 1936.

————. *Lo sviluppo storico del fascismo.* Rome: Sandron, 1928.

ZINCONE, Vittorio, ed. *Hitler e Mussolini: lettere e documenti.* Milan: Rizzoli, 1946.

II. THE HISTORY OF FASCIST INSTITUTIONS

ACERBO, Giacomo, *et al. Lo stato Mussoliniano.* Rome: La Rassegna Italiana, 1930.

AMBROSINI, Gaspare. *Il Consiglio nazionale delle corporazioni.* Rome: Littorio, 1930.

AQUARONE, Alberto. *L'organizzazione dello stato totalitario.* Turin: Einaudi, 1965.

La Camera dei fasci e delle corporazioni. Florence: Sansoni, 1937.

Codice corporativo e del lavoro. 3 vols. Milan: Hoepli, 1940.

CORSINI, Vincenzo. *Il Capo del governo nello stato fascista.* Bologna: Zanichelli, 1935.

FIELD, G. Lowell. *The Syndical and Corporative Institutions of Italian Fascism.* New York: Columbia Univ. Press, 1938.

HAIDER, Carmen. *Capital and Labor under Fascism.* New York: Columbia Univ. Press, 1930.

JAEGER, Nicola. *Principii di diritto corporativo.* Padua: Milani, 1939.

LUNELLI, Italo. *Riforma costituzionale fascista.* Milan: Treves, 1937.

MANOILESCU, Mihail. *Die einzige Partei als politische Institution der neuen Regime.* Berlin: Stollberg, 1941.

PAOLONI, Francesco. *Sistema rappresentativo del fascismo*. Rome: Littorio, 1937.

PITIGLIANI, Fausto. *The Italian Corporative State*. London: King, 1933.

RAUE, Ernst. *Beitraege zur neuen Staats- und Wirtschaftsauffassung in Deutschland und Italien*. Berlin: Junker und Duenhaupt, 1934.

SCHMIDT, Carl. *The Corporate State in Action*. New York: Oxford Univ. Press, 1939.

SERMONTI, Alfonso. *Diritto sindacale italiano*. 2 vols. Rome: Littorio, 1929.

SOTTOCHIESA, Gino. *Il nuovo regime rappresentativo dello stato fascista*. Turin: Paravia, 1939.

STEINER, H. Arthur. *Government in Fascist Italy*. New York: McGraw-Hill, 1938.

TEMPEL, Wilhelm. *Aufbau der Staatsgewalt im faschistischen Italien*. Leipzig: Hirschfeld, 1933.

WELK, William. *Fascist Economic Policy*. Cambridge, Mass.: Harvard Univ. Press, 1938.

ZANGARA, Vincenzo. *Il partito unico e il nuovo stato rappresentativo in Italia e in Germania*. Bologna: Zanichelli, 1938.

III. PROTO-FASCISM AND THE SOCIOLOGICAL TRADITION

ANDREU, Pierre. *Sorel: il nostro Maestro*. Rome: Volpe, 1966.

ARCARI, Paola Maria. *Socialismo e democrazia nel pensiero di Vilfredo Pareto*. Rome: Volpe, 1966.

BARTH, Hans. *Masse und Mythos, die Theorie der Gewalt. Georges Sorel*. Hamburg: Rowohlt, 1959.

BITELLI, Giovanni. *Filippo Corridoni e il sindacalismo operaio antebellico*. Milan: Modernissima, 1925.

BORGESE, Giovanni. *D'Annunzio*. Milan: Bompiani, 1932.

CLOUGH, Rosa Trillo. *Futurism: The Story of a Modern Art Movement*. New York: Philosophical Library, 1961.

CORRADINI, Enrico. *Discorsi politici (1902–1923)*. Florence: Vallecchi, 1923.

———. *L'ombra della vita*. Naples: Ricciardi, 1908.

———. *La patria lontana*. Milan: Treves, 1910.

———. *Sopra le vie del nuovo impero*. Milan: Treves, 1912.

———. *La unità e la potenza delle nazioni*. Florence: Vallecchi, 1912.

————. *La vita nazionale*. Florence: Lumachi, 1907.

————. *Il volere d'Italia*. Naples: Perrella, 1911.

DELLE PIANE, Mario. *Gaetano Mosca: classe politica e liberalismo*. Naples: Edizioni Scientifiche Italiane, 1952.

GUMPLOWICZ, Ludwig. *The Outlines of Sociology*, trans. F. W. Moore. Philadelphia: American Academy of Political and Social Science, 1899.

————. *Der Rassenkampf*. Innsbruck: Wagner, 1883.

————. *Rechtsstaat und Socialismus*. Innsbruck: Wagner, 1881.

————. *Die sociologische Staatsidee*. 2nd enlarged ed. Innsbruck: Wagner, 1902.

————. *Sozialphilosophie im Umriss*. Innsbruck: Wagner, 1910.

HOROWITZ, Irving Louis. *Radicalism and the Revolt Against Reason: The Social Theories of Georges Sorel (with a Translation of his Essay on "The Decomposition of Marxism")*. New York: Humanities, 1961.

HUMPHREY, Richard. *Georges Sorel: Prophet Without Honor*. Cambridge, Mass.: Harvard Univ. Press, 1951.

JOLL, James. *Three Intellectuals in Politics: Blum, Rathenau, Marinetti*. New York: Harper and Row, 1960.

LA FERLA, Giuseppe. *Ritratto di Georges Sorel*. Milan: La Cultura, 1933.

LE BON, Gustave. *The Crowd: A Study of the Popular Mind*. London: Benn, 1952.

MARINETTI, Filippo Tommaso. *Futurismo e fascismo*. Foligno: Campitelli, 1924.

MEISEL, James. *The Genesis of Georges Sorel*. Ann Arbor: Wahr, 1951.

————. *The Myth of the Ruling Class: Gaetano Mosca and the "Elite."* Ann Arbor: Univ. of Michigan Press, 1958.

————. *Pareto and Mosca*. Englewood Cliffs, N.J.: Prentice-Hall, 1965.

MELIS, Renato, ed. *Sindacalisti italiani*. Rome: Volpe, 1964.

MICHELS, Robert. *First Lectures in Political Sociology*. New York: Harper and Row, 1949.

————. *Lavoro e razza*. Milan: Vallardi, 1924.

————. *Political Parties*. New York: Dover, 1959.

————. *Sozialismus und Faschismus in Italien*. Munich: Meyer & Jessen, 1925. 2 vols.

————. *La teoria di C. Marx sulla miseria crescente e le sue origini*. Turin: Bocca, 1922.

MOSCA, Gaetano. *Elementi di scienza politica*. 5th ed. 2 vols. Bari: Laterza, 1953.

————. *Storia delle dottrine politiche*. 6th revised ed. Bari: Laterza, 1951.

OLIVETTI, Angiolo Oliviero. *Questioni contemporanee*. Naples: Partenopea, 1913.

————. *Il sindacalismo come filosofia e come politica*. Milan: Alpes, 1924.

ORIANI, Alfredo. *Rivolta ideale*. Bologna: Capelli, 1943.

PAPINI, Giovanni. *Pragmatismo*. Florence: Vallecchi, 1943.

PARETO, Vilfredo. *Corso di economia politica*. 2 vols. Turin: Einaudi, 1949.

————. *Manuale di economia politica*. 2nd ed. Milan: Libreria, 1919.

————. *Les Systèmes Socialistes*. 2 vols. Paris: V. Giard et E. Briere, 1902.

————. *Trasformazioni della democrazia*. Rocca San Casciano: Cappelli, 1964.

————. *Trattato di sociologia generale*. 2nd ed. 2 vols. Milan: Communità, 1964.

PASINI, Ferdinando. *D'Annunzio*. Rome: Augustea, 1928.

SCHULER, Erwin. *Pareto's Marx-Kritik*. Tuebingen: Becht, 1938.

SIGHELE, Scipio. *Idee e problemi d'un positivista*. Palermo: Sandron, 1908.

————. *L'intelligenza della folla*. Turin: Bocca, 1922.

————. *Pagine nazionaliste*. Milan: Treves, 1910.

————. *Le scienze sociali*. Milan: Vallardi, 1903.

SOREL, Georges. *D'Aristote à Marx*. Paris: Rivière, 1935.

————. *L'Avenir socialiste des syndicats*. Paris: Jacques, 1901.

————. *Degenerazione capitalista e degenerazione socialista*. Milan: Sandron, 1907.

————. *L'Europa sotto la tormenta*. Milan: Corbaccio, 1932.

————. *Les illusions du progrès*. Paris: Rivière, 1908.

————. *Insegnamenti sociali della economia contemporanea*. Milan: Sandron, 1906.

————. *Introduction à l'économie moderne*. Paris: Jacques, 1903.

————. *Matériaux d'une théorie du prolétariat*. Paris: Rivière, 1919.

————. *Le procès de Socrate*. Paris: Alcan, 1889.

————. *Reflections on Violence*, trans. T. E. Hulme and J. Roth. New York: Free Press, 1950.

————. *La ruine du monde antique*. Paris: Jacques, 1902.

————. *Saggi di critica del marxismo*. Milan: Sandron, 1903.

————. *De l'utilité du pragmatisme*. Paris: Rivière, 1921.

IV. THE DOCTRINE OF FASCISM

BALLARINI, Franco. *Dal liberalismo al corporativismo*. Turin: Einaudi, 1935.

BARDÈCHE, Maurice. *Che cosa è il fascismo?* trans. E. Beltrametti. Rome: Volpe, 1963.

BIAGI, Bruno. *Scritti di politica corporativa*. Bologna: Zanichelli, 1934.

————. *Lo stato corporativo*. Rome: Istituto Nazionale Fascista di Cultura, 1934.

BORTOLOTTO, Guido. *Dottrina del fascismo*. Milan: Hoepli, 1939.

————. *Faschismus und Nation*. Hamburg: Hanseatische, 1932.

————. *Massen und Fuehrer in der faschistischen Lehre*. Hamburg: Hanseatische, 1934.

————. *Lo stato e la dottrina corporativa*. Bologna: Zanichelli, 1930.

BOTTAI, Giuseppe. *La Carta del Lavoro*. Rome: Diritto del Lavoro, 1928.

————. *Esperienza corporativa (1929–1935)*. Florence: Vallecchi, 1935.

————. *Pagine di critica fascista 1915–1926*. Florence: Le Mónnier, 1941.

CAMBO, Francisco. *En torno del fascismo italiano*. Barcelona: Catalana, 1925.

CANEPA, Antonio. *Sistema di dottrina del fascismo*. 3 vols. Rome: Formiggini, 1937.

CARLI, Filippo. *Le basi storiche e dottrinali della economia corporative*. Padua: Cedam, 1938.

La concezione fascista della proprietà privata. Rome: Confederazione Fascista dei Lavoratori dell'Agricoltura, 1939.

CORSO, Giovanni. *Lo stato fascista*. Rome: Littorio, 1929.

COSTAMAGNA, Carlo. *Dottrina del fascismo*. 2nd ed. Turin: UTET, 1940.

————. *Elementi di diritto costituzionale corporativo fascista*. Florence: Bemporad, 1929.

La cultura fascista (Partito Nazionale Fascista). Rome: Libreria dello stato, 1938.

D'AMBROSIO, Manlio. *Economia politica corporativa*. Rome: Littorio, 1930.

DE MARSANICH, Augusto. *Lo stato nel ventennio fascista (1922–1943)*. Rome: Aniene, n.d.

DE MONTEMAYOR, Giulio. *Lo stato fascista*. Palermo: Sandron, 1928.

L'economia fascista (Partito Nazionale Fascista). Rome: Libreria dello stato, 1938.

ERCOLE, Francesco. *Le origini dell'Italia fascista*. Rome: Alberti, 1927.

FANELLI, Giuseppe Attilio. *Saggi su corporativismo fascista.* Rome: Secolo Fascista, 1936.

FERRARI, Santo. *L'Italia fascista.* Turin: Italiana, 1942.

FILARETI, Generale. *In margine del fascismo.* Milan: Unitas, 1925.

FONTANELLI, Luigi. *Sentimento della rivoluzione.* Rome: UESI, 1941.

FRANCK, Louis. *Les étapes de l'économie fasciste italienne.* Paris: Libraire sociale et économique, 1939.

GAUCHER, François. *Il fascismo ed il mondo di oggi,* trans. A. Romualdi. Rome: Volpe, 1966.

GIGLIO, Carlo. *Partito e impero.* Rome: Palazzo Brancaccio, 1939.

GOEBBELS, Paul Joseph. *Noi tedeschi e il fascismo di Mussolini,* trans. A. Luchini. 2nd ed. Florence: Beltrami, 1936.

GOMÈZ HOMEN, Pier Filippo. *Antecedenti teorici del corporativismo fascista.* Palermo: Sandron, 1929.

GORGOLINI, Pietro. *Il fascismo nella vita italiana.* Turin: Silvestrelli, 1923.

———. *Il fascismo spiegato al popolo.* Rome: Paravia, 1935.

———. *La rivoluzione fascista.* Rome: Paravia, 1928.

GRAVELLI, Asvero. *Panfascismo.* Rome: Nuova Europa, 1935.

LANDINI, Pietro. *La dottrina del fascismo.* Florence: Nuova Italia, 1936.

———. *La nuova coscienza nazionale.* Rome: ano. tipo. ed., 1933.

———. *Lo stato imperiale fascista.* Pistoia: Tariffi, 1937.

MANCINI, Ezio. *Fascismo e democrazia.* Rome: Piccinelli, 1945.

MANOILESCO, Mihail. *Le siècle du corporatisme.* Paris: Alcan, 1938.

MARPICATI, Arturo. *Il Partito Fascista.* Milan: Mondadori, 1938.

MARTINOLI, Ettore. *Funzione della mistica nella rivoluzione fascista.* Udine: Trani, 1940.

MELETTI, Vincenzo. *Civiltà fascista.* Florence: Nuova Italia, 1941.

MUSSOLINI, Benito. *Opera omnia.* 36 vols. Florence: La Fenice, 1951–61.

OLIVETTI, Angiolo Oliviero. *Lineamenti del nuovo stato italiano.* Rome: Littorio, 1930.

OLIVETTI, Ezio Maria. *Sindacalismo nazionale.* Milan: Monanni, 1927.

ORANO, Paulo. *Dal sindacalismo rivoluzionario allo stato sindacalista.* Rome: Camera, 1925.

L'ordinamento dello stato fascista (Partito Nazionale Fascista). Rome: Libreria dello stato, 1938.

PANUNZIO, Sergio. *Che cos'è il fascismo.* Milan: Alpes, 1924.

———. *Il diritto sindacale e corporativo.* Perugia: Nuova Italia, 1930.

———. *Popolo nazione stato.* Florence: Nuova Italia, 1933.

———. *Lo stato fascista.* Bologna: Cappelli, 1925.

———. *Stato nazionale e sindacati.* Milan: Imperia, 1924.

———. *Teoria generale dello stato fascista.* Padua: Cedam, 1939.

Il Partito Nazionale Fascista (Partito Nazionale Fascista). Rome: Libreria dello Stato, 1938.

PELLEGRINI-GIAMPIETRO, Domenico. *Aspetti storici e spirituali del fascismo.* Rome: Vallerini, 1941.

PIGHETTI, Guido. *Fascismo, sindacalismo, corporativismo.* Milan: Scientifico, 1930.

————. *Sindacalismo fascista.* Milan: Imperia, 1924.

PREZZOLINI, Giuseppe. *Le Fascisme,* trans. G. Bourgin. Paris: Bossard, 1925.

PUCHETTI, Antonio Cesare. *Il fascismo scientifico.* Turin: Bocca, 1926.

QUAGLIO, Chiarissimo. *Orientamenti della rivoluzione fascista.* Lucca: L'Artiglio, 1937.

RAGUSO, Stefano. *Elementi di scienza politica corporativa.* Florence: Nuova Italia, 1935.

ROCCO, Alfredo. *La dottrina politica del fascismo.* Rome: Aurora, 1925.

————. *La trasformazione dello stato.* Rome: La Voce, 1927.

ROMANINI, Luigi. *I principii del fascismo nel campo dell'educazione.* 2nd ed. Turin: Paravia, 1939.

ROSSONI, Edmondo. *Le idee della ricostruzione.* Florence: Bemporad, 1923.

SAMMARTANO, Nino. *Idee e problemi della rivoluzione fascista.* Florence: Vallecchi, 1932.

SCHNEIDER, Herbert. *Making the Fascist State.* New York: Oxford Univ. Press, 1928.

SPINETTI, G. Silvano. *Mistica fascista.* Milan: Hoepli, 1936.

TURATI, Augusto. *La dottrina fascista.* Rome: Littorio, 1923.

UNGARI, Paolo. *Alfredo Rocco e l'ideologia giuridica del fascismo.* Brescia: Morcelliana, 1963.

ZANGARA, Vincenzo. *Rivoluzione sindacale: lo stato corporativo.* Rome: Littorio, 1927.

V. THE PHILOSOPHY OF FASCISM

AEBISCHER, Max. *Der Einzelne und der Staat nach Giovanni Gentile.* Freiburg: Kanisiusdruckerei, 1954.

BELLEZZA, Vito. *L'esistenzialismo positivo di Giovanni Gentile.* Florence: Sansoni, 1954.

CARLINI, Armando. *Studi gentiliani.* Florence: Sansoni, 1958.

DE SARLO, Francesco. *Gentile e Croce. Lettere filosofiche di un "superato."* Florence: Le Monnier, 1925.

Selected Bibliography

Di GIAMBERARDINO, Oscar. *L'individuo nell'etica fascista.* Florence: Vallecchi, 1940.
EVOLA, Julius. *Il fascismo.* Rome: Volpe, 1964.
————. *Imperialismo pagano: il fascismo dinnanzi al pericolo Euro-Cristiano.* Rome: Atanor, 1928.
————. *Rivolta contro il mondo moderno.* Milan: Hoepli, 1934.
————. *Gli uomini e le rovine.* Rome: Ascia, 1953.
GENTILE, Giovanni. *Che cosa è il fascismo?* Florence: Vallecchi, 1925.
————. *Dottrina del fascismo:* Idee fondamentali. Milan: Hoepli, 1935.
————. *Fascismo e cultura.* Milan: Treves, 1928.
————. *Filosofia del fascismo.* Rome: Littorio, 1929.
————. *Filosofia italiana contemporanea.* Florence: Sansoni, 1941.
————. *Fondamenti della filosofia del diritto con aggiunti due studi sulla filosofia di Marx.* 3rd ed. Florence: Sansoni, 1955.
————. *Genesi e struttura della società.* Florence: Sansoni, 1946.
————. *Guerra e fede. Frammenti politici.* Naples: Ricciardi, 1919.
————. *Introduzione alla filosofia.* Rome: Treves, 1933.
————. *Origini e dottrina del fascismo.* Rome: Littorio, 1929.
————. "The Philosophic Basis of Fascism," in *Readings on Fascism and National Socialism,* Denver: Swallow, n.d.
————. *Preliminari allo studio del fanciullo.* 6th ed. Florence: Sansoni, 1958.
————. *Riforma dell'educazione.* 5th ed. Florence: Sansoni, 1954.
————. *Teoria generale dello spirito come atto puro.* 4th ed. Bari: Laterza, 1924.
Giovanni Gentile: la vita e il pensiero. 9 vols. Fondazione Giovanni Gentile per gli Studi Filosofici. Florence: Sansoni, 1948–1961.
HARRIS, Henry Silton. *The Social Philosophy of Giovanni Gentile.* Urbana: Univ. of Illinois Press, 1960.
HOLMES, Roger. *The Idealism of Giovanni Gentile.* New York: Macmillan, 1937.
MARCUSE, Herbert. *Reason and Revolution: Hegel and the Rise of Social Theory.* 2nd ed. New York: Humanities, 1954.
MAZZETTI, Roberto. *Quale umanesimo?* Rome: Armando, 1966.
MEHLIS, Georg. *Italienische Philosophie der Gegenwart.* Berlin: Junker und Duennhaupt, 1932.
MUELLER, Ferdinand-Lucien. *La pensée contemporaine en Italie et l'influence de Hegel.* Geneva: Kundig, 1941.
PANNESE, Gerardo. *L'etica nel fascismo e la filosofia del diritto e della storia.* Rome: Voce della Stampe, 1942.
SPINETTI, G. Silvano. *Fascismo e libertà.* 2nd ed. Padua: Cedam, 1941.

SPIRITO, Ugo. *Capitalismo e corporativismo*. Florence: Sansoni, 1933.

————. *Il comunismo*. Florence: Sansoni, 1965.

————. *Critica della democrazia*. Florence: Sansoni, 1963.

————. *La filosofia del comunismo*. Florence: Sansoni, 1948.

————. *Idealismo italiano e i suoi critici*. Florence: Le Monnier, 1930.

————. *Inizio di una nuova epoca*. Florence: Sansoni, 1961.

————. *Machiavelli e Guicciardini*. Florence: Sansoni, 1945.

————. *Dal mito alla scienza*. Florence: Sansoni, 1966.

————. *Note sul pensiero di Giovanni Gentile*. Florence: Sansoni, 1954.

————. *Nuovo umanesimo*. Rome: Armando, 1964.

————. *Il pragmatismo nella filosofia contemporanea*. Florence: Vallecchi, 1921.

————. *Scienza e filosofia*. 2nd ed. Florence: Sansoni, 1950.

————. *La vita come ricerca*. Florence: Sansoni, 1937.

TRIPODI, Nino. *Commento a Mussolini: note sulla "Dottrina del fascismo."* Rome: Bocca, 1956.

————. *Vita e ideali di Giovanni Gentile*. Rome: MSI, 1954.

VETTORI, Vittorio, ed. *Giovanni Gentile*. Florence: La Fenice, 1954.

VI. THE RACIAL DOCTRINE OF FASCISM

ACERBO, Giamcomo. *I fondamenti della dottrina fascista della razza*. Rome: Ministero della Cultura Popolare, 1940.

BANZI, Antonio. *Razzismo fascista*. Palermo: Agate, 1939.

BIASUTTI, Renato. *Razze e popoli della terra*. 3 vols. Turin: UTET, 1941.

CANELLA, Mario. *Lineamenti di antropobiologia*. Florence: Sansoni, 1943.

————. *Principi di psicologia razziale*. Florence: Sansoni, 1942.

————. *Razze umane estinte e viventi*. 2nd ed. Florence: Sansoni, 1941.

CAPASSO, Aldo. *Idee chiare sul razzismo*. Rome: Augustea, 1942.

COGNI, Giulio. *Il razzismo*. Milan: Bocca, 1937.

DE FELICE, Renzo. *Storia degli ebrei italiani sotto il fascismo*. Turin: Einaudi, 1962.

DE FRANCISCI, Pietro et al. *Politica fascista della razza*. Rome: Istituto Nazionale di Cultura, 1940.

DE MARTINO, Salvatore. *Lo spirito e la razza*. Rome: Signorelli, 1940.

DE ROSSI DELL'ARNO, Giulio. *L'ebraismo contro l'Europa*. Rome: Maglione, 1940.

EVOLA, Julius. *Il mito del sangue*. Milan: Hoepli, 1937.

FRANZI, Leone. *Fase attuale del razzismo tedesco*. Rome: Istituto Nazionale di Cultura, 1939.

GINI, Corrado. *Nascita, evoluzione e morte delle nazioni.* Rome: Littorio, 1930.

KORHERR, Riccardo. *Regresso delle nascite: morte dei popoli.* Rome: Littorio, 1928.

LEONI, Enzo. *Mistica del razzismo fascista.* Padua: Cedam, 1941.

LODOLINI, Armando. *La storia della razza italiana da Augusto a Mussolini.* Rome: U.E.I., 1939.

MAGGIORE, Giuseppe. *Razza e fascismo.* Palermo: Agate, 1939.

MARRO, Giovanni. *Caratteri fisici e spirituali della razza italiana.* Rome: Istituto Nazionale di Cultura Fascista, 1939.

———. *Primato della razza italiana.* Milan: Principato, 1940.

MASTROJANNI, Gabriele. *Marte e Israele.* Bologna: Cappelli, 1943.

MOMIGLIANO, Eucardio. *Storia tragica e grottesca del razzismo fascista.* Verona: Mondadori, 1946.

ORANO, Paolo. *Gli Ebrei in Italia.* 2nd ed. Rome: Pinciana, 1938.

———, ed. *Inchiesta sulla razza.* Rome: Pinciana, 1939.

PESCI, Ernesto. *Lotta e destino di razza.* Terni: Alterocca, 1939.

PISANO, Giorgio. *Mussolini e gli Ebrei.* Milan: F.P.E., 1967.

PODALIRI, Guido. *De Republica Hebraeorum.* Osimo: Barulli, 1941.

PRETI, Luigi. *Impero fascista, Africani ed Ebrei.* Milan: Mursia, 1968.

VII. FASCIST SOCIALIZATION

AMICUCCI, Ermanno. *I 600 giorni di Mussolini.* Rome: Faro, 1949.

CIONE, Edmondo. *Storia della Repubblica Sociale Italiana.* Caserta: Il cenacolo, 1948.

DEAKIN, Frederick. *The Brutal Friendship: Mussolini, Hitler and the Fall of Italian Fascism.* New York: Harper and Row, 1962.

DRIEU LA ROCHELLE, Pierre. *Socialisme fasciste.* Paris: Gallimard, 1934.

PERTICONE, Giacomo. *La Repubblica di Salò.* Rome: Leonardo, 1947.

SARACRISTA, Vito. *Con la Repubblica Sociale Italiana al servizio del paese.* Milan: Manara, n.d.

TARCHI, Angelo. *Teste dure.* Milan: S.E.L.C., 1967

VIII. THEORIES OF FASCISM

ARENDT, Hannah. *The Origins of Totalitarianism.* New York; Harcourt, Brace, 1951.

BAUER, Otto, Herbert MARCUSE, and Arthur ROSENBERG. *Faschismus und*

Kapitalismus: Theorien ueber die sozialen Urspruenge und die Funktion des Faschismus. Vienna: Europaeische, 1967.

DE FELICE, Renzo, ed. *Il fascismo e i partiti politici italiani.* Rocca San Casciano: Cappelli, 1967.

DUTT, R. Palme. *Fascism und Social Revolution.* New York: International, 1934.

FETSCHER, Iring."Zur Kritik des sowpetmarxistischen Faschismusbegriffs," in *Karl Marx und der Marxismus.* Munich: Piper, 1967.

LIPSET, Seymour Martin. " 'Fascism'—Left, Right and Center," in *Political Man: The Social Bases of Politics.* Garden City, N.Y.: Doubleday, 1959.

LUKÀCZ, Georg. *Die Zerstoerung der Vernunft.* Berlin: Aufbau, 1954.

MOORE, Barrington. *Social Origins of Dictatorship and Democracy.* Boston: Beacon Press, 1966.

NATHAN, Peter. *The Psychology of Fascism.* London: Faber and Faber, n.d.

NOLTE, Ernst, ed. *Theorien ueber den Faschismus.* Berlin: Kiepenheuer und Witsch, 1967.

PARSONS, Talcott. "Some Sociological Aspects of Fascist Movements," in *Essays in Sociological Theory.* Revised edition. New York: Free Press, 1954.

PIRKER, Theodor, ed. *Komintern und Faschismus: 1920–1940.* Stuttgart: Zeitgeschichte, 1965.

TROTSKY, Leon. *Fascism: What It Is, How to Fight It.* New York: Pioneer, 1944.

Index

Index

Index

Racism (*cont.*)
  Mussolini and, 259, 281
    colored races and, 269–70
    populationist definition of, 275, 277
    racism justified, 245–49
    racism opposed, 245–49
    State anti-Semitism and, 278–81
    as nationalism, 245–49
  Nazi, 260–67
    Fascist imitations of, 11, 15
    Fascist racism compared, 242, 259, 281–82
    racial differences and, 21–22
    racism and alliance with, 277–78
    Nordicism in, 262–65
Raguso, Stefano, 183
Rahn, Rudolf, 291, 294
Rationalism, Marxist, 105; *see also* Antirationalism; Transrationalism
Religion, decline of, 1
Reason, 123–24
Red Guard, 175
Representatives, selection of, 234–35
Revolution
  in backward countries and production, 353–55
  Bolshevik and Fascist, 352–53
  defined, 6–7
  Engels and elite led, 108
  Fascism as conservative, 293–94
    Fascism assumes power, 2, 166–68
  Fascism and nationalistic, 10
  ideas and, 6
  initiation of socialist, 105–6
  Marxist view of, 348–53
  Mussolini on, 116
  proletarian, 348–52
    bourgeoisie in, 104, 108
    capitalism and, 350–51
    production and, 349

strike and, 110, *see also* Strike
  world-wide, 2–3
  See also Mass movements; Revolutionary socialism; Revolutionary syndicalism
Revolutionary socialism
  class struggle and, 54
  anarchism in, 93, 94
  Fascism and, 97
  as heritage, 164
  historic circumstances for, 36
  spread of, 33
  in working class movement, 93
Revolutionary syndicalism
  Blanqui's cvonception of, 108
  of Corradini, 75–76, 81
  defined, 110–11
  of Labriola, 97, 201, 378
  mass-based party and, 87–88
  Mussolini and, 100, 101, 108–9, 127
  pragmatism of, 200
  principal theoretician of, 54
  theory and practice of, 110
Right totalitarianism, 330–33; *see also* Totalitarianism
Rights
  equality of, 46; *see also* Equality
  Gumplowicz on, 46, 57
  to strike, 376
Rocca, Massimo, 133, 174
Rocco, Alfredo, 163, 207, 208
  on society, 184–86
Rokeach, M., 332
Rosenberg, Alfred, 262, 264, 277, 279, 280
Rossi, Cesare, 307
Rossoni, Edmondo, 163, 294–95, 378
Roux, Georges, 28
Ruling class
  elitism of, 43–44; *see also* Elitism
  as necessity, 88
  ruled and, 39
  State as instrument of, 357–59; *see also* State